"Something Dreadful and Grand"

"Something Dreadful and Grand"

AMERICAN LITERATURE AND THE IRISH-JEWISH UNCONSCIOUS

Stephen Watt

OXFORD

UNIVERSITY PRESS

OXFORD
UNIVERSITY PRESS

Oxford University Press is a department of the University of
Oxford. It furthers the University's objective of excellence in research,
scholarship, and education by publishing worldwide.

Oxford   New York

Auckland   Cape Town   Dar es Salaam   Hong Kong   Karachi
Kuala Lumpur   Madrid   Melbourne   Mexico City   Nairobi
New Delhi   Shanghai   Taipei   Toronto

With offices in

Argentina   Austria   Brazil   Chile   Czech Republic   France   Greece
Guatemala   Hungary   Italy   Japan   Poland   Portugal   Singapore
South Korea   Switzerland   Thailand   Turkey   Ukraine   Vietnam

Oxford is a registered trademark of Oxford University Press
in the UK and certain other countries.

Published in the United States of America by
Oxford University Press
198 Madison Avenue, New York, NY 10016

© Oxford University Press 2015

Library of Congress Cataloging-in-Publication Data
Watt, Stephen, 1951–
"Something dreadful and grand" : American literature and the Irish-Jewish
unconscious / Stephen Watt.
pages cm
Includes bibliographical references and index.
ISBN 978–0–19–022795–1 (cloth) — ISBN 978–0–19–022796–8 (updf)   1. American
literature—Irish influences.   2. Jews in literature.   3. Irish in literature.   4. Popular
music—United States—Irish influences.   5. Popular music—United States—Jewish influences.
6. United States—Civilization—Irish influences.   7. United States—Civilization—
Jewish influences.   I. Title.
PS173.I75W38 2015
810.9'89162—dc23
2014040771
ISBN 978–0–19–022795–1

1 3 5 7 9 8 6 4 2
Printed in the United States of America
on acid-free paper

{ CONTENTS }

{ PREFACE }

In a 2013 essay that serves as the introduction to his play *Outside Mullingar*, John Patrick Shanley, an Irish-American writer who grew up in The Bronx, recounts his 1993 trip to County Westmeath with his Irish-born father. He recalls the harrowing experience of driving for some hundred miles "on the wrong side" of cramped lanes to reach the family farmhouse outside the village of Killucan, of first experiencing the estranging silence of the farm when he and his father finally arrived there, and of overhearing a dispute among his relatives in speech so "utterly different" he couldn't decipher a single word. His cousin Anthony was a bit different, too, a "strange mixture of calm and storm." In fact, Shanley reflects, as he and Anthony later visited a nearby graveyard and approached a "forbidding Victorian tombstone" with the name "SHANLEY" engraved upon it, *all* of his Irish relatives were strange. Yet for all this cultural dissonance—challenging driving conditions, verbal incomprehensibility, and a pervasive feeling of strangeness—while kneeling at the headstone in this, his first visit to Ireland, he "felt a bond with something dreadful and grand." "*These are my people,*" he thought.

This epiphany, in all of its uncanniness and ambivalence, intimates the larger project of this book. And so, too, does *Outside Mullingar*, first produced by the Manhattan Theatre Club in January 2014 at the Samuel J. Friedman Theatre. The production elicited both enthusiastic and tepid reviews, and both kinds of response are revealing. While Marilyn Stasio in *Variety* found it a "tender family drama" performed by a "letter-perfect cast," other commentators lacerated its traversing of "predictable rom-com territory" and its "comforting" and "charming but phony" Irish familiarity (Jesse Green in *Vulture*). Most critics agreed, however, that much of the play's charm is generated by the fractious middle-aged neighbors Anthony Reilly (Brendan F. O'Byrne) and Rosemary Muldoon (Debra Messing), who walk well-trodden conventional ground on the way to a kiss that, true to the complications of romantic comedy, seemed at times so unlikely to occur. And, in the play's final moments, sunlight pierces through the gloom and rain that had so dominated their lives to augur a brighter future for both of them.

Both supportive and indifferent reviewers alike, however, tended to agree with Green's observation that *Outside Mullingar* was rooted in a tradition of both "Irish literature" and "blarney": in other words, Shanley's play evoked a long history of the Irish play on the American stage and the characters who helped define it, but also recalled something else, something excessive, anterior, and perhaps fictive, represented by the term "blarney." Charles Isherwood in the *New York Times* hints at this latter quality, detecting in the play's dialogue echoes of "lost loves, deaths, and other grim subjects dear to the hearts of the Irish, or at least those who populate Broadway stages." The play itself seemed haunted by previous nights at the theater and ancestors of the characters Isherwood saw, so, for example, the dynamic between O'Byrne's character and the tempestuous Rosemary as played by Messing paid "gentle tribute" to the volatile affection of Jim Tyrone and Josie Hogan in Eugene O'Neill's *A Moon for the Misbegotten*. Although less enthralled critics heard in Messing's Irish dialect the echoes of Darby O'Gill, not O'Neill's complicated pair, they nonetheless endorsed the performances of two Irish-born actors (O'Byrne and Dearbhla Molloy, who played Aoife, Rosemary's ailing mother), one Irish-American (Peter Maloney, who played Anthony's aging father), and Messing, a Jewish-American actress whose rise to fame included her portrayal of interior designer Grace Adler in the long-running situation comedy *Will & Grace*. Joe Dziemianowicz in the *New York Daily News* found Messing's Rosemary "feisty, fiery, and very amusing"; Isherwood applauded her "bossy irritability"; and Stasio regarded her performance as "amazing." Seeming to channel J. M. Synge's Pegeen Mike from *The Playboy of the Western World*—or perhaps Maureen O'Hara from John Ford's film *The Quiet Man*?—Messing's Rosemary struck Stasio as "fiercely independent," a standout performance that was irreducibly "Irish and stubborn to the core."

Except, of course, that neither the talented actress nor *Outside Mullingar* is exactly Irish "to the core," however much the latter may be laden with flourishes of blarney and prompt comparisons with or be haunted by other "Irish" plays, films, and performances. It is, among other things, an American drama that *performs* Irishness in both familiar and, occasionally, inventive ways. Moreover, both the script and premiere of *Outside Mullingar*, like so many of the texts discussed here, are the results of Irish, Irish-American, and Jewish-American collaboration: of traditions, histories of immigration, uncanny relationships, and performances that are, alternatively, dreadful and grand.

Illuminating these texts, performances, and genealogical hauntings is the project of this book, which is the result of several intellectual pressures bearing down on its author at seemingly the same moment. While I was completing *Beckett and Contemporary Irish Writing* (2009), trying to refine and expand senses of the Beckettian in the work of Brian Friel, Derek Mahon, Marina Carr, Paul Muldoon, Bernard MacLaverty, and others, a dispiriting sense struck me that, in the process of addressing one set of questions, others had arisen and been abandoned. It was impossible not to notice, for example, particularly in Muldoon and MacLaverty, the creation of sometimes elaborate analogies between Irish and Jewish diasporic histories, between Irish and Jewish subjectivities, and between analogous contours of collective memory, cultural trauma, and feeling. These recalled for me, not surprisingly, moments in James Joyce's *Dubliners, A Portrait of the Artist as a Young Man,* and particularly *Ulysses*; Douglas Hyde's analogies between learning Hebrew and learning Irish while stumping for the Gaelic League in the 1890s; and many more texts replete with suggestions, however implicit or unstated, of an unusual relationship between these peoples that goes well beyond comparisons of their respective diasporas. Yet, although intrigued by these intimations, I was also apprehensive about venturing further into this analogical territory: for one thing, "Irish" and "Jewish" essentialize people whose origins, class affiliation, educations, life experiences, and so on are enormously different. How can we presume to know precisely what these terms mean, as their mere utterance seems to erase the differences inherent to them?

While these reservations were lodged uneasily in my thoughts and the temptation to neglect the questions to which they were attached grew increasingly attractive, books like Michael Rothberg's *Multidirectional Memory: Remembering the Holocaust in the Age of Decolonization* (2009), Declan Kiberd's *"Ulysses" and Us: The Art of Everyday Life in Joyce's Masterpiece* (2009), and George Bornstein's *The Colors of Zion: Blacks, Jews, and Irish from 1845 to 1945* (2011) reactivated my fascination with them. In their very different ways, they returned me to Joseph Roach's *Cities of the Dead: Circum-Atlantic Performance* (1996), the subtitle of which, as you will see, I have revised for my own purposes here. All of these seemed to lobby for a revised understanding of human experience, history, and cultural production, suggesting and at times urging more explicitly that cultural understanding demanded an "always already" pluralism. That is to say, while some historical narratives might focus productively on the experience of one group, class, or community of people, a different and potentially valuable reading might be achieved by a more expansive critical juxtapositioning. Projects like Bornstein's, Kiberd's, and Rothberg's complemented analogies Muldoon and MacLaverty advanced, providing evidence of the richness of a combined ethnic study. Jewish-Irish studies, or Irish-Jewish studies, we might say, could produce a fresh purchase on cultural phenomena ranging from nineteenth-century theater to modernist literature, from popular music to comedy, which neither Jewish studies nor Irish studies could produce alone.

Increasingly, the evolution of drama on the modern American stage from around 1850 until 1950 captured my attention, but so, too, did tenement fiction, popular music, and other cultural forms of this period. Bornstein's book also pushed me in the direction of immigrant culture, as did Mick Moloney's album *If It Wasn't for the Irish and the Jews: Irish American Songs from Vaudeville and Early Tin Pan Alley* (2009). Moloney's title song, composed by an Irish and Jewish songwriting team in 1912, convinced me that, like *Outside Mullingar*, American popular culture writ large owed much to Irish and Jewish America in particular—and to Irish and Jewish artists and thinkers as well—and this debt was not confined to Tin Pan Alley. Stated slightly differently, American culture was never *just* American—*is* never just American, as Shanley's play and its origins confirm—but is, in this case, a site in a reciprocal cultural system that includes Ireland, the United Kingdom, and Europe more generally. Just a few years before Moloney's album was released, for example, while writing an essay on Brendan Behan I revisited Ulick O'Connor's 1970 biography of Behan and his claim that "New York humour was largely an Irish-Jewish creation." Here, O'Connor was alluding to Cold War America, the ascent of American television in the 1950s, and its frequent booking of nightclub "Borscht Belt" entertainers for popular variety shows. My hypotheses continued to grow: If popular music in the era of vaudeville was an Irish-Jewish creation and American comedy in the 1950s and 1960s was similarly indebted to these two immigrant groups, what other cultural realms did they influence and shape? One answer advanced recently by Sally Barr Ebest in *The Banshees: A Literary History of Irish American Women Writers* (2013) is the ascendant feminism of the 1960s, marked by the publications of both Mary McCarthy's *The Group* and Betty Friedan's *The Feminine Mystique* in 1963. Another is, of course, tenement fiction. The posthumous publication of Henry Roth's *An American Type* (2010) fueled my already keen interest in this genre, just as his first novel *Call It Sleep* (1934) had done so many years ago. But, finally, another cultural form seemed to me the most obvious Jewish-Irish creation: American drama and theater, from the post-Famine era of the mid-nineteenth century through the rise of O'Neill and the Provincetown Players, the founding of the Group Theatre during the Great Depression, and the rise to prominence of Arthur Miller in the 1940s and 1950s.

The pages that follow address all of these matters. The first chapter introduces theoretical and historical dimensions of an uncanny Irish-Jewish affinity and, on occasion, concomitant hostility—on the dreadful *and* the grand, both of which are recognizable by their excessive qualities—stopping along the way at Joycean representations of Jewishness, the Freudian uncanny, theories of performance and affect, immigrant culture, and notions of the allo-Semitic and what I call the allo-Hibernian. The last chapter continues this conversation, illustrating the continuing explanatory potential of these discourses through a series of wanderings through more recent Irish-Jewish interactions. In between these ruminations, three chapters chart a genealogy of modern American drama from representations of Irishness and Jewishness on the nineteenth-century stage to those on the modern stage, arguing that modern Irish drama and Irishness more generally not only resonated importantly with such playwrights as Elmer Rice, Clifford Odets, and Arthur Miller, but are also woven permanently into the fabric of American culture.

{ ACKNOWLEDGMENTS }

Books are like children, or so many arguments against prepublication censorship like John Milton's *Areopagitica* assert. If this is so, then they are like children conceived at the urging of friends and colleagues without whose support the project would be impossible. I am grateful to have enjoyed the support of such a community.

Three friends at Indiana University helped make it possible for me to have the time to write: former Dean of the College of Arts and Sciences, Bennett Bertenthal, Executive Dean of the College Larry Singell, and Associate Executive Dean Jean Robinson. But they also did a lot more than merely approve a research leave, encouraging me to pursue this project and actually listening to talks I gave as my argument evolved. During the summer of 2011, the Dorot Foundation supported my study at the Harry Ransom Center at the University of Texas at Austin; that opportunity, aided by Thomas Staley, the Center's Director, and the expertise of his superb staff, led me to believe my research might actually lead somewhere. Librarians and archivists, particularly Erika Dowell at the Lilly Library at Indiana University, Erin Harris of the Richard Avedon Foundation, Amy Stolarczyk at ArenaPAL, Jim Bantin at the Southern Illinois University Library—Carbondale, Madeline Long at Steppenwolf Theatre, and the staff at the Harvard Theatre Collection and the Eclipse Theatre Company in Chicago have all helped me enormously in assembling the archive and securing illustrations for this book. The Robert A. and Sandra S. Borns Jewish Studies Program at Indiana University provided an audience for my first formal discussion of this work, and its journal *Musica Judaica* offered me a forum for writing on Irish and Jewish contributions to popular American music.

Equally important were the number of conversations, formal and informal, with friends and colleagues that I have enjoyed in developing my thoughts about Irish, Irish-American, and Jewish-American culture. There have been so many of these that I am almost certain to have forgotten one or another important interlocutor, an oversight for which I offer a preemptive apology. These include Tony Roche, Nelson Ritschel, Christopher Murray, Susan Gubar, Margaret Kelleher, Christie Fox, John Brannigan, Brooks Hefner, Ed Comentale, Paige Reynolds, Richard Rankin Russell, Alvin Rosenfeld, Diane Hotten-Somers, Mary Trotter, Christoph Irmscher, William Demastes, Art Simpson, and a wonderful group of residential fellows at the Ransom Center with whom I was privileged to work.

I have also benefited enormously from the research assistance of three former graduate students, Sharyn Emery, Lynn Ramert, and Kara Kendall Morwick, and from the eagle-eyed proofreading—and gentle suggestions for revision from time to time—of my daughter, Caitlin Watt. Any errors that remain are not her responsibility in any way, but entirely mine.

Books need editors, too, and Brendan O'Neill and his staff have been superb throughout the editorial process, making my experience of developing this book the best I have ever enjoyed in my thirty years of academic publishing. I am deeply appreciative of them and of the sage advice of anonymous reviewers who provided excellent readings of an earlier draft.

My greatest thanks are reserved for my family: my wife Nonie, Caitlin, and my son Brendan. And I know they would quickly agree that this book must be dedicated to my father Robert Watt—known in his football days before World War II as Hard Hittin' Bob Watt—who died in the same week that Brendan O'Neill informed me the book manuscript had received strong support from the reviewers. When my brother Rob, sister Sally, and I were growing up in Springfield, Illinois, my father ran a corner drugstore in a neighborhood dominated by Irish Catholic families—my mother Virginia Mary, half Irish Catholic herself, raised us in this religion—and sprinkled with Jewish families, some of whose sons worked in my father's store. One of dad's friends helped manage Joe Fishman's pawnshop downtown; and Joe, a large man—oddly resplendent in his dress shirt, bow tie, bulging suspenders, and omnipresent cigar—was much in my thoughts as I wrote this book. Perched on a stool at the pawnshop's counter, gumming his stogie into a pulp, he teased us "minnow munching" Catholic kids every Saturday morning when we paid him a visit trying to hawk whatever items we could rummage. Cackling uproariously yet trying to feign indifference, he almost always agreed to buy some of the beat-up golf balls we had found in the weeds or creek of a public golf course or, in the winter, other stuff we managed to acquire, but only after a raucous negotiation that was the highlight of our day and, I'd like to think, of Joe's day, too. He now resides with my mom and dad in my memories.

Versions of two sections of chapter 5 have been published previously: "MacLaverty's Holocaust: Affect, Memory, and the 'Troubles,'" in *Bernard MacLaverty: New Critical Readings*, ed. Richard Rankin Russell (London: Bloomsbury, 2014), 89–100; and "Brendan Behan, Borscht Belt Comedian," in *Irish University Review* 44 (Spring–Summer 2014): 149–64.

Introduction

PERFORMING THE IRISH-JEWISH UNCONSCIOUS

There's Fanny, Annie, Jenny,
And the dance they do
Would make you wish that you
Were in a harem with Pat Malone [Abie Cohen].[1]

— IRVING BERLIN, "IN MY HAREM" (1913)

Rose Mary. Abie, you're a dear! You know sometimes [*Lapsing into brogue.*] I think you've a bit of the Irish tucked away in you somewhere. Faith, I believe you're half Irish.
Abie. [*Right back at her with a brogue.*] To be sure Mavourneen, my better half is Irish.
Rose Mary. [*Laughing.*] And my better half is Jewish. [*Puts right hand on his cheek.*]
Abie. What could be sweeter? [*Kiss.*][2]

— ANNE NICHOLS, *ABIE'S IRISH ROSE* (1922)

It was Arnie who'd been the brain behind running rum
to those thousands of Irish schlemiels
who dug the canal.[3]

— PAUL MULDOON, "AT THE SIGN OF THE BLACK
HORSE, SEPTEMBER 1999"

Taken together, these three passages are representative of the diverse archive of cultural texts that chronicle the unique, often uncanny relationships between the Irish and Jews in America. Widely heard in World War I–era

America, "In My Harem," a song that Irving Berlin's friend George M. Cohan once jokingly dubbed the songwriter's "autobiography," relies upon the kind of interchangeability of and affinity between Irish and Jewish characters that define these relationships. That is to say, Berlin's composition of one line so that the name "Pat Malone" can be replaced with "Abie Cohen" represents an exchange or "surrogation" that accrues significance in the chapters that follow.[4] More broadly, lyricists of Tin Pan Alley–era songs frequently returned to the topic of Irish-Jewish interactions, including their uncanny relationships, as such songs as "Yiddisha Luck and Irisha Love" (1911), "If It Wasn't for the Irish and the Jews" (1912), and "There's a Little Bit of Irish in Sadie Cohn" (1916) exemplify.[5] Often denigrated as inferior commodities, these songs and the term "Tin Pan Alley" itself, as Keir Keightley observes, confront the notion of "otherness as inferiority," in the process "signaling widespread anxieties about modernity, social change, and the industrialization of culture."[6] One of these recurrent anxieties focused on the increasing presence of and interactions between immigrant groups, including intermarriage and its opposite sentiments, bigotry and hostility; in this context, the Irish-Jewish themes of popular music emerge from a larger formation, a repository or unconscious that might be regarded as underlying modernity itself (see figure 1.1).

The particular anxiety of intermarriage is soothingly dispelled in Anne Nichols's post–World War I comedy *Abie's Irish Rose*. Upon their return to New York from war-torn Europe, Nichols's two young lovers—Abie Levy, wounded in battle, and singer cum field nurse Rose Mary Murphy—have secretly married and brace themselves for strenuous paternal objections to their union. Shortly after entering the home of Abie's father, they contrive to convince him that Rose Mary "Murpheski" is actually Jewish, and a sympathetic rabbi and Irish Catholic priest who both served as chaplains during the war do all they can to support the young couple. Opposition to the pair's marriage is based entirely on prejudice and paternal obduracy: Solomon Levy's animosity toward "Irishers" and his resolve that his son Abie will never marry a "schickie" are rivaled by the determination of his pugnacious counterpart Patrick Murphy that his daughter will marry an Irish Catholic. Yet, in a line that received the most enthusiastic approbation from Nichols's audience, Father Whalen, supported by his friend Rabbi Samuels, explains that with "all the shells bursting, and the shrapnel flying, with no one knowing just what moment death would come," soldiers of all religions "forgot their prejudice and came to realize that all faiths and creeds have about the same destination after all" (78–79).[7] This thesis receives poignant corroboration in Nichols's 1927 novelization of her comedy when, succumbing to injuries in the Battle of the Argonne Forest, Abie's Irish-American buddy Patsy Dunn dies in then Chaplain Samuels's arms.

FIGURE 1.1 *Alfred Bryan and Jack Stern, "There's a Little Bit of Irish in Sadie Cohn" (1916)*
Courtesy, The Lilly Library, Indiana University, Bloomington, Indiana

But Nichols's play will not admit such heartache. The irresistible charms of twin infants in the play's concluding act melt the frost of their grandfathers' hearts; and the play's other attractions—the vaudevillian schtick of the Irish and Jewish fathers, the utopian sentiment of a world without prejudice, the celebratory trajectory of romantic comedy—combined to create a popular sensation.[8] No matter that critics disparaged its clichés and ethnic stereotypes, one deriding it as the "worst play of the year" and predicting that it would alienate Irish and Jewish theatergoers.[9] *Abie's Irish Rose* was produced across the country and set what was then a Broadway record for longevity, opening on May 23, 1922, and closing over five years later after 2,327 consecutive performances. By 1927, this now largely forgotten comedy was heralded in a promotional "blurb" on the novelized version's dust jacket as "the most phenomenally successful play of modern times."[10] And in some ways it was. It inspired two film adaptations, a six-film series *The Cohens and the Kellys*, a 1940s radio series, and much more (see figure 1.2). This success aside and more to the point of this project, what if we were to take seriously the notion in the epigraph that, like Sadie Cohn in the Tin Pan Alley song, the play's young Jewish and Irish lovers harbored parts of each other's heritage within them? What larger interpretive yield might be mined from the veins of such an uncanny Irish Jewishness or Jewish Irishness?

Some eighty years after the premiere of Nichols's play at New York's Fulton Theatre, transplanted Northern Irish poet Paul Muldoon revisited Irish Jewishness in "At the Sign of the Black Horse, September 1999" in his Pulitzer Prize–winning volume *Moy Sand and Gravel* (2002). Set the day after Hurricane Floyd and over a foot of rain had battered New Jersey's Raritan River basin, the poem's speaker, a figure for Muldoon himself, watches a current of floodwater rush down what was once the road in front of his house, and his gaze travels to a pram beside him in which his infant son Asher sleeps. He notices both the Irish lace border of the shawl in which the child is wrapped and the exquisite bonnet fashioned by his Jewish great-grandmother, Sophie. Like the origins of these garments, Asher embodies the union of Irishness and Jewishness, the son of a Northern Irish poet and Jewish writer, Muldoon and his wife, Jean Hanff Korelitz. As the morning proceeds in a demonstration of what Muldoon elsewhere terms the "ungetroundable," a kind of conceit in which disparate phenomena meld into a single formation in the writer's imagination, the speaker reflects upon this Irish Jewishness or Jewish Irishness.[11] Other aggregations form as a result of the flood, as the flotsam of objects bobbing in the water evokes both historical events and more recent, even trivial, antecedents in his memory—from Nazi atrocities during World War II to cautionary signs at local businesses like "Please Examine Your Change" and "Do Not Fill Above This Line." Seemingly random epiphenomena of the spectacle flash through Muldoon's mind before he arrives on those "thousands of Irish schlemiels" who, over a century earlier, had dug the Delaware and Raritan Canal that has just so violently breached its banks.

As American and world histories merge, as memory and the day residue of more mundane transactions combine, the connections between Irishness and Jewishness thicken. The abandoned spectacles, rags, and clay transported so violently by the flood waters congeal to form historical images that for Muldoon are hard to get around, recalling both the waterway's Irish construction workers and the horrors of the Holocaust, and maybe—just maybe, he thinks—it was the infant's great-uncle Arnie "who'd been the brain behind

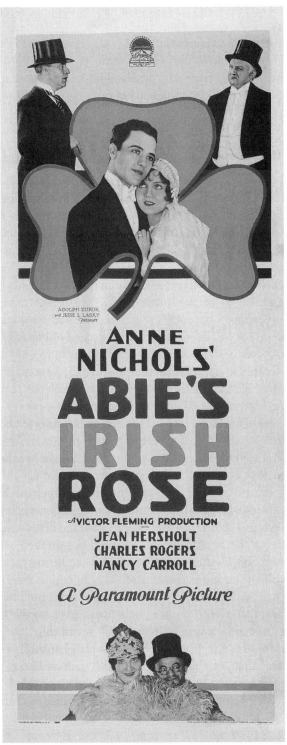

FIGURE 1.2 *Film Poster,* Abie's Irish Rose
Courtesy of Matinee Classics

running rum / to those thousands of Irish schlemiels / who dug the canal"
(94). Earlier, Muldoon identifies Uncle Arnie as Arnold Rothstein, forever
associated with one of American professional sports' most infamous episodes, the so-called "Black Sox Scandal" of 1919:

> This was the Arnold Rothstein who had himself fixed the 1919 World Series
> by bribing eight Chicago White Sox players, Keep Back
> Fifty Feet, to throw the game. (87)

Uncle Arnie, however, did not orchestrate the fix by himself, as the scam is
believed to have been contrived by Rothstein and Joseph "Sport" Sullivan, a
Boston-Irish bookmaker, with the assistance of former world featherweight
boxing champion Abe "The Little Hebrew" Attell. As it happens, this was
also the same Arnold Rothstein who helped Nichols produce *Abie's Irish
Rose*, investing in the production when others declined to do so. Such histo-
ries parallel the heritage of the infant boy; and, for me, the notions of Irish
Jewishness, and the Jewish Irishness invoked in "At the Sign of the Black
Horse, September 1999," became "ungetroundable," as irrevocably linked as
Abie and Rose Mary in Nichols's play, as interchangeable as the Jewish—or
Irish—harem owner in Berlin's Tin Pan Alley tune.

At least two other inferences might be made from these examples. The first
is that what might be termed the Irish-Jewish "unconscious" underlies a vast
array of cultural forms—drama, fiction, popular music, poetry—throughout
the modern period and well into our own century. And for very good reason, given the histories of Irish and Jewish immigration to America that are
intimately connected to this cultural production. Because of the odd "devia-
tions" and "minute accidents" inherent to genealogical progress,[12] the next
two chapters return to mid- and later nineteenth-century America, particularly the stage, when Irish and Jewish immigration reshaped such cities as New York, Boston, Philadelphia, and Chicago. Throughout the book
and especially in the fourth chapter, discussion remains largely focused,
as it will be here, on the first half of the twentieth century; and, insofar as
the Irish-Jewish unconscious remains of value to us, the final chapter considers later twentieth-century texts and several from our own century. It
should be added that, of the various phenomena arising from this construction, the often uncanny nature of Irish-Jewish relationships is foregrounded
with equal prominence in texts as popular as *Abie's Irish Rose*—for some, a
"synthetic farce" that "might have reminded Jewish audiences of the popular Yiddish *shund* (trash) play"[13]—and as dense as high modernist writing
with the complex intertextuality and playful allusiveness of a Muldoon poem.
Reviewing his earlier volume *The Annals of Chile* (1994), for example, Helen
Vendler admitted to both "admiration" and "exasperation" at the "Joycean
game of baffle-the-reader" in which Muldoon appeared to indulge.[14] Because
both Joycean and Muldoonian texts, whatever their levels of exasperating

opacity, contain crucial examples of the Irish-Jewishness explored here, the binarism high/low in regard to cultural hierarchy has little relevance for this endeavor. James Joyce in particular, but also such Irish writers as Dion Boucicault, Bernard Shaw, Sean O'Casey, and Brendan Behan—and several English writers and performers as well—will be considered in my excursus of this dreadful and grand construction, even if, unlike Muldoon, they did not move to America or visit here for any length of time.

A second inference might now seem obvious: namely, that although my archive is largely constituted of American texts and performances, national borders cannot be observed in its construction, as European texts, performers, and histories merge and (re)circulate in an ever-modernizing America. Much like the "circum-Atlantic" world so productively explored by Paul Gilroy, Joseph Roach, Patricia Yaeger, and others, what might be called a "circum–*North* Atlantic" world is similarly defined by diasporic populations and histories. As Roach asserts in *Cities of the Dead*, the "concept of a circum-Atlantic world (as opposed to a transatlantic one) insists on the centrality of the diasporic and genocidal histories of Africa and the Americas, North and South, in the creation of the culture of modernity."[15] This "region-centered" theoretical instrument, moreover, privileges a circulation and creolization of cultures, not the reign of a monolithic or singular national culture; a modernity in which performance sustains memory;[16] and a ruthless economy in which the bodies of laborers—most particularly slaves—constitute a prized commodity. Africa and the Caribbean rim, the black and circum-Atlantic world that Roach, Yaeger, and Keith Cartwright find so generative of carnival in New Orleans and cultural life in the American South more generally, is not the same circum–North Atlantic with which I am concerned.[17] But the similarities between them are striking, and, as historian J. H. Elliott explains, "slavery and migration, both voluntary and involuntary, are particularly appropriate for a pan-Atlantic treatment because, by their very nature as the story of people in movement, they transcend the history of single nations and continents."[18]

A vast difference exists, of course, between the brutalities of slavery and the exploitation of immigrant workers, between the deplorable conditions of living each endured and the suffering each experienced, yet the ruthlessness of capitalism and its effects on laboring bodies (and minds) are much in evidence in both Atlantic worlds. In both, an exodus from poverty and genocide—the Great Famine in Ireland has been indicted as a genocidal, not "natural," disaster much the same way that the "revolting deeds" perpetrated against Jews in Kishinev in 1903 were motivated by ethnic hatred[19]—led to the horrific irony that most desperate immigrants struggling to reach America did not immediately benefit from the superabundance that many imagined existed here. For Yaeger, "superabundance" and excess as realized across a range of cultural practices and material goods define both the circum-Atlantic world and such literary representations of the American South as Eudora Welty's and William Faulkner's. Such putative abundance also informs "myths of New World plenitude"—the notion that the Americas are a veritable paradise where streets are paved with gold, sidewalks with silver—and is mirrored by a myriad of other excesses: from the violence perpetrated by slave owners and the blood rituals indulged in by participants in slave rebellions, to the constructed worlds of beauty "beyond a history of scarcity" registered in the extravagant styles of artists of color.[20] A similar excess marks circum–North Atlantic texts.

The circum–North Atlantic, like the Atlantic world to its south, is marked by a circulation of cultures, texts, and bodies, although given the mass exodus of peoples from Ireland and eastern Europe in the nineteenth and twentieth centuries, it is also true that, at various moments, such transferences scarcely formed a perfect geometrical shape. Irish and Jewish vernacular, music, and other cultural traditions traveled with immigrants; and, even as it evolved with native talent, the American theater was, at least in part, a cultural satellite for touring stars from the European and London stages. This would seem to suggest a westward-leaning unidirectionality, not a reciprocity or vibrant cultural exchange, but this was hardly the case. American cultural forms—fiction, drama, popular music, film—circulated widely in the North Atlantic world as well, a topic about which Sean O'Casey's "Captain" Jack Boyle comments in act 2 of *Juno and the Paycock* (1924): "Take the real Dublin people, f'r instance: they know more about Charlie Chaplin an' Tommy Mix than they do about SS. Peter and Paul!"[21] Growing up between the world wars in Cork, David Marcus (1924–2009) enjoyed both the songs of composers like Berlin and a newer, jazzier American music played by such musicians as Benny Goodman, Louis Armstrong, and Art Tatum.[22] Taken together, both Captain Boyle and Marcus confirm the accuracy of Diarmaid Ferriter's observation in *The Transformation of Ireland* (2005) that popular Irish tastes in the early twentieth century were "dominated by Anglo-American culture," thereby undermining claims of the new republic's cultural chauvinism.[23] In addition, Irish writers when placed in a circum–North Atlantic context not only can be seen to exert a powerful influence on Jewish-American fiction and theater, but at times are also identified as Jews themselves. Indeed, as immigrants like Berlin and Muldoon have contributed to this significant history, so too have such nonimmigrants as Joyce and Shaw who, like several of their characters, *perform* an Irish Jewishness subtended by both a psychoanalytically and politically constituted unconscious that determines conceptions of identity and the operations of human affect. Much like the texts captured by my epigraphs, then, Joyce's fiction, even Joyce himself, illustrates the presence of the Irish-Jewish unconscious, characteristics of which might be inferred from a brief survey of Jewishness in Joyce, a topic several Jewish-American writers, as we shall see, found "ungetroundable."

The Performance of Excess and Joyce's "Irish Jews"

> Though [Mr. Harford] had never embraced more than the Jewish
> ethical code his fellow-Catholics, whenever they had smarted in
> person or by proxy under his exactions, spoke of him bitterly as an
> Irish Jew and an illiterate and saw divine disapproval of usury made
> manifest through the person of his idiot son. At other times they
> remembered his good points.[24]
>
> —JAMES JOYCE, *"GRACE" FROM DUBLINERS (1914)*

Like the excerpts above, this passage from Joyce's "Grace" intimates, as do
many events in *Ulysses* and *A Portrait of the Artist as a Young Man* (1916), the
larger and often contradictory interactions with which this project is concerned.[25] That is, on the one hand, while *Ulysses* cultivates parallels between
the Irish and Jews—and several characters express a profound respect for
Jewish culture and history—on the other Joyce's novel and oeuvre are replete
with examples of antagonism, not affinity, between them, including moments
of thoughtlessness, bigotry, and overt anti-Semitism. To complicate matters
further, one need not be Irish or Jewish to be characterized as such—or as
both, as in Mr. Harford's case in "Grace." One may simply engage in a religious or other practice, exhibit a style of dress or employ a mode of speech,
or possess an object that can be "read" in this way, including an "idiot son."
As in Harford's case, the perceived embrace of the usurious code of a Jewish
business partner, however illusory or fantastical the embrace and the code
might be, can motivate the fiction of a monstrous identity, one evil enough
to elicit "divine disapproval." And, oddly, the monster might exhibit some
"good points" from time to time as well.

Much like the designation of Harford as an "Irish Jew," "Jew" and "Irish"
seem to promise a precise, essential knowledge they can never truly
deliver. A Northern Irish Orangeman and a Catholic nationalist may be
countrymen—both may be born and raised in Belfast or Carrickfergus—but
labeling them both Northern Irish holds little interpretive potential. Similarly,
in a remarkable chapter of *Hélène Cixous Rootprints: Memory and Life Writing*
(1997), Cixous, "born in an age of nationalisms, of re-nationalisms" and raised
by her immigrant parents in Algeria, describes "destinally European" Jews,
"*so different from each other*, who were Hungarian, Austrian, Czechoslovakian,
Romanian, Polish," and so on (my emphasis). Like Franz Kafka, she notes,
these Jews shared German as a common language and then acquired the second language of the country in which they lived.[26] Further connotations of
both nationality and ethnicity accrue importance as well, as Cixous discovered after moving to Paris, where she found the colonially based "logic" of the
French to be "accompanied by behaviours that have always been unbearable."

This discovery, coupled with "the explosion, the odour of misogyny" she found there, led to an almost Joycean epiphany in which she shed the "obligation" of her French and "Jewish identity" and repatriated to an illusory place she had long inhabited: "From 1955 on, I adopted an imaginary nationality which is a literary nationality."[27] For her, therefore, "Jewish" both ascribes a similarity to people who may differ radically from one another and also promotes an identity that one can choose either to enact or deny. Or, as in the case of Mr. Harford's monstrous identity, "Jewish" may signal the existence of what Slavoj Žižek terms a "conceptual Jew": like the maternal phallus, the conceptual Jew "doesn't exist" and for this reason, "I fear him even more—in short, *the very nonexistence of the Jew in reality functions as the main argument for anti-Semitism* [emphasis in original]."[28] "Jewish" and "Irish" can be enacted or perceived in a myriad of ways ranging from the gestural to the consumption of cultural texts, from the promulgation of certain business practices to the simple courtesy of buying a drink, as in the bar scene from Joyce's "Counterparts": "O'Halloran stood a round and then Farrington stood another round, Weathers protesting that the hospitality was too Irish" (90).

Stated in another way that extends the observations made, respectively, by Lionel Pilkington and Aoife Monks, "Irish" is partially constituted of what the former calls a "histrionic" element. My articulation of "Irish" with "Jewish" and emphasis on their performative fungibility—their ability to be exchanged for other terms as the context requires—are in part intended as a counterbalance to the more often discussed relationship between Irish and African-American performance, both on the nineteenth-century minstrel stage and in the contemporary music scene, where, in describing the 1990s rap group House of Pain, Mark Quigley writes, "Irishness comes to the fore as the performative foil of an unruly blackness, while whiteness retires to the space of pure spectatorship."[29] As Pilkington outlines, "Irish" also exhibits a paradoxical valence when modifying certain nouns. So in the phrase "Irish confetti" the adjective undercuts the celebratory connotations of the noun to define stones or other objects converted into weapons, a version of what Ciaran Carson in "Queen's Gambit" from *Belfast Confetti* (1989) sees in violence-ravaged city streets "splattered with bits of corrugated / iron and confetti" during the "Troubles."[30] For Pilkington, the Irish in "Irish coffee" works similarly, doing more than merely modifying the noun it precedes: "An Irish coffee, of course, is just the thing for intoxicating your sobriety, or sobering up your intoxication."[31] "Irish" and "Jew" unlike, say, "Italian" or "Polish," are uniquely tied to performance, action, and movement. Indeed, both can be used as verbs or infinitives: the derogatory phrase to "Jew down" as a synonym for cheat or haggle has existed since the early nineteenth century; and, as Monks notes, the phrase "Irish up" indicates a process of energy infusion, as in the addition of whiskey to coffee.[32] This dimension of "Irish" bears similarity to the functioning of "Jewish" both as Cixous uses it by destabilizing what was thought to be a known identity and as Žižek explains in the creation of imaginary figures and illusory bogeymen. Thus, while both Monks and Pilkington underscore the uniquely performative capacity of "Irish," "Jew" often performs in similarly hyperbolic ways, even though speakers employing the term may wield it as concrete, specific, and definitive. Often "Irish" and "Jewish" communicate a prosaic facticity, no doubt; but they also can perform much more—or less.

Not surprisingly, both of these terms and expressions proximate to them surface in Joyce's fiction in ways ranging from the common to the more abstruse. In the "Ithaca" episode of *Ulysses*, for instance, Joyce's narrator gestures to a commonly held *essential* difference between the Irish and Jews when referring to Bloom and Stephen Dedalus's late-night conversation, asking, "Did either openly allude to their racial difference?" and responding, "Neither" (*U* 17.525–26). This use of "race" to describe both Jews and Irish was common at the fin de siècle (and before and after it as well);[33] it was employed by Jews and Gentiles alike—and their respective antagonists—for various reasons, one of which concerned some parents' fears that their children's commitment to their heritage might be imperiled as they assimilated into their new homes. Eric Goldstein points to an 1884 editorial in the *American Hebrew* advocating the maintenance of racial purity and refers to Friedrich Kolbenheyer's novella "Jewish Blood," published serially between April and September 1896 in the *American Jewess*, in which an immigrant father urges his son not to marry a Catholic girl because of their "dissimilarity of race."[34] (In this instance and unlike the refulgent conclusion of *Abie's Irish Rose*, such counsel leads to disaster: the death of another brother devoted to the girl, her untimely death, and her beloved's inconsolable sorrow.) As was common at the time, Abraham Neider, the wealthy immigrant-father in "Jewish Blood," elides distinctions between "race" and "nation," admonishing his son that the girl is "of another race" and that "national suicide" is the inevitable result of marriages to non-Jews.[35] This elision accrued importance as the nineteenth century drew to a close, motivating a dialogue between Viennese Zionist Theodor Herzl and London writer Israel Zangwill, whose play *The Melting Pot* (1908) was produced with considerable success across America. Zangwill, like Joyce's narrator in "Ithaca," regarded Jews as a race, while Herzl rejected the notion, insisting that Jews were a "nation with anthropological diversities. . . . No nation has uniformity of race."[36]

But the "Ithaca" episode's intimation of a potentially divisive distinction between the Irish and Jews eventually grows even more malignant than this "scientific" debate might suggest. As Marilyn Reizbaum phrases it, one of the "more enigmatic" moments in *Ulysses* occurs in this episode when, after chanting lines from the Hatikvah, Bloom invites Stephen to respond by reference to a "strange legend on an allied theme" (*U* 17.795–96). Stephen does so by reciting lines from "The Ballad of Harry Hughes," the title of which invokes

Hugh of Lincoln, a thirteenth-century child thought to have been murdered by Jews in an infamous instance of "blood libel." Expanding the repertoire of Jewish evil to foreground the seduction of the innocent, Stephen includes a verse in which a Jewish girl entices a Christian boy into a remote room "where none could hear him call" and then ruthlessly decapitates him (*U* 17.824).[37]

Blood libel, the myth that Jews murder Christian children so as to extract their blood to use as an ingredient in matzah eaten on Passover, is still an incendiary allegation today, as Caryl Churchill discovered in responses of outrage to her 2009 one-act play *Seven Jewish Children: A Play for Gaza*.[38] More to the point, this and other equally predictable accusations informed the discourse of anti-Semitism in the turn-of-the-century circum–North Atlantic, and they inform *Ulysses* as well. The most strident anti-Semites in the novel are Dominic Deasy, Stephen's employer in the "Nestor" episode, and the hypernationalist Citizen in "Cyclops," the latter of whom accuses Jews of "Swindling the peasants . . . and the poor of Ireland" (*U* 12.1150–51). Later in the episode, the conversation turns to Bloom's father, "Old Methusalem Bloom, the robbing bagman" who committed suicide after "swamping the country with his baubles and his penny diamonds" (*U* 12.1581–83).[39] More meaningful in terms of the complicated subjectivities of immigrant Jews and the relationship of the Irish and Jewish diasporas, topics of significance in the coming pages, Joyce's bullying Citizen, like Abraham Neider in "Jewish Blood," tends to employ "nation" as a synonym for "race" in his interrogation of Bloom:

—What is your nation if I may ask? says the citizen.
—Ireland, says Bloom. I was born here. Ireland.
The citizen said nothing only cleared the spit out of his gullet and, gob, he
spat a Red bank oyster out of him right in the corner. (*U* 12.1430–33)

Often accompanying the stereotype of unethical or usurious business practices associated with Mr. Harford, this indictment—that Jews are foreign or comprise a "nation within a nation"—underlies anti-Semitic discourse at the end of the century from Joyce's Dublin and early twentieth-century Limerick to Émile Zola's Paris, implying Jewish indifference to nationalist causes and a parasitic internationalism corrosive of the body politic.[40] Yet, contrary to Deasy's feeble witticism earlier in *Ulysses* that Ireland never persecuted Jews because it never admitted them, the Jewish populations of Dublin, Cork, Limerick, and Belfast were growing at the turn of the century,[41] so much so that Dubliners like Bloom could as justifiably claim an Irish nationality as any other habitué of Barney Kiernan's public house.

More useful for my purposes than the hackneyed indictments in "Cyclops," evidence of the larger repository of cultural meaning associated with Jewishness often emerges suddenly in Joyce's fiction. Reizbaum, for example, cites the moment in *A Portrait of the Artist as a Young Man* when an adolescent Stephen Dedalus, inflamed with desire and in rebellion against the repressiveness of Catholicism, wanders at night "up and down dark slimy streets," hoping to "sin with another of his kind, to force another being to sin with him and to exult with her in sin." He finds himself in a "maze of narrow and dirty streets" where he hears the "drawling of drunken singers" and wonders "whether he had strayed into the quarter of the jews."[42] Like Bella Cohen, the madam of the bordello in the "Circe" episode of *Ulysses*, the woman to whom Stephen surrenders in this scene—Jewish or not—does more than *represent* sexual excess; with "the proud conscious movements of her perfumed head," she *performs* it, as does the mise en scène of her "warm and lightsome" room furnished with a "copious easychair beside the bed" where a "huge doll sat with her legs apart" (95). The scene appropriates well-traveled fantasies of the Jewess as a figure of exoticism, seduction, and—in this context—transgression. "The girl as temptress, symbolically the Jew as urban host," Reizbaum writes, "takes us back to the many sites of such hosting in the Jewish quarters of Joyce's Dublin, places of temptation and threat, degradation and capitulation."[43] Extended in "Circe" through Bella/O Cohen, the body of the Jewess becomes for Reizbaum a figure both of grotesquerie and of sexual fantasy, including the masochistic fantasies of Leopold von Sacher-Masoch's *Venus in Furs*.[44] In these ways, Jewishness in Joyce's writing is frequently connected to the body, sexuality, and excess, to desires lurking beneath a middle-class veneer of Catholic respectability, and to a kind of enormity that dwarfs or overpowers.

Stephen's assignation in *Portrait* prompts a consideration of finer distinctions between theatricality and performativity in the discourse of Irish Jewishness. So, for example, his silent recitation of lines from Edward Bulwer-Lytton's *The Lady of Lyons* prior to his liaison in the "quarter of the jews" juxtaposes what Janelle Reinelt characterizes as the "lingering traces of the theological stage"—the "text-dominated, logocentric stage of European theatre and culture"[45]—with emergent meanings as performed both by the woman Stephen meets and by the objects with which she is associated: a "livesome" room, copious easy chair, and a huge doll with its legs splayed promiscuously. As he wanders into this almost surreal scene, Stephen carries with him codes of behavior promulgated by romantic drama; this influence from the dominant culture is opposed by the performance of a slatternly actor from everyday life, one whose gestures produce subversive meanings arising as the scene unfolds. Particularly relevant here is Reizbaum's observation that the "surprise of the Jew is that s/he is always the proxy relation," an analogue of Roach's contention that performance operates through surrogation insofar as most definitions of performance "commonly assume that performance offers a substitute for something else that preexists it." The process denoted by the term is perhaps most visible, as Roach describes, in the similarities between an effigy and performance: "*Effigy*'s similarity to *performance* should be clear enough: it fills by means of surrogation a vacancy created by the absence of an original."[46] In a vertiginous spiral of surrogation in this scene, the doll amounts to an effigy of a woman; the seductive woman, an effigy of the fantasy represented by the Jew.

In the paralytic Dublin of *Dubliners*, and as a supplement to the implications of Stephen's encounter in *Portrait*, the Jewess was often construed not only as a figure of illicit desire but also as an emblem of a fulfilling emotional life that was impossible to attain. Near the end of "A Little Cloud," the humbled protagonist Little Chandler gazes into the eyes of a photograph of his wife, the coldness and "composure" of which "repelled" and "defied" him. By contrast, the "dark Oriental eyes" of the rich Jewesses about whom his friend Gallaher boasted convey "passion" and a "voluptuous longing," metonyms of a "rapture" he will never know.[47] A significant difference obtains, I would argue, between the totalizing narrative of plays on the late Victorian stage and the excess intimated by "voluptuous longing," precisely because the performance of this surplus can only be an ersatz surrogation, rapture being irreducible to a single gesture, scene, or script. Perhaps more important, while the seduction scene in *Portrait* with its suggestive setting underscores the woman's—and by extension, the Jew's—perverse excess, the voluptuous Jewess Little Chandler imagines serves to nurture the fantasy of a sexually fulfilling life and thereby counters the emotional aridity of Dublin life. In Joyce's Dublin, then, as in the circum–North Atlantic world, this sexualized figure of the Jew represents a profound ambivalence, not unlike Harford's cache of good points that partially mitigate his monstrosity in "Grace."

In this scene in *Portrait*, Joyce's narrator also hints at the affective reach of popular culture, in this case of the theater that both the young Joyce and Stephen Dedalus attended whenever they could afford the price of a ticket. Because both were avid "fans" of the drama, it is scarcely surprising that Stephen's encounter with temptation and ooze, material and psychical, is preceded by the revelation that before arriving at this site, he was mouthing lines from a play. But lines from Lord Lytton's *The Lady of Lyons*? First performed by William Charles Macready in 1838, Bulwer's romance was regarded as a vehicle for "feeble sentiment" by Helen Faucit, who starred opposite Macready in its premiere, and disparaged as a "well-worn piece of fustian" by a critic today.[48] Nevertheless, it served reliably in the repertories of London stars like Henry Irving, a major attraction in Dublin's fin de siècle theater, and in those of lesser talents as well. But, in an exemplary instance of textual circulation, much like Bloom's father who found Irish-American writer Augustin Daly's melodrama *Leah, the Forsaken* (1862) so profound—"Every word is so deep, Leopold" (*U* 5.206)—Joyce's teenage protagonist regarded Bulwer's drama with reverence. In particular, Claude Melnotte, the noble peasant whose "soft speeches" rose to Stephen's lips and "eased his unrest," embodies an idealism far removed from the damp, earthy reality of the scene of Stephen's assignation (94). Possessing a single aspiration—to prove himself worthy of his beloved Pauline, the beautiful daughter of a wealthy merchant—Melnotte cultivates "high thoughts—bright dreams—the hope of fame," goals he eventually achieves through his valor as a war hero.[49] Stephen's valorization of Melnotte's utterly orthodox ideology including the love of home and a Victorian code of the gentlemanly confirms the power of residual texts, even such jejune and musty ones as this, to inform—even penetrate with genuine force—the subjectivity of one of modernism's most discussed characters.[50] As we shall see in the cases of American immigrants, Stephen is hardly unique in this regard.

It should be noted, however, that the plays Joyce and his characters enjoyed did not always endorse the Victorian restraint of characters like Bulwer's Melnotte. On the contrary. In the opening paragraph of *James Joyce: A Biography* (2011), Gordon Bowker describes an incident similar to the one in *Portrait* in which popular drama exerts an entirely different kind of effect on Joyce. The sixteen-year-old playgoer, Bowker writes, leaves a performance of *Sweet Briar* in 1898 "strangely aroused" by what he had seen and afterward meets a "shadowy figure," a woman who eventually seduces him. If Bowker is correct that, because of this incident, Joyce's "Jesuitical conscience now had something serious with which to contend,"[51] then we might speculate that this contending force was one in which the theater, performance, sexuality, and Jewishness proved ungetroundable. In *Ulysses and Us: The Art of Everyday Life in Joyce's Masterpiece* (2009), Declan Kiberd implies as much by asserting that a chance meeting in the city like the one Bowker finds so compelling "connects the reader with his or her inner strangeness, helping us make friends with our buried selves, epitomized perhaps by the Wandering Jew."[52] But if the Jew facilitates our acceptance of our own "buried" identity, Kiberd suggests that the opposite affective process may also be intimated by *Ulysses*: "In making the central character of *Ulysses* an ordinary Jewish citizen, [Joyce] may have foreseen that the Jews could easily become victims of the general disenchantment with the complications of modernity."[53] This dark scene in *Portrait*, then, simultaneously conveys the operations of two antithetical subjective processes: an affective pull *toward* a figure associated with Jewishness, frequently implying the uncanny familiarity of the Irish subject and Jewish object of desire, and a potent opposing force that both repulses and catalyzes a movement *away* from her.

Yet, as I have mentioned, numerous moments in *Ulysses* also advance a formidable counterdiscourse both to this contradiction and to Deasy's and the Citizen's anti-Semitic outbursts. Joyce's novel in fact alludes to what, by 1922, was a well-developed homology between Jewish and Irish culture, between Irishness and Jewishness more generally. That is to say, well before Joyce's writing of the novel, cultural nationalists in the years after the Great Famine period (1845–55) "continually 'reminded' their audiences that the Irish were

being 'driven out of Erin,' like the 'children of Israel.'"[54] During the Celtic
Revival, Douglas Hyde adduced other similarities between the Irish and
Jews, arguing against blinkered notions of cultural homogeneity and asserting that selective cultural appropriation did not compromise the formation
of national identity. In his 1892 speech "The Necessity for De-Anglicizing
Ireland," Hyde maintained that an "educated Irishman" not knowing his
own language would be "at least as disgraceful as for an educated Jew to be
quite ignorant of Hebrew."[55] The "Irish race" at the turn of the century, however, was "ceasing to be Irish without becoming English," languishing in the
"most anomalous position" of "imitating England and yet apparently hating
it." Hyde's decolonizing agenda did not mandate a purifying erasure of everything English from Irish life; in fact, he deemed any devaluation of "what is
best in the English people" to be "absurd."[56] Rather, as a first step both to resist
thoughtless assimilation *and* to reform a contemporary Irish cultural production distinguished only by its "hideousness," Hyde and the Gaelic League
advocated a return to the Irish language, which, in turn, would spark a
renewed commitment to "the traditions of the past." Perhaps most important,
as Gregory Dobbins has explained, this commitment to a past emblematized
by the Irish language did *not* demand a renunciation of political engagement,
but was wholly consistent with the "collective project" of Irish cultural and
social activity at the time: namely, a modernization in which tradition could
serve as a "guarantor" of an ongoing "national essence that persists through
time."[57]

Some characters in *Ulysses* hypostatize an even closer bond between Irish
and Jewish cultures, even if, unlike Hyde, they find little in English culture to
admire. For them, Irish and Jewish traditions constitute examples of cultural
and intellectual achievement, something made visible when compared to the
corrupt cultures of Rome and England. In the "Aeolus" chapter, Professor
MacHugh mockingly summarizes this counterdiscourse to imperial hubris
by noting that "The Roman, like the Englishman who follows in his foot-
steps, brought to every new shore . . . only his cloacal obsession. . . . [A]nd he
said: *It is meet to be here. Let us construct a water closet*" (*U* 7.491–95). The Jew,
by contrast, built an "*altar to Jehovah*" and refused to succumb to the "arro-
gant admonition" of Egypt's high priests; instead, Moses ascended Mt. Sinai,
returning with God's commandments "*graven in the language of the outlaw*" (*U* 7.864, 869). The anti-imperial politics of this juxtaposition are clear,
and Irish nationalists at the time often compared Moses to Charles Stewart
Parnell, the "uncrowned king" of Ireland who, like Moses, died before he
was able to witness the liberation of his people.[58] In *Ulysses*, then, what Joyce
once diagnosed as a "contempt for the unknown"—Irish hostility toward
Jews, even imaginary ones like Mr. Harford in "Grace," and other "foreigners"—and uncanny affinity exist side by side. For MacHugh and his listeners, the Irish and Jews created cultures comparable to that of ancient Greece,

which was also one of Douglas Hyde's contentions, and this achievement merited respect. Moreover, as Little Chandler's fantasies reveal, daily life in Dublin had become so enervated that an exoticized Jewishness represented a desirable alternative.

Given all of this, the most famous Irish Jew of the modern era may well have been Joyce himself. For, if the figure of the Jew in various guises appears in his fiction, she does so with equal persistence in recent studies of Joyce.[59] To be sure, in his monumental biography *James Joyce* (1959, revised 1982), Richard Ellmann devotes considerable attention to Joyce's Jewish friends, his attraction to a young Jewish student Amalia Popper, the Jewish sources for Bloom, and a host of related topics. But more recent books like Kiberd's and Bowker's emphasize Joyce's Jewishness from their very beginnings. For Kiberd, borrowing terminology from Freudian dream analysis, if the "manifest content" of the *Odyssey* is the "scaffolding which eventually falls away to reveal the latent content of *Ulysses*, such a technique isn't necessarily taken from Marx or Freud. It can be found where they probably discovered it too—in the Torah as the source of Jewish tradition." The "strongly autocritical element" in Joyce's novel manifested by passages that "help to supply the very apparatus by which the book might be interpreted" and the notion of a text as a work in progress provide further evidence of Joyce's Jewishness.[60] For Bowker, Joyce's "Bloom side" rendered him "intensely curious about Jews and Jewish life" (9), and his "reading Israel Zangwill's *Ghetto Tragedies* prompted him to draw parallels between the Irish and the Jews, a people with whom he found it easy to identify" (172). At the same time, Joyce was not nearly so sanguine about the Irish nationalist movement, confiding in a letter to his brother Stanislaus that he was "nauseated by [Nationalists'] lying drivel about pure men and pure women and spiritual love" (qtd. in Bowker, 161).

In sum, Joyce's Irish Jews—and perhaps Joyce himself—betray the contradictions inherent to performances of the Jew as illicit and usurious, but also desirable and shrewd; supposedly inferior, but culturally laudable; and, explicit in the analogy between Moses and Parnell, Jews and the Irish were both construed as an "outlaw" people justly seeking their freedom. Such a mottled construction with all of its complexities, its conceptual nooks and crannies, is well captured by Zygmunt Bauman's term "allo-Semitism":

> The Jew is ambivalence incarnate. And ambivalence is ambivalence mostly because it cannot be contemplated without ambivalent feeling: it is simultaneously attractive and repelling, it reminds one of what one would like to be but is afraid of being, it dangles before the eyes what one would rather not see. . . . It is an insight into the truth of being which all ordering bustle is trying hard, though in vain, to hide.[61]

Bauman's diction in this passage is evocative, particularly in its braiding of feeling and the exposition of concealed truth. The Jew renders "incarnate"

something that was previously hidden and is unusually generative of feelings, including intensely ugly ones—think here of Sianne Ngai's discussion
of the "insistent and intolerable" nature of disgust in *Ugly Feelings* (2005)
or Sara Ahmed's unpacking of disgust's "sticky" and performative inten-
sifications in *The Cultural Politics of Emotion* (2004).[62] A similar variety of
ambivalence defined newly arrived immigrant Irish and Jews in America, to
whom I now turn. In particular, American tenement literature at the turn
of the century through the 1930s proves a wealthy trove of allo-Semitism
and allo-Hibernianism as well—that is, intense bigotry on the one hand,
powerful attraction on the other. Moreover, the privileged relationship of
these two diasporic peoples exists not only in the psychical depths of characters languishing and struggling for survival on New York's Lower East
Side—American counterparts to Joyce's Little Chandler, Stephen Dedalus,
and perhaps Joyce himself—but also in a larger political unconscious, a "fundamental history" of a "buried reality" that needs to be excavated in all of its
ambivalent dimensions.[63]

Immigrant Subjectivity and the Irish-Jewish
Unconscious in America

We are going to America, to New York, to the New Jerusalem....
There are more Irish here than in Dublin and more Jews than in all
of Palestine.[64]

—PHILIP WEISENFREUND (1900)

Through the smell of the arbutus she caught for a second the
unwashed smell of immigrants, of Ellis Island, of crowded tenements.
Under the nickelplated, goldplated streets enameled with May, uneasily
she could feel the huddling smell, spreading in dark slow crouching
masses like corruption oozing from broken sewers.[65]

—JOHN DOS PASSOS, *MANHATTAN TRANSFER* (1925)

Philip Weisenfreund's sentiments about immigrating to America typify
the immigrant's belief in a superabundant and pluralistic America, a New
Jerusalem of possibility. An itinerant actor who eked out a meager living in
rural Austria-Hungary during the 1890s, Weisenfreund ultimately made several strategic decisions. One was to anglicize his first name, from Nachum
Favel to Philip, something his young actress-wife later did, changing her
name (Salche) to Sallie; another was to move his growing family—he and
his wife had three young sons—from Budapest to London's East End, where
he found life in impoverished Whitechapel surprisingly rewarding and even
hopeful. Supported by a shopkeeper, Philip and Sallie rented a small theater

that, producing comic fare in Yiddish featuring the *schlemiels* and *shmendriks* his audiences enjoyed, became so successful that Philip eventually bought it and for the first time was able to save for the future. But his prosperity was short-lived. The neighborhood was plagued by gangs, and after a murder occurred outside the door to his theater, Philip's nascent enterprise was ruined. So, like many other fathers before him and after, Philip Weisenfreund traveled alone to America in 1900, later summoning his family to join him in the New Jerusalem better known as New York. His youngest son, Muni, was only five then, and years later, as the actor Paul Muni, he would be nominated five times for an Academy Award, winning one in 1936 for his performance in *The Story of Louis Pasteur.*

Weisenfreund's exuberance evinces the power of the myth that the streets of America were paved with gold and that an ideal cosmopolitan community of different peoples traveled them. David Quixano, the quixotic, hence aptly named young Jewish musician in Zangwill's *The Melting Pot*, summarizes this fable to Vera Revendal, with whom he is falling in love, with all the optimism with which it was typically expressed: "All my life I had heard of America—everybody in our town had friends there or was going there or got money orders from there. . . . America was beckoning, shining—the place where God would wipe away tears from off all faces" (286). David visits Ellis Island to watch the "weary, sea-tossed wanderers" arrive from "the starving villages of Italy and Ireland," the "swarming stony cities of Poland and Galicia," or the "ruined farms of Roumania" (287). Inspired by such sights, he believes—and his "American symphony" reflects this belief—that his new country is a "great Melting Pot where all the races of Europe are melting and re-forming . . . Germans and Frenchmen, Irishmen and English, Jews and Russians—into the Crucible with you all! God is making the American" (288). With such paeans to America and allusions to its welcoming democracy recurring throughout the play, it is little wonder that *The Melting Pot* was one of President Theodore Roosevelt's favorites and that he counted its author as his friend.[66]

David's optimism is sorely tested, however, by the revelation that Vera's father was a Russian officer who participated in the internationally condemned massacre at Kishinev in April 1903 that claimed among its victims his father, mother, and sisters, an outrageous episode of rampant anti-Semitism that included rape, arson, and widespread looting.[67] Equally problematic, Vera fears that her kiss will "leave blood" upon his lips and force him to remember this horror; gently dismissing her fear, he is confident "it will make me forget" (362). The play ends with a brilliant performance of his symphony at Vera's Settlement House; a panorama including the torch of the Statue of Liberty appears in the backdrop; and the "*softened sounds of voices and instruments joining in 'My Country, 'tis of Thee'*" is heard as the curtain falls slowly (363). As if to testify to the wisdom of David's faith in an annealing American melting pot, Zangwill creates two entertaining minor characters: David's Yiddish-speaking and devoutly religious great-aunt, Frau Quixano, and her antagonist, Irish housekeeper Kathleen.[68] As the opening scene begins, Kathleen fumes in the offstage kitchen about the confusing particulars of kosher preparation: "Pots and pans and plates and knives. Sure, 'tis enough to make a saint chrazy [sic]" (272). Entering the living room, she complains, "Bad luck to me, if iver I take sarvice again with haythen Jews" and threatens to give her employers a one-week notice (273). Yet, by the end, this comic antipathy has been transformed into an affectionate Irish Jewishness. Kathleen speaks broken Yiddish with a brogue, dotes on her employer, who after the performance of David's symphony is momentarily lost, and embarks upon a search for her with a line reflective of her new identity in the great American melting pot: "Begorra, we Jews never know our way" (355).

The America that greeted 28 million arrivals between 1880 and 1920—and 2.1 million Irish decades earlier during the Famine—hardly matched the idealized place David Quixano envisioned.[69] The epigraph from Dos Passos's *Manhattan Transfer* hints at the harsh reality that awaited the majority of immigrants by way of both familiar metaphors and a trope of depth relevant to this history: America's "goldplated" streets actually papered over a corruption reminiscent of the filth of Joyce's Nighttown. This was especially true of New York's Lower East Side, which attracted newcomers from across Europe and Asia, and African-Americans as well who migrated by the thousands to northern cities prior to the Civil War. The numbers of Jews escaping eastern Europe rose sharply after 1881, as Irving Howe and other historians document, with the death of Alexander II in Russia. Much like the Irish who escaped the Famine of 1847–51, Jews leaving eastern Europe in the 1880s were not always embraced by an earlier generation of more educated, successful émigrés who tended to advocate a "mildly restrictionist approach" that would grant admission to the country only to skilled workers and the able-bodied.[70] For their part, as David Fitzpatrick puts it, and although Ireland in the nineteenth century was "far from homogenous," many Irish-Americans hailed from Connaught in Ireland's southwest and "characteristically left behind them an unusually backward rural economy in which they had little chance of employment, only to find all but the squalid margins of American society apparently closed to them likewise." This austere reality applies equally to Famine-era Irish and to those who came to America later between 1876 and 1895. As a result, like Muldoon's canal-digging "Irish schlemiels," in the best cases these Irish succeeded only in "securing the best of the worst jobs" in their new home.[71] Howe, too, provides some sense of this "good bad luck" (a phrase of which Eugene O'Neill's James Tyrone in *Long Day's Journey into Night* was fond) when depicting an overcrowded Lower East Side that by 1890 had 522 inhabitants per acre, a figure that a decade later exploded to more than 700, making the density of the population "greater than that of the worst sections of Bombay."[72] From such data and the accounts of "greenhorns" or recent arrivals, Howe creates a sense of an immigrant's first days in the city: the "fortunate" landing of a menial job, the suffering of pangs of acute loneliness, and a restless night's sleep on dirty sheets splattered with dried blood and infested with fleas (68).

Nevertheless, as Howe mentions, appreciable differences distinguish Jews arriving in the 1880s from those who came even two decades later, confirming again the danger of using such terms "Jew" and "Irish" that might efface distinctions of class, origin, gender, and much more. This negative potential notwithstanding, in the majority of instances below I will direct my attention to immigrant experience, particularly tenement experience, and to the often uncanny and intense psychical realities intimated by the term "unconscious" starting with the oppressive conditions of Lower East Side New York in the 1880s and thereafter before moving to the pool halls and baseball diamonds of Studs Lonigan's Hyde Park on the South Side of Chicago.

Writers from Stephen Crane and Anzia Yezierska to Henry Roth and, later, Frank McCourt have represented in at times excruciating detail the hardship of tenement life in New York. But such literature depicts more than the poverty and dysfunction of the Johnson apartment in Crane's *Maggie, A Girl of the Street* (1893/96); more than Sonya Vrunsky's memories in Yezierska's *Salome of the Tenements* (1923) of being "tied to a machine" in a factory with barred windows and iron doors; and more than desperate young women "scratching out each other's eyes in the mad pushing" to get to the head of a line of applicants at a shirt factory in Yezierska's *Bread Givers* (1925).[73] These snapshots capture a riven human subject whose inner realities are at times as hidden as the "corruption" residing just below the streets in *Manhattan Transfer*. What David Quixano hailed as America's great, welcoming "mother-hand" was nowhere in sight, for example, when Genya Schearl in Roth's *Call It Sleep* (1934) arrived with her young son in New York in May 1907. Roth begins his masterwork with a reiteration of the same opposition Dos Passos's narrator perceives, for after an epigraph that reads "I pray thee ask no questions / this is that Golden Land" the novel's first sentence conveys a very different reality: "The small white steamer, *Peter Stuyvesant*, that delivered the immigrants from the stench and throb of the steerage to the stench and throb of New York tenements, rolled slightly on the water beside the stone quay."[74] Standing on deck with her son David and viewing her pitiably gaunt husband Albert for the first time in seventeen months, she ironically remarks, "And this is the Golden Land. . . . You must have suffered in this land" (11).[75] As Genya infers from her waiting husband's appearance, the lure of a "shining" America too often concealed a different reality, lives in extremis that recall the "Little Ireland" section of mid-Victorian London that Marx and Engels decried.

Throughout the early pages of *Call It Sleep*, Albert Schearl exhibits behaviors that provide a window onto an immigrant subjectivity shared by many

Irish- and Jewish-Americans—and by some of Joyce's Dubliners as well. Albert's complicated subjectivity erupts with disturbing clarity when he meets his wife and son, and more than material deprivation is responsible for it. In "Bowery Afternoon" from *The Ghetto and Other Poems* (1918), transplanted Irish poet Lola Ridge portrays the deadening routinizations of modernity that workers like Albert know all too well: "Drab discoloration / Of faces façades, pawn-shops. . . . Deadly uniformity / Of eyes and windows / Alike devoid of light."[76] More than just "drab," life in Ridge's Bowery is "rancid" and "mangy," an existence endured in "dingy bee-hives swarming with humanity" (82). Even more devastating, ghetto life leads to a depredation of the spirit that must be recuperated, and for this reason Albert, like Crane's Maggie, becomes uncommonly invested in the theater. He tells his foreman Joe Luter, who for a time rents a room in the Schearl apartment, that long ago in the old country he was "moved . . . greatly" by a Yiddish play called *Revenge of Samson* (34). Not long after this, "like a drunkard his dram," Albert "seized hold of the theatre," even to the point, as Genya reports, of his "gnashing his teeth at a certain character" while he slept beside her at night (42). Attending lighter entertainments, Crane's Maggie enjoys Irish songs—both comic tunes and patriotic ballads that glorify Ireland's resistance to English colonial rule—and is drawn to one of melodrama's most potent attractions: "She rejoiced at the way in which the poor and virtuous eventually overcame the wealthy and wicked."[77] She wonders if the "culture and refinement she had seen imitated, perhaps grotesquely, by the heroine on the stage, could be acquired by a girl who lived in a tenement house and worked in a shirt factory" (125). In other words, like Joyce's Rudolph Virag, who found deep meaning in *Leah, the Forsaken*, Maggie and Albert engage with popular theater in an uncommonly strong way. For immigrant and provincial theatergoer alike, then, recalling that Joyce's Dublin even after the rise of Irish Literary Theatre in 1897 was, in part, a satellite of the London stage, plays and other forms of an incipient circum–North Atlantic culture "moved" popular audiences, so much so that, as in Albert's case, it visited their dreams and inflected their fantasies.

The preface of *Call It Sleep* also reveals a second characteristic of an immigrant subjectivity that might be juxtaposed to what James Clifford theorizes as a "diasporic subjectivity," remembering that both groups are socially heterogeneous and that both are contingent historical formations "in process."[78] For Clifford, and for the Famine-era Irish immigrants Kerby Miller describes in *Ireland and Irish America: Culture, Class, and Transatlantic Migration* (2008), diasporic subjectivity is inherently fractured. That is, "diasporic forms of longing, memory, and (dis)identification are shared by a broad spectrum of minority and migrant populations." Such groups, as Clifford explains by allusion to contemporary migrants with camcorders and other electronic devices for carrying vivid representations of their pasts with them, "increasingly find themselves in border relations with the old country": they maintain memories of their homeland, often believe they cannot be successfully assimilated into their new society, and even desire an eventual return to their country of origin.[79] Or, as in the case of O'Neill's father James, these "border relations" can manifest themselves in devastating ways. Like James Tyrone in *Long Day's Journey into Night* (1956), the elder O'Neill was abandoned by his father, who returned to Ireland, died soon thereafter, and doomed his children and wife who remained in America to lives of poverty and hardship.[80] Although James O'Neill eventually achieved stardom on the American stage and acquired a degree of wealth, he maintained a keen interest in Ireland and Irish politics, so much so that, for one biographer, although James was a "faithful member of the church, his religion was almost as much Irish nationalism as Catholicism."[81] Indeed, his attachment to Ireland may have been stronger, as Jamie mockingly observes of his father's hypocritical trumpeting of the "one true faith of the Catholic Church" in *Long Day's Journey*: "I don't notice you've worn any holes in the knees of your pants going to Mass" (77).

Of course, some Jewish émigrés felt a similar nostalgia, although the intensity of this longing may be overstated as the rates of *return* immigration for both Irish- and Jewish-Americans is exceptionally low compared to that of other groups.[82] In this regard, the Irish and Jewish diasporas are hardly identical, as Jews moved to North America from a number of countries, not just one, requiring serial assimilations for some and a muting of allegiance to their former homelands for others. Some, like Reb Smolinsky's wife in Anzia Yezierska's *Bread Givers*, insist that "There ain't in America such beautiful things like we had home" (33); and, even more seriously, for "Honest Abe" Levy, "shrewdest bargain driver that ever shrugged his shoulders" in *Salome of the Tenements* (59), all the wealth he has amassed cannot disguise the fact that life in his native village "had purpose and meaning" because, as the cantor at a synagogue, he was "the soul and spirit of his people" (60). Having lost his voice in a botched operation and thus forced to relinquish his position of centrality in his village, he moved to America with just one goal: to feed his newfound "obsession" for gold.

Unlike this internally divided diasporic subject, however, a younger second-generation seldom experienced this precise nostalgia-driven conflict so acutely. As a teenager growing up on Chicago's South Side, for example, James T. Farrell's Studs Lonigan celebrates America's victory in World War I in the early pages of *The Young Manhood of Studs Lonigan*, the second of Farrell's trilogy of Lonigan novels published between 1932 and 1935. On a crowded Chicago elevated train, trying his best to "brush up" against an attractive "jane" and extract a cheap thrill or two, Studs learns that Germany has been defeated. Just then, a "cabbage-faced woman with a brogue" hollered, "Bully for Wilson and Ireland," and a "monkey-faced mick blubbered tears, whining that Padraic Pearse was dead, whoever that guy was." Pearse, of course, was executed soon after the Easter 1916 rising in Dublin, not in 1918 at the end of the war, but no matter—Studs has little interest in Irish politics or history. As he proclaims later celebrating in the streets of the Chicago "Loop," "I'm an American."[83] His father, by contrast, lounges on the front porch of the trilogy's first novel *Young Lonigan* smoking a stogy and dreaming of the time he and his wife might visit the "old sod," tour the birthplace of the great tenor John McCormack, "take a squint at the Lakes of Killarney," kiss the Blarney Stone, and meet their relatives (19). And unlike Studs, who hums popular Tin Pan Alley hits, his father sings traditional Irish ballads to himself. Quite different subjectivities thus coexist in the same households in the decades described by Farrell, Roth, O'Neill, and Yezierska, often sparking conflict between father and sons, and mothers and daughters like Ridge's Sadie in "The Ghetto," whose mother is harshly unwelcoming of her daughter's Gentile lover (19).

Like Studs, Roth's Albert Schearl, though he hardly feels at home in New York as genuinely as Farrell's feckless teenager does in Chicago, maintains no connection to Europe. After he goes on board the *Peter Stuyvesant* to meet his wife and two-year-old son, Albert notices that Genya has allowed David to wear a blue straw hat adorned with polka-dot ribbons sewn on by his former nurse, which from Albert's perspective is the source of derisive laughter from a small group of "idiots" watching them. "They're mocking us!" he explodes. "What will the others do on the train? He looks like a clown in it!" (15). Uttering the words in a "harsh voice" accompanied by a "wrathful glare," Albert seizes the boy's hat and hurls it onto the green waters below. As rationalized by Roth's narrator, who seems to have insinuated himself into Albert's psyche, the boy's "costume" seems "distinctly foreign"—a glaring sign that they were "newly arrived immigrants" (10), and, Albert snarls, Genya "should have left it behind!" (15). Depicting the entrance of a 1950s Irish immigrant in his novel *Brooklyn* (2009), Colm Tóibín similarly understands the capacity of objects like this unfortunate hat to announce—indeed, to perform—ethnic or national difference. Eilis Lacey, leaving her home in Enniscorthy as victims of the Famine had a century before, is advised by a fellow passenger as their ship approaches New York to discard her suitcase before their arrival as it is obviously "too Irish." Later, at the boarding house at which she has taken a room, another girl constantly complains that the food served by the Irish-American proprietor is "too Irish."[84] These and other efforts to assimilate notwithstanding, including marriage to her Italian suitor, Eilis is never completely successful at breaking ties to Ireland, hinting at the inherent difficulty of this subject position. Returning to Enniscorthy for what was supposed to be a brief visit, she dreads returning to the monotonous ordeal of working on the shop floor in Brooklyn and a life "with strange people, strange accents, strange streets."[85] But, resolved to do her duty, she returns, knowing that doing so will grow to haunt her more and more as the years go by. Nostalgia, as these examples attest, is an uneven phenomenon, afflicting some strongly and barely affecting others.

Perhaps more important and regardless of their relationship with their former homelands, immigrants like Roth's Albert Schearl, Yezierska's Sonya Vrunsky, and Tóibín's Eilis Lacey *feel* more acutely, experience life more intensely than natives, especially wealthy Americans of Anglo-Protestant heritage. And this capacity comprises a third characteristic of an immigrant subjectivity undergirded by the Irish-Jewish unconscious, along with the immigrant's intense attraction to and penetration by popular cultural texts, and the internal pressures resulting from an often unresolved relationship to the country of origin or cultural practices associated with it. A passage in Roth's preface to *Call It Sleep* extracts ironic humor from this affective reality when relating the spectacle of immigrants landing in America:

> The most volatile races, such as the Italians, often danced for joy, whirled each other around, pirouetted in an ecstasy; . . . Jews wept, jabbered, almost put each other's eyes out with the recklessness of their darting gestures; . . . and after one pecking kiss the English might be seen gravitating toward, but never achieving an embrace. (11)

This affective calculus informed colonialist discourse by feminizing the colonized and thereby rationalizing the colonizer's domination: the Irish are a feminine race, for example; therefore English rule brought a necessary rationality and restraint to governance, or so this logic runs. But in the context of nineteenth- and early and mid-twentieth-century immigration, this sense of an intensity of feeling, of an at times uncontrollable hypercathexis, accrues a very different significance. In some instances, this intensity—and theories of affect privilege *intensity*[86]—is associated with such negative feelings as shame and envy, which were bred in the squalor of tenement life; in others, it characterizes the ebullience and naive optimism inherent to the conception of an American melting pot.

Few novelists understand immigrant affect better than Roth and Yezierska. From their opening paragraphs, Yezierska's *Salome of the Tenements* and *Bread Givers* foreground the affective surplus that rages in many tenement households. Yet it is often a surplus one neither needs nor wants: too many buns and not enough hot dogs. Complementary commodities like hot dogs and buns, as economists are wont to note, are imbricated differently in a "value network" than opposing or competitive items: one brand of mustard as opposed to another. At the risk of considerable vulgarity, feelings might be theorized similarly. For example, as Seth Moglen describes, American "modernization had produced, above all, an affective crisis—a crisis in the possibility of love."[87] This crisis, not unlike that portrayed in the conclusion of "Eveline," the forced marriage of "The Boarding House," or the acute loneliness of "A Painful Case" in Joyce's *Dubliners*, finds part of its origins in abject poverty and modernity's alienations, Irish corollaries of what Moglen labels the "injuries of American capitalism." And, in the injurious America of Dos Passos's *Manhattan Transfer* and *U.S.A.* money—capital itself—is consistently linked to gender and the gratifications of love; indeed, it often functions as a prerequisite for both the achievement of full manhood and the attainment of a lover. Jimmy Herf's Uncle Jeff chastises him for not exhibiting "sufficient responsibility about money matters" and thus "making good in a man's world" (101); returning from the war, Joe O'Keefe complains that because former soldiers cannot find work their "girls have gone and married other fellers" (242). Without consistent work and the salary it brings, a man isn't really a man, and his prospects of finding a woman with whom to share his life are poor to nonexistent. The value network of *Manhattan Transfer* therefore does more than delineate the complementarity of work, money, gender, and the possibility of love; the former pair is a prerequisite to the full achievement of the latter pair. The lovers Dutch and Francie, attempting to short-circuit the network, resort to armed robbery so as to recapture the good times they can no longer afford, and receive twenty years in prison for their trouble.

Yezierska's heroines struggle with love as well, but this crisis is overshadowed by a discourse in both *Salome of the Tenements* and *Bread Givers* of surplus feeling, not emotional desiccation. In *Salome* Sonya Vrunsky proclaims herself a creature of intense longing: "I am a Russian Jewess, a flame—a longing. A soul consumed with hunger for heights beyond reach. I am the ache of unvoiced dreams, the clamor of suppressed desires" (37). Preparing for the climactic scene in which her wealthy suitor John Manning arrives at her refurbished tenement apartment, Sonya was a "planet on fire" and a "flame of unrest": "In her intensity of emotion, she was the Russian Jewess rapacious in her famine to absorb the austere perfections of the Anglo-Saxon race" (65–66). Drawn by the "intensity of spirit of the oppressed races," Manning is "pierced through the very roots of his being" (101). As his "cultured restraint" and "cold austerity" yield to Sonya's intensity, he imagines "The oriental mystery and the Anglo-Saxon clarity that will pioneer a new race of men" (108).

This utopian ambition, however, is never realized, as Sonya never feels at home in his "stolid" and "unimaginative" world, an epiphany triggered by her hosting a social reception as Manning's wife. Irritated by the procession of wealthy dowagers and their spoiled daughters who parade past her, Sonya can abide neither this sterile pageant nor her deferential role as hostess in it. And her beauty and style cannot disguise her humble background: "Her gesticulating hands show her origin," one snide guest remarked (121).[88] Unable to countenance this charade and retreating to her room, Sonya is reprimanded by Manning, and the "crumbling temple" of their love is the inevitable result: "Sonya and Manning, tricked into matrimony, were the oriental and the Anglo-Saxon trying to find a common language. The over-emotional Ghetto struggling for its breath in the thin air of puritan restraint" (132). The optimism with which both pursued their dreams showed itself to be, *pace* Lauren Berlant, cruel: "A relation of cruel optimism exists when something you desire is actually an obstacle to your flourishing. It might involve food, or a kind of love; it might be a fantasy of the good life, or a political project."[89] Consistent with the affective surplus of much tenement literature, Berlant's definition captures Sonya's triad of ambitions: finding of a man to love, social ascendancy, and the pursuit of a progressive politics. Unfortunately, Sonya's Puritan husband, not unlike Eveline's suitor Frank in Joyce's "Eveline," cannot facilitate an escape from poverty without exacting a psychically fatal cost (both women fear a loss of self). And both young women's naive optimism and intensity of feeling make this reality even crueler.

Like Sonya, Sara Smolinsky in *Bread Givers* experiences life in flames of sensation; sadly, these are largely negative affects, particularly her acute sense of shame. From the novel's opening page, shame functions as a leitmotif: because Sara's family depends upon her sister Bessie's earnings, her unsuccessful search for a job would mean being "thrown into the street to shame and to laughter" (1); if this occurred, each penny "thrown into the plate was another stab into our burning shame" (2); Sara is "shamed" by her father's ill-treatment of one of her sister's suitors, and so on. "Shame" or some lexical variant of it recurs throughout the novel, a negative affect that Sara Ahmed equates to a jolting exposure—"another sees what I have done"—but it "also involves an attempt to hide," a turning away from others and retreat into the self.[90] This pattern is broken in the novel only by envy when one neighbor determines that another has benefited from a sudden windfall. Given her poverty, hence not surprisingly, Sara experiences an equally strong feeling of elation when she earns money for the family; at the end of the opening chapter, she buys and sells herring at a profit and is overwhelmed by her success:

> It began dancing before my eyes, the twenty-five herring that earned me my twenty-five cents. It lifted me in the air, my happiness. *I couldn't help it*. It began dancing under my feet. And I couldn't stop myself. (22–23; my emphasis)

Later, languishing in her family's ill-fated shop, bought on a whim by her father, she recalls the feeling she had once so enjoyed: "The pay envelope. The joyous feel of money where every little penny was earned with your own hands" (129). Crane's narrator in *Maggie, A Girl of the Streets* attributes a similar feeling to Maggie's brother, Jimmie: "When he had a dollar in his pocket his satisfaction with existence was the greatest thing in the world" (113). Even when working for modest wages (or worse), capital drives feeling in the tenement subjectivity; it invades interiority and dominates psychical life.

Like subjective fracturing and an intense engagement with popular culture, this affective surplus or excess of feeling defines everyday immigrant experience. Affective surplus, however, does not denote a surfeit of *emotion*, nor does it necessarily refer to feeling generated by causally constructed or linear narratives. Sara's elation at receiving her wages cannot be helped; it dominates her being and she cannot resist. For Brian Massumi, such intensity is equated with affect and marks the emergence of an "expression-event" that is in many ways ineffable. Massumi might object to my use of "unconscious" in connection with the origin of this constellation of feeling and the subjective affinities between the Irish and Jews, for while he regards affect or intensity as autonomic and therefore "non-conscious," he maintains that it is not part of a "depth reaction."[91] Expanding upon this notion and that of an affective "situation," Berlant similarly theorizes a "sense of emergence of something in the present that may become an event"—that is, may become an occasion upon which "*something* that will perhaps matter is unfolding."[92] Fair enough. Massumi's insistence that this intensity is "narratively delocalized," "disconnected from meaningful sequencing, from narration," describes several of the examples I have offered here.[93] That is to say, there is a difference between feeling shame as the result of eviction—Sara Smolinsky's fear—or of the humiliating chastisement Stephen Dedalus receives at Clongowes Wood in *A Portrait of the Artist as a Young Man*, and the flooding of intense torrents of feeling for no obvious reason, as Sonya experiences in *Salome of the Tenements*. Such intensities, for good or ill, not only define figures of the Irish and the Jew, but also surface frequently in their interactions with each other. Performative figures, Irish and Jews are thus not only ambivalent figures in themselves; they are hybrids produced by relationships that are equally ambivalent and highly cathected, and at times strangely familiar and close—even when they are hostile to each other.

Allo-Semitism ↔ Allo-Hibernianism: On Ambivalence and the Uncanny

> Like a river addled
> With its hot tide of flesh
> That ever thickens.
> Heavy surges of flesh
> Break over the pavements
> Clavering like a surf—
>
> —LOLA RIDGE, *THE GHETTO*

Like Muldoon gazing at the flood waters coursing before him in "At the Sign of the Black Horse September, 1999," Lola Ridge recognized in the human tide on Hester Street histories of both recent and more distant pasts. From one point of view, Hester Street was "Heaped like a dray / With the garbage of the world" (15), a site of unimaginable overcrowding and abject poverty; from a longer or typological perspective, the "brood" of women on Hester Street stand in for the "ancient mothers" who had seen the "dawn break over" Egypt, "turned their cakes upon the dry hot stones / And went on" (16). And from this performance, yet another perspective—of both Jewishness and modernist poetry—is enabled: "nearer seen / This litter of the East / Takes on a garbled majesty" that neither T. S. Eliot's nor Ezra Pound's representations of the Jew exhibited (24).[94] The figure of the Jew and, as I will delineate in the following chapters, that of the Irishman perform a similar "garbled majesty." And this ambivalence finally proves more resonant and *uncanny* as newly arrived and first-generation Irish- and Jewish-Americans begin to interact with each other, hence the addition of "allo-Hibernianism" to Bauman's allo-Semitism. Both terms grow even more garbled in majesty, dreadful and grand at the same time, when juxtaposed to each other.

To be sure, at the turn of the century and later both Jews and the Irish were stereotyped in mindless screeds like Uncle Jeff Herf's in *Manhattan Transfer*: "I tell you, Wilkinson," he complains, "New York is no longer what it used to be. . . . City's overrun with kikes and low Irish" (85). In this paranoid analysis strikingly similar to the discourse of immigration in twenty-first-century America, "Jew lawyers and Irish judges" will "run" Americans "out of their own country" (143, 85). Or so Dos Passos's malcontent grumbled. Achieving such a purposeful and powerful solidarity to achieve this imperial goal, however, was hardly a simple project for new arrivals to New York or anywhere else for that matter. As photographer Jacob A. Riis explains in *How the Other Half Lives* (1890), urban poverty was accompanied by ethnic tensions that scarcely qualified as utopian or facilitated the formation of the indomitable political blocs bigots feared. Through his often stunning photography and accompanying commentary, Riis, an émigré from Denmark, catalogs a notorious Fourth Ward Alley that once housed some 140 Irish and Italian families and chronicles the history of struggle that obtained there:

> The once unwelcome Irishman has been followed in turn by the Italian, the Russian Jew, and the Chinaman, and has himself taken a hand at opposition, quite as bitter and quite as an ineffectual, against these later hordes. Wherever these have gone they have crowded him out, possessing the block, the street, the ward, with their denser swarms. But the Irishman's revenge is complete.[95]

This revenge came in the form of tenement ownership, which allowed nouveaux riches Irish to exploit less fortunate arrivals who came after them. Nevertheless, the articulation between these two diasporic peoples grows in meaning at the fin de siècle and throughout the opening decades of the twentieth century.

A mapping of allo-Semitism and allo-Hibernianism extends the param-
eters of a scholarly literature written, to a considerable extent, from a critical
race studies perspective on the black-Irish relationship or on the particulari-
ties of Irish/African- American cultural exchange: Noel Ignatiev's *How the
Irish Became White* (1995), Peter O'Neill and David Lloyd's anthology *The
Black and Green Atlantic* (2009), and Lauren Onkey's *Blackness and Trans-
Atlantic Identity: Celtic Soul Brothers* (2009) come immediately to mind.
Others scholars have profitably excavated a black-Jewish formation, as represented by Lori Harrison-Kahan's *The White Negress: Literature, Minstrelsy, and
the Black-Jewish Imaginary* (2011), which expands upon the work of Michael
Rogin and Jonathan Freedman, and Willis Barnstone's *We Jews and Blacks*
(2004), a memoir with poems by Yusef Komunyakaa. Another kind of multi-
foliate approach distinguishes George Bornstein's *The Colors of Zion: Blacks,
Jews, and Irish from 1845 to 1945* (2011), which announces its intention to consider "what these three groups might have had in common at the turn of the
previous century and perhaps still do."[96] Citing Bryan Cheyette's influential
work, Bornstein recognizes the "protean instability of 'the Jews' as a signifier"
and thus its inherent ambivalence.[97] Still, his primary ambition is to trace the
"congruencies" between blacks, Jews, and Irish, illuminating "positive links"
and "parallels" between them.[98] A worthy project, Bornstein's study follows a
trajectory quite different from the narrative of uncanny affinity and affective
surplus—an inventory of cultural collaborations and both positive and "ugly"
feelings—I hope to adumbrate here.

Here, "uncanny" is intended to echo Freud's essay on the topic. Given his
synopsis of the etymology of the uncanny (the *unheimlich*)—its connotation
of the homely and familiar, yet also of the secret, concealed, or terrifying;
the dreadful and the grand—it is not difficult to imagine its applicability
to immigration to, and the cultural archive of, the circum–North Atlantic
world. Indeed, creating or finding a new home and, at the same time, feeling fully oneself there, *is* the immigrant project writ large. Equally relevant,
from the opening sentence of his essay, Freud regards the uncanny as inextricably tied to feeling: "It is only rarely," he begins, "that a psycho-analyst
feels impelled to investigate the subject of aesthetics, even when aesthetics
is understood to mean not merely the theory of beauty, but the theory of the
qualities of feeling."[99] *Making* a home and *feeling* at home are not synonymous phenomena, however, as Una Chaudhuri explains in *Staging Place: The
Geography of Modern Drama* (1995) while excavating the problematic of place
in the plays of Henrik Ibsen, August Strindberg, and others. In her reading
of *Long Day's Journey into Night*, for example, the Tyrones, especially Mary,
exhibit "geopathic symptoms" or problems with place both in their relationships and within their own troubled psyches. Mary confides to one of her
housekeepers that she "never felt at home in the theatre" when she accompanied her husband, the matinee idol, on tours from city to city (102); and

she similarly regards the family's summer home as "lonely" and hardly the place of "peace" her doctor has prescribed (95, 93). Her husband is at least partially responsible for her symptoms: "He doesn't understand a home" (61), she complains to Jamie, an allegation that both of her sons implicitly endorse. Like Mary, Chaudhuri observes, characters on the modern stage often harbor "incommensurate urges" to stay in one place and to escape it, to make a "stable container for identity" but to ensure it is not a prison and flee if it devolves into one, thus giving rise to the "problematic of home." And, much like the Freudian "uncanny," Chaudhuri's geopathology comes closer to explaining the peculiarities of the allo-Semitic–allo-Hibernian relationship than critical emphases on congruencies or hostilities alone can unpack and inventory.

An uncanny geopathology marks the lives of Irish and Jewish Americans in the early twentieth century. Years before he edited the *Liberator* and *New Masses* and wrote *Jews without Money* (1930), for example, Michael Gold held a variety of jobs on the East Side: soda jerk, errand boy, shipping clerk, and more.[100] In 1905 at age twelve, he began working to help support his family, eventually finding steady employment with Adams Express, a freight operation where he did everything from move heavy cargo to serve as a receiving clerk and assistant truck driver. He would occasionally experience wanderlust and take what appeared to be a more promising job elsewhere, only to return to Adams Express and his Irish New Yorker boss who possessed the uncommon ability to make almost any task seem "romantic." Gold's father, however, an émigré from Romania and by the second decade of the century an invalid, constantly complained about his son's association with the Irish:

> So you are off again, woe to us all! To work on the wagon again with the Irishers. It was the only dream of my life in America that my sons would be educated people! . . . Here the poorest Jewish children can become rabbis, doctors, lawyers! But my son spits on education! He is a basketball bum, a fighter, he comes back from that dirty Irish gym with a black eye, a broken nose, every night like a bloody wolf! ("Childhood" 294)

Gold attributes his father's censure not to prejudice but to a generational "misunderstanding," for in addition to his job as a laborer, Gold was caught up in the "craze for sports" sweeping over the East Side that was unimaginable in the older European ghettoes. And, as they had for "The Little Hebrew" Attell, raised in an Irish neighborhood in San Francisco before moving to New York to pursue his career as a prizefighter, sports in general and boxing in particular brought Jewish and Irish boys together. Gold was one of these. He learned to box in a basement gym jerry-built in a nearby Catholic church, often sparring with a gaunt printer's apprentice called "Kid O'Reilly," whose real name was Aaron Cohen ("Childhood" 301).

Jewish and Irish immigrants lived in stifling proximity in Gold's tenement, and in *Jews without Money* he depicts the almost nightly fights of the O'Briens, who resided on the top floor of his building, including the "anguished screams of the Irish mother" being beaten by her husband.[101] For her part, Gold's mother wasn't in any way startled by the ruckus (or, "ructions," in a more Irish register), as she regarded all Christians with equal disdain. "It is worse than the whores . . . having Christians in a tenement is worse" (169), she once observed. But if his mother disparaged Christians—and if his father lectured his son about squandering his opportunities with "Irishers"—Gold took a much broader view. In fact, while contemplating and then deconstructing ethnic stereotypes, he remarks, "My father, for instance, was like a certain kind of Irishman more than the stenciled stage Jew" (81). More important, when recalling his days working at the Callahan Transfer Express, Gold makes a comparison between Jewish and Irish laborers that underscores both their affinity with and occasional hostility toward each other: "Between jobs these citizens of the two leading persecuted and erratic small nations of the world loafed on a bench. They fought, philosophized and drank buckets of beer together in the sunlight" (269).

This paradoxical relationship informs much of Gold's writing and life, as his Irish friends and acquaintances at times perceived him in terms similar to the way he envisioned his father—that is, as an Irishman. In a 1961 article on Irish labor leader Jim Larkin, James T. Farrell recalls that the Dublin activist often referred to Gold as "Mickey" and, when asked to help broker a truce between rival Irish-American labor groups, Larkin invited his friend Mickey to accompany him to a meeting of the disputants.[102]

When Gold's aspirations to become a writer matured, as biographers of Eugene O'Neill note, he contacted the emergent Provincetown Players and George Cram "Jig" Cook, asking him to read a one-act play he had written and consider producing it. Cook did both, earning Gold's respect, and the aspiring playwright joined a social circle comprised of political activists, theater workers, and writers. During the harsh winter of 1917–18 Gold introduced O'Neill to Catholic activist Dorothy Day, which led to their friendship and nights drinking at The Golden Swan, an Irish saloon known as the "Hell Hole." Arthur and Barbara Gelb describe drinking sessions there as enlivened by Gold's impromptu dissertations on art and revolution, Hippolyte Havel's reminiscences, and O'Neill's recitation of the Catholic poem "The Hound of Heaven." After the saloon closed, Gold, O'Neill, Day, and others would stroll down the waterfront, Gold entertaining his companions with Jewish songs. Whether it was such entertainment, the conversation, his attraction to Day, his disaffection from his family, or a welcome fog induced by the booze—or some combination of all of these—O'Neill grew fond of nights at the Hell Hole. There were disputes, of course, and emotional complications; nevertheless, as the Gelbs put it, the Hell Hole "became one of the few places where [O'Neill] found himself completely at home"—not unlike the benches where Gold sat in the sunlight with his Irish coworkers.[103]

Life in New York is similarly complicated by Irishness for Ira Stigman, the protagonist of Henry Roth's four-book series *Mercy of a Rude Stream* (1994–98). The first installment, *A Star Shines over Mt. Morris Park*, chronicles Ira's early years, beginning in the summer of 1914 when his parents moved the family from the Lower East Side to Harlem. At first, Ira hates the move and lobbies his parents to return to the old neighborhood, even if only for a visit: "So persistently had Ira nagged Mom to revisit 9th Street, to revisit the East Side—out of a longing grown all the more intense now that he found himself in Irish-dominated 119th—that she finally consented" (23). At school his teenaged uncle Harry had become "the object of derision, of Irish derision (and what derision had a sharper edge?)" (16); and some toughs had picked fights with young Ira as well, until he administered "as hard a wallop on the cheek as he could" to a neighborhood bully named Heffernan (30). This is the first of many battles Ira waged with Irish adversaries, and his chronicle is hardly unique. In *Because I Was Flesh* (1959), Edward Dahlberg recalls life as an eleven-year-old in 1912 at the Jewish Orphan Asylum in Cleveland, the monotony of which was relieved every January when the "Irish Micks came from Kinsman Road and the slums of Superior Avenue to fight with the orphans."[104] For these kids, such skirmishes—often contested with damaging snowballs formed around rocks—become as much of a winter ritual as ice skating and sledding. Perhaps for this reason, in his autobiographical novel *Bottom Dogs* (1930) Dahlberg's narrator recalls these days with an alloy of nostalgia and seriousness: "Well, the kids were always ready for fightin' of any sort; that was one home tradition they stuck by through thick and thin. It was no joke foolin' with micks."[105] Later, he would bemoan the decline of the institutional "myths" to which he had become inured and from which he wrested an unusual sense of comfort: the kids now seemed too "lax"; the teachers, too old; and "the micks didn't come around anymore" (204). And, while traveling the country, he would at times inexplicably seek out the "mick section" of a new city, as he does after arriving in San Francisco, where he found a hotel room and "turned in right away" (273). As he grew older, Dahlberg found himself surrounded by Irish friends and married to an Irishwoman; and he was at a loss to explain how this all happened.[106]

Ira in *A Star Shines over Mt. Morris Park* also cultivates friendships among the Irish, and his sense not only of being American, but of happiness itself undergoes a profound change. With his friend Eddie Ferry, who possessed "Irish boldness" and "only rarely" flung ethnic slurs like "Yuh lousy Jew," Ira begins to range outside his neighborhood, fighting opponents and participating in the harmless capers in which adolescent boys are involved (34). Eddie's Irish-American world quickly becomes the "world Ira now yearned for" (35), and Jewish things like kosher food and custom grow ever more unappealing.[107] His sense of well-being, in short, evolves to include an incipient Irishness that represented his new country and a new identity, a sense underscored in Roth's novel when Ira's mother rewards him for a promotion at school:

> Mom gave him a nickel when he was promoted to 5A, and the Irish kid he had once fought . . . sat beside Ira in the backyard at 114 East, waiting for Ira to decide how the nickel was to be spent. . . . Ah, the euphoria of sitting in the shade of a wooden fence in the backyard at the end of school! . . . He was promoted, with a nickel in his pocket, and an Irish friend beside him, who said yes to whatever he said. (52)

Like Albert Schearl, Ira despised greenhorns or new arrivals to America, especially Jewish greenhorns whose "crudity and ignorance," unsightly teeth, and aura of "oppressive orthodoxy" repulsed him (19). For boys like Ira, assimilation involved shedding every vestige of the greenhorn—and, ultimately, of the Jew—which in turn formed a potent antidote to feelings of alienation and geopathic anxiety. Perhaps most important, and by contrast from the perspective of contemporary affect study, the feeling of "euphoria" Ira experienced with his Irish friend is hardly so calculated; it is an autonomic reaction that transcends careful plotting or a unified narrative. As such, it hints at the uncanny familiarity subtended by the Irish-Jewish unconscious and, in this instance, the concentration of feeling to which it gives rise.

This process of Ira's finding a home in Irish culture continues in the second installment of *Mercy of a Rude Stream* set in 1920s New York, *A Diving Rock on the Hudson* (1995). As he did in its precursor, in *Diving Rock* Ira forms a strong friendship with an Irish schoolmate, Farley Hewin, who, as the elder Ira recalls, became a "staunch refuge from ruined Jewishness" (7). Introduced to recordings of the Irish singer John McCormack at Farley's house, Ira likes to "wind up the phonograph" and "drift off into enchanted reverie under the spell of the Irish tenor and his mellifluous brogue" (11). Later, after noticing the "unity" and "pride of the Irish" exhibited by an Irish cop (53), Ira emulates the officer and "basked in the glow of Farley's victory" at a citywide track meet (59); and although his friendship gradually fades, Ira recalls Farley and his parents with great affection. Here, I think, metaphor is important. As Harrison-Kahane observes, references to "blackest poverty" in *Bread Givers* exemplify the repeated use of "black" in Yezierska's novels to "deepen the negative connotations of the noun that follows."[108] By contrast, Jewish-Irish interactions are at times glowing, something in which one might "bask"; or, if not refulgent, as in Gold's case when loafing on a bench "together in the sunlight" and drinking beer with Irish coworkers, this sensation might be experienced in a luxuriant shade, as in Ira's feeling of "euphoria" lounging in the backyard with his Irish friend.

But, following Bauman's delineation of allo-Semitism, philo-Hibernianism can similarly be accompanied by or devolve into a calcified anti-Hibernianism, as both Dahlberg and Roth's views of Joyce demonstrate. As aspiring writers and avid readers of modernist literature, both expressed an almost religious devotion to Joyce, and this often surfaces in the authorial interpolations the elder Roth weaves into the narratives of his youthful protagonist throughout his four-novel epic. In *From Bondage* (1996), for example, immediately after Ira recalls a scene between young lovers that struck Ira as especially Irish he reflects upon his "many years among the Irish on an Irish-dominated street" (73). In an autobiographical aside, Roth continues the thought and intimates Joyce's ascent to the status of a veritable Old testament God:

> But as the days passed, and [Ira/Roth] read and wrestled, read and floundered, the strange conviction took firmer and firmer hold of him, that within himself was graven a crude analogue of the Joycean model, just as he felt within himself a humble affinity for the Joycean temperament, a diffident aptitude for the Joycean method. (74)

As his ambition to write pressed more urgently, Roth increasingly turned to Joyce—and, at times, to Bernard Shaw and J. M. Synge—even if the Great Master inscriber had become an inescapable force from which no fledgling writer could escape: "James Joyce, the bastard is like a literary black hole. You aren't meant to go on writing after that, after you've come in contact with him. You can't escape him, once you've entered his stupendous gravitational field; you're lost" (*Diving Rock* 114).

From the earliest interpolations in the tetralogy where the aging writer reflects upon the chronicle he is composing, however, Roth's antipathy for Joyce and the Joycean grows almost exponentially. In *A Star Shines over Mt. Morris Park*, a more politically attuned Roth can no longer tolerate Joycean surfaces under which "the havoc inflicted by deprivation" is concealed. He wonders aloud if the concealed havoc originated in "cruel social relations" or class inequities Joyce didn't bother to explore. In fine, Roth "rebelled against Joyce" (73), in part because glittering Joycean "riches" amounted to little more than baubles with a contemptible "surface allure" (72, 157). As Roth's interest in Israel and Jewishness grows, his sympathy for Joyce, "Pontiff [Richard] Ellmann," and the "erudite Jewish worshipers" of the Irish master wanes (*Diving Rock* 149). His "people were Israel" (*From Bondage* 69). Now the Irish writer who had helped Roth access his own psychical depths seemed "pathological and pathetic" (70).

Dahlberg's odyssey with Joyce parallels Roth's, leading eventually to his accusation of Joyce's anti-Semitism. But it was not always so. As Harold Billings observes, in the late 1920s Dahlberg regarded Joyce as drawing a blueprint for a new American literature that might be used to reimagine the skyscrapers, dancehalls, and features of the modern city "as images for a vernacular American *Ulysses*."[109] Dahlberg relates his enthusiasm for Joyce's unflinching, sensually rich variety of modernism in his 1929 essay "Ariel in Caliban," lauding the synesthesia of Joyce's prose:

> James Joyce has done with ordinary Dublin what no artist has with the subway and surface cars of New York. He has found Ariel in Caliban. Joyce is the poet of smell, color and sound. . . . Joyce's writings are inferential and highly sensory. He excludes no phase of experience, and just because it is experience, it has an artistic value.[110]

For the younger Dahlberg of the late 1920s, such texts as *A Portrait of the Artist as a Young Man* made a "direct appeal to the olfactory sense which has been long neglected." That is to say, Joyce finds no smell "repugnant"; hence, his writing exerts a more "reminiscent appeal to modern experience." From this earthy Caliban, a literary Ariel arises, transposing Dublin into a "mechanized and diabolical cosmos" and elevating Joyce's achievement above anything yet produced by American modernism: "No one up to the present time has given us an impressionistic study of misshapen American cities" (*Bottom Dogs, etc.* 131). No American writer, in other words, has created such a Caliban, or realized such purely "poetic motives" in a minutely detailed portrait of modern urban life (132).

Such high praise makes Dahlberg's later excoriation of *Ulysses* as a "street urchin's odyssey of a doddering phallus" and a "twenty-four hours' journey through ordure" in his collaboration with Sir Herbert Read *Truth Is More Sacred: A Critical Exchange on Modern Literature* (1961) even more bizarre.[111] Joyce's deployment of the olfactory that Dahlberg applauded in 1929 became in *Truth Is More Sacred* a reduction of man to "unheroic dimensions," "bad smells," and "ugly habits" (18). Worse, the language of the novel grew "lubricious" (21); its author's style, a "canting riff-raff English"; and whenever Joyce "was about to be serious he could not be contemplative because he thought it more important to be humorous" (35). Once the "pinchbeck novelties of language in *Ulysses* are dropped, platitude is the King"; and what has "passed for an unusual assortment of words and originality are neologisms, bombast, solecisms, and perverse and corrupt sequences of words" (36). These "feculent droppings of the Yahoos that stir upon the branches" reduced *Ulysses* to little more than an "*Iliad* of everyday disgusts" featuring a "wittol" (Leopold Bloom) as its protagonist (42). Like Roth, Dahlberg also recognized the uncanny attraction Joyce exerted on Jewish academics: "It is odd that the sodality of atheistical scribbling Nimrods, pining for the old debaucheries in the Plains of Shinar, should have turned to James Joyce whose book was gnawed to pieces by . . . his own foul desires" (*Truth* 54). However much he was surrounded by Irish friends, as he conceded to Kay Boyle in a 1967 letter, Dahlberg could no longer muster a scintilla of admiration for Joyce. His philo-Hibernianism could not extend that far.

The allo-Semitic/allo-Hibernian relationship so central to Gold's, Roth's, and Dahlberg's writing similarly informs James T. Farrell's *Young Lonigan*, the first installment of the Studs Lonigan trilogy (1932–35), albeit in a less literary and academic fashion. Set in 1916 in the Washington Park neighborhood on Chicago's South Side, Farrell's narrator hints at Studs's Irish Jewishness: "Studs was a small, broad-shouldered lad.... His long nose was too large for his other features, almost a sheeny's nose" (5). In case a casual reader might have skimmed over this detail, it is repeated later when Studs admires his face in the mirror: "He took a close-up squint at his mug and decided that it was, after all, a pretty good mug, even if he almost had a sheeny's nose" (61). As Freud and his former student Otto Rank underscore, the uncanny frequently involves the appearance of a double, a character who is the mirror image of the protagonist. What the fourteen-year-old Studs sees in the mirror, whether he likes it or not, is an Irish Jew, a highly ironic motif that runs throughout the trilogy given Studs's and his father's recourse to ethnic slurs. In the opening chapter of *Young Lonigan*, the elder Lonigan recalls taking his wife to a dance and, while returning, almost getting "into a mixup with some soused mick because the fellow had started to get smart-alecky, like he was a kike" (16). As this passage implies, ethnic stereotyping targets the Irish too. Studs's friend Davey Cohen, who participates with Studs in mild violence against other Jewish kids in the neighborhood, grows to regret his bullying and in a revealing introspection disparages his Irish running mates: "The Irish were lousy all right," he thinks. "A race of beer-guzzlers, flat-feets, red mugs and boneheads. Why, they even had to take a Jew Christ and . . . make a dumb Irishman out of him" (159). Such sentiments, however, are coterminous in the *Studs Lonigan* trilogy with the uncanny affection and familiarity found in Gold's and Roth's writing. In *The Young Manhood of Studs Lonigan*, Davey has been away from the South Side for two years living in Toledo. After winning money shooting dice with sailors and dockworkers, Davey longs to return to Chicago in triumph to see Studs, Tommy Doyle, and all "of the old guys, the best gang in the world" (234). Unfortunately, his "beefy-faced," craps-shooting adversaries follow him, retrieving their lost money, stealing his, and deflating Davy's fantasy of his grand return to his old Irish friends.

Young Lonigan also reveals the influence of popular culture in Studs's working class Irish-American neighborhood on the South Side during the years of World War I. In this instance, however, popular music, not theater, much of it from New York's Tin Pan Alley, permeates the consciousness of Studs and his friends. Songs associated with vaudeville and Tin Pan Alley, as I have mentioned earlier, were regarded by many cultural critics as inferior mass-produced commodities, and by some as not even music at all.[112] Such critical considerations, not surprisingly, are entirely absent from a small gathering at the Lonigan home celebrating Studs's graduation from the eighth grade, where partygoers gather around a piano to sing what amounts to an Irish-Jewish medley: "Alexander's Ragtime Band," The River Shannon Flowing," "It's a Long Way to Tipperary," "Dear Old Girl," "Dance and Grow Thin," and other songs taken from an Irish / Tin Pan Alley catalog. Both "Alexander's Ragtime Band" and "Dance and Grow Thin" were hit songs for Irving Berlin, who wrote the former and collaborated on the latter, and when the pianist begins to play Berlin's "In My Harem," Studs's friend Bill Donoghue moves to the center of the floor, mimes a "shocking hula-hula," and redacts the lyrics in a crude, if altogether sadly predictable way:

> And the dance they do . . .
> Is enough to kill a Jew . . .
> Da-Da-Dadadada-Da . . .
> In my harem with Pat Malone. (50)

Given their ignorance and cultivation of an inchoate anti-Semitism, Studs and his friends were unaware that Berlin wrote the song so that the names Pat Malone and Abie Cohen could be so seamlessly interchanged.

Throughout the trilogy, Farrell's young protagonist and his friends repeat the lyrics of popular music as intently as Joyce's Stephen Dedalus mouths Claude Melnotte's speeches before his foray into "the quarter of the Jews." The cases of such subjective penetration, however, are significantly different: Joyce's teenager recites soliloquies from a relic from the Victorian stage, while Farrell's adolescent constantly hums or recalls lines from contemporary culture. Joyce's characters often do as well, but not at the same accelerated pace as Farrell's South Siders, who have memorized a songbook of tunes about girls and World War I. In addition, like the boxing ring—or the back room at the "Hell Hole" that O'Neill and Gold, for a time, frequented—the variety stage formed another venue for Irish Jewishness in early twentieth-century America. But all was not necessarily sweetness and light. For almost a decade after scoring a hit with "In My Harem," Berlin abandoned his own harem to pursue Ellin Mackay, daughter of wealthy Irish-American industrialist Clarence Mackay. The two met at a party in the spring of 1921, and, according to one biographer, "thus began one of the most arduous, publicized, and embattled romances of the Jazz Age."[113] At the end of the nineteenth century, Ellin's grandfather, an Irish immigrant, built a financial empire that was later presided over by his son, who adamantly refused to allow his daughter to marry a Jew. Mackay's animosity toward Berlin quickly became fodder for gossip columnists, and eventually the disputants sought legal remedies: Mackay, interestingly enough, retained the services of a Jewish attorney, Max Steuer; Berlin, the prominent Irish attorney Dennis O'Brien.[114] No matter. On January 4, 1926, Ellin and Irving were married at City Hall, and a few days later boarded a ship for London. Ten months later, their first daughter Mary Ellin was born, and to celebrate the occasion, Berlin wrote one of his most enduring songs, "Blue Skies."

The widespread popularity of *Abie's Irish Rose* notwithstanding, as the Jazz Age sank into the Great Depression and fascism was on the rise in Europe, the unique relationship of blue skies between American Jews and the American Irish were darkened by the strain. Indeed, some Catholics of Irish descent fomented a far more virulent anti-Semitism than Studs Lonigan and his father could ever have imagined. Father Charles Coughlin, to take a notorious example, a Canadian-born priest who by the mid-1930s inveighed against capitalism and an international conspiracy of Jewish bankers to a massive radio audience, went so far as to rationalize Nazi violence against Jews. His Sunday afternoon broadcasts, much like the hateful ranting of talk radio personalities today, eventually exerted their exorbitant effects. In his history of Boston, Thomas O'Connor chronicles an "outbreak of anti-Semitic violence" in the late 1930s and early 1940s perpetrated mainly by "Irish youths [who] ranged up and down . . . the Jewish district . . . harassing shop owners, beating up Jewish boys on their way home from school, scrawling swastikas and ugly graffiti on their homes and temples."[115] And not all Boston Jewish boys were willing to play the victim, as Willis Barnstone recalled in *We Jews and Blacks* while describing his father: "Dad grew up in the streets, and to survive on his own in Boston as a kid . . . of course he had to be a street-fighter. Now he always fights for underdog causes." And he "really loses his temper over Nazi-lovers" like Father Coughlin, "who are the scum of the earth."[116] The blissful union of young lovers in *Abie's Irish Rose* was thus opposed by the counterforce of a demagoguery that sought to undo its larger implications, not merely in Boston but across the country. Catalyzed by fear and in some cases an overweening nationalism, this polemic began to overwhelm senses of affinity, sensual attraction, and desire. Carefully manipulated ugly feelings superseded autonomic and euphoric ones. Coughlin's anti-Semitism was so widespread that by 1944 in *Dialectic of Enlightenment* Theodor Adorno and Max Horkheimer listed him in the same roster with the architects of European fascism:

> The leader [of the discourse of ethnic hatred] acts as a representative; he portrays what is forbidden to everyone else in actual life. Hitler can gesticulate like a clown, Mussolini strike false notes like a provincial tenor, Goebbels talk endlessly like a Jewish agent whom he wants murdered, and Coughlin preach love like the savior whose crucifixion he portrays—all for the sake of still more bloodshed.[117]

It was precisely at this moment, however, that at least some Jewish- and Irish-American writers found strength in each other. Committed to the ongoing struggle for workers' rights and other progressive issues of the 1930s, James Farrell and Jack Conroy, author of *The Disinherited: A Novel of the 1930s* (1933), joined Michael Gold and Edward Dahlberg in several causes, including attendance at an April 1935 meeting of American "revolutionary"

writers—the First American Writers' Congress—called by the *Daily Worker*.
Only a few months before, Farrell and Dahlberg had picketed with nearly
one hundred women in support of better working conditions and the Office
Workers Union.[118] Farrell in particular grew to become a staunch defender of
both Jews and the founding of the state of Israel, which he visited in 1956. Later,
he gushed, "The Israelis are something to be proud of—not simply because
they are Jews—but because they are giving the finest example of democracy
the world has ever seen."[119] Two years later, Farrell published an account of
his trip, *It Has Come to Pass* (1958), which advances a similar argument about
Israeli efforts to cultivate a principled democracy. Nation-building in Israel
involved other desiderata, and perhaps one of the most ironic of which given
the anti-Semitic slurs in the *Studs Lonigan* trilogy is the dismantling of ethnic
stereotypes: "Israel represents a tremendous protest against the Ghetto," he
maintained, and its people "seem determined to refute all stereotypes about
the Jew in the Ghetto, as well as all other stereotypes about and prejudices
against the Jew."[120] In this sense, he contended, Israelis are not Jews, underscoring in the process the performative figurations of Jewishness. If Roth's
Ira Stigman, with his love for Irish tenor John McCormack and many things
Irish, at least for a time early in his life, was a Jewish Paddy, Farrell in the
1950s became an outspoken, pro-Israel Irish Jew.

The chapters that follow probe many of the issues outlined here. Chapter 2,
"The Cultural Work of Immigrant Melodrama," concerns the representation of recently arrived Irish and Jewish immigrants in popular melodrama
from 1850 through the 1880s and attempts to construct a critical genealogy
of modern American drama that maps a more complete route to ground-
breaking plays of the 1920s and 1930s by John Howard Lawson, Elmer Rice,
Clifford Odets, Eugene O'Neill, and others. In so doing, it argues for a redaction of the common history of the nineteenth-century stage that takes the
influential work of Dion Boucicault, particularly his play *The Colleen Bawn*
(1860), as the beginning of a uniquely Irish drama in America. While most of
the immigrant plays were written or performed by transplanted Irishmen or
first-generation Irish-Americans—James Pilgrim, John Brougham, Augustin
Daly, George Henry Jessop, and others—some were not, for, as George
Bornstein persuasively observes echoing Cornel West's work on American
jazz, "popular culture is incorrigibly hybrid." Much like performance, culture
inevitably involves "the weaving of antecedent cultures,"[121] and such was frequently the case on the modern American stage, which sews into its textures
characters and conflicts from the nineteenth-century drama that preceded it.

Chapter 3, "Allo-Semitism and the Performative Uncanny: Leah and
Shylock, Svengali and the Count of Monte Cristo," traces the appearance
of four crucial figures on the late nineteenth-century stage in some of the
most widely seen plays and revivals of the period: Augustin Daly's *Leah, the
Forsaken*, so importantly referenced in *Ulysses* and seen frequently in early

twentieth-century theaters on both sides of the Atlantic; *The Merchant of Venice*, particularly as adapted by Henry Irving; Paul Potter's adaptation of George Du Maurier's blockbuster novel *Trilby* (1895); and James O'Neill's portrayal of Edmond Dantès in *The Count of Monte Cristo*, a role he played some six thousand times. All four of these figures transform and complicate received notions of the figures of the Jew and the Irish, and—in Svengali's case—link the figure of the Jew to a discourse of psychical depth and uncanny familiarity.

Chapter 4, "The Jewish-Irish Modern American Drama," attempts to tease out the myriad connections between such Irish playwrights as Bernard Shaw and Sean O'Casey and two architects of American modern drama: Elmer Rice and Clifford Odets. Both Rice and Odets represent tenement life and the social activism it produced as influenced by their Irish predecessors, one of whom—Shaw—is regarded in some quarters as anti-Semitic. Thus, more than influence is at issue here, as the allo-Semitism and allo-Hibernianism outlined in in this introduction—ambivalence, affect, and uncanny affinity—resurface in these relationships. "Irishness" takes on a decidedly different status in an often-neglected play by Arthur Miller, *A Memory of Two Mondays* (1955) and in Stella Adler's acting workshops on John Millington Synge's *Riders to the Sea*, leading to a resolutely antimodernist vision of Irishness rife with political connotation. The chapter concludes with an assessment of the Irish melodramatic tradition in Eugene O'Neill's *A Touch of the Poet* and *A Moon for the Misbegotten*, an atavistic return to the theater of his father that seems almost counterintuitive given the pronounced antagonism between the two over the younger O'Neill's interest in a modernist writing totally reviled by the elder.[122]

The final chapter, "The New Wandering Rocks," takes its formal inspiration from the narrative shape of episode 10 of *Ulysses*. That is to say, in an effort to bring the excursus of Irish Jewishness and Jewish Irishness into the present, I have followed Joyce's lead by developing short "floating" sections on individual writers and relaxing the focus on American drama in the previous chapters. Works by John Banville, Brendan Behan, Harold Pinter, Howard Jacobson, and Bernard MacLaverty—and a final coda on contemporary immigrant literature including Brian Friel's *Philadelphia, Here I Come!* (1964) and Gish Jen's *Mona in the Promised Land* (1996)—are discussed in this capstone chapter, which circles back to the very issues outlined here: immigration, the Freudian uncanny, ambivalence, performativity, affect, and the priority of Irish Jewishness and Jewish Irishness in the circum–North Atlantic world.

The Cultural Work of Immigrant Melodrama

Each and every artistic event occurs in relation to certain aspects of
its heritage. The idea of *artistic heritage* includes the artistic traditions,
conventions, norms and codes of not only drama and theatre but all of
the arts. Every artistic event has a relation to the artistic tradition or
heritage in which it operates, to which it refers, and out of which it shapes
its own separate identity—sometimes in homage, sometimes in revolt.

—THOMAS POSTLEWAIT, *THE CAMBRIDGE
INTRODUCTION TO THEATRE HISTORIOGRAPHY* (2009)

Moments in two American plays separated by nearly sixty years provide both a
context and primer for a reassessment of the cultural work of nineteenth-century
Irish- and Jewish-American melodrama and its relationship to the modern
political theater. Hardly necessary to advance the play's action, the first scene
might be dismissed as comic falderal, so much diverting banter prefatory to its
main melodramatic business. Set in the Tombs Police Court in New York, act
2, scene 2 of Augustin Daly's *Under the Gaslight* (1867) opens with two justices
arraigning defendants charged with minor criminal offenses. After a juvenile
pickpocket's case is dispatched, a policeman turns to Rafferdi, an Irish street
musician accused of disturbing the peace by playing his street organ and putting on a raucous entertainment with his pet monkey. Seizing the opportunity to prize a quick fifty cents from a hapless immigrant and incredulous that
an Irishman would be working as an organ grinder, a shyster named Splinter
attaches himself to Rafferdi, introducing him to the court as a "native of sunny
Italy" who came to "our free and happy country" with but one ambition: "to
earn his bread." Recognizing the defendant as Irish, the magistrate is initially
angered by the deception, but after an amusing conversation about the disposition of the monkey in the event of its owner's incarceration, the tension is eased.

Rafferdi gets off with only a warning, a happier verdict than that meted to the suspect who follows him, a "bureau nigger" named Sam arrested for being drunk and disorderly. Splinter also takes his case and, while conceding that Sam was "slightly intoxicated" in public, argues that as "the equal of the white man," his client should not suffer any legal consequences.[1] His brief falls on deaf ears, and Sam is sentenced to ten days in jail.

Produced by the Theatre Guild several decades later, a moment in John Howard Lawson's *Processional: A Jazz Symphony of American Life in Four Acts* (1925)—an experimental work replete with arresting moments—also serves, albeit quite differently, as an exemplum of much American drama from the mid-nineteenth century through the years of the Great Depression. In act 2, scene 2, soldiers brought to a West Virginia town to quash a coal miners' strike pursue an escaped criminal to a nearby hilltop where they happen across an imposing structure Lawson names "The Labor Temple" and wonder aloud about its purpose:

Bill

What's this place?

MacCarthy

We're way up the hill.

Bill

Is this a church? [*He approaches it examining lettering on wall*] Got writin' on it.

"To the Spirit of American Industry, Coal . . . Steel . . . Oil . . ."

MacCarthy

Banana oil!

Bill

One a' these statues is Capital an' the other is Labor. "American Manhood" it says.[2]

What the temple to "American Manhood" does *not* enshrine with capital, labor, and gender, but what Lawson's text foregrounds, are immigrant workers and the construction of ethnicity in such popular cultural forms as vaudeville—not to mention, though I will, their centrality to the polemics of the Ku Klux Klan (see figure 2.1). In act 4 the Klan's King Kleagle calls for the protection of "Native-born Americans, Patriotic Protestants, regular citizens" and their "morals" from the incursions of immigrants: "Clean up the dirty foreigners, make 'em kiss the flag! Skin the Jews, lynch the niggers" (182, 183). In what ways do these plays from different eras—the former deprecated by the *New York Herald* as a "stage carpenter's drama" of which "nothing good can be said";[3] the latter, an experimental text much admired by Eugene O'Neill, John Dos Passos, Fanny Hurst, and other notable figures

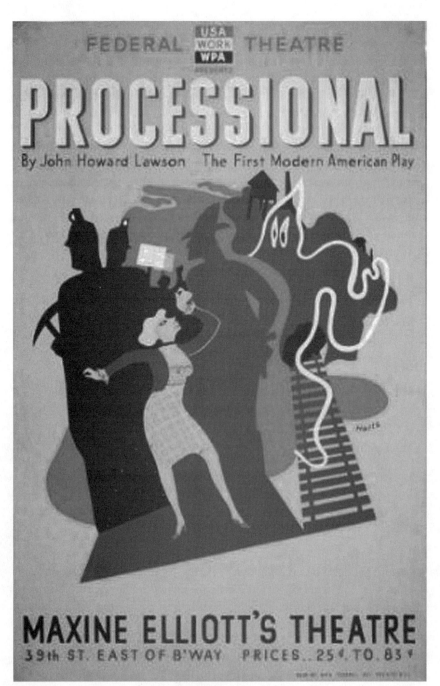

FIGURE 2.1 *Program for Federal Theatre Production of* Processional *(1936)*
The Library of Congress.

FIGURE 2.2 *Set Design for John Howard Lawson's* Processional
Mordecai Gorelik Papers, Special Collection Research Center, Southern Illinois University–Carbondale.

in American modernism—represent both the cultural work of immigrant melodrama on the nineteenth-century American stage and its importance in the development of modern American drama (see figure 2.2)? How do these plays facilitate access to modern drama's Irish-Jewish unconscious?

Both plays anticipate the "ungetroundable" constellation of factors presented by Paul Muldoon's Irish-Jewish navvies: ethnicity, gender, and labor, with all that labor connotes materially and affectively to immigrants. To these matters, as intimated by figures of the law in both plays—courts and bailiffs in *Under the Gaslight*, a sheriff and soldiers enforcing martial law in *Processional*—a fourth is added: the dispensation of justice in a multiethnic and class-riven America, a social goal inherent to the ethics of cosmopolitanism. As promiscuously deployed as it is highly theorized, "cosmopolitanism" connotes a range of cultural practices and philosophical positions, as, among others, Rebecca Walkowitz reminds us. It may even be the case, as the editors of an anthology expounding the term assert, that "specifying cosmopolitanism positively and definitively is an uncosmopolitan thing to do."[4] I'll have to risk it. For however conceptually slippery, "cosmopolitanism" connotes both a communitarian ethics and at times a disruptive, even decadent, cultural practice that resonate in the plays I want to read here. And, although contemporary cosmopolitanism casts a wary eye on modernization and its presumption of social progress, it also addresses the dialectic of individualism and community inherent to the politics of Irish- and Jewish-American melodrama. This is not to say that the forms of such melodrama originate in "deviant cultural strategies" or have much to do with such later nineteenth-century phenomena as Wildean dandyism or the experiences of urban flâneurs. But, as I hope to show, the politics of this drama parallels that of one of the philosophical foundations of cosmopolitanism: namely, its premise of the inherent "attachment of all humanity" and its resultant "commitment to intercultural understanding."[5]

Moreover, while contemporary uses of "cosmopolitan" suggest an aesthetic associated with wealth and social privilege, a penchant for the cultural products of a diverse population, "cosmopolitanism" insists upon the necessity of a single or "universal standard" of justice.[6] And, although this sense of cosmopolitanism's ethical imperative seems more urgent in our post-Holocaust world, I want to argue that it informs nineteenth-century Irish- and Jewish-American melodrama as well and not in an inchoate way. Rather, a significant body of this melodrama develops a narrative in which labor, gender, and justice are braided together in an imperfect capitalism often subjected to sharp critique. Equally important, through representations of immigrants' integrity and earnest desire for work, these popular plays refute stereotypes of the Irish and Jews: the former, to paraphrase Joyce's abusive priest in *A Portrait of the Artist as a Young Man*, little more than "lazy, idle schemers"; the latter, avaricious and unscrupulous in their business practices. Perceptually blinkered by a version of this stereotyping, Daly's lawyer in *Under the Gaslight* presumes that only Italians "make their bread" as street musicians, just as Lawson's Klansmen assume that Sadie Cohen, the pregnant teenage daughter of a local Jewish merchant, is a "jazz kid" infected by a mysterious "bug" that must be exterminated (184). Near the play's end, the "Responsive Chorus" in *Processional*, sharing the Klan's biases, attempts to saddle Sadie with the same gender politics and affect to which Sara Smolinsky in *Bread Givers* is susceptible—shame—but Sadie will have none of it: "I ain't ashamed, I'm glad" (186). She continues her rhythmical swaying in the "jazz wedding" in the play's final scene, vowing defiantly to raise her unborn child regardless of the social disapprobation she might suffer.

Because of its blending of parades, call and response, jazz, and an ironic romantic comic emplotment, *Processional* is properly regarded as a hybrid modernist text wrought from the conventions of European avant-garde drama *and* American popular culture, even if Lawson disavows European influence in his preface to the play.[7] Instead, he underscores the play's American origins, asserting that "native craftsmanship" exists "only in the fields of vaudeville and revue"; the dramatic method gleaned from these fields, he asserts, is "as far removed from the older realism as from the facile mood of Expressionism" (v). Critics since then have troubled this self-described "theoretical explanation." As Ryan Jerving argues, vaudeville served *Processional* in 1925 as both "metaphor and medium for exploring labour and ethnicity and their articulation under industrial capitalism," although the play's revival in 1937 as part of the Federal Theatre Project (FTP) required redactions of the vaudevillian and "outdated" representations of Jews and blacks in the original.[8] In *Expressionism and Modernism in the American Theatre* (2005), Julia

Walker queries both Lawson's disdain of expressionism in his preface and the critical tendency to emphasize the vaudevillian elements of *Processional* while ignoring those derived from other sources. At the risk of playing the "contrarian," Walker recounts Lawson's viewing of the 1917 ballet *Parade* by Jean Cocteau and Erik Satie with design by Pablo Picasso and argues for its inspiration of the then young ambulance corps driver.[9] Moreover, although acknowledging parallels between Lawson's play and vaudeville, she examines often overlooked relationships between *Processional* and such well-known minstrel sketches as "The Radio Jazz Hounds," with their blackfaced jazz performers, typical jokes, and racialized puns. Walker trains particular attention on Lawson's portrayal of Rastus Jolly, who first appears "lazily twanging [a] banjo" (9) and later, following the familiar stereotype of African-Americans, "trembles and goes down on his knees" in an extravagant display of fear and superstition (63). This "problematic use of race," as I have mentioned, which is rendered more complicated near the end of the play when Rastus is revealed to be a member of the Klan, was revised in the later FTP production just a dozen years after *Processional*'s premiere.[10]

Romantic comedy, expressionism, the minstrel tradition, even Freudian psychoanalysis and Brechtian epic theater—Lawson's *Processional* borrows from all of these. But the play's "artistic heritage," Thomas Postlewait's term, is even richer than this list suggests.[11] Other influences exist, too, some of which Lawson acknowledges while others remain largely unexamined. In his preface, he alludes to the "Vaudeville Jew or Irishman" who resides "on any street corner" contributing to a "grotesque of the American environment" in part through a "colorful exaggeration of the American language" (vi). However such figures contribute to this grotesque, however much they constitute "montages, born of the conflation of vaudeville and Dada,"[12] they also share a long history on the nineteenth-century stage. The opening minutes of *Processional* venture near this antecedent theater with the introduction of Cohen, a local shopkeeper, and his daughter, Sadie. Grumbling about closing his store on the Fourth of July, Cohen is also disturbed that martial law has been declared to contain the miners' strike and, as a result, the strikers have organized a march accompanied by music. Given the prevalent figure of the Jew as crass materialist, Cohen's response is predictable: "There it is for the Fourth of July . . . Coal dust an' blood . . . oi! There's no money in it!" (6). His dismissal of the excitement created by the labor action recalls the psychical makeups of stage Jews on the nineteenth-century stage who, unlike their emotionally charged daughters, often exhibited a stolid impassivity originating in a cold-blooded materialism. Jewish underworld boss Mordie Solomons endorses this cool rationality in an exchange with Terence O'Halloran, an unhappy confederate anxious to leave the gambling rackets and reform himself, in John Brougham's *The Lottery of Life: A Story of New York* (1868): "There, there! There never was such a funny boy. Now let us talk reasonably. You know

I never get into a passion—it don't pay."[13] Dicey Morris, the Jewish gambler and proprietor of the Silver Hell in Dion Boucicault's *After Dark: A Drama of London Life in Four Acts* (1868), reveals a similar disposition. Amazed that Tom, a vagrant who has squandered his last sovereign at the gaming tables and last sixpence at the bar, would reject his offer of charity, Morris exclaims, "Refuse a shilling! It's shocking what intemperance will bring a fellow to! I can't make him out!"[14] As Elin Diamond observes, "every performance, if it is intelligible as such, embeds features of previous performances,"[15] and such is the case with the ghostly presence of stage Jews in *Processional*. To borrow a metaphor from Marvin Carlson in *The Haunted Stage* (2001), this "haunted-ness" seeps into a variety of theatrical phenomena, including the evocation in an actor's performances of well-known theatrical types, the ghosts of previous plays and performers.

From Sadie's perspective, however, the miners' strike provides a welcome respite from both the monotony of daily life and her father's despotism, a view that parallels the discontent of daughters in the canon of tenement and immigrant literature from Stephen Crane's *Maggie* to Anzia Yezierska's *Bread Givers*.[16] As Cohen orders Sadie to come into the house instead of fraternizing with the strikers, she laments her predicament: "I don't do nuthin' I hadn't oughter, but popper's always got the blues, he's always scoldin'" (11)— or worse. Predictably enough, this precise conflict has a long history on the nineteenth-century stage, revealingly so in the myriad of adaptations of Sir Walter Scott's novel *Ivanhoe* (1819) produced in Britain and America throughout much of the century.[17] One exchange in Henry J. Byron's burlesque *Ivanhoe, An Extravaganza* (1862), which opened simultaneously on St. Stephen's Day in London and Liverpool, is especially telling. In it, Jewish money lender and clothing merchant Isaac of York is confronted by his daughter Rebecca over his questionable business practices and her complicity in them:

> I hate the shop—I hate myself and you—
> And all our money-grubbing, cheating crew.
> I wasn't born to stand at a shop door,
> Saying, "That bonnet, miss, is five-and-four;
> It's this year's fashion," when I know it's not,
> I tell you that I'm sick of such a lot.[18]

That Sir Walter Scott's medieval England could be burlesqued in such anachronistic ways—Were bonnets in style then? Did a Barthesean type of fashion system exist?—is less important than the ways in which residues of both Victorian stereotypes of unscrupulous, "money-grubbing" Jewish merchants and conventional conflicts between them and their daughters persisted in modern and modernist drama.

Perhaps surprisingly, another issue significant to the representation of immigrants and to modern writing as well also emerges in this passage, for in this otherwise frivolous mid-Victorian entertainment Byron portrays Rebecca as an arbiter of style and, ultimately, a figure of desire. One exemplar of this familiar modern type is Sonya Vrunsky in Yezierska's *Salome of the Tenements*, who inspires the creations of a celebrated fashion designer and, later in the novel, becomes a talented designer herself. In delineating the characteristics inherent to what she terms "assimilative empathy" in Yezierska's fiction, Ann Mikkelsen emphasizes the major part immigrants and first-generation American played in remaking mainstream fashion in the early twentieth century, particularly insofar as Jewish management of the garment and nascent movie industries is concerned. For Mikkelsen, "working-class Jews could aspire to a mode of sartorial equality that belied their economic condition and presaged their entry into and transformation of the American middle class"; following Walter Benjamin, she further argues that this privileged relationship to fashion signaled a new affective relationship between the immigrant subject and the commodity form.[19] This assertion seems both accurate and just a bit mysterious: How do tenement dwellers like Sonya, cultural outsiders often despised or demeaned by the wealthy, possess social cachet sufficient to inflect fashion trends and shape notions of taste? How does a shopgirl like Rebecca in Byron's burlesque of Scott *know* what is fashionable while her presumably more affluent customers do not? In this way, what Mikkelsen identifies as an "emergent, earlier twentieth-century discourse about empathy that defined this concept quite differently from current usage"—that is, as a "relationship among bodies, objects, and desires within capitalism"[20]—might be regarded as having a history, or prehistory, that includes the mid-Victorian popular stage.

It is a short leap from exemplar of taste to figure of exoticism, and the two are frequently linked in a manner more complicated than Byron's *Ivanhoe* might suggest. In an *Unsocial Socialist* (1884), Bernard Shaw's Henrietta Jansenius with her alluring "olive complexion," dark eyes, and "delicately sensuous lips" displays "Oriental taste" in the colors of her "close fitting" costume, her straw hat, and "tan-colored gloves . . . decorated with a profusion of gold bangles."[21] Is it any wonder her husband found life with this "beautiful and luxurious creature" such a diverting "carnival of love" that, after barely six weeks of marriage, he needed to leave her so as to return to more serious work? In Lawson's *Success Story* (1932), Sarah Glassman, a former Lower East Side tenement resident who works as an office secretary in an advertising firm, is described as "*handsome in an Oriental way. Sleek back hair, olive skin, full bodied and vigorous,*" a clear contrast to both another office worker, Dinah McCabe, a "*thin girl with a peaked face, inefficient, gossipy and unprepossessing,*" and Agnes Carter, the "*blonde, beautiful, and slightly artificial*" floozy who, after marrying Lawson's protagonist Sol Ginsberg, spends money as quickly as he can earn it.[22] That Sol's meteoric rise to success began with the creation of a promotional campaign for an expensive beauty product called Glamour

Cream only reinforces this relationship between capital, fashion, and immigrant sensibility transformed into assimilative empathy, as Mikkelsen might phrase it. For like Sonya Vrunsky, Sarah and Sol in *Success Story* are Russian Jews, "the world's most gifted and most difficult people" (17), as financier Rufus Sonnenberg expresses it. In *Processional*, Sadie Cohen possesses a similar intuition for style, as Lawson's initial description of her emphasizes her deployment of fashion *"calculated to fill out her childish figure."*

Somewhat similarly, the Irishman in *Processional* evokes the celebrity style of Tin Pan Alley composers. A self-announced and self-fashioning Irish Jew, the dapper reporter Phillpots—depicted in the stage directions as a *"very George M. Cohan sort of newspaper man"* with a straw hat and *"neat made-to-order clothes"* (26)—has come to West Virginia to report on the strike. His first meeting with Sadie reveals her dancing skills as the two sway to music playing on a Victrola inside the Cohens' house. That Cohen interrupts the dance—"you ain't been introduced," he tells the journalist (28)—opens the possibility of a conventional romantic comic plot complete with a paternal blocking figure or senex suppressing a relationship between his daughter and her big-city lover. But this never occurs. Instead, Sadie enjoys a brief fling with "Dynamite" Jim Flimmins, an escaped criminal, and carries his child at the play's concluding "Jazz Marriage" ceremony. Near the end of *Processional*, Phillpots and an uncharacteristically emotional Cohen speculate about the larger cultural implication of the event:

Cohen
    She ain't my Yiddisher Rose no more.

Phillpots
    She's an American beauty now.

Cohen
    [*wipes a tear from each eye*]
    Babies they will have an' babies . . . .

Phillpots
    And their children's children will be shouting oi, oi! (215)

This prediction recalls David Quixano's idealism in Zangwill's *The Melting Pot*, the final tableau of which represents this ideal on stage. In David's annealing crucible, Yiddish roses are transformed into American beauties, and immigrant linguistic markers are assimilated into the American vernacular. As a result, David and his beloved Vera can forget the past and bask in the democratic glow of the Statue of Liberty, which rises in the background as the curtain falls.[23] Set on the Fourth of July, Lawson's ironic comedy *appears* to replicate Zangwill's social utopia, jazz in this instance replacing strains from David's American symphony in the closing tableau of *The Melting Pot*.

But this utopian vision of an ascendant social order potent enough to topple the brittle patriarchy in *Processional* and counter its corrupting hegemony proves to be misleading. For, as Julia Walker observes, when Phillpots refers to Sadie as "Desdemona" and claims that she "bears the burden of 'the black monster's hand,'" he is not so much comparing Jim to Othello as he is predicting that Sadie's unborn son will be exploited by the monstrous coal mines just as ruthlessly as his father was.[24] Further, while America may be ecumenical enough to assimilate a Yiddisher Rose, it is incapable of cultivating a single standard of justice. On the contrary, the putative resolution of the miners' strike, announced simultaneously with Sadie's bann of marriage, is revealed to be the contrivance of the Man in the Silk Hat, who appears in an "upper box" and announces, "I have here a telegram from Calvin C. Coolidge stating that all men are brothers" (214). Hoodwinked by this proclamation, Phillpots grabs a megaphone declaring, "Gentlemen, Industrial Peace has come . . . Cemented in this marriage! A pact, a compact, an agreement, a document! The nation is rejoicing! There's going to be coal to keep 'em warm!" (214). Yet only moments earlier, the Man in the Silk Hat had instructed the Sheriff to "Make a list of the marked men and we'll get them in their beds tonight!" (212). The ceremony, we come to understand, has been staged for the "motion picture machines," making reporters like Phillpots complicit in concealing the machinations of the ruling class as it prepares its brutal reprisal against striking workers.

The influence of nineteenth-century melodrama on *Processional* is perhaps most evident in stereotypical characters like Cohen and the Man in the Silk Hat—and in the predictable conflict between fathers and daughters—but surfaces in other ways as well. One of these concerns what Joyce Flynn terms the "iconology of the subterranean" in Irish-American drama by Daly, John Brougham, and Edward Harrigan, who often create scenes "central to theme and plot in dark, confined spaces." Such spaces—basements, cellars, and steerages on overcrowded immigrant or "coffin" ships—are often indexed in a vertical mapping of American society: wealthy Americans luxuriating at the top, poor immigrants and laborers at the bottom surviving in cramped and unhealthy conditions.[25] As Flynn speculates, such a mise en scène can forge a solidarity and sense of companionship among the poor; and in act 2, scene 3 of Daly's *A Flash of Lightning* (1868) set in "Jacob's Ladder," an "all night's lodging cellar" in which sailors, immigrants "of the poorer class," and thieves find shelter, this subterranean space becomes a site for a sensational escape facilitated by newly arrived Irish.[26] Yet, as in *Under the Gaslight*, basement rooms also house desperate young women eking out a living; and Daly juxtaposes such spaces both to parlors in the cheaply ornamented home of nouveau-riche Irish-American Garry Fallon in *Flash of Lightning* and to rooms in expensive houses or posh restaurants like Delmonico's in *Under the Gaslight*. This proxemics of verticality informs *Processional* as well. The Labor Temple *must* be located, as one of the soldiers describes, "way up the hill" where such abstractions as capital and American manhood reside above the fray of human enterprise and the dangerous means of production. By contrast, in response to Phillpots's question, "What sort of place is this?" Cohen portrays the lower regions of this class-based verticality in the starkest of terms: "It's rotten! Look at me: I come up here from Charleston when the mines opened, it looked like a million dollars, an' I tumbled into a valley where Death lives" (29). Jake Psinski, a Polish miner-musician on strike, adds perspective to Cohen's picture: "Go up that big hill, see all the graves a' men died sweatin' in the mines, little stones standin' like an army, but there on the other side a' town a temple built by a rich man" (30). Analogues of the defendants in Daly's Tombs courts, the corpses in these graves symbolize a buried justice that failed to protect miners from their politically connected exploiters.

Through its own subterranean architecture, Michael Gold's one-act play *Money* (1929), set in a *"gloomy East Side cellar, a cobbler's shop by day, now the in the deep of the night, the sleeping place of five weary men,"* constitutes an even more direct expression of the nexus of labor, masculinity, and the plight of the immigrant.[27] As the play begins, Moisha, proprietor of the cobbler shop and landlord of the cellar where poor men rent beds, is overwrought because he has lost the money he has been saving to bring his family to America from Poland. His distress is so palpable that one of his nocturnal tenants, the sickly peddler Yonkel who has stolen the small pouch of money, eventually feels guilty, apologizes, and returns it to him. For Moisha, this money represents his wife and children, whom he has not seen for five years; for Yonkel, it represents the quintessence of an America that terrifies him: "I was afraid—afraid of Money. What was it—this beast that God had put into the world." In Poland he disdained money; there, people "helped each other, they were friends." By contrast, he pleads, "I am different now. See how thin and unhappy I am now. But I have money" (223). Meditating upon his transformation, Yonkel recalls an epiphanic moment after arriving in New York: "Something said to me, something in this land—get money! It is not enough to study the Talmud, to work, to be a man. You must have money" (224). For Yonkel, money thus not only destroys the ethos of communal life, but also deforms the human subject. Near the end of the play, a policeman appears at the top of the stairway leading to the cellar, and yells down, "What are you Yits up to anyway?" (227). Satisfied that the disturbance has been quelled, the policeman leaves, laughing over the very notion that a "lot of Yits" are awake arguing in the middle of the night about money. But the beat cop's sneering inference is scarcely accurate, for this dialogue concerns much more than petty squabbles by invoking the dialectic of individual and collective, the corrosive nature of capitalism, and the hardships "foreign coolies" like these poor workers endure.[28]

The iconology of the subterranean, therefore, resonates equally for doomed miners and for Jewish and Irish immigrants; it vertically maps a justice system implicated in fostering America's worst biases; and it reveals, in part by the juxtaposition of extreme hardship to nouveau-riche comfort, even opulence, an emergent class consciousness both in nineteenth-century melodrama and in more politically progressive texts like Gold's *Money* and Lawson's *Processional*. A critical genealogy must illuminate this variegated and forward-looking affinity, joining Postlewait in challenging an already "suspect history" of an American theater in which melodrama is narrowly regarded as leading inevitably—and solely—to realism. In a redacted theater history, popular ethnic melodrama of the middle nineteenth century might be reassessed as the precursor of more overtly political drama of the modern stage, much of which is resolutely nonrealistic.[29] And this project begins by reconsidering the cultural work achieved by ethnic melodrama in the years after the Great Famine, when the numbers of Irish immigrants arriving in America soared, and then continuing on to a reading of Jewish melodrama—and melodramas featuring Jewish characters—later in the century across the circum–North Atlantic theater.

A Critical Genealogy

This revision of the narrative of American theater history will actually be threefold. First, the story of Irish drama on the American stage is commonly related as beginning with Dion Boucicault's *The Colleen Bawn*, which opened at Laura Keene's Theatre on March 29, 1860, and closed on May 12 before moving to Philadelphia, returning to New York, then on to London's Adelphi Theatre and Dublin. In *Dion Boucicault: Irish Identity on Stage* (2012), Deirdre McFeely observes that Boucicault himself "subtly" claimed that *The Colleen Bawn* was *the* first Irish play, and it was received as an Irish national drama when it was first produced later in Dublin.[30] It was also, not coincidentally, the most popular Irish drama of the nineteenth century, traveling back and forth across the circum–North Atlantic world for more than fifty years after its inaugural production.[31] McFeely's account chronicles Boucicault's move to America in the 1850s, his failed theatrical management in New Orleans, and his breakthrough successes in New York with *The Poor of New York* (1857), *Jessie Brown; or, The Relief of Lucknow* (1858), and *The Octoroon; or, Life in Louisiana* (1859). After adapting contemporary events in these three plays— the so-called commercial panic, the Sepoy mutiny in India, and contemporary debates over slavery—Boucicault then turned his attention to Irish rural life in *The Colleen Bawn* and to Irish themes more broadly in such plays as *Arrah-na-Pogue; or, The Wicklow Wedding* (1864), *The Rapparee* (London, 1870), *Daddy O'Dowd* (New York, 1873), and *The Shaughraun* (New York, 1874). Correcting earlier historians' oversimplifications concerning the patriotic melodrama *Robert Emmet* (1884), including my own, McFeely adds significantly to our understanding of Irish drama on the American stage, particularly through her reading of the much-neglected text *Daddy O'Dowd*, revised by Boucicault and retitled *The O'Dowd* in 1880.[32]

Albeit illuminating, this narrative of the Irish play in America is not especially helpful either in tracing the ancestry of gender, labor, and capital inscribed on the industrial capitalist's temple in *Processional* or in understanding how the nineteenth-century stage forms part of the genealogy of plays like Lawson's or Gold's. And I am not the first student of melodrama to recognize this. John P. Harrington, for example, briefly surveys mid-nineteenth-century Irish plays in the opening chapter of *The Irish Play on the New York Stage, 1874–1966* (1997), yet as his title implies, this study effectively begins with the production of Boucicault's *The Shaughraun* in 1874. Expanding this history, Harrington's later anthology *Irish Theater in America* (2009), which features essays on Boucicault and on Edward Harrigan's collaborations with Tony Hart and David Braham in inaugurating the American musical comedy, includes Maureen Murphy's meditation on a different kind of ethnic drama that preceded *The Colleen Bawn*. Here, following Boucicault's own formulation, Murphy distinguishes between the popular "Irish play," which not only concerns "Irish subject matter," but also is "invariably rural and Catholic,"[33] and the immigrant plays written by Dublin-born John Brougham (1810–80), British playwright James Pilgrim (1825–79), and, to a lesser extent, Daly (1838–99), a first-generation Irish-American. This latter group entertained audiences with a very different drama set in urban environments far removed from the rural Killarney of *The Colleen Bawn* or the Wicklow of *Arrah-na-Pogue*, which begins with a vista in Glendalough including the *"The ruins of St. Kevin's Abbey, the Round Tower, the Ruined Cemetery, the Lake and Mountains beyond"* (3). Murphy cites Brougham's *Temptation; or, The Price of Happiness* (1849)—revised as *Temptation; or The Irish Emigrant* in 1856—as a popular play that represents the Irish immigrant as an "honest working man."[34] Thus, while Harrington properly regards characters in Pilgrim's plays as confirming a general "unhappiness with the stage Irishman,"[35] it is also the case that Pilgrim, Brougham, and Daly contributed to a thesis about Irishness in general and Irish masculinity in particular that was both progressive and inherently modern. Paradoxically and significantly, I think, while such plays attempted to convince audiences of immigrants' importance to a burgeoning modern economy, they frequently advanced a pointed critique of capitalism's inequities developed more forcefully on the modern stage.

One result of this articulation of Irish- and Jewish-American melodrama, then, is a revised understanding of the middle nineteenth-century American stage. As Daly did in such plays as *A Flash of Lightning*, Brougham and Pilgrim, who came to America in 1842 and 1849 respectively, capitalized on the changing demographics of American cities in the post-Famine era. In his appearances in the 1850s at Brougham's Lyceum, later Wallack's Theatre, the Bowery, the

Metropolitan Theatre, and the Winter Garden, Brougham offered audiences a diverse menu of entertainments. And, after a hiatus in England between 1860 and 1865, his return to New York and Philadelphia featured Irish-themed plays, social comedy, and such burlesques as *Much Ado About a Merchant of Venice* (1869) in which he starred as Shylock. Nonetheless, as influential critic William Winter phrases it, whether he was playing Sir Lucius O'Trigger in Richard Brinsley Sheridan's *The Rivals* (1775) or other roles, Brougham enhanced them with a "Celtic sparkle," rendering his lines in a "rich, rolling voice with a touch of the brogue in it."[36] Winter particularly enjoyed Brougham's impersonations of characters like O'Trigger, for whom "fortune always, sooner or later, slipped through his fingers," a result of his "buoyant Hibernian recklessness" (143). Although perhaps attractive and skillfully performed, such portrayals of feckless Irish gallants—their "honeyed cadence" and engaging demeanor notwithstanding[37]—were opposed by representations of immigrants in which earnestness, hard work, and honesty leavened the excessive qualities Irish characters typically exhibited. And this genre of Irish-American and Jewish-American melodrama, however reminiscent of Boucicauldian Irish drama, communicates a very different picture of the immigrant character. That is to say, following Edward Said, if identity is not only "what we impose on ourselves through our lives as social, historical, political and even spiritual beings," but is also "the process by which the stronger culture . . . imposes itself violently upon those who, by the same identity process, are decreed to be lesser people,"[38] then immigrant melodrama on the mid-nineteenth-century stage acted as an entertaining counterdiscourse to this imperialism.

This genre, to move to a second revision of the history of nineteenth-century American theater, rose to popularity in the late 1840s and early 1850s as the wave of Irish escaping the Famine arrived in unprecedented numbers in America. But its cultural and political work is often overlooked in histories of immigration that privilege a nostalgic attachment to a homeland among the multiple challenges to assimilation. As I have mentioned previously, in *Ireland and Irish America* Kerby Miller regards the progress of assimilation as complicated not only by nativist animosity toward the Irish, but also by Irish émigrés' own sense of themselves as exiles. During the Famine period of 1845–55, by Miller's estimation, roughly 1.9 million Irish emigrated to North America for reasons varying from eviction, "sheer panic," and fear of death to the more general aspiration to better themselves economically; relying upon annual reports from the Immigration and Naturalization Service, Leonard Dinnerstein and David Reimers set the number of Irish entering the United States between 1840 and 1860 at 1.7 million.[39] For Miller, an assiduous student of the letters of recently arrived Irish, the exilic image and its premise of involuntary leave-taking underlie a history dominated by hardship and emotional trauma. The persistence of this image, in turn, has led commentators to advance parallels between newly transplanted Irish and other immigrant peoples, especially Jews, characterized as the banished "Children of Israel." The figure of the "unhappy exile" informs letters written by many new arrivals in America to relatives who remained in Ireland, the symptoms of which included "acute home sickness" and a longing to return home, however unrealistic such a return might be.[40] As a result, for Miller the "diasporic subjectivity" is marked by an emotional struggle born of the contradiction between an attachment to an older home and the need to adapt to a new one. Mick Moloney's *If It Wasn't for the Irish and the Jews* includes songs like John O'Brien and Al Dubin's "'Twas Only an Irishman's Dream" (1916) and Teresa Brayton's "The Old Bog Road" (early 1900s), both of which convey immigrants' senses of nostalgia and connection to Ireland. One refrain in the former summarizes this sense best: "Oh you never miss the land you love until you're far away / Oh you never know what homeland means until you're away to stay."[41]

Not surprisingly, then, as Pnina Werbner explains, diasporas seem "both ethnic-parochial and cosmopolitan"; and, like performance, contain a backward glance that often manifests itself in cultural production and representation:

> The diasporic subjectivities invoked by creative artists (or religious leaders) are shaped *in tension with* prior or more widespread hegemonic diaspora discourses and modes of institutional organization; they are never simply a response to exile and alienation per se or to the sense of marginality and cosmopolitanism these engender.

For this reason, analyses of diaspora should aim "to reveal the dialectics between diaspora, aesthetics, and 'real' political mobilization."[42] But political mobilization in middle nineteenth-century America required economic mobilization, for without it immigrants had no realistic possibility of a broader social assimilation. Inherent to this assertion is another kind of dialectic: while often requiring the opportunity and equitable conditions of employment that might derive from collective mobilization, economic mobility is also an individual project (and is almost always reductively portrayed as such in melodrama). That is to say, the majority of Famine-era Irish immigrants fled a rural life in extremis in which "the religious and secular sanctions against explicit individualism [were] so intertwined . . . that the effects of the two can scarcely be separated."[43] This demography continued later in the century, leaving David Fitzpatrick with the unenviable task of explaining how "particularly 'backward' emigrants should have chosen the more expensive passage to America rather than Britain."[44] More to the point, how did such new arrivals succeed in America, as both diasporic longing and the demography Miller and Fitzpatrick outline are hardly predictive of social advancement? As I hope to show, immigrant melodrama played a central role in this ascent by depicting Irish workers and entrepreneurs rising in

American society in ways similar to the way successful Jews were portrayed later in the century, although of course neither depiction was without its liabilities and regrettable accessions to caricature.

Insofar as the Irish are concerned, such portrayals not only refute stereotypes of an indolent, belligerent, and simianized "race," but also find a basis in economic fact. Examining the bank accounts of Irish-Americans in New York's Emigrant Savings Bank, founded in 1850 by Irish-American professionals and businessmen, historian Tyler Anbinder (and his graduate students) learned that "nearly 40 percent of Irish immigrant depositors saved the modern equivalent of $10,000 usually after less than a decade in America," concluding that for many Irish the rags-to-riches "myth" was "not such a myth after all."[45] Resident Americans advanced more quickly than recent arrivals, and English and German immigrants typically outpaced the Irish financially; still, a "substantial segment" of the "laboring class" of Irish made "notable economic progress," much as Daly's irascible and Irish-hating immigrant Garry Fallon did in *A Flash of Lightning* (Daly's stage directions describe him as "American by choice, Irish by birth").[46] A number of variables complicate Anbinder's rosy picture—the movement of Irish westward from eastern cities, for example, and the unreliable nature of self-reported employment and real estate ownership in nineteenth-century censuses—yet his emphasis of Irish-Americans' financial success nonetheless challenges the portraits of Irish Americans painted by historians like Miller who emphasize immigrant suffering and their desire to return home. Most didn't.[47] Consistent with Anbinder's thesis, popular drama countered the Anglo-American press's creation of an unassimilable "Teague," "Paddy," and "Biddy," "whose qualities made him or her ... the supposed antithesis of the 'respectable' and 'civilized' (hence, Protestant) English or American man (or woman)."[48] So, even while many plays of the 1850s and 1860s rely upon unfortunate stereotypes of Irish immigrants, they also work to collapse chauvinistic constructions, featuring characters too busy pursuing their economic goals to languish in nostalgia and too attractive to be ignored. The same might be said of melodramas featuring Jewish protagonists later in the century.

Third, and finally, apropos of Jewish characters on the mid- and later nineteenth-century stage, it is important to recognize the extent to which Irish and Jewish characters were interchangeable in popular plays of this period or, returning to Joseph Roach's term, one stood as a *surrogate* of the other. Lawson's allusion to types of Jews and Irish in his preface to *Processional*, in other words, is hardly arbitrary. Indeed this trope of substitution, of one ethnic immigrant standing in proxy for another, still exists today and was critically lampooned in a recent production of Lawson's *Loud Speaker* (1927) when New York gubernatorial candidate Harry U. Collins addresses a Jewish crowd, then an Irish one in an attempt to garner support for his campaign. As revived by the ReGroup Theatre in March 2013, the candidate's strategic donning first of a Hasidic fur hat and side curls, then a "cheap green party hat" commonly worn on St. Patrick's Day, makes this point about surrogation clear.[49] A critical *genealogy* of this substitutive operation, used here in the sense that both Roach and Jonathan Arac before him understand the term, amounts to an excavation of the past in an effort both "to account for how we got here" and to ascertain how this past may be useful "for conceiving alternatives to our present condition."[50] An alternative history of politically progressive American drama of the 1920s and 1930s might therefore return to the mid- and later Victorian stage that Brougham, Boucicault, Zangwill, and many others knew so well and carried with them to America.

Examples of Irish-Jewish surrogation abound in Victorian drama, as is made ridiculously clear in Byron's burlesque of *Ivanhoe* when the nefarious Sir Brian De Bois Guilbert secretly pours poison into Rebecca's goblet and hands it to her. At just the right moment, a "portion of the roof" providentially collapses, knocking the fatal liquid from her hand. In a highly metatheatrical vein, Rebecca then calls for the limelight and promptly receives it, for "scenes sensational" like these demand such prominence. She then threatens to emulate well-known Irish heroines by throwing herself off a high platform. Sir Brian calls her his "Kathleen Kavanagh, Eily O'Connor, whichever you like" and refers to himself as Danny Mann, the misguided creature who hurls Eily into one of the Lakes of Killarney in *The Colleen Bawn*. Rebecca's father, Isaac, is then discovered on the roof of a turret, and the audience quickly learns it was he who knocked the poison from his daughter's hand, having taken his cue, he boasts, from the popular Irish melodrama *Peep O' Day*.[51] Ivanhoe and King Richard then enter to rescue Rebecca, who delivers the play's last lines: "Without a sneer or frown, / Pray bring our curtain down / With a regular Christmas chee-ar!"[52] In this context, Rebecca's Jewishness and that of her father are momentarily subsumed by the Irishness of Boucicault's popular characters, leading to their participation in Christmas "cheer" (reasonably enough, as Byron's burlesques often appeared as holiday entertainments). As we shall see, this surrogation is central to Jewish immigrant melodrama, as the doubling of Jewish characters and Irish ones becomes increasingly common on the nineteenth-century stage.

These three revisions of theater history, then—the notions that a vital Irish-American immigrant drama preceded *The Colleen Bawn* that differs significantly from a more familiar Boucicauldian or Irish melodrama; that it performed cultural work supportive of a revised thesis about the successful assimilation of Irish men in particular in midcentury America and later; and that an Irish-Jewish surrogation evolved as part of this cultural work—define the critical genealogy that follows. In addition, such plays, even as they emphasized the suitability of immigrants for roles in a modernizing economy, commonly advanced a political critique of modern capitalism foreshadowing that of modern American political drama, the Provincetown Players, the Group Theatre, and beyond.

Teague, Brougham, and Pilgrim; or, The Genealogy of the Genealogy

> Men must not be poor; idleness is the root of all evil. . . . Fortune has taken the weak under her protection, but men of sense are left to their industry.

In act 1 of *The Beaux' Stratagem* (1707), Archer, one of George Farquhar's two Cavalier gentlemen of "broken fortune," delivers a homily to his friend Aimwell expounding upon this theme: men should not be poor, and the remedy to the condition resides within the liberal humanist ambit of their own abilities and industry. He asserts further that they are both men of "intrinsic value who can strike our fortunes out of ourselves," in part because they "have heads to get money and hearts to spend it."[53] This formulary—manhood, self-reliance, and the delicate calculus of heart and head in the operations of human industry—similarly defines many Irish and Jewish characters on the nineteenth-century stage and is exhibited in their pursuit of the one thing they typically require and conspicuously lack: money. Money, of course, as Michael Gold and a host of proletarian writers would later demonstrate, is hardly an uncomplicated thing, and it isn't a simple matter in melodramas or comedies of manners either. Too often, for example, as in *The Beaux' Stratagem*, a surfeit of it is possessed by an undeserving character like Squire Sullen, who "says little, thinks less and does . . . nothing at all" except pursue his desires as a "man of pleasure."[54] But this is hardly money's worst quality or ramification. In the works of Lawson, Gold, Clifford Odets, and Eugene O'Neill, money creates or frequently exacerbates as many socially and psychically deforming "vices" as inhabit Farquhar's Squire Sullen; and, on occasion, even the most predictable melodramas anticipate socialist critiques by underscoring both the class inequities capital produces and, as in Gold's *Money*, the monstrous reshaping of the human subject it eventuates.

A later scene in *The Beaux' Stratagem* is also relevant to this discussion in which Aimwell meets Foigard, presumed to be a Belgian chaplain, and in an aside recognizes a deception: "a foreigner! A downright Teague, by this light!"[55] More specifically, by the turn of the eighteenth century "Teague" was synonymous with "Irishman," a conflation largely attributable to the comic footman Teague in Sir Robert Howard's *The Committee*, first published in 1665 but performed as early as 1662 when John Evelyn saw it (Samuel Pepys reports having seen it the following year).[56] Almost immediately, Teague was received with great enthusiasm by Restoration audiences, and *The Committee* remained prominent in repertories for decades. More important, as some have argued, whatever his shortcomings or stereotypical qualities, Teague constitutes an early example, perhaps the inaugural example, of a sympathetic portrayal of the impoverished Irish immigrant and, ultimately, his value to a modernizing society.[57]

Unlike his counterparts in Irish melodrama—Myles-na-Coppaleen in *The Colleen Bawn*, say, or Shaun in the Post in *Arrah-na-Pogue*—Teague enters the scene in act 1 of *The Committee* completely destitute. To be sure, Boucicault's comic Irishmen are hardly wealthy, but they are both "employed"—Myles, a former horse-dealer, as a poacher and smuggler; Shaun, as the driver of a mail car—live happily among friends in rural Ireland, and are more or less contented at the beginnings of these plays. Shaun enters singing in celebration of his wedding day, his breast "so big" with love for Arrah Deelish that "I feel like a fowl wid her first egg" (10–11). By contrast, Teague, whose master has recently died, enters the scene alone, a figure of exile and abjection wearing only a blanket for clothing. And, unlike Boucicault's peasant characters that possess a variety of specific skills, Teague responds almost disparagingly to a question about his work background: "Bo, bub bub bo, a trade, a trade! An Irishman a trade! An Irishman scorns a trade: . . . I will run for thee forty miles, but I scorn t'have a trade."[58] He offers, in other words, unflinching loyalty and energy, not vocational expertise. And on the rare occasion when he does have money, which he likens to a "wild colt," he is "obliged to drive it up in a corner to catch it." Prone to do the "undiplomatic thing," he also benefits his employer through an unvarnished honesty that, on occasion, clashes indecorously with prevailing notions of etiquette and social custom.[59] Teague makes this clear when recalling his retort to an Englishman who claimed there were no stars in Ireland: "I told him he told two or three lies. . . . There were as many stars in Ireland as in England, and more too" (477); later, when the aristocratic Mrs. Day calls him a "bloody rascal," he responds honestly and immediately: "You are a foolish brable-bribble woman, that you are" (496). By the play's comic conclusion, however, impediments are overcome, and Colonel Careless, Teague's employer, both expresses his appreciation and encourages others to do the same: "So friends, thank honest Teague—Thou shalt flourish in a new livery for this" (525). In this way, anticipatory of Boucicault's (and Pilgrim's) efforts some two centuries later to revise the figure of the comic Irishman,[60] Teague presents an entertaining variation of the fine broths of boys whose blarney, blather, inebriety, and shillelaghs came to define the stage Irishman. A loyal, honest, and industrious character, he complements his social betters and thwarts supercilious adversaries in a setting far removed from the peasant cottages, green hills, and crystal lakes of rural Ireland.

This is not suggest that Howard's representation of the displaced Irishman is devoid of the stereotypical defects commonly presented to English audiences of the period, or that Howard acknowledges the audience's complicity in Teague's (and Ireland's) impoverishment as a more politically driven dramatist might attempt. Instead, as Helen Burke justifiably complains, in *The Committee* Howard indulges in a process of historical "erasure" of the "memory of why a character such as Teague might have arrived in English territory in the first place": namely, colonialist domination in the Cromwellian era that led to a "massive confiscation and redistribution of native land" and, as a result, thousands of displaced persons.[61] Further, as Burke emphasizes, Teague exhibits other regrettable traits as well; his verbal blundering, for example, and his entrance as a beggar, hat in hand, cast the immigrant Irishman as "purely an object of charity for the British spectator."[62] Just as obviously, his lack of a trade confirms the aspersion that he, like most of his countrymen, is qualified for only the most menial of jobs at the bottom of the employment hierarchy: a *foot*man. For this reason, one might read the play's celebratory conclusion as tempered by Colonel Careless's announcement that while Teague may flourish in his new role, his success will nonetheless be achieved "in livery."

Popular midcentury playwrights like John Brougham and James Pilgrim refine the figure of Teague, retaining in their immigrant protagonists his most attractive features and, albeit an imperfect transformation, improving upon some of his defects. In *Temptation; or The Irish Emigrant* (again, 1849/1856), Brougham introduces Tom O'Bryan, a recent arrival from Ireland seeking work, not charity. O'Bryan, often played by Brougham himself, arrives at the door of Tom and Polly Bobalink, who are hardly wealthy themselves, exhausted and seeking a place to rest. *Temptation* includes several instances of ethnic slurring, some mild and others more severe, and these begin immediately after O'Bryan's entrance. Polly, for instance, pities O'Bryan, even though he is "only an Irishman," and offers him a chair; her husband repeats this mild deprecation only minutes later. When challenged by Bobalink, who presumes O'Bryan is merely another Teague—"Wouldn't it be better for you to be at work than lounging about in idleness"—O'Bryan quickly responds, "It would indeed be better, but where is a boy to find it?"[63] When Bobalink replies, "Anywhere—everywhere," O'Bryan wittily responds, "Faith, sir, that's exactly the place I've been looking for the last three weeks and there was nobody at home." Polly, who recognizes the affective benefit of work, encourages her husband to help O'Bryan: "Point out to him how he can get some employment; all the money you could give him would be no use. See if you can't get him a chance to earn his living, and his heart will be continually jumping" (7). O'Bryan and Bobalink eventually join forces, and Polly's prediction about the excitement of meaningful work is confirmed by her husband's report: "This poor Paddy is ready to jump out of his skin for joy that he's got something to do" (10). Further, while the lack of specific vocational skills may have disqualified Teague from any but the most humble of occupations, for O'Bryan it serves as a platform to demonstrate his versatility. So, when Bobalink asks him if he knows how to "put the horse up," O'Bryan exclaims, "If I can't I can learn. There's nothing in the way of an *honest* living that I won't have a try at" (12, my emphasis).

This issue of honesty, of acquiring wealth in an ethical way as intimated in the play's title, is reinforced when Bobalink finds a wallet containing $5,000 and, for a time, conceals his discovery. The money would have saved a desperate couple down on their luck that searches frantically for the missing wallet. As Tom considers keeping this unexpected windfall, the weight of his predicament drastically alters his behavior: he begins to drink too much and treats his wife callously, a stark change from his previous abstemiousness and loving demeanor. Given to more modest hopes, O'Bryan daydreams about acquiring just a "trifle of money" to get himself "some duds" and fantasizes about being "so full of fun and industry" if he only had cash at the ready (17). When he happens across the wallet, he refuses to touch it believing it was placed there to tempt him: "They say money that isn't earned is the devil's wages, and I don't want him for my master any way" (20). Bobalink eventually reaches the same conclusion and returns the $5,000 to its rightful owners, refusing to take even a penny as a reward. And when, near the end of the play, a crusty landlady denigrates O'Bryan as an "ignorant Irishman" and moments later as a "savage," he rejoins her insult with displays of both his natural courtesy and witty equanimity: "I know enough anyway to keep me from saying anything agin a female, when she tries to forget that she's a lady" (21).

Plays like *Temptation; or The Irish Emigrant* thus redact the figure of the newly arrived Irish in ways compatible with the emergent "business class theatre for the respectable" outlined by Bruce McConachie in *Melodramatic Formations* (1992). As he explains, the 1840s witnessed the emergence of entertainments designed both to delight and to instruct, hence the founding of P. T. Barnum's famous American Museum in New York and Moses Kimball's Boston Museum, which "developed entertainments respectable enough to preserve and enhance the reputations of their establishments, yet affordable enough to attract the millions."[64] Each museum housed theaters, adding drama to the exhibitions, lectures, and concerts that drew "native-born," mostly Protestant crowds of "moderate means," including entire families. Here, such values as self-control and "sensibility" were cultivated, along with more economic virtues like frugality and industry,[65] values Brougham foregrounded in plays like *Temptation*. His brief comanagement of Brougham and Bland's Boston Adelphi Theatre was marked by promotion of the same civic and personal virtues, as the *Evening Transcript* reported in the spring of 1847: "This elegant little place of amusement is now thoroughly established in public favor; full and fashionable audiences visit it nightly. There is not a vestige of the ancient rowdyism apparent."[66] And similar "sensibilities" obtained in his nondramatic performances as well. In *Annals of the*

New York Stage (1931), George C. D. Odell recalls Brougham's "Irish Evenings" at the Society Library in the spring of 1846, in which the actor and raconteur, accompanied by his wife on the piano, offered songs and stories associated with "Pat's Peculiarities" and delivered a lecture on temperance. Odell muses that it seemed "strange that men like Brougham could find but little place, in those hard times, in the theatres. But we must remember that the public was quite avid for lectures, concerts, and platform entertainments." In fact, times *were* hard: Brougham leased a larger Boston theater briefly after leaving the Adelphi and returned to New York in 1848 to star in *The Irish Lion*, where ticket prices had been lowered in several houses in an effort to attract larger crowds.[67] Equally important, in the nondramatic performances Odell chronicles, particularly that in which a celebrated Irish actor lectures on temperance, Brougham contributed to a broader counterdiscourse on Irishness for audiences to consider.

In December 1850, he opened Brougham's Lyceum, later Wallack's Theatre, and in early 1851 offered audiences a variety of entertainments, including adaptations of Charles Dickens's novels. And by the mid-1850s, he had garnered a measure of success. Odell lauded Wallack's as "the most interesting theatre then in New York" for the 1855–56 season, in part because Brougham's *The Game of Love* ran uninterrupted for a month in the autumn of 1855. He followed this with the "biggest success of the winter, here or anywhere," his "excruciatingly funny" burlesque *Pocohontas, or, The Gentle Savage*. This "absurd trifle with its puns, its anachronisms, [and] its immense seriousness caught the town" (Odell 6.443). Later, in the spring of 1856, he played Dogberry in Shakespeare's *Much Ado About Nothing*, Sir Harcourt Courtly in Boucicault's *London Assurance*, and others. But, as was the case with the origin of William Winter's admiration of Brougham, it was his appearance in Irish roles that elicited the praise lavished on him by commentators like Joseph Ireland, who maintained that excepting only Tyrone Power, who made several starring visits to New York in the 1830s before his untimely demise in 1841, Brougham played the "Irish gentleman" to perfection, with all his "chasteness" and "finish of character."[68]

Another relative of Teague, one less gentlemanly than Brougham's Irishmen, also rose to prominence in the 1840s and 1850s. Unquestionably, the most successful purveyor of this character in midcentury New York, Philadelphia, and Boston was the Cork-born actor Barney Williams (1823–76), who initiated his conquest of the American stage as a teenager in *Pat Rooney* at the Franklin Theatre in the summer of 1840. Joseph Ireland remarked that "the brogue was ever inseparable from [Williams's] tongue," and he "has not been excelled in the use of it by any actor on the American stage, Power only excepted" (2.331). Although Ireland commended the young actor with superlatives like these—being mentioned in the same sentence with Tyrone Power is no mean achievement—he also observed that Williams did not excel in the more refined roles so brilliantly assumed by Power, Brougham, and John Collins. Rather, Williams was unrivaled in playing the "conventional stage Irishman of low life, the ranting, roving, blarneying blade, or the more dull and stupid grade of bogtrotters"; as a result, "he has gained a popularity on our stage unequalled by any rival, although a host of imitators and competitors have arisen to dispute the palm with him" (Ireland 2.332).

This assessment begs an obvious question: how could ranting "bogtrotters," dull ones at that, accomplish the positive cultural work described here? Equally curious, how could Odell, referring to the 1850–51 season at the National Theatre, lionize Barney Williams and his wife as "pillars of the American stage" alongside such stars as Edwin Booth and Joseph Jefferson (see figure 2.3)? More broadly, what sort of perverse theatrical culture would countenance the production of plays featuring such miserably jejune characters in the "Temple of the Legitimate," as the Broadway Theatre was hailed in August 1853, when Williams appeared there? His long New York run the following spring in April 1854 featured, among other Irish titles, productions of J. H. Amherst's *Ireland As It Is* (1848?) and three plays by James Pilgrim,

FIGURE 2.3 *Mr. and Mrs. Barney Williams—American Actors. Etching from a photograph by Mayall. Adelphi Theatre, Strand, London, July 1856.*
Credit: Mander and Mitchenson / University of Bristol Theatre Collection/ArenaPAL.

one of the most prolific and popular dramatists of the 1850s: *Shandy Maguire; or, The Bould Boy of the Mountain* (1851), *Irish Assurance and Yankee Modesty* (1854), and *Paddy Miles, The Limerick Boy*, also known by such other titles as *The Limerick Boy; or, Paddy's Mischief* (1836, rev. 1855). In his commentary on the 1854 run of Williams and his wife, Odell lists seven Irish titles simply to "show how large was now the repertoire of these popular plays" (6.284) and how immensely successful they were at attracting crowds, as Williams confirmed when returning to close the theater season for three weeks between June 19 and July 8, 1854.

It is surely not coincidental that Brougham's, Pilgrim's, and Williams's rise to prominence paralleled the population explosion of Irish in America. In *Boston Catholics: A History of the Church and Its People* (1998), for example, Thomas H. O'Connor notes that in 1847 alone the city of Boston, that had accommodated some 4,000–5,000 immigrants a year, received 37,000 new arrivals. Thousands of Irish arrived "pallid and weak," unskilled, half-starved, and impoverished; and because mills had recently been built in Lowell and Lawrence, O'Connor notes, few jobs for unskilled laborers existed. As a consequence, many immigrants settled near docks and wharves where men sought work as day laborers and women served as domestics in nearby hotels.[69] The predicaments of Irish émigrés in Philadelphia and New York were similar; as a consequence, while residual texts from an earlier era featuring an irresponsible Irish gallant continued to flourish in some venues and for some audiences, it is scarcely surprising that other depictions of a peasant class arriving in America eager for work would emerge during this period. The middle or "business" class audiences who frequented the National, Bowery, and Wallack's theaters in 1850s New York—or Boston's new National Theatre (opened in 1852)—could scarcely have failed to contemplate the ramifications of this huge influx of émigrés.

To be sure, many of Pilgrim's plays, like Boucicault's, reiterate well-tested formulas of plot and characterization and, deferring to Joseph Ireland's enthusiasm for the roles Williams played, some of these feature the predictable capers of a stage Irishman and other conventions of the Irish play in America: the significance of shame as attached to a heroine placed not only in physical distress, but also in dilemmas contrived to ruin her virtue, for instance. (In this regard, the heroines of melodrama anticipate Crane's Maggie and Yezierska's Sara, who are especially susceptible to shame and vulnerable to the machinations that would produce it.) Both conventions inform *Eveleen Wilson, The Flower of Erin* (1858), a melodrama set in several locations in Ireland and, in the final act, in New York. Bernard Wilson, infatuated with his orphaned cousin Eveleen, schemes to ruin her virtue, which he might have done were it not for the refusal of two associates to cause the "living death" of someone so innocent—namely, the infliction of "shame!"—and the intervention of Pilgrim's comic Irishman, Barney O'Slashem.[70] Predictably,

Eveleen first appears in front of a cottage contemplating her "loneliness" and "desolation"; and Barney soon thereafter displays the pugnacity and inebriety of the conventional stage Irishman. One speech later in the play typifies this characterization as Barney, steeling himself to confront his antagonists, enters "drunk" and staggering: "Ould Ireland foriver! Who's afeard? Let the bla yards come, we'll tickle their hides for them! (*Takes bottle from pocket.*) This is the stuff to make a boy sing in the middle of the night!" (21). As is typical of sensational melodramas, Eveleen is finally spared the life of enforced concubinage her cousin hopes to contrive,[71] in part because, as if by magic, the stage Irishman who has difficulty even managing his pony in the old country arrives in the big city to secure her spectacular rescue. In sum, *Eveleen Wilson* is fabricated from familiar materials indeed, and this includes the residual Irishman Williams impersonated so brilliantly.

In several respects, plays like *Eveleen Wilson* resemble other popular cultural forms, midcentury sentimental fiction, for example, far more than they do the more secular, male-dominated, and labor-centered plays that form the nucleus of immigrant theater. Most obviously, Eveleen finds counterparts not only in Eily O'Connor in Boucicault's *The Colleen Bawn*, but also in the heroines of such sentimental novels as Mary Anne Sadlier's *Bessy Conway; or, The Irish Girl in America* (1861). Sadlier (1820–1903), born in Ireland and an immigrant first to Canada in the 1840s and then New York in 1860, published essays and fiction regularly in Irish-American periodicals, attempting through such novels as *Bessy Conway* and *The Blakes and the Flanagans* (1858) to create, as Marjorie Howes phrases it, "a popular Catholic literature that could compete with other popular American cultural forms of the period."[72] As Howes explains, Sadlier's fiction served to counter both anti-Irish sentiment from the nativists and Know-Nothings, which was notoriously conflated with anti-Catholicism, and such assaults on Catholicism as *The Awful Disclosures of Maria Monk* (1836), a titillating and popularly read book in antebellum America available decades later to Leopold Bloom at a seedy bookshop in *Ulysses*. Sadlier's fiction, by contrast, constituted a primer for Irish immigrants that underscored the importance of religious education and warned of the spiritually dangerous circumstances of girls seeking employment in America, as the preface to *Bessy Conway* underscores: "There is no class more exposed to evil influences than the Irish Catholic girls who earn a precarious living at service in America." For whatever material advantages awaited these young women, the "great Babylons of the west" disguised "the awful depth of corruption weltering below the surface, and the utter forgetfulness of things spiritual."[73] Like Eveleen Wilson, the heroines of Sadlier's fiction possess an innate "moral and spiritual worth" (Howes's characterization); so, when Bessy's pursuer Henry Herbert gives her a "peculiar smile," her cheek automatically turns "scarlet" in response (20). Such inherent virtue is in constant peril in America. Fortunately, given the sentimental tradition in

which Sadlier's fiction is steeped, Bessy finally does not require the intervention of a stage Irishman, although a deformed hunchback (Paul Brannigan)
watches over her protectively. In the end, Henry, about whom Paul once said,
"The devil himself is no blacker" (52), undergoes a conversion experience, the
result of a nearly fatal attack by his criminal companions. Saved from a fatal
stabbing by Paul, Henry is ministered to by nuns who restore him not only to
physical health, but to spiritual reformation as well. In the novel's final chapter, he proposes to Bessy and she gladly accepts.

By contrast, *Paddy Miles* and *Irish Assurance and Yankee Modesty* are very
different texts, as the focus on spiritual redemption and religion in Sadlier's
fiction is replaced in these plays by commercial ambition and social assimilation. Both plays begin with a young Irishman arriving in either London or an
American city seeking any work he can find. He is hired by a native resident
requiring assistance in financial and/or amatory matters, and is thus thrust
into the business of comic intrigue at which he excels. By his own description,
Paddy Miles arrives from Limerick "wid one shilling" in his pocket, just as
Pat enters the city in *Irish Assurance and Yankee Modesty* asking Buffer, his
future employer, "Good luck to your honor. Can you give a poor Irishman
a job of work?"[74] Like Paddy, Pat has led an unfortunate life and failed at
numerous occupations: farmer, jockey, footman, fisherman, postman, and so
on. Neither character is well educated or even literate, which allows for further comic business; as Pat admits when trying his hand at delivering mail,
"I did not understand reading, so took all the letters to the wrong places"
(5). Nevertheless, in *Irish Assurance and Yankee Modesty* Buffer, who claims
that "every" dollar he possesses was gained by his own "perseverance and
industry" (3), hires Pat to help him solve two problems: a meddling maiden
sister from whom he would like to be freed, and a beautiful daughter named
Susan being pursued by Clifton, a prissy Englishman he cannot abide. Clifton
is particularly fearful of confronting Pat, whom the old maid sister dislikes
intently and would like to see banished from the house, necessitating her hiring a vivacious housekeeper named Nancy to keep his brother's Irishman in
line. By the end of the comedy, however, one filled with complications Pat
cleverly engineers, Pat and Nancy announce their love for each other; Susan
is able to marry the man she wants; and Clifton and his old maid confederate are trounced. Buffer awards Pat a check for $500 for his contrivances
and at the closing curtain Nancy asks the audience, "Ladies and Gentlemen,
Pat is rather bashful . . . [but] If his progress has merited your approbation,
convince him with a good round American applause" (24). And as played by
Barney Williams at the Broadway Theatre, the New Boston Theatre, the Arch
Street Theatre in Philadelphia, and other venues, Pat received that heartfelt
American response.

Two additional conventions of immigrant melodrama distinguish it from
the better-known Irish drama. First, most of these plays advance a thesis of

immigrants' eventual assimilation and economic success in America, projects that leave little time for nostalgia or dwelling on the past. As Paddy Miles explains, "Sure, I'll niver [sic] forget Limerick, where pratties cost nothing and buttermilk half the price; but it's no use thinking of days gone by" (5). More positively, Jimmy Finnegan in *Ireland and America* considers himself a "fair specimen" of America's abundant "goodness," because after only three years in residence and by virtue of his "industry and perseverance"—the precise traits Buffer possesses in *Irish Assurance*—he has thrived in the news business.[75] Importantly, his success also reveals an inherent entrepreneurial ability to create businesses and manage them, not merely work as a menial laborer. As Jimmy, entering in act 2 "fashionably dressed," proclaims, "Jimmy Finnegan the newsboy that was, is Mr. James Finnegan, the boss that is" (20). Such moments form a powerful rebuttal to emphases of diasporic longing and exilic subjectivity; further, it is difficult to imagine that audiences would have universally agreed with Joseph Ireland's assessment that Williams played mainly stupid, ranting "bogtrotters" in these plays. Quite to the contrary, Pilgrim's plays strongly suggested that the Irish could be assimilated into American society and, as in Jimmy Finnegan's case, make contributions to it in what Bruce McConachie terms an "ideology of modernization" that stressed, among other things, Irish self-reliance.[76]

And, while Pat in *Irish Assurance* may resemble Teague in lacking a trade—he laughingly informs Buffer that he has done "anything and everything," most of them unsuccessfully (5)—his skill at outwitting his adversaries is impressive. One of these, Clifton, is as vain as he is cowardly, a not uncommon portrayal of English characters on the mid- and late-century American stage. In the opening scene of Daly's *Horizon* (1871), for example, the "English nobleman" Arthur Wellesby Vere de Vere Smith prepares to leave the "elegant salons" of New York and travel to the western frontier. Although he may be "no snob," as one character puts it, he is nonetheless smugly confident that during his journey he will be "protected" by the British flag, and later fatuously promotes his ability to speak to the "noble savage" because he has read James Fenimore Cooper's Leatherstocking stories.[77] By contrast, the Irish immigrant family he meets in the West harbors no such pretentions, proving far more adaptable in their interactions with a phalanx of fellow-workers that include Chinese, Native, and African-Americans.

Equally important, and second, Pilgrim represents a familiarly emotive Irish masculinity that, in a colonial context, helps rationalize imperial domination yet, when juxtaposed to English prissiness and recontextualized in an American setting, reads quite differently. That is to say, self-reliance and self-restraint—particularly in pointed expressions of romantic ardor—are not synonymous, and the self-control Joseph Valente privileges in *The Myth of Manliness in Irish National Culture, 1880–1922* (2011) is scarcely evident in

Pilgrim's peasant dramas. Valente offers the following definition of a hegemonic masculinity during this period:

> In increasingly polarized opposition to the feminine norm of "passionlessness" [and] "submissiveness . . . ,'" masculinity came to be defined in terms of the possession and regulated deployment of robust "animal spirits," the source of conventionally "masculine" fortitude, tenacity, assertiveness, and stamina. The ethos of manliness . . . involved turning those inward and thus converting these cruder "animal" virtues into the higher order spiritual attainments of integrity, self-possession, and self-control.[78]

As the possessors of strong, unchecked passions, Pilgrim's immigrants productively complicate this definition. Paddy Miles sings about pretty girls in the city, and Pat in *Irish Assurance and Yankee Modesty* admits to a passion that is impossible to suppress: "The indispensable desire to make love to all the women that chance throws in my way has ruined me entirely . . . and sent me on my travels, a pilgrim of Love" (9). In short, for Valente, although an idealized late Victorian masculinity required "*strong passions strongly checked*" (3, my emphasis)—one reason an actor like Henry Irving was often hailed as having given an impressively "manly" performance—such an act of restraint was hardly demanded of the midcentury Irish immigrant on the American stage, where an *unchecked* masculine desire became a privileged attribute because it allowed new arrivals to reanimate an enervated upper class that frequently lacked such vitality.

In these admittedly imperfect ways, playwrights like Brougham and Pilgrim, aided by talented actors like Barney Williams, contributed to an effective refutation of widely circulated anti-Irish sentiments and in so doing anticipated the multicultural melting pot that became modern America. At the same time, on occasion these popular playwrights also leveled a critique of capitalism developed more fully in modern and modernist drama. Early in Brougham's *Temptation*, for example, Bobalink, eager to help Tom O'Bryan in his hour of need, regrets that he cannot "put my hand in my pocket and make this poor devil's heart jump for joy" and makes a prescient comment to Polly: "I'm more discontent than ever, to think that a few hundred swindling schemers or fortunate fools should monopolize the rights of millions" (7). Here, Brougham's kindly husband isn't alluding to junk bond dealers or the multimillionaires at AIG or J. P. Morgan Chase who bundled and marketed worthless mortgages during the banking crisis of 2008–9, but to the much smaller managerial class of antebellum America as represented by Granite, the unethical businessman in the play, whose fortune, as the audience learns in the opening scene, has passed the quarter-million-dollar mark. As detestable as he is, Granite, when comparing his happiness to that of an old employee, at least understands that his fortune has come at an exorbitant subjective cost: "I would almost give [the money] up to be permitted *to feel* as he does" (4; my emphasis). Unfortunately for him, his greed quickly overrides this sentiment, and tragedy ultimately befalls him. In a similar vein, the most strident anti-Irish invective in the play is mouthed by a heartless landlady, Mrs. Grimgriskin, who even when faced with profound human suffering that she could ameliorate operates by one simple maxim: "Business, you know, is business" (8).

An even more targeted scrutiny of capital—more specifically, of alienated labor—informs Daly's *A Flash of Lightning*. Convinced that he must make his fortune before he can seek Bessie Fallon's hand in marriage, Jack Ryver ventures west to work on the railroad only to return no wealthier than when he left. Mrs. Dowderry, recently arrived from Ireland with her family, asks Jack about the wisdom of making the same trek, where she has heard that "there's goold [sic] and silver to be picked up there." Jack advises her to consider the plan more carefully:

> I've tried it and I know. If you will go West, seek the spot where you can hew the forest, till the land, and rear your own home in the wilderness. The western farmer lives like a king—the laborer on the railroad like a slave. The one works for himself and rears his children among the laughing meadows. . . . The other toils in the railroad ditch, till the ague seizes on his vitals, and he drops into the grave he has dug. (72)

Alienated labor, in other words, amounts to an all-too-quickly-imposed death sentence. In this regard, just how different are exploited railroad workers dying in ditches from Lawson's coal miners in *Processional*, buried under coal dust in a valley of death? How different are they from Gold's desperate workmen in *Money* or Elmer Rice's Mr. Zero in *The Adding Machine* (1923)? And how starkly different from all of these is the utopian ranch life Jack describes, or the American west Biff Loman experiences in Arthur Miller's *Death of a Salesman* (1949)?

In these ways, mid-nineteenth-century melodrama confronts the same issues of social inequality, alienated labor, class structure, and the relationship between work and human subjectivity interrogated by modern politically inflected literature. Equally important, immigrant characters on the midcentury American stage, like Teague before them, provided vehicles for writers like John Brougham, James Pilgrim, and Augustin Daly to represent Irish immigrants' potential to succeed in a modernizing economy on the one hand, while exposing, on the other, this same economy's more sinister consequences. And melodramatists frequently borrowed conventions from plays like these to make an analogous case for Jewish immigrants as well.

Irish-Jewish Surrogation and the Circum–North Atlantic

Is it not hard to see plenty before your very eyes, and feel the pangs of Hunger within us? Does not the land yield golden grain enough for

all? Does not nature bless us with bounteous harvests, and flocks and
herds in plenty? But man—greedy, grasping man—stands like a fiend
between the food of life and his fellow creatures.

—C. H. HAZELWOOD, *JESSY VERE; OR, THE RETURN OF THE
WANDERER* (1856)

This epigraph might have been taken from the writings of Karl Marx or
Friedrich Engels, for both believed that the introduction of machinery during the Industrial Revolution and the drive for ever-increasing surplus value
altered the human and natural landscapes. For so many workers, as Engels
lamented, the mechanical age and modernity itself transformed a "pass-
ingly comfortable life," a "righteous and peaceful life," into an existence that
scarcely benefited from "bounteous harvests" and "herds in plenty."[79] In fact,
however, this plaintive observation is made by a laborer, Jacob Thorne, in the
opening scene of C. H. Hazelwood's *Jessy Vere; or, The Return of the Wanderer*,
which had its premiere in February 1856, at the Britannia Theatre in Hoxton.[80]
And it is not difficult to understand why this sentiment would resonate with
the ever-expanding audience that supported this theater. As Jim Davis and
Victor Emeljanow describe, the rapid population growth of London's East
End at midcentury led, in turn, to the reconstruction of the Britannia in
1858 to accommodate some 4,700 spectators. The nearby Pavilion Theatre
in Whitechapel, destroyed by fire in 1856, was rebuilt and enlarged to seat
an audience of some 3,500–3,700, which made it 1,000 seats larger than the
new theater in Covent Garden.[81] Contrary to depictions of grimy playhouses
frequented by an ill-mannered hoi polloi, the Britannia typically attracted a
diverse audience, as Davis and Emeljanow delineate, of skilled laborers (car-
penters, upholsters, tailors) and merchants that grew both more highly educated and prosperous as the century came to a close. This diversity included,
increasingly, immigrant Irish and Jews. The population of Jews in London
grew from 20,000 in 1850 to 50,000 in 1887, and to 160,000 in 1900; by the
1880s, some 80 percent of Jewish immigrants lived in the East End.[82] And,
as was the case with American immigrants and tenement dwellers, many
relocated Jews and Irish were avid theatergoers, as the Report of the Select
Committee on Public Houses (1854) emphasized: "If you were to go to the
theatres near the Jews' quarters, you would find the gallery and pit filled with
Jews and Jewesses."[83]

Like the midcentury museums of Boston and New York, the Britannia
regularly featured exhibitions—a playbill for Easter week, 1869, trumpeted
the appearances of "REAL SIAMESE TWINS," "THE CELEBRATED CIRCAS-
SIAN LADY AND THE NOVA SCOTIAN GIANTESS!"—and produced a variety
of musical performances, dance, opera, and more. Yet, on most evenings
the Britannia presented melodramas or, in season, pantomimes that were

"often ideologically in line with the likely attitudes and aspirations of its local community," including "passages critical of social injustice."[84] In this latter respect, East End melodrama paralleled the politics of the midcentury American immigrant drama, and many featured Irish and Jewish characters. Between 1858 and 1862, for example, *The Colleen Bawn* and *Kathleen Mavourneen* were among the most popular presentations at the Pavilion Theatre in Whitechapel;[85] and from the later 1850s on through the 1880s, Jewish and Irish plays were well supported at the Britannia. Many were written by C. H. Hazlewood, best known for his adaptation of *Lady Audley's Secret* (1863), whose Irish plays include *Eily O'Connor; or, The Bride of Killarney* (1861, adapted from Boucicault), *The Ballanasloe Boy; or, The Fortunes of an Irish Peasant* (1867), *Erin-go-Brach; or, The Wren Boys of Kerry* (1870), and *For Honour's Sake* (1873), all of which had their premieres at the Britannia. Other playwrights like George Dibdin Pitt and W. H. Pitt produced Irish dramas at the Britannia like the latter's *Biddy O'Neal; or, The Daughter of Erin* (1869), and on occasion offered plays with Jewish antagonists—*Jewess of the Temple* (1863), for instance—as Hazlewood did with *The Stolen Jewess; or, The Two Israelites* (1872). Jewish characters would also occasionally find their ways into Irish plays, as the "Honest Israelite—The Money-lender and the Borrower" Ephraim Haydon, a "kind-hearted Jew" who shelters a poor Irish girl—does in Dibdin Pitt's *Flowers of Erin*, reprised at the Britannia on Easter Monday, 1872. Such plays promised excitement and spectacle, and playbills advertising them helped shape the audiences' expectations. The dramatic action of *Flowers of Erin*, for instance, moved from Ireland to England and finally to America, where, as the playbill promoted in bold type, neither an "ATTACK OF THE CHEROKEE INDIANS" nor a harrowing incident in the "BLACK ROCK CAVERN!!" could sully the unflinching "DEVOTION OF THE IRISH GIRL."[86]

One frequent East End playgoer was Israel Zangwill, born in 1864 to immigrant parents who had escaped the anti-Semitic hostility of czarist Russia. Like James Joyce and Sean O'Casey after him, the adolescent Zangwill was drawn to the theater, particularly to the Britannia and the nearby Pavilion, where he was likely to see the kind of surrogation of Jewish and Irish characters he so amusingly invented for *The Melting Pot*. As I mentioned in the previous chapter, after battling comically with her Jewish employer throughout much of the action, Kathleen, the Irish housekeeper, eventually refers to herself as a Jew and endearingly acquires a vernacular in which English, Yiddish, and Irish expressions meld together, as in "*Wu geht Ihr*, bedad?" and "Begorra, we Jews never know our way" (355). Viewing its 1908 American premiere in Washington, DC, President Teddy Roosevelt proclaimed *The Melting Pot* a "great play" and three years later counted it among the "very strong and real influences upon my thought and life."[87] To be sure, one of Zangwill's ambitions in the play—perhaps his chief one—is to dispel, through its protagonist David Quixano, the myth of the money-hungry stage Jew; another aim, following his own conviction, was to endorse the intermarriage of Jews and Gentiles.[88] This section of the chapter seeks to expand this list of objectives by suggesting that Irish-Jewish surrogation represented in *The Melting Pot* facilitates broader assimilative and counterdiscursive projects, and as such forms part of a larger strategy of mediation Zangwill experienced in East End theaters and brought with him to America.

By "mediation," I mean to underscore the kind of *transcoding* Fredric Jameson outlines in *The Political Unconscious: Narrative as a Socially Symbolic Act* (1981). This highly influential book is so well known that inclusion of its subtitle might seem superfluous; informed readers already know the rough contours of Jameson's argument as well as they know New Critical well-wrought urns and the Freudian dreamwork. But, when it comes to the cultural work of immigrant melodrama, the terms "narrative" and "socially symbolic" are too evocative to ignore. Consistent with the terms of Jameson's subtitle, the conventions of melodrama help us—and helped audiences at the time—create an interpretive "code," the strategic deployment of which allows for the articulation of "two quite distinct types of objects or 'texts'" in the narratives of popular plays. This code allows us to "read" the socially symbolic connotations of such plays, which is to say to arrive at some understanding of them in relation to the other levels or modes of production Jameson identifies: culture, ideology, the juridical, the political, the economic, the relations of production, and the forces of production. A "device of the analyst," mediation allows for a momentary overcoming of the "fragmentation and autonomization," the "compartmentalization and specialization, of the various regions of social life."[89] By positioning Jewish characters in familiar narratives, particularly ones in which Irish characters had previously occupied central roles, Jewish-Irish surrogation encouraged audiences to reconceive or transcode the foreign as the familiar, the exotic as the domestic: in short, the Jewish as the Irish and, later, vice versa. Thus arose the inevitable paradox that, for Jewish and Irish immigrants struggling for acceptance, their embrace and performance of a bourgeois sensibility—one easily decoded as such by audiences—was a socially progressive project. And this is precisely the reading or decoding popular theater encouraged.

This is not to claim that *every* appearance of Jews in nineteenth-century melodrama is modeled after an antecedent or contemporary representation in Irish plays. In Hazlewood's *The Stolen Jewess; or, Two Children of Israel*, set in Spain during the Napoleonic Wars, the Jewish couple Balthazar and Miriam function generically, for the most part, as innocent victims, in this instance wrongly accused of complicity with invading Napoleonic forces. From their first appearance in the play's opening scene, their ethnicity and

inherent virtue are made as clear as their adversaries' propensities for evil, as
Balthazar explains:

> What hand is not ready to be raised against our race! But I will not wander
> from here, where our father lived and died, and our only child, now twelve
> months old to-day was born. My homestead is the altar of my affections,
> and under the shadow of my own fig tree will I sit, desiring peace and good-
> will with all men.[90]

Unfortunately, other than the friendship of Sybilla, a heroic young woman
who advises the couple to be cautious of those for whom "the unoffending
Hebrew is ever a mark for insult" (7), little good will is extended to them
in the play's early scenes. Their infant daughter Ruth is kidnapped and Don
Carlos, Balthazar's chief tormentor, manufactures a case of treason against
him, accusing him and all Jews of usury—"Money! That's all your race can
think of!" (12). Balthazar is eventually dragged to the chopping block and
certain death before he is saved spectacularly at the end of the opening act.
In subsequent acts set eighteen years later and in spite of daunting complications, their missing daughter is recovered and her identity confirmed; her
Christian suitor discovers he is also really a Jew; the evil Don Carlos is mor-
tally wounded, and the long-suffering family is reunited. Even an avalanche
on an "elevated Alpine pass" cannot deter a happy ending. In the final tableau
and after the avalanche has been reduced to a gently falling snow, the virtue
of the wronged Jewish couple is recognized by all, and Balthazar and Miriam
bless their daughter's impending marriage.

There is, as this synopsis indicates, nothing particularly Irish about *The
Stolen Jewess*, although, like Brougham's and Pilgrim's immigrant plays,
Hazlewood's melodrama explicitly challenges stereotypes: the relationship
between usury and Jewish identity, for example. Hazlewood's earlier *Never
Too Late to Mend* (1859), however, might be regarded as moving the project of surrogation forward, however modestly. In this melodrama, Frank
Winchester and the protagonist George Fielding hope to wed their respective loves, but have no money; George, in fact, has been engaged for three
years to Susan, who loves him selflessly in spite of his penury. In the opening
scene, Frank announces his intention to go to Australia, "where little money
turns to a great deal, instead of dissolving like a lozenge in the mouth, as it
does in London," and tries to convince George to accompany him; there, he
believes, "by industry we shall both come home rich."[91] This plan is complicated by John Meadows, whose lust and capacity for evil are as definitive
of his character as Susan's goodness is of hers. His malevolence extends to
the abuse and threatened eviction of an elderly Jewish tenant farmer, Isaac
Levi, who has lived in his cottage for twenty years. At one time, Isaac had
led a desperate "wandering life" and never found rest until arriving at this
home, where, as he says, "the god of my fathers gave to me my wife [Leah]" (8).

Sadly, both Leah and their two children have died and are buried on the property, making Isaac all the more determined to keep it. Deaf to Isaac's pleas, Meadows presses for eviction, hoping to turn him out "bag and baggage" (8). But Meadows's evil transcends mere greed, as he not only wants no "Jewish dogs" lying in his house, but also plans an unthinkable exhumation to make certain none are "buried in my garden" (9). His anti-Semitism thus informs his more general corruption, which includes cowardice as George observes when spoiling Meadows's attempt to beat Isaac with the butt end of a whip: "You are joking, Master Meadows. Why this man is twice your age" (9). Not surprisingly, Isaac and George grow to be fast friends, and from this point on the elderly Jew becomes Susan's savior and blocks Meadows's designs to ruin her at every turn.

In the process, Isaac revises stereotypical depictions of Jews by invoking, then dismantling, their derogatory connotations, and by assuming a variety of familiar melodramatic roles. In act 3, for example, while foiling another of Meadows's and his gang's schemes, Isaac announces that "Our people find out all things where money is concerned" (50) and reverses the notion that often accompanied this aspersion: that is, that because of their greed— or, in a few cases, their obsessive engagement with religious exegeses and scholarship[92]—Jewish men lacked appropriate feeling. In fact, George and Isaac enjoy such a close relationship that at one moment the younger man exclaims, "Bless you, old man—my friend—my more than father" (50). In the last act, Susan is pressed by her father to marry Meadows, who has lied and spread the rumor that George has married another woman in Australia. George returns to England in the nick of time, as does Isaac who enters to make things right: "The old Jew has been despised and insulted in many lands, but now it is his time and he can give blow for blow" (64). Susan and her beloved are reunited, and as the final curtain descends, George repeats publically his affection for Isaac: "My friend—my more than father—we owe everything to you" (64).

Like *The Stolen Jewess*, *Never Too Late to Mend* depicts Jews as virtuous and possessive of admirable values, including meaningful ties to both family and the land. Indeed, Balthazar and Isaac, in their separate but similar ways, overstate their affection for their homes in ways Victorian audiences could understand, in part to rejoin any notion that Jews are inherent wanderers and to dispel all the negative characteristics associated with rootlessness. (Not unlike Irish Travellers or "tinkers," wandering Jews were susceptible to charges of dishonesty, sexual promiscuity, witchcraft, criminality, and a hefty catalog of other vices.) Hazlewood knows this and knows his audience. Writing less than a decade after the Great Famine, he is also aware that such topics as eviction from the family home, for many playgoers, will be decoded within a context that includes recent events in Ireland. Moreover, by introducing Isaac as a widower threatened with eviction, Hazlewood locates him in a

narrative position generally occupied by sympathetic women: Mrs. Cregan in
Boucicault's *The Colleen Bawn* and Judge Peyton's widow in *The Octoroon*, to
name just two. At the same time, as in many of the plays discussed here, by also
positioning Isaac in high-energy and curtain-lowering moments that allow
him to save heroes and heroines alike from the machinations of their adversaries, Hazlewood creates sensation scenes similar to Boucicault's in which
the comic Irishman saves the day. African and other ethnic figures occasionally effect similarly spectacular interventions—the black servant Jacky in
Never Too Late to Mend, for example—but in mid-nineteenth-century melodrama Isaac anticipates what decades later a writer like John Howard Lawson
describes as a phenomenon visible on any New York street corner: stage
Irishmen and stage Jews who, whatever their unique qualities, could stand in
for each other much as Michael Gold could become "Mickey" at labor meetings over which his Irish friend Jim Larkin presided.

This is the case, I would submit, with the Jewish protagonist in George
Henry Jessop's *Sam'l of Posen; or, The Commercial Drummer* (1881), one of the
earliest plays on the American stage to advance a similarly flattering portrayal of Jewish-American masculinity. As Harley Erdman outlines both in a
fine essay on the play and later in *Staging the Jew* (1997), the play's success was
the result of a collaboration between Jessop (1851?–1915), an Irish-born graduate of Trinity College and author of several Irish romances, and Jewish actor
Maurice Bertrand Strellinger (1852–1921), who took the stage name M. B.
Curtis.[93] Jessop eventually went on to collaborate with Brander Matthews,
commonly regarded as the first professor of drama in America, in writing
a play entitled *The Gold Mine* (1908) in which an effete Londoner expresses
her equal disdain for Irishmen and Americans; yet by the end of the play
she is engaged to a wealthy California gold baron and her niece is engaged to
the Irish leading man. Here, again, the American and Irish men possessed
in abundance "animal" attractions British suitors lacked, as in Pilgrim's and
Daly's melodramas. And, for his part, Curtis enjoyed widespread popularity
in a variety of roles, particularly as the immigrant Samuel Plastrick in *Sam'l
of Posen*, who, as Erdman notes, works assiduously in the play to exhibit all
the attributes of a "jolly good fellow": an "honest heart, a clear head, and the
attributes of manliness."[94] These are precisely the attributes of the Irish immigrants who preceded Samuel on the American stage.

Sam'l of Posen, written to entertain the flood of Jewish immigrants pour-
ing into New York during the 1880s—between 1880 and 1900, over 2.3 million immigrants came to American from Russia and the Baltic states, with
300,000 Jews living on the Lower East Side by 1900—is in many respects an
unexceptional vehicle for a skilled actor.[95] More broadly, Irving Howe regards
the play's protagonist as anticipating comics like Frank Bush, who also impersonated Irish characters on the vaudeville stage in the early decades of the
twentieth century.[96] Samuel Plastrick, like so many of Pilgrim's characters,

enters the drama seeking employment, although he has earned a modest living peddling men's garters and shoulder braces. In the play's inaugural scene, he attempts to hawk his wares to employees of a jewelry store and immediately projects an unflattering stereotype absent the beard and exaggerated nose commonly associated with it: that is, he replicates the stereotype of a crafty businessman who extracts funds from gullible customers. But then several things occur to mute this depiction: he meets the beautiful Rebecca Heyman, with whom he falls in love; he is reintroduced to the flawed but likeable Jack Cheviot, who immediately recognizes him as the man who found and returned a ring he had lost; and Jack commends Samuel to his colleagues as an "honest and industrious young fellow, and I am proud of him as a friend."[97] Jack similarly describes Samuel to Mr. Winslow, wealthy diamond merchant, as of "Hebrew type" and "honest, trustworthy and industrious" (161); and although Winslow informs Samuel that he has no openings, he is quickly won over and offers him work. When asked by Winslow what he can do, Samuel responds confidently, much like the Irish characters who precede him, "I don't know so much about that until I try. I think I could do a great many things" (162). Eventually, he is entrusted with jewels that villains attempt to steal; in the end he helps expose their rapacity, resolve the impasses that prevent Jack from marrying his fiancée, and is rewarded with both Rebecca's hand and the promise of a new business of his own. This narrative formula worked for Brougham, Pilgrim, and Barney Williams; and it was similarly successful for Jessop and Curtis.

Like Pilgrim's Paddy Miles and Jimmy Finnegan, Samuel possesses an abundance of vitality and humane sympathy that counter both the dissipation of his friend Jack and the nastiness of his eventual adversary, Frank Bronson. In the play's opening scene his industry is contrasted to both the indolence of a "crowd of horrid loafers" on the streets outside the store and the crassness of Mr. Fitzurse, who, after spying Rebecca, is immediately smitten by her beauty: "She is beautiful, Jack, beautiful. Will you introduce me, Jack?" (155). This exotic Jewess, a character much-discussed already in the preceding chapter with more to come in the next, exhibits only a professional interest in Fitzurse and proves immune to his flirtations; she responds courteously and appropriately to his questions about diamond rings, although their tastes differ, and nothing more. When Samuel enters, he quickly sizes Fitzurse up as a gull and just as quickly establishes a rapport with Rebecca that by the play's second act evolves into love. Perhaps just as important, in the play's final act Jessop introduces two minor, but significant characters: Rebecca's uncle, the elderly pawnbroker Uncle Goldstein, who bears little resemblance to Samuel; and a starving Irish widow, Mrs. Mulcahey, who attempts to pawn her shawl to buy bread for the youngest of her fourteen children. While Goldstein is away from the store, Samuel is left in charge, and he prevails upon Mrs. Mulcahey to keep her threadbare shawl, takes two dollars out of his pocket to give her, and asks Rebecca to prepare a "Jewish picnic" basket of food for her. The grateful widow responds, "Well, the Lord bless you both!" to which Sam'l quips as she exits, "But not with twins! Good-bye" (184). This kindhearted and quick-witted young immigrant thus shares many attributes with the protagonists of Pilgrim's Irish plays: all are gifted with wit and verbal dexterity, and all are inherently honest and compassionate, whatever residue of negative stereotypes remains.

Harley Erdman contextualizes other aspects of Curtis's performance with familiar representations of Jewishness. Erdman notes, for example, that several popular plays of the 1860s and 1870s by such Irish-American writers as John Brougham and Edward Harrigan feature a Jewish protagonist that, "in order to be liked," must "perform himself as a less-than-masculine money grubber who borders on a laughing stock." That is to say, to escape the roles of a Fagin or Shylock, Jews gradually cultivated a "comic spiel which effaces dignity and self-respect" as a means of gaining the spotlight of audience sympathy and support.[98] Not so with Jessop's play. Samuel Plastrick's dignity is never placed in such jeopardy; indeed, he even walks and talks much differently than previous Jewish characters on the American stage. And his masculinity, what Erdman terms his "healthy heterosexuality," not unlike that of Pilgrim's Pat and Paddy Miles, the self-described "Pilgrim of Love," is validated throughout by his affection for Rebecca and her affection for him, which lead happily in the final scene to his announcement of their impending marriage. Like old Isaac's brave actions in Hazlewood's *Never Too Late to Mend*, Samuel's intervention has also saved Jack Cheviot's relationship with his beloved Ellen, a turn of events Jack acknowledges at the play's closing: "Sam, you have made a new life for me, and have given me a world of happiness [*Embraces Ellen*] (185). Thus, the play's final curtain, which, in one version, includes the other characters lauding Rebecca and Sam'l as "Our Hebrew Friends," confirms the entire play's project to reverse stereotypical aspersions and intimate what attractive friends these two young immigrants will be. Adding humor to the scene, in the last lines of the play Samuel ironically invokes the conventional notion that Jewish drummers prey on the unsuspecting by selling them goods of degraded value. Joking with the audience sitting in the "front" and holding up a "big piece of cut glass," he offers to sell it as a diamond for fifty cents if anyone is interested (185).

After opening at New York's Haverly's Fourteenth Street Theatre, *Sam'l of Posen* enjoyed great success outside of New York, broadening its appeal beyond an audience of largely immigrant Jews. As one Boston reviewer observed in December 1882, M. B. Curtis was greeted at the Globe Theatre "by a full house, for the great and deserved reputation which he has made in this role." While the reviewer may have justly assessed the play as having only minimal merit, he lavished praise on Curtis's "cleverness" and on the "fidelity and completeness" of his "delineation of the Hebrew character."

The admiring critic concluded, "Mr. Curtis's week at the Globe will be limited in prosperity only by the capacity of the theatre,"[99] perhaps one reason why this December appearance marked his third at the theater in 1882 alone. But the facts that this *was* Curtis's third appearance at the Globe in 1882, and that the theater, remodeled and expanded in 1874, could seat as many as 2,180 playgoers, confirm the widespread success of this performance of the new Jewish immigrant. Further, this success was not solely attributable to the play's attracting a large Jewish audience, although it certainly did, for a playhouse the size of the Globe could not be filled nightly by mounting plays that appealed only to one or another ethnic group. And, in fact, the Globe promised audiences a wide variety of entertainments during this period, including a visit from Edwin Booth in *Hamlet, King Lear,* and other attractions in February 1884.[100] Jessop's perhaps unremarkable play about a Jewish immigrant, then, appealed to theatergoers in one of America's most Irish cities, one later torn by anti-Semitic violence in the 1930s and 1940s. But in the early 1880s, in part because of the surrogation of Jewish and familiar Irish characters, *Sam'l of Posen* achieved a major commercial success.

Epilogue

In all of these ways, Jewish and Irish drama of the middle and later nineteenth century formed a response to domination and prejudice made more legible in the immigrant context. And, much like those admiring Boston crowds who flocked to the Globe Theatre to see M. B. Curtis, immigrants and an ascendant middle class alike in New York, Philadelphia, and elsewhere did much the same thing, watching attractive young Irish- and, later, Jewish-American protagonists make their fortunes and win the hands of their beloveds. "Men must not be poor," as Farquhar's Archer advised, and "men of sense" must rely on their own "industry," which is precisely what they often did in popular immigrant melodrama on the American stage. For unlike a number of earlier plays and later popular songs of the Tin Pan Alley era, in the majority of these popular melodramas *diasporic* nostalgia or subjective fracturing is consistently superseded by the immigrant's desire to succeed in a new country. On the London, New York, and Boston stages such plays—directed at Irish, Jewish, and larger audiences—performed similar, if not precisely the same, cultural work. C. H. Hazlewood's popular dramas in East End London worked to overturn stereotypes in part through a process of surrogation that contextualized Jewish characters with the more familiar roles of Irish melodrama, while Brougham, Pilgrim, and Jessop provided audience with plays in which Irish and Jewish immigrants alike prospered in their new country, employing a similar Irish-Jewish surrogation that evolves more variously on the modern American stage.

But such an assimilative project is never complete, it seems. If it were, characters at the conclusions of Clifford Odets's *Waiting for Lefty* (1935) and Langston Hughes's *Don't You Want to be Free?* (1937) wouldn't have needed to join voices or hands with audiences in a utopian brotherhood to shout "STRIKE" or proclaim one larger unity that abolishes distinctions between black and white, Jew and Gentile. This assimilative brotherhood would already have been formed. And Boston radio audiences in the 1930s, many of whose parents or relatives enjoyed Curtis as Samuel of Posen at the Globe, wouldn't have turned on their sets on Sunday afternoons to listen to Father Charles Coughlin. Manhood, Capital, Labor—Lawson's temple rebuilt—and its connection to ethnicity and feeling drive immigrant melodrama on the nineteenth-century stage and some of America's most important modern texts as well.

Perhaps more immediately relevant, midcentury melodramatists could never accomplish the goals of assimilation *and* a cosmopolitan social justice by themselves. Other performances, adaptations, and dramatic genres rose to contribute to this discourse. For this reason, in the next chapter I move to monumental figures and representations of Jewishness prominent in the latter half of the century—Leah, Shylock, and Svengali—and to a single romantic hero played by nineteenth-century Irish-America's greatest star: the Count of Monte Cristo as played by James O'Neill. Like the importance of melodrama in the genealogy of modern American political theater, plays featuring these figures reveal and, in Shylock's case, continue to illuminate the dreadful and grand operations of the Irish-Jewish unconscious. And with these figures the project of an ethical cosmopolitanism—of equity and justice for all people concretized and enshrined in a single standard—moves forward, as the figures of the Jew and the Irishman grow more complicated, more psychically resonant, and significantly more challenging to those audiences who haven't yet moved beyond stereotypes.

Allo-Semitism and the Performative Uncanny

LEAH AND SHYLOCK, SVENGALI AND THE COUNT OF MONTE CRISTO

Who was a Jew, and how could you know for sure?

—JAMES SHAPIRO, *SHAKESPEARE AND THE JEWS* (1996)

You flattered the daylights out of them, with your silver-tongued charming peasant rascals. . . . You conjured up a never-never Emerald Island, fake heroics and mettlesome beauties and villains made of pasteboard, outwitted through eternity by the bogus grinning peasant rogue as only you could play him—with the blather and codology and the gaslight moonshine.

—JOHNNY PATTERSON TO DION BOUCICAULT IN STEWART PARKER'S *HEAVENLY BODIES* (1986)

In the late 1880s . . . the earnest rigour of Victorian debate was replaced by a more abrasive dialectic. Those who questioned received opinion did so with more delight and less angst. . . . Fundamental to the assault on traditional values was a recognition of the power of the unconscious.

—GEORGE TAYLOR (1992)

Referring to the quandary of the Inquisition in exposing hidden Jews—some converted to Christianity by choice, others by force—James Shapiro privileges the performative dimensions of the term "Jew."[1] Who was a Jew? How could one know if a convert was genuine or plumb the depths of a person's psyche to discover what resides there? Because Jewishness, much like Irishness, "no less than Christianity, was a role to be assumed or shed"—because, as the subject of scrutiny, a Jew might "temporize" a role as circumstances demanded[2]—the Inquisition's project of ascertaining the fidelity of true "conversos" required reading or, to employ a term introduced earlier, *transcoding* behaviors by way of a more familiar Christian rubric. In this way, Inquisitors resembled playgoers endeavoring to comprehend what transpires on stage, and neither group initiates the process as veritable blank slates. For, among other things, a spectator's understanding of the performance event is mediated by a host of contexts, however subconsciously. In this chapter, I want to illuminate several contexts in later nineteenth-century America and, on brief occasion for comparative purposes, England and Ireland, within which Jewishness and, in my conclusion, Irishness were performed and read by audiences. These range from the theatrical—the "conventions, traditions, canons, codes, styles, norms, genres, and recurring patterns of drama and theater that any specific text draws upon and uses"[3]—to an ever-expanding discourse of celebrity, an emergent fan culture, and the two concepts identified in the title of this chapter: allo-Semitism and the uncanny, both of which lead to the regions of unconscious George Taylor identifies as ascending to discursive prominence at the end of the nineteenth century.[4]

Although both of these terms have already been introduced, a brief recapitulation here might prove useful. As Zygmunt Bauman explains, "allo-Semitism" does not "unambiguously determine either hatred or love of Jews, but contains the seeds of both, and assures that whichever of the two appears is intense and extreme." As such, it denotes a "radically *ambivalent* attitude."[5] How did Jews, Bauman asks, ever become "ambivalence incarnate"?[6] Such ambivalence, intensive and affectively resonant, finds a parallel in Freud's theorization of the uncanny, which, on the one hand, signals "what is familiar and agreeable, and, on the other, what is concealed and kept out of sight" (*SE* 224–25). In what might be termed a *performative uncanny*—the ways in which uncanniness is conveyed on stage and, in some instances, in performances outside the theater—such ambivalence is played and received not merely as foreign or alien, but as "strange." Freud would surely concur with this assertion, as his etymology of the uncanny foregrounds the copresence of the *heimlich*, that "belonging to the house, not strange, familiar, tame, intimate, friendly, etc.," and the *unheimlich*: "concealed, kept from sight . . . withheld from others" (*SE* 222, 223). When associated with animals, the uncanny perches on the binarism domestic/wild, and in religious discourse it describes a veiling or concealment of the "divine." In a more spectral vein, the uncanny connotes ghosts: *heimlich* promises a place "free from ghostly influences"; the *unheimlich* is "eerie," "weird," and might arouse "gruesome fear" (*SE* 224), often hinting that "automatic, mechanical processes" are at work "concealed beneath the ordinary appearance of mental activity" (*SE* 227). *Heimlich*, then, is a word that moves "in the direction of an ambivalence until it finally coincides with its opposite, *unheimlich*" (*SE* 226). The uncanny resides at this point of coincidence.

Most of the later nineteenth-century plays and productions discussed here, unlike midcentury immigrant melodrama, develop this farrago of opposites. And they do so through a variety of narrative and performative strategies that, alternatively, reaffirm and unsettle viewers' expectations; when contextualized within extraperformative phenomena, the interpretive challenge for audiences becomes even more formidable. By contrast, mid- and later-century immigrant melodramas rarely foregrounded this degree of ambivalence or afforded glimpses into secret (or latent) desire, into the coexistence of the dreadful and the grand. Instead, in these vehicles, Irish- and Jewish-American figures—John Brougham's honest Tom O'Bryan, James Pilgrim's entrepreneurial Jimmy Finnegan, George H. Jessop's resource-ful Sam'l of Posen—exemplified hard-working, multicultural America at its assimilative best. Such characters espoused bourgeois values with which middle-class audiences could easily identify: a desire for upward mobil-ity through honest work, aspirations to marry and start families, and an attractive industriousness to complement an upper class grown enervated or complacent. At the opposite end of the human spectrum, Jewish gamblers like Dicey Morris in Dion Boucicault's *After Dark* and Mordie Solomons in Brougham's *The Lottery of Life* were similarly transparent in their less admi-rable ambitions and ethics. Such characters *knew* themselves and were fully cognizant of what they wanted, as figures in melodrama most often are, making the audience's interpretive task less onerous. However predictable, therefore, the heroes of immigrant melodramas fail to corroborate the charge leveled at the fictional Dion Boucicault in Stewart Parker's Faustian-inspired *Heavenly Bodies* that audiences were "flattered" by his "silver-tongued" peas-ants, so many "pasteboard" Irishmen designed to entertain, not challenge dominant ideologies or counter the stereotypes that immigrant melodrama sought to dismantle.[7]

Other genres and performances on the later nineteenth-century stage advanced more complex understandings of Jewishness and Irishness, even if, as cultural theorists like Stuart Hall and Lawrence Grossberg insist, popu-lar texts participate in a dialectic of containment and resistance to both the dominant ideology and the "mainstream culture" of which several plays considered here were parts.[8] At the same time, these plays rendered the transcoding process more arduous, in part because the subjectivities rep-resented in them could hardly by denigrated as "pasteboard" constructions designed to flatter spectators. Rather, consistent with Freud's theorization of the "uncanny," three of the most widely seen Jewish characters on the later nineteenth-century stage—Leah in Augustin Daly's *Leah, the Forsaken* (1862); Shylock in Shakespeare's *The Merchant of Venice*, particularly as impersonated by Henry Irving, who began his tours of America in 1883; and Svengali in stage adaptations of George Du Maurier's novel *Trilby* (1894)—possessed paradoxi-cal qualities that required carefully calculated theatrical production to convey and concerted attention to read. At the same time, Leah and Shylock in particular elicited great sympathy from audiences and exhibited the ambivalence captured by the term "allo-Semitism." There is no more telling description of this ambivalence than that expressed in Jules Lemaître's rapturous praise of Sarah Bernhardt, who initiated her series of nine tours of America in 1880–81 as Victorien in Sardou's *Fédora* (1883) and featured A. Albert Darmont's French adaptation of *Leah, the Forsaken* in the repertory of her 1892 tour:

> Mme Sarah Bernhardt, by her character, her allure, and her kind of beauty is eminently a Russian princess, unless she is a Byzantine empress or a begum of Muscat; feline and impassioned, gentle and violent, innocent and perverse, neurotic, eccentric, enigmatic. . . . Mme Sarah Bernhardt always seems like a very strange person returning from very far away; she gives me the feeling of the exotic. . . . I like her for everything hidden that I feel to exist in her.[9]

"Innocent and perverse," "gentle and violent," strange and exotic, possessive of hidden or secret impulses—these descriptors, particularly those tending toward the oxymoronic, define the performative uncanny on the later nineteenth-century stage. Further, Lemaître's use of "neurotic" implies a level of psychical convolution in Bernhardt's repertory of characters that Boucicault's Eily O'Conner and Jessop's Sam'l Plastrick lacked. As Harley Erdman notes, critics in the 1880s observed much the same thing, ranking Sam'l as "feeble and worthless" in comparison to Shylock.[10] He was not, in other words, strange or fascinatingly enigmatic like Bernhardt's protagonists—or Shakespeare's.

But more than the ability to rival Shylock in stature is at issue in the articulation of performance, allo-Semitism, and the Freudian uncanny: How was allo-Semitic ambivalence created in performance? Within what interpretive contexts was it understood? The answers to such questions extend beyond the enduring popularity of immigrant melodrama well into the 1880s and beyond, as *Sam'l of Posen*—and its surrogation of Irish and Jewish immigrants—underscores.[11] And, just as the emergence of immigrant melodrama coincides with the enormous rise in the numbers of Irish arriving in America in the 1840s and 1850s—over 300 percent and 400 percent increases, respectively, from the decade of the 1830s[12]—the present triangulation of performance, allo-Semitism, and the uncanny similarly finds its provenance in the history of immigration. For while Irish immigrants poured into America between 1840 and 1870, only some 3,500 people from Russia and the Baltic states arrived during the same period, whereas between 1881 and 1910, nearly 2.3 million immigrants, a substantial percentage of them Ashkenazim, came from this region to America. A similar trend with slightly larger increases in immigration from Austro-Hungary obtained during these decades as well.[13] As a consequence, and not surprisingly, interest in Jews and the performance of Jewishness rose as well.

This interest was heightened by productions of Daly's *Leah, The Merchant of Venice*, and Paul Potter's 1895 theatrical adaptation of *Trilby*, which contributed to the mania Du Maurier's novel created across the circum–North Atlantic. It was further amplified, in Bernhardt's case and that of American actress Adah Isaacs Mencken, by the publicity and sensation that adhered to the "Belle Juive," and by the lavish reception accorded actors of Irving's stature. Such figures piqued the imaginations not only of American playgoers, but also of impresarios and newspaper reporters eager to prize open the private lives of theatrical royalty, foreign and domestic. Thus, while the preceding chapter charted a genealogy of both a dramatic form and a type of American immigrant character, this chapter focuses on allo-Semitic performances of Jewishness that anticipate the more psychically resonant characters of modern realistic drama and tenement fiction, for example, and their location within a rapidly expanding celebrity culture that extends to Joyce's *Ulysses* and beyond. Stated slightly differently, if American political drama evolves from nineteenth-century melodrama, much modern and modernist writing contains within in it vestiges of an allo-Semitic and uncanny representation conveyed by cultural artifacts produced decades earlier. Much the same claim might be made for a new stage Irishman, a more philo-Hibernian one, who emerges in the later nineteenth century both from Irish history through personages like Robert Emmet and, perhaps unexpectedly, through the protagonist of Alexandre Dumas's (*père*) novel *The Count of Monte Cristo* (1844) impersonated by James O'Neill for nearly thirty years in the stage version, *Monte Cristo*. This chapter will conclude with a brief consideration of this heroic antithesis to Boucicault's "grinning peasant rogue" who, if not so uncanny as Leah or Shylock, nonetheless redefines Irishness in more complicated ways for theater audiences.

Leah, the Forsaken and the Haunted Stage

> MY GOOD PUBLIC—You don't know why a young lady, who boasts
> of so few years as does Miss Bateman, should have a biographer. . . .
> But, it is a historical fact, that RACHEL had appeared in public but a
> few months when M. Jules Janin—the father of all those happy dogs
> of feuilletonists, like myself—thought her worthy of a biography;
> and RISTORI, by some ardent memorialist, was written down a
> great artiste the instant she was written up one. . . . These great
> luminaries must be memorialized.[14]

Addressing the "good public" with this salutation, Augustin Daly, writing more in the capacity of press agent than historian or biographer, thus began his 1863 sketch of Kate Bateman (1842–1917), who, only twenty years old at the time, was already an accomplished performer. She made her New York debut at six as Richmond in *Richard III* and assumed child roles—Fleance in *Macbeth*, for example—at the Louisville theater her father managed, which featured appearances by, among other notables of the day, the famed Shakespearean actor Edwin Forrest. When barely nine in 1851, Kate toured London, Edinburgh, Glasgow, and Dublin, where she won both critical praise and the adoration of Irish playgoers, who "managed to cram the theater up to the gallery every night" of her visit and affectionately referred to her as the "Little Princess" ("Memoir" 7). At seventeen, and after more than a three-year hiatus from the stage, she achieved considerable success at the Winter Garden Theatre in New York in her mother Frances's adaptation of Henry Wadsworth Longfellow's epic poem *Evangeline*, appearing in it for three consecutive weeks before moving to the capacious Boston Theatre, where Longfellow himself was in attendance and is said to have remarked, "You *are* Evangeline" (qtd. in "Memoir" 10).[15] Later that year, she traveled to Chicago and starred in another of her mother's plays, *Geraldine*, earning praise for her playing of the "proud agony" and "self-abrogating death of the heart-broken woman" ("Memoir" 11).[16] She also graced the opening of a new theater in Montgomery, Alabama, playing Juliet opposite John Wilkes Booth as Romeo, and reprised the part some weeks later in New Orleans.

There is little question, however, that her portrayal of Leah, a wandering Jewess leading a small band of exiles, in *Leah, the Forsaken* marked the zenith of her career (see figure 3.1). Opening in New York on January 19, 1863, at Niblo's Garden (it enjoyed its premiere in Boston the month before with a slightly different title); this is the play, over forty years later, Bloom contemplated seeing (again) in *Ulysses*. As Joyce knew, Leah had become a reliable attraction in the repertories of actresses great and otherwise: Mrs. Millicent Bandmann-Palmer (1845–1926) in Joyce's Dublin, for example, who played it in repertory with *Hamlet*; Fanny Janauschek (1830–1904), Shakespearean actress and a decade older than Bateman, who starred in such roles in New York as Jaques in *As You Like It* and, more famously, Medea; and such lesser lights of the later nineteenth-century American stage as Lucille Western, Sara Neville, Bessie Byrne, and many others. Although an infrequent attraction in her repertory—not significant enough to merit even a reference in most biographies—Sarah Bernhardt, as I have mentioned, played Leah on her American tour of 1892.[17] Commenting on the play and actress who made it famous some twenty years after its premiere, Lawrence Hutton observed that "'Leah' and Miss Bateman became at once the fashion"; the play was a "universal success" wherever she performed it, allowing her the "greatest scope for the display of intense melodramatic powers of which unquestionably she is possessed."[18] Echoing Daly, he adds: "Miss Bateman is an exception to all established dramatic rules, not only because she was a phenomenal child who became a great woman, but because she is a brilliant star who was never in

FIGURE 3.1 *Kate Josephine Bateman (as Leah), at the Adelphi Theatre, London, 1863*

Credit: Mander and Mitchenson / University of Bristol Theatre Collection / ArenaPAL

stock."[19] By the end of the decade, Kate's luster had dimmed considerably, even if just the year before her marriage in 1866 Leopold Bloom's father "waited all the afternoon to get in" to see her at London's Adelphi Theatre (*U* 5:198).

But in 1860, that foreboding "Year of Meteors" as Walt Whitman termed it, a year before the shelling of Fort Sumter in 1861, the planets seemed to align in inaugurating a decade of long-enduring plays, characters, and actors. Indeed, March 1860 by itself was an auspicious month in the annals of the American theater. Boucicault's *The Colleen Bawn*, discussed in the preceding chapter, opened in March at Laura Keene's Theatre, earning greater fame for its author than he had previously enjoyed in his new country; it was produced throughout the northeast United States in the 1860s and 1870s, and was revived almost annually in Ireland well into the twentieth century.[20] In the same month, Adah Isaacs Mencken appeared in New York and Philadelphia, among other cities, serving secondarily as a salacious punching bag for the press; meanwhile her second husband, Irish-American heavyweight boxer John Heenan, was training to fight for the heavyweight crown in England. Her early biography clouded by uncertainty—Was she a Jew? If not, how did she appear to know Hebrew? When exactly was she born?—Mencken was sensationalized in newspapers as "a bouncing voluptuous looking Jewess, with a well-developed figure, which she takes great delight in exhibiting, a profusion of dark curls, and wicked black eyes."[21] Pregnant and abandoned by Heenan, Mencken responded to such comments by announcing her preference of death to further journalistic abuse: "These happy dead have rest and peace. . . . They have not vile darts of slander hurled at their defenceless bodies, by cruel vampyres, who live on the innocent blood of wives and mothers."[22] And, as I have mentioned, in March 1860, seventeen-year-old Kate Bateman appeared in her mother's adaptation of Longfellow's *Evangeline*. Although the play and production did not rank as an unqualified success, she was warmly received for her "innocent" advancement of the "chaste, beautiful, and true school" of performance ("Memoir" 10). It is in the juxtaposition of Mencken's and Bateman's fame that a distinction emerges between what, in another context, Sharon Marcus terms the "celebrity of impudence"—associated with "feminine artifice and the shameless public display of actions that should be kept private"—and the "celebrity of exemplarity," a fame that led to the idolization of stars like Bateman.[23]

Like allo-Semitism, such opposing contexts as a heightened public fascination with the intimate details of an actor's sexuality, on the one hand, and a theatrical repertory of self-sacrificing and "chaste" roles, on the other, suggest the complex, even contradictory, discursive formations within which Daly's *Leah* and the figure of the Jewess might be read. Yet another interpretive frame, a historical dimension not mentioned in this brief list, is outlined by Harley Erdman: namely, the ascent and decline of the "Belle Juive." As Erdman notes, such characters as Rebecca in adaptations of Scott's *Ivanhoe* (1819) and Rachel Mendizabel in the French opera *La Juive* (1835) were well-known to nineteenth-century American audiences, and the latter text at times anglicized as *The Jewess* remained prominent in repertories until the 1880s. There is little reason to doubt Erdman's claim that "these two products of European Romanticism shaped the century's performance of the Jewess. She is a beautiful woman with an unhappy destiny who lives in a rural area of premodern Europe." Perhaps more important, her strange beauty makes the alluring stage Jewess the "object of gentile male longing, an exotic and sometimes dangerous creature whose end is pathos and whose effect is frustrated desire."[24]

Where does this orientalized fantasy construction originate? From such sites as the theater, which itself was inflected in the nineteenth century by the epiphenomena of a celebrity culture that included prurient reporting about the intimate lives (and bodies) of actresses like Menken and, later, Bernhardt, who during her first tour of America in 1880–81 was both the subject of penny dreadfuls like "The Loves of Sarah Bernhardt" and the target of a group of mothers in New Jersey hoping to protect their sons from the wiles of this "European *courtisane*." Her giving birth to a son out of wedlock was widely reported—indeed, her son Maurice often accompanied her on tour—and stories circulated that she actually had four illegitimate sons, the products of her seductions of European monarchs and even the pope.[25] Like Mencken, who was thought to take "great delight" in exhibiting her pulchritude on stage, Bernhardt, at least in Bernard Shaw's memory, often appeared in the "old days" in "splendacious" costumes that both reflected her study of French painting and "far too scantily upholstered" her figure.[26] At the same time, however, she was greeted in America in contradictory ways that produced another feminine body and a decidedly different woman. In late October as reported by the *New York Times* and *Daily Graphic*, she was, alternatively, "ethereal yet womanly" and possessive of a "charming grace," but she was also caricatured anti-Semitically with an exaggerated nose, a bald head, and a skeletal frame that necessitated the ministrations backstage of an army of assistants with wigs, makeup, and padded costumes. An unwed mother and a "shrewder Shylock" in her business dealings, she was foreign, strange—other.[27] Yet, as Cornelia Otis Skinner phrases it, due in part to a massive publicity campaign before her arrival in America, "The Bernhardt" became "The Thing." Her "every move was reported in the papers," ranging from sketches of the gowns and jewelry she wore to conjecture about her sexual peccadillos.[28] There are stars like Kate Bateman and then there are brilliant novae like the Divine Sarah.

Two decades earlier, however, well before the divine one's conquest of America, *Leah* emerged in the nexus of similarly provocative contradictions. In the play's exposition, a young man proclaims his passion for a mysterious young woman and relative stranger named Leah; and, from its opening moments, the play builds an opposition between a village repressive of desire and an outlying forest of libidinal possibility where Leah has taken refuge. The first scene takes place on Good Friday with peasants leaving a village church after attending a service. In keeping with this time of devotion, they sing a chorus that advocates Christian self-denial:

> All blessings on this holy day,
>   That teaches us to know
> What great rewards await above
>   Good actions done below;
> How pain to pleasure turneth there,
>   How bleeding feet are shod.[29]

Madelina, niece of the parish priest, exits the church prayer book in hand and, in emulation of Christ's suffering on Good Friday, professes her desire for self-sacrifice: "Would that I could suffer for humanity" (3). Perhaps, she tells her uncle, she could perform a "good work" by proffering aid to a wandering Jewess and her tribe encamped on the outskirts of their village. Madelina, we learn, has met the Jewess, who related the story of her people's flight from Hungary after their "miserable huts" had been burned down, hence their need to seek shelter "among the beasts of the field" (6). Madelina also explains that a poor Christian woman with an infant sought aid from Leah, who provided her comfort; thus, Madelina's own self-sacrificial impulses originate not only in Christian teaching, but also in Leah's example.

Conspicuously absent from the Good Friday religious observance, Madelina's longtime friend and future husband Rudolf has also met Leah and been transformed by the experience. As Madelina relates in act 2, he is no longer "at peace in his father's house" (11); and once he hears that a mob incited by the play's villain, a hidden Jew named Nathan passing as a Christian schoolteacher, plans to attack Leah, Rudolf immediately runs to her protection. Fearing that his deception will be revealed, Nathan exploits the villagers' ignorance with old stereotypes and fears, including the allegation that in celebrating "their accursed Passover" Leah and her band will "devour little children as a sacrifice" (9). Rudolf finds her waiting in a nearby forest, which, again, serves as more than a place to hide; absent the repressive apparatus of the Church, the forest represents a haven where desire can be given full expression. Now devoted to a secular religion of love, Leah prays for Rudolf, "the adored one whom I worship, for whom my soul liveth!" (12). Arriving after her soliloquy, and by stark contrast Rudolf expresses his ardor for Leah in terms riven by ambivalence, the existence of which implies the workings of a sinister and dominating process:

> Thou givest me no rest nor peace—in my sleep thy image is ever present—thy dark eyes are ever gazing in my soul—thy gleaming hair ever twining round my hands draws me to thy heart. . . . Thou has taken me from all that

was once so dear and I hate thee—yet thou hast given the more than thou hast taken, and I pity thee—and hate, fear, and pity are my love! (13)

The action of the scene culminates with a kiss and their plan for Leah to flee to America with Rudolf, marry, and begin a family, a dream eventually undone by Nathan's machinations.

This passionate exchange and the scenes leading to it are overdetermined by a number of intertexts and contexts. The most obvious of these concerns anti-Semitic stereotyping, particularly Nathan's earlier accusation of blood libel. Daly's play works to refute such notions, as Leah both offers succor to an anonymous woman and her infant and, in the play's final act, blesses Madelina and Rudolf's marriage that has produced their daughter, also named Leah. The opposition between a repressive community and the wilds of the forest, superego versus id, the social versus the primitive (civilization and its discontents), defines another context, one analogous to the opposition of the city and the "green world" in romantic comedy.

Yet, darker implications inhere in this convention as well, one of which relates to Rudolf's allusion to Leah's effect on him. As an apparition that visits him nightly, Leah possesses a preternatural power, her "dark eyes" gazing into his soul and hair "ever twining around his hands" with the result that Rudolf is helplessly drawn to her. This metaphoric connection of Jewishness and vampirism was resonant in the 1860s long before the publication of Bram Stoker's *Dracula* (1897), as Adah Mencken's aspersion of journalists as "vampyres" who would suck the blood from the innocent partially suggests. As Lori Harrison and others explain, this association persists throughout Joyce's *Ulysses* and beyond, as the "nationless Jew" was often disparaged as a "bloodsucker (literal and allusive), sexual threat, and corrupter of Christian morality."[30] Like vampires who suck blood from their victims, Jews were regarded as parasites that could drain nations dry of resources,[31] a fear villagers discuss in the play's opening act:

> LUDWIG: . . . If they once get fast, ten devils can't move them. Let in one or two, and then Cousin Abraham, and Uncle Moses will be smuggled in. Cousin Abraham will open a tailor's shop on Monday, and Moses will begin a bakery on Tuesday, and both will sell their miserable wares at half price. (8)

Another more Gothic image pattern in *Leah* illustrates this vampiric connection. Prior to Rudolf's arrival in act 1, scene 2, Leah appears against a backdrop rich with signification: "*A Forest. Night; the moon not risen; a large ruined cross on platform, in centre.*"[32] Here, the forest of desire is opposed to both a "ruined" symbol of Christianity and a moon that has not yet risen, the larger meaning of which is revealed in Leah's soliloquy: "Welcome, night! . . . Ah, welcome, thrice welcome, Luna! Thy beams rest on me as they did in childhood" (12). The moon is figured as a metonym of Leah's Jewishness, but after meeting Rudolf, as she proclaims later, its priority has been supplanted by the warmth of love: "You placed me in the revivifying sunlight of love. . . . I began to feel that I was a woman—not that hideous blot upon the face of nature, a Jewish outcast!" (15).

This *revivifying* "sunlight of love" restores her to life by transforming a Jewishness that thrives in moonlight much as vampires were thought to do, a motif theatergoers would have remembered from Boucicault's *The Phantom*, which opened at Wallack's Theatre in 1856.[33] In *The Phantom*, Boucicault played Alan Raby, the fiendish and undead inhabitant of the ruined Raby Castle, where unfortunate travelers approaching at nightfall, as local residents knew all too well, often met with a horrific fate as evidenced in the mysterious conditions of their bodies upon discovery: "a wound in [the] throat in the right side from which they have evidently bled to death" and "the face is white and fixed, as if it had died of horror."[34] Young women, not unlike Rudolf overwhelmed by Leah, feel ensnared by Raby, an enthrallment he demystifies for one of his victims: "It is my will; mine eyes fix upon thy heart as if with fangs, while my soul entertwines thine within its folds" (10). Further, and unlike the folklore later surrounding vampiric reanimation, Raby does not so much fear the sun as require the moon, as Raby's adversary Dr. Rees discovers: "After death, his body must be kept from the moonlight, or by virtue of its rays he will revive" (12). For this reason, in the play's final tableau, Rees hurls Raby into a chasm "where the light of heaven never visited" (14).

Leah's powerful effect on Rudolf parallels this preternatural overpowering, which Daly's dialogue and mise en scène reinforce. And this metaphorization is entirely consistent with Leah's imminent difference, that of vampires, and Freud's emphasis of strangeness in the etymology of "uncanny." In the play's opening scene, Father Herman asks Madelina if she would really comfort "*strange* Jews who might become a burden to the village," and she reminds him that they are "erring suffering fellow-beings," a point he condescendingly agrees not to dispute (4). Madelina refers to Leah as the "*strange* woman" whom she saw on the outskirts of the village offering aid to a disconsolate Christian woman (6); and Rudolf hails Leah as "*strange* woman" when he embraces her at the edge of the forest (13). The power of love—which Leah believes is as "strong as death" (23)—has even made Rudolf strange to Madelina, who remarks to him, "You remind me so much of that Jewess" (12). Such comments gesture toward the thesis Freud postulates: "It may be true that the uncanny [*unheimlich*] is something which is secretly familiar that has undergone repression and then returned from it, and that everything that is uncanny fulfills this condition" (*SE* 17:245). In *Leah*, this hidden, repressed, and later emancipated thing is desire. And, brought into the clear and repressive light of day, it resonates strangely.

But more is hidden as well. For, sexual frisson aside, Kate Bateman's impersonation of Leah also occurs within the diametrically opposite context of pathos and self-sacrifice that Madelina evokes in the play's opening moments and Leah's compassionate reunion with Rudolf and his family recalls in the final scene. After having been duped into believing Leah has left him for money, Rudolf marries Madelina, which motivates the speech that audiences and reviewers alike waited to hear when the deeply wronged woman later returns to the village: her curse. Entering a cemetery behind the village church where Rudolf and Madelina are being married, her long hair "streaming over her shoulders," Leah initiates the much-awaited soliloquy that summarizes the injustice she has suffered. Waiting seven days for Rudolf and abandoning her people, she is devastated by his broken promise. Hoping to find Rudolf and learn why he has forsaken her, she approaches the church, overhears the joyous sounds of a nuptial benediction, and—ignorant of the identities of the newly wedded couple—generously blesses the union.

Inching closer to catch sight of the ceremony, she *"goes to a window, looks in, screams, and comes down—speaks very fast*: "Do I dream? Kind Heaven, that prayer, that amen, you heard it not. I call it back. . . . 'Tis he! Revenge!" (34). Rudolf enters, rose wreath in hand in celebration of his marriage, oddly distracted by the thought that he might have seen Leah's face through the stained-glass window. She confronts him, refuses to accept his apology, and then shrieks her curse in a curtain-lowering tableau that thrilled audiences and critics alike:

> May you wander as I wander, suffer shame as I now suffer it. Cursed be the land you till, may it keep faith with you, as you kept faith with me! Cursed be the unborn fruit of thy marriage! May it wither as my young heart has withered. . . . Cursed, thrice cursed may you be evermore, and as my people on Mount Ebal spoke, so speak I thrice, Amen! Amen! Amen! (35–36)

Upon hearing this, Rudolf drops to his knees as the curtain falls and, we learn later, lapses into a dangerous illness.

The intensity and speed with which Leah delivers the curse reveal a frightening dimension to her psychical makeup: From what depths does it emanate? How does one understand the explosive and frenetic pace of the diction? To my way of thinking, the scene suggests the existence of what Freud terms "automatic processes at work" (31), invoking the image of the Jewess as related to the uncanny or, at the very least, possessive of a surplus of feeling that, at times, she is unable to contain (not unlike Sonya Vrunsky in *Salome of the Tenements*, for example). As numerous reviewers at the time and later observed, the scene demands accomplished acting, especially exquisitely calibrated vocal control and range. Equally important, at this moment the performative uncanny and allo-Semitism burst into the play conjoined as

Leah's scream and frenetic speech imply a fearful psychical reality that here-tofore has been hidden from sight—from Rudolf's and ours; it is, as Freud's etymology of the uncanny adumbrates, "eerie" and "blood-curdling," dread-ful and theatrically grand at the same time.

Just as the play's action works to undo anti-Semitic prejudices—the false accusations of blood libel and usury, the offensive phrasing of Leah as a "huckster" of "maddening charms" (29)—the final act of *Leah* reverses this curse and vitiates its implications, returning Leah to the status of a helpless innocent. Set five years after the curse, act 5 reveals that Rudolf and Madelina now have a four-year-old child, whom they have named Leah. The act begins in pastoral splendor with reapers singing as they harvest a bountiful crop on a beautiful day. A sense of evil permeates this serenity, however, as two villag-ers discuss Nathan's unrelenting anti-Semitism, a hatred many in the village do not share. In fact, Rudolf's father Lorenzo deeply regrets his uncharita-ble actions toward Leah five years earlier and denounces the "accursed hate which is handed down from father to son!" (38). In the same scene, Madelina fears the worst as Rudolf has been gone from home for several days, yet he returns with the joyous news that the emperor has revoked the "laws of exile" prohibiting the extending of comfort to Jews; henceforth, "all subjects should be equal" (42). Leah's small band has returned to the area of the village and is preparing to emigrate to America when she meets her namesake and gives her the now withered rose wreath Rudolf had carried on the fateful day of his wedding. Leah blesses the child and recants her curse, collapses from exhaus-tion, and appears near death, but not before she can expose Nathan, who has once again incited the villagers to violence against her. In Daly's pub-lished version, satisfied that justice has been served and determined not to ruin Rudolf's happiness, Leah exits the stage to "wander into the far-off—the promised land" (44).

Significantly, I think, most reviewers in the 1860s and 1870s did not dwell upon or even recognize Leah's "strangeness" or, understandably enough, detect signs of the uncanny, but rather saw her as a tragic and pitiable figure. An "admirably filled" house greeted Kate Bateman at Niblo's Garden in 1863 with "hearty applause," and playgoers were not disappointed, even though the *New York Times* deemed the "literary merits" of the play as "not of the highest order." "Nicely balanced between gracefulness of pose and power of interpretation," Bateman was "called out after every act" to acknowledge the audience's applause. And, unlike the script in which in the final moments Leah goes off "slowly and feebly," in performance the "poor girl's heart is broken" and the drama, "terminating in her death, becomes a tragedy."[35] Consistently in the decades and myriad productions that followed, reviewers saw only this "poor girl," not the exotic figure of libidinal fantasy Erdman describes or a strange, fearful emanation from the Freudian uncanny. When Mme. Elizabeth von Stamwitz played Leah at the Broadway Theatre in 1878,

for example, she did so, as the *New York Times*' reviewer noted, in the tradition of Bateman and Fanny Janauschek by creating a "thoroughly sympathetic" character, a figure of deep pathos and the "most intense passion."[36] But
not every actress could pass critical muster in this role. Lesser talents, even
budding stars like Clara Morris, whom Daly groomed to play Leah in the
fall of 1875 and who, as Patricia Marks notes, "specialized in high emotions,"
failed to win critical approbation.[37] Others fared even worse: Bessie Byrne's
disastrous performance in 1887 moved the *Times*' reviewer to conclude that
Leah really "ought to be forsaken" and that the actress might consider a vacation in the Rocky Mountains, where she could direct her verbal thunder "to
the crags and peaks, and give the gallery a long, long rest."[38]

The relationship between success in the role, an audience's perception of
Leah as a tragic heroine, and the actress's deft use of gesture and voice is made
clear in responses to Sarah Bernhardt's 1892 appearance as Leah in Chicago.
And this effusive praise may seem surprising given the lurid exaggerations
of her sexual life in the newspapers, her exotic and erotic persona (Gottlieb's
characterization), and the anti-Semitism that she occasionally confronted.[39]
Yet, while other actresses had disappointed Chicago playgoers as Daly's
Leah before—Katharine Rogers, for example, at Hooley's Theatre in 1874,
almost a decade before she played Mercedes opposite James O'Neill in *Monte
Cristo*—Bernhardt and her rendering of the curse enraptured spectators, as
the *Chicago Daily Tribune* reported on March 1:

> Surpassing in pure tragical force any effort that nowadays may be seen
> upon the boards . . . was Bernhardt's delivery of the famous curse in the
> fourth act of "Leah, the Forsaken." The audience . . . was not only moved, it
> was fairly lifted to its feet.

Pursued by a mob in an early scene, dressed in a "poor and travel-stained"
gown, Bernhardt, now almost fifty, was transformed for this reviewer into
a "young girl—positively young, for it is an ingenuous girl's soul that looks
out of the black scared eyes—who is invested with the pathos of a harmless
and helpless animal that is about to be destroyed." Her Leah possessed a pronounced "sweetness," a "spiritual grace" without even a "thought of physical charm." More important, while Bernhardt's Leah spoke in a "plaintive,
musical voice" that in the love scenes countered the play's more "lugubrious
tones," her "high-pitched" curse ascended to an emotional crescendo wherein
"the very genius of Hebraism seemed to find expression."[40]

That Bernhardt could communicate so much vocally is more impressive
when one considers that she played the part in French, rendering the precise meaning of the lines she delivered inaccessible for most of her Chicago
audience. Instead, her voice itself seemed "to be endowed with the will to
'say something' with an inner intentionality."[41] In this way, a successful
performance of Jewishness may not require lexical precision so much as a

finely trained voice to communicate the "genius of Hebraism." Londoners agreed. Mrs. Patrick Campbell, who played Mélisande to Bernhardt's Pelléas in 1904, even quoted from an effusive review in the *Guardian* that praised the timbre of Sarah's voice, noting that she "found her note and kept it, low in tone, and rich in music."[42] Most concurred that Bernhardt, who entered the Comédie Française in 1860, where vocal study was of paramount importance in the curriculum, possessed a remarkably versatile voice. Professors at the Comédie likened the voice to a musician's instrument, and within their teaching the older style of declamation (*chant*) was challenged by a new *verité*, as the modern repertory demanded facility with both poetry and prose.[43] The tenderness *and* fury of the latter system prepared actors to change cadence and rhythm, to explore the possibilities inherent in the octaves of their voice. And it is this criterion of communicating through the voice that a lesser talent like Margaret Mather failed to meet in her 1883 appearance as Leah at McVicker's Theatre in Chicago, showing the "strain of effort" to rise to the passion required in the curse scene where, sadly, she "had no reserve force for the climax."[44] Similarly, although a skilled actress, Mme. Von Stamwitz elicited criticism from the *New York Times* for her "thin, monotonous" tones "incapable of expressing deep emotion," a liability the *Theatre* in 1878 summarized bluntly: "Her voice is decidedly against her."[45] Voice, therefore, and in particular a kind of vocal intensity resonant with an "inner intentionality" that serves as more than an instrument of language transmission, is a defining trait of the performative uncanny.

Needless to say, more than voice, costume, and gesture are responsible for the sympathetic response to Leah. Enthralled by Bernhardt's portrayal of innocence wronged, the reviewer for the *Chicago Daily Tribune* alludes to yet another context within which Leah and Jewishness were performed and decoded on the nineteenth-century stage: "The spectator immediately reconstructs his ideal of Leah left in his mind by the preceding actresses. She is not, he discovers, a vigorous little spitfire, but a much-wronged, deeply-loving woman whose sorrows lift her ultimately to the dignity of a type." Anticipating Marvin Carlson's argument in *The Haunted Stage*, this reviewer regards the (male) playgoer's memory as always already inhabited or "ghosted" by other Leahs who shape and reshape the Jewess before his eyes, or by other famous roles an actor has played. Because of the nineteenth-century practice of frequent revivals of actors in popular roles, close connections became forged between actor and role; for example, Bernhardt frequently reprised her role as Marguerite Gautier in *La Dame aux Camélias*, abbreviated as *Camille* in America. Precisely because the "physical theatre" is "among the most haunted of human cultural structures,"[46] playgoers carry with them memories not only of other actors in the same role, but also of celebrities like Kate Bateman and Bernhardt in other parts. And because this residue remains in the viewer's memory to inflect responses to a subsequent performance, the repertory in which a play is situated provides a rich context for reading and rereading.[47] If the role happens to fall into one or another stock type, the new performance might also be judged by way of previous incarnations of the type.[48] In some instances, an actor can become narrowly tied in the popular imagination to a single role—David Garrick with Lear, Charles Chaplin with the Little Tramp—and, as we shall see, James O'Neill with Edmund Dantès, the Count of Monte Cristo.

It is thus hardly a coincidence that for her first American tour Bernhardt played almost exclusively pathetic, long-suffering women who died at or near the end of the play; as Robert Gottlieb notes, six of the eight "vehicles" she selected for American audiences are describable in this way: Meilhac and Halévy's *Froufrou*, Victor Hugo's *Hernani*, Eugène Scribe and Ernest Legouvé's *Adrienne Lecouvreur*, and so on.[49] (I should note that Shaw would most likely refute this line of argument, as he famously complained that Bernhardt "does not enter into the leading character; she substitutes herself for it.")[50] Similarly, before and soon after impersonating Leah for the first time, Kate Bateman seized the public's attention as three heroines designed to elicit sympathetic responses: Shakespeare's Juliet; Geraldine, who, again, must suffer the "madness of infuriate jealousy, and the self-abrogating death of the heart-broken woman"; and Longfellow's protagonist in *Evangeline*, a text inordinately similar to *Leah* in several respects.

Of particular importance in this repertory, I think, and also to Bateman's performance of Jewishness is the theatrical adaptation of Longfellow's five-part poem *Evangeline: A Tale of Acadie* (1847) in which she starred. To be sure, Longfellow's protagonist sheds but faint direct light on allo-Semitism or the uncanny. Rather, the subtitle suggests the long-suffering heroine as a figure of an entire people, in this case a people whose homes and land are destroyed by imperial brutality. As is Rudolf and Madelina's village at the beginning of the fifth act of *Leah*, Longfellow's Acadie is blessed by material plenitude, happiness, and pastoral beauty. "Distant" and "secluded," Evangeline's Grand-Pré can boast of pastures and flocks "without number"; villagers reside in "strongly built" houses with thatched roofs, enjoying the "tranquil evenings of summer" in "peace and contentment."[51] Like the devout villagers in *Leah*, Evangeline and her neighbors attend church services regularly; and, as in *Leah*, metaphors of religious fervor also describe youthful ardor and libidinal attraction to seventeen-year-old Evangeline: "Many a youth, as he knelt in the church and opened his missal, / Fixed his eyes upon her as the saint of his / deepest devotion," and "Happy was he who might touch her hand or the hem of her garment" (80). But only Gabriel Lejeunesse, son of the blacksmith and Evangeline's closest friend, wins her affection, and the happy pair prepares to marry in the idyllic first part of the poem. Like the sumptuous orchards laden with fruit, "She, too, would bring to her husband's house delight and abundance, / Filling it full of love and the ruddy faces of children" (81).

Then, the invaders came, and the temperate summer's yielding to a cold autumn augured their ruthless intent to evict the villagers from their homes and seize their land. The parish priest had long advocated peace and urged his congregation to abandon any martial ambitions and tend to their flocks and fields; hence, the residents of Grand-Pré were unable to resist. Herded like cattle into waiting ships, parents were forcibly separated from their children and young lovers torn from each other's arms. Ever stoic, Evangeline was "Not overcome with grief, but strong in the hour of affliction, / Calmly and sadly she waited, until the procession approached her" (86). In the throng, she found Gabriel, whom she attempted to console: "Gabriel, be of good cheer! For if we love one another / Nothing, in truth, can harm us, whatever mischances may happen!" (87). Remaining with her father while Gabriel boarded a ship, Evangeline watched, just as Leah had done, as her village was burned to the ground. So did her former neighbors, both those on board and those steeling themselves to leave:

> Started the sheeted smoke with flashes of flame intermingled
> These things beheld in dismay the crowd on the shore and on shipboard.
> Speechless at first they stood, then cried aloud in their anguish,
> "We shall behold no more our homes . . . ." (87)

The rest of the poem chronicles Evangeline's extraordinary efforts to find Gabriel in the New World, a project she finally achieves when, ill and dying, he falls into her arms and receives her kiss for the last time. And, for this small mercy, Evangeline offers a prayer of thanks.

Such a character and narrative might be fruitfully juxtaposed to Daly's *Leah*: the centrality of Christianity to village life, the dissolution of a pastoral utopia, the plight of young lovers separated only to be reunited years later, and all the pathos that accrues from this reunion. In this context, Leah, the "strange" Jewess, plays the role of a familiar Christian martyr, not unlike the figure Madelina hopes to be. But, most striking, both Evangeline's neighbors and Leah's are forced from their homes, which are destroyed so as to prevent their ever returning. And it is not difficult to imagine that in the later 1840s when the poem was published and certainly by 1860 in its theatrical adaptation that Irish immigrants and other playgoers would make a connection between this atrocity and the Great Famine that forced many into exile. At the time, Irish nationalists attributed the Famine both to absentee landlords—some of whom ordered the "tumbling" of peasant cottages to ensure their inhabitants could not return—and to English colonial legislation; much later, Brendan Behan and historian Tim Pat Coogan would argue that the Famine furthered England's pursuit of a ruthless genocide analogous to the Holocaust of World War II.[52]

Evangeline, much like Shakespeare's Juliet, provides another context (or *contexts* given the implicit anti-imperial politics of the poem) for responding to the performance of Jewishness in *Leah*, a play situated in the crucible of such significant nineteenth-century theatrical discourses as the construction of repertory, the generic boundaries of melodrama and tragedy, theatrical celebrity (or notoriety), and the larger contexts of allo-Semitism. When combined with elements of the performative uncanny—intimations of a hidden psychical reality capable of explosive, seemingly autonomous, eruption; vocal variations of unusual pace and register; image patterns connected to horrific and unholy characters like vampires; allusions to strange familiarities and familiar strangeness—the performance of ethnic alterity accrued even greater depth and dimension in performance and the bodily presence of the well-known actor, especially in provincial theaters when the distant star is momentarily brought close to an often adoring audience. And like Leah, Shylock on the nineteenth-century stage, particularly as played by a celebrity like Henry Irving, extends our understanding of allo-Semitism and the uncanny.

Shylock, Interiority, and Henry Irving's Provincial Audiences

Shakespeare spells ruin, and Byron bankruptcy.
—OFT-REPEATED VICTORIAN TRUISM

Alien by both religion and nation the conversos—like Shylock—might doubly serve as figures for the stranger within. [Sir Thomas] More's appeal to the English [to empathize with the position of Jews] in fact plays exactly on this sense of uncanny "within-ness."[53]
—JANET ADELMAN, *BLOOD RELATIONS: CHRISTIAN AND JEW IN "THE MERCHANT OF VENICE"* (2008)

I ceased finally to be a "forgiver" [of *The Merchant of Venice*] when, in 1973, watching Laurence Olivier's oi-yoi-yoi portrayal of Shylock in Jonathan Miller's production at the National Theatre I was struck by the play's irredeemable anti-semitism. It was not an intellectual evaluation but the immediate impact I actually experienced.[54]
—ARNOLD WESKER, PREFACE TO *THE MERCHANT* (1983)

The aphorism that Shakespeare "spells ruin" informs numerous accounts of the Victorian theater—the tenures of actor-managers like W. C. Macready, Charles Kean, Samuel Phelps, and a few others notwithstanding—and is often attributed to Colonel H. L. Bateman, Kate's father and manager of London's Lyceum theater in the early 1870s when Henry Irving began his conquests of the English, Irish, and American theatrical worlds.[55] My conflation of these stages is intentional, as later nineteenth-century American playgoers often

resembled Dublin and other provincial audiences flocking to the theater to
see London's brightest stars (and such exotic visitors as "The Bernhardt").
Such luminaries as Irving and Frank Benson made regular visits to Dublin's
Gaiety Theatre and Theatre Royal,[56] and audiences at and near the fin de siècle
viewed other celebrated performers as well—Martin Harvey, for example, the
"matinée idol" whom both Gerty McDowell and Molly Bloom recall so fer-
vidly in *Ulysses*—in the "more tightly organized programmes" that came to
define the provincial tour.[57] Similarly, beginning in 1883 Irving made the first
of his eight tours of America, the last of which was in 1904. How Shylock
was contextualized by Irving's "tightly organized programs" on tour—and
how American audiences responded to him as a celebrity—is the subject of
much of what follows, as are the allo-Semitic and uncanny dimensions of his
performances.

Before embarking upon this theatrical tour, I want to meditate very briefly
upon the admonition that "Shakespeare spells ruin." Though the admonition
was regarded by some mid- and late-Victorian theater managers as an incon-
trovertible truth, by the 1880s William Archer, distinguished drama critic and
translator of Henrik Ibsen, began to doubt its inviolability. Writing in 1884,
he pronounced Shakespeare the most successful dramatist of the day; indeed,
with several revivals of his plays running at West End theaters that season,
Archer quipped, Shakespeare spelled ruin only for those "modern dramatists
who have to compete with him."[58] Times had changed and the lion's share of
credit for this cultural shift went to Irving, who, albeit never one of Archer's
favorite actors,[59] played *Hamlet* a decade earlier to nearly universal acclaim,
sparking a resurgence of interest in both Shakespeare and the "legitimate"
theater. And, in the preceding decade, Irving revived seven other plays as
well: *Macbeth, Othello, Richard III, The Merchant of Venice, Romeo and Juliet,
Much Ado About Nothing,* and *Twelfth Night.* During his first visit to New
York, he readily agreed with a reporter that Shakespeare was now more popular than in the past, in part because of the founding of Shakespearean "societies," hence the very real possibility that Shakespeare's works were being read
more widely.[60] *The Merchant of Venice*, in fact, *was* being read more widely,
as Linda Rozmovits explains, because the play was not only a "late Victorian
popular obsession," but clearly a "preferred vehicle" for a child's "induction
into the serious study of literature."[61] And Irving was hardly alone in reviving
Shakespeare. Herbert Beerbohm Tree produced *The Merry Wives of Windsor*
in 1889, and his *Julius Caesar*, which according to Hesketh Pearson had not
appeared on a West End stage in half a century, ran for five months in 1898,
thus confirming for Pearson that "Shakespeare spells success."[62]

Whatever advances had been made in presenting a larger canon of
Shakespeare to the public, there is little question that *Hamlet* and *The
Merchant of Venice* ranked as the most significant—and most widely
viewed—Shakespearean plays in the later nineteenth century and at the fin

de siècle in those two cities in which I am most interested here: New York and Dublin. My elevation of *The Merchant of Venice* to the "pleasant seat" occupied by *Hamlet* in the hierarchy of Shakespearean productions is hardly based on intuition, but on a more objective aggregation of data. At a 2010 conference "Performing Shakespeare in Ireland, 1660–1922" held at the National University of Ireland–Galway, Deidre McFeely presented the statistical results of her exacting study of performances of Shakespeare in Dublin for most of the eighteenth and the entire nineteenth century. Just five plays—*Hamlet, Macbeth, Richard III, Othello*, and *Romeo and Juliet*—account for one-half of all the Shakespeare performed during this period; thus, in a decade-by-decade listing of the three most-produced plays, some combination of these five nearly always appeared. The principal exception occurs in the decade 1891–1900, when *The Merchant of Venice* ranks as the second most-produced play, the *only* time it made the top three in over 180 years of Shakespearean production.[63] Given the explosive growth of the comparatively small Jewish population of Ireland between 1881 and 1911, this anomaly seems entirely predictable.[64] And if, as Bryan Cheyette argues, Jews both represented the forces of "modernity and change" in later Victorian literature and evoked senses of "invasion and violation," this greater interest in Shylock across the circum–North Atlantic seems inevitable.[65] Crucial to this discourse was a sense that cultural forces were progressing uncontrollably; but, as an American critic's praise of Irving's Shylock implies, so too was fascination with an all-consuming, if sublime, passion that defined the performance of tragic Jewishness on stage.[66]

What analogies can be made across later nineteenth-century theatrical events in, London, Dublin, and New York? Invoking Michael Rothberg's phrase, what "multidirectional memory" or strategic juxtaposition might enrich our understanding both of Shylock in America and of American drama's Irish-Jewish unconscious? To begin, theatrical repertory—the plays and protagonists that "haunted" productions of *The Merchant of Venice*—is of immediate relevance, much as *Evangeline* is when assessing responses to Kate Bateman's star turn in *Leah*. Irving's initial four-week repertory in New York in 1883 was hardly dominated by Shakespeare; on the contrary, it was chockablock with melodrama and sensation, opening with Leopold Lewis's *The Bells*, followed by Dion Boucicault's *Louis XI, The Merchant of Venice*, W. G. Wills's *Charles the First*, Charles Reade's *The Lyons Mail*, and Hannah Cowley's *The Belle's Stratagem*. In his return to New York in the spring of 1884, he added *Much Ado About Nothing* and *Hamlet*, and for subsequent tours included *Macbeth, Twelfth Night*, and *Henry VIII*. Yet, in the twilight of his career in the 1890s, Irving dropped much of the Shakespeare, leaving in one tour of Dublin, for example, a variation of the gallimaufry of plays he played in his inaugural and subsequent visits to New York: *The Merchant of Venice, The Bells*, Tennyson's *Becket, Louis XI*, Sardou's *Robespierre*, W. G. Wills's *Faust*, and Arthur Conan Doyle's one-act play *A Story of Waterloo*. My point is that rather than being read within the context of Hamlet or Macbeth, Irving's Shylock was more often contextualized with Wills's martyr-king Charles the First, Lewis's guilt-plagued Mathias, and Boucicault's ruthless, yet weirdly sympathetic, monarch. American critics often objected to this offering of undistinguished "modern" plays: for one reviewer, *The Bells* was little more than a "tawdry melodrama," one Irving would eventually appear in over eight hundred times, nearly two hundred of which were in America;[67] for another, *The Lyons Mail*, resembled a "Bowery melodrama" that had long since lost its luster. More important, for some commentators like Bernard Shaw, Irving's success playing Shylock—during the 1879–80 London season he appeared for 250 consecutive nights in the role—did not mean that it was Shakespeare's Shylock.[68] It was something else, some demurred, even if his longtime collaborator Ellen Terry bridled at the notion, insistent that Irving knew as "well as most" what or who Shakespeare's character was.[69]

This "something else" is the result of several factors, only one of which is the provincial repertory. Other factors include Irving's "improvements" of Shakespeare—the reduction of the text by some 20 percent and the scenic, musical, and gestural additions—the stage history of the play Irving hoped to turn on its head, and an acting style designed to portray Shylock as Irving saw him: a complex amalgam of "rage and mortification" that occasionally "get the better" of him, a victim reduced to a helpless state by the end of the famous trial, and a type of "an injured race." This was the vision of Shylock he had performed with such great success to English audiences. Yet, although received as an international star in America and feted wherever he appeared, Irving quickly realized that transporting productions "as they were done in London"—the goal he announced to reporters prior to his first appearance in New York—was not without difficulty. After leaving New York and Philadelphia in the winter of 1883, he arrived in a snowy Boston, appearing at the Boston Theatre in *Merchant*. There, Irving recognized that while the play had gone "well, very well, indeed," his audience was not altogether "with" him. He attributed this tepid response to his acting style, hypothesizing that American audiences were accustomed to have the part of Shylock "strongly declaimed," a muscular style inimical to his impulse for understatement and nuance.[70]

Yet more than the difference between declamation and *verité* distinguishes Irving's characterization, as he also strenuously objected to portrayals of Shylock that reduced him to a "Jewish butcher." The stage history of *The Merchant of Venice*, then, is of immediate relevance in understanding Irving's conception of the character, which—as for Macready before him—far more closely resembled Hamlet than Christopher Marlowe's Barabbas: that is to say, Irving's Shylock was far more tragically complex than he appeared in the eighteenth century as either a "stock evil buffoon" or as a figure of "unrelenting malevolence," as in Charles Macklin's impersonation first undertaken in 1741.[71] Countering a long-standing portrayal of Shylock as a comic figure, Macklin's assumption of the role offers a useful counterpoint to Irving's, and his performance not only affected the repeal of the 1753 Jewish Naturalization Act in England, but in the process transformed Shylock from a mere "stage character to one who steps out of the theater into the daily lives of English men and women, whose influence extended out of the City into the countryside."[72] James Shapiro describes both impacts—including the request from London Jews that Macklin and the play *not* appear during the 1753–54 season, as the very name Shylock connoted "rapacious Jew"—and in a richly suggestive essay entitled "Celebrity Shylock," Emily Hodgson Anderson outlines both Macklin's overthrowing of previous comic adaptations of the play and the ways in which the actor himself was overtaken by the role.[73] Macklin's Shylock was so malevolent that, in yet another uncanny instance (a non-Freudian one) of Irish Jewishness—Macklin hailed from County Donegal and emigrated to England in the 1720s—King George II is said to have responded to Robert Walpole's wish that the House of Commons could be frightened into compliance with, "What do you think of sending them to the theatre to see that Irishman play Shylock?"[74] To be fair, this anecdote may not communicate the entirety of Macklin's representation of Jewish identity. For from 1759 until the close of the century, as Michael Ragussis describes, the tandem of *Merchant* and Macklin's afterpiece *Love à la Mode* was performed regularly in patent theaters, the latter serving as a "paradigm of a new kind of comedy, the multiethnic spectacle." An engaging if excessive suitor in the play—competing with Irish and Scottish rivals—not a ruthless money lender, Macklin's Beau Mordecai may have helped destabilize notions of Jewish identity by expanding this identity well beyond the dimensions of Shakespeare's merchant.[75]

Irving's nuanced, at times understated, style coupled with carefully designed stage pictures virtually guaranteed that spectators would *not* regard him as a character dominated by malevolent intent.[76] This is not to suggest that Irving avoided large gestures, but only to note that his Shylock was also capable of expressing a spectrum of feelings, some dreadful and others grand. In response to his successful 1872 premiere as Charles the First, for example, an innocent martyr and doting father oppressed by a villainous Cromwell, the *Morning Post* critic applauded the impersonation's "dignity, and refinement, and pathos beyond praise."[77] His acting style, which some naysayers found irritatingly eccentric, also allowed Irving to convey psychical depth more subtly, a quality evident in his portrayal of Matthias in *The Bells*. Haunted by his murder of a Polish Jew before the action of the play begins, Irving's Matthias seemed almost capable of turning ashen on command, as Ellen Terry recalls; Terry also underscores the intensity of his performance that, in turn, created a stress the aging—and ailing—actor could not survive.

In fact, his doctor advised him not to play the part, *not* to play the death of the guilt-ridden murderer with "such [a] horrible intensity" that "his face grew gray" and "his eyes disappearing upward."[78] Irving could also communicate his intensifying anxiety as Matthias through other gestural and vocal means. Eric Jones-Evans remembers Irving's pause while drinking a glass of wine at the end of act 1 when the subject of the Polish Jew, missing for fifteen years, was introduced. And then, as "far off jingling" sleigh bells are heard outside, he whispers, "The Bells! The Bells!" and is jolted back in time to the scene of his crime. Jones-Evans confided, "The sense of fear and horror conveyed by Irving in that whisper still has the power to make me shudder."[79] As the action ensues, Matthias can no longer effectively suppress his anxiety, and the staging communicates this, culminating in the famous stage picture of his hallucination of stalking his victim, ax in hand, while the Polish Jew navigated his sled through a driving snow. The gauzy realism of the effect predates Tennessee Williams's use of the same technique in *The Glass Menagerie* to represent a modern world of dreams, fantasy, and—in this case—horror.[80]

This combination of pictorial effect and meaningful gesture enhanced Irving's *Merchant of Venice*. And a decade after his inaugural appearance in America, New York critics continued to underscore both of these elements of his production. Appearing in the play at Abbey's Theatre in late November 1893, and immediately after playing the martyred Archbishop in Tennyson's *Becket*, Irving was praised by the *New York Times* for a "fine, subtle, thoughtful, and picturesque impersonation," even if the performance was slightly marred in two scenes by "finicky" mannerisms that muddled the clarity of the plot. Equally praiseworthy were new scenes of Venice painted by Hawes Craven, leading the reviewer to conclude that Irving's was not the Venice of history but that of "poetry," realized beautifully in "architecture and atmosphere." As a consequence, the *Times* hypothesized in 1893, spectators are not "at all occupied by contemplation of the sinister moods" or the "malicious purpose and fanaticism of the Jew," but instead are immersed in the splendor that was Venice.[81] Yet, however stunningly visual the production, as almost every student of Irving's production notes, his portrayal of Shylock was the sum of calculated subtraction from the text and strategic addition to it. He shortened the love story and Belmont scenes considerably, for example, reducing Morocco's first scene, editing Bassanio's casket scene, and eliminating Aragon altogether. Charles Shattuck underscores the importance of further textual excisions in bolstering Shylock's stature, such as cutting the brief act 2, scene 3 in which Jessica's refers to Shylock's house as "hell" (2.3.2) and asks, "Alack, what heinous sin is it in me / To be ashamed to be my father's child?" (2.3.16–17).[82] (As it does in melodrama and tenement literature, shame plays a role in *Merchant*, here reversed in Shakespeare's text to be associated with the despised father, not the rebellious or sexually liberated daughter, and thus jarringly antithetical to Irving's depiction.) He also deleted the line in act

3, scene 5 in which the Clown warns Jessica that she will be damned because she is Shylock's daughter and mockingly adds, "Marry, you may partly hope that your father / got you not, that you are not the Jew's daughter" (3.5.10–11).

His additions proved perhaps even more effective in portraying Shylock not as a saint or martyr—not as a Charles the First or Becket—but as something Beerbohm Tree would later insist upon in *Thoughts and Afterthoughts* (1913): a mixture of both "demon and savior" whose love of his daughter "commends him to our sympathies," yet whose "cruel nature commands our censure."[83] Tree's latter presumption of the character's "cruel nature" is something Irving would doubtless refute, since he once hailed Shylock as "almost the only gentleman in the play, and the most ill-used." In Irving's vision of the character, Shylock is driven by his daughter's elopement into a "passion of rage and disappointment" and is a man "beside himself with vexation and chagrin."[84] This powerful combination of fatherly disappointment and intense feeling distinguishes Irving's Shylock from Macklin's and draws it closer to the domain of an allo-Semitic tragic hero like Leah, a revision enhanced by one of Irving's most effectively designed mise en scènes. Following an earlier tradition, Lorenzo and Jessica elope in the midst of the music and celebration of a street carnival; Lorenzo "steals Jessica away with his comrades over the canal bridge while a gondola carrying serenaders crosses the stage and disappears into the distance."[85] Having cut the brief appearance of Antonio in 2.7, Irving has the curtain brought down with revelers celebrating and a burst of music. A few moments later, the curtain is raised again and Shylock is seen returning alone from his dinner with Antonio. He appears weary and preoccupied—much like both Matthias and Louis XI—and his stooped figure is partially illuminated by a lantern he is carrying. Crossing the bridge slowly, he is the last to know that his daughter is gone. As he approaches his now empty house, the curtain is lowered again in a stage-effect that moved even some of Irving's harshest critics.

But this wasn't enough, so Irving experimented with this scene to heighten its pathos. This interpolated scene's action was preceded by Shylock's departure for dinner, his order for Jessica to lock his doors, and his halting ascent up a flight of stairs to cross the bridge, "leaning heavily on his stick" and "pausing at the top" to glance back "at the home he is loath to leave" (qtd. in Cockett, 142).[86] As the sound of his tapping stick reverberates in the distance, Jessica, alone, confides, "If my fortune be not crossed / I have a father, you a daughter, lost" (2.5.57–58). The walking stick's tapping announces his return and, after crossing the bridge again and approaching his house in early performances, as I have mentioned, the curtain fell a second time. But this ingenious piece of stage business evolved. William Winter, America's preeminent drama critic at the time, recalls that Shylock "descended the steps, crossed to his dwelling, raised his right hand, struck twice upon the door with the iron knocker and stood like a statue waiting—while a slow-descending curtain

closed in one of the most expressive pictures that any stage has ever produced."[87] Laurence Irving recounts yet another refinement of this scenic
interpolation:

> A second and third knock echoed through the empty house. The cur
> tain fell again, as without word or sign, Irving conveyed to the audience
> Shylock's crushing realization of the perfidy of his daughter.[88]

In performance, these details accrue in meaning, communicating a depth of
character without the utterance of a single word. A similar example revelatory of Shylock's internal conflicts occurs early in act 3 when he enters raging
about his stolen jewels, inquiring about Jessica, and then exploding, "I would
my daughter were dead at my foot, and the jewels in her ear; would she were
hearsed at my foot" (3.1.87–89). Appalled by his own curse, Irving's Shylock
hides his face in his hands and sobs, "No, no, no, no, no!,"[89] implying that his
imprecation had emanated from a dark psychical place he was appalled to
inhabit.

This is also the internal domain Matthias inhabits in *The Bells*, one reason
the play remained so prominent in Irving's touring repertory until the end of
his career in 1905.[90] So, too, did Boucicault's *Louis XI*, W. G. Wills's *Charles the
First*, and, somewhat later, Tennyson's *Becket*. How might Irving's Shylock be
haunted by the protagonists in these plays? More profoundly, I believe, than is
captured by the thesis that Irving was merely following in an "apologist" tradition inaugurated by Macready's revival of *The Merchant of Venice* in 1823 by
imbuing Shylock with the "dignity and humanity" of a tragic hero.[91] William
Archer in particular chastised the Lyceum audience for applauding Irving's
every "jerk" and "spasm," noting that his acting style "utterly precludes the
possibility of dignity, grace, or even ease."[92] This censure diminishes Irving's
potential for tragic heroism. Rather, Irving's Shylock, much like Arnold
Wesker's a century later, may well have been, as a reviewer in the *Spectator*
described, a Jew who in "intellectual faculties" and "spiritual discipline" was
"far in advance of the time and country in which he lives."[93] He was neither
saintly like Wills's Charles the First, nor given to murderous inclination like
Boucicault's Louis XI. He was inevitably—and allo-Semitically—both. And
like Louis XI, who suffered from an "ulcered soul, / Creeping with terrors and
alive with crime" that woke him nightly from a "fever'd sleep,"[94] Shylock bristles with ambiguity. While not "alive with crime," Shakespeare's character
was wracked by discouragement and a profound sense of loss that underwrite
his insistence upon Antonio's payment of his bond. Conversely, he enters the
trial scene "dignified and quiet," much like Charles the First as Cromwellian
forces surround him, yet "under his quietude he was not now incipiently
malevolent, he was burningly so." Exiting the court in defeat, Irving's Shylock
"nearly fell, but with a fierce effort he drew himself up to his full height" in
one final display of will and personal dignity.[95]

In a play in which, as Janet Adelman puts it, the "discourse of interiority is everywhere,"[96] Irving allowed audiences access to Shylock's "secreted self," much as he did with Matthias and Louis XI. And however tormented by guilt or defeated by assaults to their humanity, all three characters were also driven by internal forces—not unlike Leah in her curse of Rudolf—they could not always manage. Peter Thomson describes the matter well: "Irving's acting drew attention to the risk that, should the grip on the self slacken, another very different self might emerge from the secreted depths."[97] These secreted depths are the abode of the uncanny. They may also be too opaque to penetrate and understand, as Antonio suggests in the opening lines of the play:

> In sooth I know not why I am so sad.
> It wearies me, you say it wearies you.
> But how I caught it, found it, or came by it,
> What stuff 'tis made of, wherof it is born,
> I am to learn. (1.1.1–5)

We might extend the applicability of Antonio's lines to Irving's Shylock: What interior "stuff" triggers his collapse at the discovery of Jessica's elopement? Prior to his interpolated improvements, Irving's Shylock resembles other fathers—modern or early modern, Jewish or otherwise—in advising his daughter to lock the doors during the masque and cautioning her not to "clamber" up to the casements to "gaze on Christian fools" (2.5.34); after it, audiences painfully share his uncommon and overwhelming sense of loss. How do we measure this excessive response and Shylock's later effort to rise to full height after Portia's interrogation? Perhaps, to revise Thomson's formulation ever so slightly, in Irving's performance of Jewishness selves lurk beneath selves, poised to emerge as something alternatively dreadful or admirable, even vaguely heroic.

The complexity so central to Irving's conception of Shylock complements the larger trope of interiority in Shakespeare's text. A privileging of interiority is implicit in Harry Berger Jr.'s ingenious argument that Shakespeare's Venetian society promotes a kind of "negative usury"; as epitomized by Portia's ring-giving, the practice of negative usury involves a display of apparent generosity in a "something for nothing" exchange that, in the end, protects some and "savages" others.[98] Negative usury lurks just below the surface of social decorum, in other words, disguised as benevolence and coterminous with the exchange represented by Antonio's "bond." Remarkably, the opening scene of Wesker's *Shylock* (1976), later *The Merchant*, invokes yet another dimension of interiority: a loosening of the reins of suppression. Convinced that Antonio and Shylock must be old friends, nearly the same age, and bibliophiles—Irving, by contrast, after trying an older actor as Antonio, finally settled on one in his thirties roughly the same age as Bassanio[99]—Wesker opens his play with the pair drinking wine and cataloging the books and manuscripts in Shylock's library, a collection Jews were prohibited from maintaining:

ANTONIO: Until I met you, old Jew—

SHYLOCK: Not so old *then*, old man, only just past fifty—

ANTONIO: —and I became caught up in your, your passion, your hoard-ings, your—your vices!

SHYLOCK: Is he complaining or thanking me?[100]

His affection for Shylock and infatuation with his vices cause Antonio not only to renounce his former life as a businessman, but also to "envy" Shylock's "free thinking" that, as a gratifying alternative to the world of commerce, has set the merchant free to pursue his desires much as Leah's arrival in Daly's play catalyzes Rudolf 's desire. Wesker's Antonio, in short, is as irrevocably "caught up" in Shylock and his bookish world of ideas as Rudolf is with Leah.

Irving's Shylock on the American stage may have exerted a similar effect in shaking *some* spectators from their familiar subject-positions, but generally not members of the social elite. That is to say, in his earlier tours the star-actor was often greeted by a provincial city's elite at lavish dinners, either at pri-vate clubs or restaurants, where he mingled with politicians, prominent busi-ness families, and the "gentlemen" of the press. Speeches of welcome would be delivered and, of course, the great man himself would typically say a few words, graciously expressing his fondness for the city he was visiting and pre-viewing upcoming attractions for his well-heeled listeners. So, before his 1883 performances in New York, he was invited to an event at the Lotos Club where some 140 members and guests crowded the dining room and salon with 50 others eating in the restaurant and even more arriving for the speeches after dinner. As Joseph Hatton recounts, conspicuously displayed on an easel in a window alcove behind the club president's chair was a portrait of Irving as Shylock (85–86), an anticipation of Anderson's useful querying of distinctions between actor and role: Which is the celebrity, Irving or Shylock? A month later, Irving was honored at a breakfast at Philadelphia's Clover Club, where he was presented with a gold watch that had once been owned by Edwin Forrest, an act of magnanimity that moved him to kiss the theatrical relic and left him nearly speechless. Hatton deemed the event "historical in the annals of the stage," a momentous affair that "calls for a special record" of its glories (204).

Other more provincial playgoers, younger ones especially, responded to the stars' visits very differently. For Joyce's teenaged Milly Bloom in *Ulysses*, as for Gerty MacDowell and her "stagestruck" friend Winny Rippingham, the handsome Martin Harvey was the topic of constant conversation—or, using Molly Bloom's metaphor, the entrée for "breakfast dinner and supper" (18.1055). Harvey's self-sacrificing role as Sydney Carton in an adaptation of Charles Dickens's *A Tale of Two Cities* was a particular favorite in fin de siècle Dublin, so much so that upon his arrival fans would gather outside the Gresham Hotel in "exuberant and somewhat hysterical little crowds" just to catch a glimpse of him. In his autobiography, Harvey also recalls the tabloid-like apocrypha that circulated about touring stars. Much like the pale romantic heroes in his repertory, he was believed to be dying of consumption or of alcoholism; and Irving, it was rumored, zealously guarded the secret of his wife's residency in a hospital for the insane.[101] Joyce's young playgoers weren't alone in their enthusiasm, as much like Beatlemania in the 1960s, theater mania at the fin de siècle spread well beyond the social stratum of barely pubescent teeny boppers. In his biography of Frank Benson, J. C. Trewin explains that one reason Benson's tours of Ireland amounted to the "happiest parts of a Benson year" was the chance to play football against local clubs in Belfast, Derry, Armagh, Newry, Waterford, and elsewhere, and Irish fans were equally pleased at the prospect.[102] The visits of star-actors thus reverberated in a myriad of ways across cultural and class lines.

It should come as little surprise that responses to performances of Shakespeare and of Jewishness could be contextualized so widely. My contention is that provincial theater in the later nineteenth century—and this includes American theater—was, in some instances, a vibrant component of youth culture, complete with connotations of intense feeling, not intellection; immediacy and impact, not staid formalities and well-rehearsed tributes. Such fealty to star actors resembles the excesses of a fan culture today that has now grown up so familiarly around rock-and-roll idols, among other popular performers. That is, unlike the local aristocrats who planned formal dinners and delivered clichéd tributes to celebrate a star like Irving's arrival, younger fans' reactions were often more spontaneous—a sign of how invigorated they felt or how invested they were in a cultural form or performer.[103] Bram Stoker's recounting of Irving's 1877 visit to Trinity College in which the star-actor read from *Richard III, Othello*, and *David Copperfield* paints a picture of such effusive improvisation, for after the reading, "He was wildly cheered in the Hall; and in the Quadrangle, when he came out, he was 'chaired' on men's shoulders all [a]round the place."[104] Irving was received with similar exuberance at the United States Military Academy at West Point a decade later when he mounted *The Merchant of Venice* in a large campus dining hall:

> The attention and understanding of the audience could not be surpassed. Many of these young men had never seen a play. . . . When the curtain finally fell there was a pause. And then with one impulse every one of those hundreds of young men with a thunderous cheer threw up his cap; for an instant the air was darkened with them.

Although the throwing of a cap was prohibited by military regulations except in those instances in which permission has been granted by a superior officer, these "splendid young fellows," as Stoker calls them, needed to find "a suitable means of expressing their feelings; and they did it in a way that they and their comrades understood."[105] Intensity, feeling, an impulse lived in the skin—these are characteristics of a fan culture and, to my way of thinking, Shylock is a very different character in the context of youthful affect than he is in the more restrained cultural registers of exclusive clubs and hackneyed encomia.

That the cadets at West Point were moved to what Stoker recognized as an act of insubordination or rebellion, albeit an innocuous one, also seems meaningful. By reference again to Emily Anderson's argument, one might ask who the catalyst is for this mild insurrection: Irving, the famous actor, or Shylock, the proud and defiant object of Portia's inquisition? In considering the question, I also want to reference the frustration Arnold Wesker outlined in a letter to the *Guardian* in 1981 with Jonathan Miller's 1973 production at the National Theatre starring Laurence Olivier, and John Barton's 1981 production for the Royal Shakespeare Company at the Aldwych Theatre starring David Suchet, the latter of which I was also fortunate enough to have seen. Wesker was repulsed by Miller's vision: the Shylock-Jessica relationship reminded him of *Fiddler on the Roof*; and Shylock's use of scales to weigh gold "just in case one forgets how he spends his time" struck him as mindless at the very least, one of a myriad of anti-Semitic clichés in the production.[106] Although also troubled by aspects of Barton's production, Wesker was moved by Suchet's facial expression of despair at the end of the trial scene and amused by his ironic laugh in response to Portia's fatuous questions near its beginning, "Which is the merchant here? And which the Jew?" (4.1.176). Dark and diminutive, dressed in black, employing a walking stick, and stooped with age—the property and posture necessities for Suchet, as at the time he, Sinead Cusack (Portia), Jonathan Hyde (Bassanio), and Tom Wilkinson (Antonio) were all in their thirties—Suchet's Shylock could hardly be misidentified.[107] I also remember, and my memory is corroborated by rehearsals of the scene available online, the interchange between Shylock and Portia when the former asks, "On what compulsion must I [be merciful]? Tell me that," and Portia responds with her famous speech beginning "The quality of mercy is not strained . . ." (4.1.186–211). In rehearsing the exchange, Barton asked Suchet to push Cusack more aggressively, leading to his emphasis of the word "compulsion" while appearing to rise in stature as he hurled it at his antagonist. Doing so, in turn, motivated Cusack almost to snarl the word "Jew" in her speech: "Therefore, *Jew* . . . consider this." Such an inflection effectively undermines any notion of Portia's generosity, "mercy," or "Christianity"; indeed, her allusions to heavenly justice ring disingenuously as she attempts to quash any sense that Shylock can claim agency or even humanity. He must be put in his place, and she does so.

And thus I wonder if, as Irving's West Point performance concluded, those exuberant cadets heard, in Ernst Bloch's phrasing, the "voice of tomorrow" echoing inside them, an "overhauling of what has previously become the adult world" in a moment of the "not-yet-conscious."[108] Were they momentarily overwhelmed by what Alan Hughes, a fastidious student of Irving's textual editing and performance, describes as the "defeated" Shylock summoning his dignity in his final moment on stage? A Chicago reviewer in 1885 applauded Irving's "superb ignoring—even to the quiver of a muscle—the taunts of the braggart Gratiano" and his uttering, "I pray you give me leave to go from hence, / I am not well" as he exited the courtroom (4.1.412–13). Then, as he crossed right, Shylock shrank from Gratiano's touch and gave him an "accompanying sneer" betraying his "unfathomable contempt," all of which made for a "magnificent exit."[109] So, again, I wonder if the cadets themselves fully understood the origins of their surge of feeling. Were they struck powerfully by the scene's "asceticism" and overwhelmed by Shylock's display of dignity and courage?[110] Did throwing their caps in the air signal a newly created solidarity with this "spare figure of the Jew"? I don't know. But I *do* know that provincial audiences, especially younger ones, get excited by the visits of stars.

Until they don't—and then all but the most loyal or obsessed fans move on, redirecting their attention and feeling to other performers, roles, or subcultures. The *New York Times*' highly laudatory review of Irving's Shylock at Abbey's Theatre in 1893, a decade after his initial American tour, implies as much about the celerity of fame by ending on an almost funereal note: "But the house was not nearly filled." Ten years after packing theaters, after being received as veritable royalty at the White House, Irving's celebrity had cooled even as Shakespeare continued to spell success for his contemporaries Martin Harvey and Beerbohm Tree. And fascination with Shylock remained constant. Moreover, audiences were still intrigued by, indeed were still susceptible to being "caught up" in, other performances of Jewishness and Irishness, and the 1880s and especially the 1890s would not disappoint them.

The Uncanny Svengali

They're always trying to wiggle up to you that fellow in the pit at the
Gaiety for Beerbohm Tree in Trilby the last time I'll ever go there to be
squashed like that for any Trilby.

—MOLLY BLOOM IN *ULYSSES* (18.1040–43)

Every seat in the house lower than the family circle had been sold
before the box office opened last night. Sidewalk speculators had
managed to secure a few seats in the upper gallery, which went off
like hot cakes before the curtain rose, at an advance of 100 percent on

the box-office price. . . . Every available inch of "standing room" was occupied.

—"PAUL POTTER'S 'TRILBY' PLAY GREETED WITH
LOUD HURRAHS," *NEW YORK TIMES*, APRIL 16, 1895

In at least one respect, it appears not to have mattered much if you went to see Wilton Lackaye as Svengali and Virginia Harned as Trilby at New York's Garden Theatre in the spring of 1895, or Beerbohm Tree and Dorothy Baird later that fall at Dublin's Gaiety Theatre. At either venue, like Molly Bloom, you might very well have been "squashed" by an overflowing crowd. However acute your state of discomfiture, though, you might have considered yourself fortunate just to be in attendance, because on opening night at London's Haymarket Theatre in October (the production had opened in Manchester in July before moving to Tree's theater), the house was not only packed with spectators, including the Prince and Princess of Wales, but some 3,000 would-be playgoers were disappointed that their applications for tickets could not be accommodated. As the *Illustrated London News* reported, "no one can get in for love or money."[111] Still, as we have seen, where celebrity and cultural notoriety are concerned, things can change quickly. A mere five years later, even though Tree continued to revive *Trilby* and starred in a film version in 1914—and even though a considerable audience "picked its way through the snow" for an "all-star" revival of the play in April, 1915 at New York's Shubert Theatre[112]—the mania had clearly subsided. By 1900, for example, the *Irish Playgoer* reported that "No more the weird figure of the lean and uncanny Svengali . . . hypnotizes the audience as well as the tone-deaf Trilby, and laughter instead of dread is the only result produced by his fantastic movements at this 'lean and slippered pantaloonic' stage of this play's career."[113]

Not so just a few years earlier across the circum–North Atlantic theatrical world. The phenomenon sparked by George Du Maurier's novel has been well documented: chapters of the book appeared in serial form in *Harper's* magazine beginning in January of 1894; the novel was published and sold in huge numbers; and by spring of the following year Paul Potter's theatrical version was refined during a short tour before arriving in New York. Tree saw the play in Buffalo and immediately purchased the rights to produce it. The novel instantiated a "Trilby" craze, complete with the marketing of such products as Trilby-related cigars, corsets, even ice cream confections.[114] As Emily Jenkins explains, numerous factors combined to fuel this popular phenomenon: higher levels of literacy, the mass circulation of magazines, increased advertising, new technology that allowed for the photomechanical reproduction of line drawings (*Trilby* contained some 122 such drawings), the rise of the illustrated "gift book," and much more.[115] Of course, the novel's unprecedented success also owed much to the relationships between Trilby O'Ferrall, a seventeen-year-old Irish-Scots model in Paris's bohemian art community; Svengali, a Jewish musical impresario twice her age who, through hypnotic manipulation, transforms her into a singing sensation; and the three young artists (Taffy, Sandy "The Laird," and Little Billee) who befriend and love her. The titillating environment of Paris's arts district, the subversive allure of sexual revolution so frequently represented in so-called "fallen women" plays of the fin de siècle like Arthur Wing Pinero's *The Second Mrs. Tanqueray* (1893) and Henry Arthur Jones's *Mrs. Dane's Defence* (1900), and the pronounced interest in the "unconscious," as George Taylor intimates in one of the epigraphs to this chapter, here manifested in the dynamic of hypnosis, all helped make *Trilby* on the printed page and on stage an international sensation.

This is not to suggest that in every respect the *Trilby* Molly Bloom, New York audiences, or the Prince of Wales saw on stage followed the novel Du Maurier wrote; in fact, most commentators recognized precisely what the *Times* reviewer emphasized: namely, because of the adaptation's "great departures" from the novel, Svengali and hypnotism become much more central to the play.[116] And this affects the play's narrative in several ways. Hopelessly in love with Trilby, Billee proposes to her some twenty times before she finally accepts; and, in the novel, after meeting his disapproving mother, Trilby is convinced that such a marriage would ruin him. In a letter to Taffy, she relates how desperately unhappy she would be if Little Billee ever grew to be "ashamed" of her and regret this *mésalliance*; thus, in a selfless decision, she elects to spare Billee this misfortune.[117] In Potter's play, by contrast, Svengali hypnotizes Trilby, who, in his broken English proclaims, "There is great fortune for you, Trilby, but there is no marriage with the Billie" (613). "Sickened" and reduced to helpless shivering when her eyes meet his, Trilby is immediately and completely controlled by him. Like the novel, the play traces the mesmerized Trilby's rise to fame as a singer and dramatizes her shocking fall from acclaim five years after she first fell under Svengali's power. On that fateful night, her real vocal talents—or the lack of them—are displayed to her incredulous public. Not surprisingly, as reviewers noted, the play provides no opportunity for Trilby to model in the "altogether" for painters and drastically reduces the novel's suggestion of her sexual activity; instead, it heightens her role as a victim of Svengali's dark and strange practice of mesmerism. Indeed, when a portrait of the dead Svengali arrives at Trilby's bedside, the question arises as to whether he is effectively dead or not, as Trilby speaks to it, sings, and then collapses fatally in front of the image of the mesmerist. Rather differently, the narrative of Du Maurier's novel continues on after her shocking death, providing a retelling of Trilby's rise to celebrity and giving an account of her friend Taffy's marriage. Potter's widely viewed adaptation contains no such intimations of future happiness.

Adherent to the original in at least one respect, however, Potter's *Trilby* seemed intent on reproducing Du Maurier's many pen and ink drawings of principal characters. Some of the most striking—and potentially anti-Semitic—of these depict an ominous Svengali manipulating Trilby's performances and thus exaggerating his "otherness," his origin "Out of the Mysterious East," as one drawing is entitled. Portrayed in New York and Boston by Wilton Lackaye, Svengali appeared "Mephistophelean"; in London, William Archer proclaimed Tree's Svengali "lineally descended from the Devil of the Miracle Plays."[118] His demise on stage, therefore, was hardly mourned by audiences: in New York; on the contrary, the "spectacle of the dead Svengali lying across a table with his hideous face inverted and his eyes staring at the spectators" at the end of act 3 was met with a "burst of cheers."[119] The moments preceding this sensational scene explain, at least in part, the audience's elation at his cardiac failure, as the dramatic tension is heightened when Svengali's assistant Gecko reveals to Billee, the Laird, and Taffy that the hypnotist may have brutalized his ingénue:

> BILLEE (*coming down*): You mean to say that he struck Trilby?
> GECKO: Struck her? Oui, she never complained to me, I never guessed it, but I heard her say it just now—so soft, so gentle. "Do not beat me Svengali."
> (*They make angry movement towards Svengali*).
> SVENGALI (*Hand to heart, very feebly totters over to table L.*): My heart, my heart! (*Falls heavily on seat*).
> (*Taffy turns away in disgust*).
> GECKO (*L.C.*): He is killing her.
> BILLEE (*C.*): Our Trilby?
> GECKO (*L.C.—solemnly*): No, it is not!
> TAFFY, LAIRD, and BILLEE (*R.C. and C.*): What?
> GECKO (*L.C.*): It is Svengali's Trilby, not your Trilby. (634–35)

Gecko goes on to ramify this last notion, postulating that when under the control of "this magician"—a control achieved by merely "one look of his eye"—the Trilby these men adore ceases to exist. This revelation occurs backstage while she is performing before a large audience, and when Svengali suffers a heart attack, Trilby's singing is immediately affected. The result is pandemonium in the audience, and the act concludes with Svengali's last "horrible grin of hatred" and a confused Trilby entering unaware of where she is and what has happened.

Svengali is a figure of evil, of course, an alien and perverse presence in the world Trilby and her artist-friends inhabit.[120] And he is strange. He admits in the play's opening act, for example, that he "loves" alleviating and then absorbing Trilby's neuralgic pain through hypnosis because "it comes from" her (600); in later scenes as portrayed by Tree, Svengali exhibited "symptoms of great exhaustion through the transfer of his [musical] powers to Trilby," intimating a psychical transference of great involution. But there was a risk in Tree's impersonation of the dreaded mesmerist, as Maurice Willson Disher explains: "The risk lay in not being able to make Svengali horrible enough. Tree made [him] more horrible. The mild eye became baleful, excruciatingly baleful. His hold over Trilby was no mesmerist's power but testimony, like another Pagnini, of being in league with the Devil."[121] In this respect, the play follows the novel's opening pages where Du Maurier links Svengali to post-lapsarian evil. That is to say, in its own eccentric way, adorned with statuary and a hanging trapeze, paintings and a newly tuned piano, the three young painters' studio/apartment constituted a "blissful abode" (5). Billee, who possessed an "almost girlish purity of mind," looked upon his two friends as "a glorious pair of chums" (8); and in one humorous scene, Svengali interrupts two of the men bathing, a "sinister" presence insinuating itself into their bohemian Eden where nudity—like Trilby's modeling in the "altogether"—is an everyday and totally innocent practice. For her part, Trilby, whose father was the son of a famous Dublin physician, "followed love for love's sake" yet, in an ambivalent allo-Hibernian fashion, might "also be said to possess a virginal heart" (36–37). This blissful—and, in Trilby's case, paradoxical—innocence is forever altered by Svengali's insinuation into their lives.

But Svengali is more than a serpent, as the *Times* implied when noting the "frenzy" with which Tree's Svengali "pursues his object." This frenetic performance of Jewishness recalls Leah's rapidly spoken, almost mechanical curse and Irving's Shylock, who automatically uttered "no, no" after wishing Jessica dead at his feet. *This* Svengali, in other words, figures an unconscious and an excessive desire too powerful to be contained—and an allo-Semitic and performative uncanny. The mechanical or automatic quality of Tree's frenzy is but one sign of the uncanny; another is Trilby's bizarre, ultimately fatal response to Svengali's portrait after his death. For Freud, here citing Ernst Jentsch, the uncanny creates "doubts whether an apparently animate being is really alive; or conversely, whether a lifeless object might not be in fact animate" (*SE* 17:226). Trilby's speaking to and singing for the portrait raises the latter possibility that Svengali still exercises his domination from beyond the grave, implying that like a vampire he is in some ways "undead." Part of Svengali's indomitability, therefore, is his mysterious ability, one associated in late Victorian culture with medical science and Jewishness, both to breach the boundaries of his being through mesmerism and to transcend those of the undiscovered country of death.[122]

This strange power, in its own way, mirrors the radical ambivalence of allo-Semitism, which posits that the Jew is at once "better and worse than us," an embodiment of extremes and "dis-order."[123] This disorderliness can possess positive or negative valences: it can, alternatively, shake Wesker's Antonio from the stolidity of commerce and awaken him to an entirely new world of intellectual self-fulfillment; or it can destroy the "blissful abode" of bohemian life. Du Maurier intimated the existence of this allo-Semitic complexity even as his narrator described Svengali as "well-featured but sinister"

(11) and constantly in search of those he might "cheat, betray, exploit" (42). However deplorable these characteristics are, Jewishness in *Trilby* is more ambivalent than a thesis of anti-Semitism can accommodate. Little Billee, for example, possesses the "faint suggestion of some possible very remote Jewish ancestor—just a tinge of that strong, sturdy, *irrepressible*, indomitable, indelible blood which is of such priceless value in diluted homeopathic doses" (6–7, my emphasis). Given this trope, Svengali might be considered *too* Jewish, not diluted enough, a relative of immigrants, customs, and things like cardboard suitcases similarly regarded as "too Irish."

This same "priceless" indomitability, as Daniel Pick discusses in returning to the matter with which this chapter began, led Victorians in the 1890s, "despite assorted apparent 'conversions,'" to believe "the Jews would not (indeed could not) convert from Judaism" and would eventually control everything "from the stock market to public taste in art."[124] This supposition of an ever-expanding cultural and financial empire, as Joseph Litvak has argued, must be portrayed as despicable—a category for which Svengali clearly qualifies as an exemplary instance—or else our "Jew envy" might be put on too obvious display. That is to say, responding to Adorno and Horkheimer's time in America in the 1940s and their characterization of the "image" of Jews as possessing "happiness without power," Litvak contends that far from lacking power, they are "alleged to have too much of it" and, further, that neurosis has replaced happiness in such representations of Jewishness.[125] In performance, this neurosis is also intrinsically *uncanny*, a term that constitutes a veritable motif in critical responses to Svengali on stage: *The Irish Playgoer* alludes to a "lean and uncanny Svengali"; a reviewer for the *Scotsman* found Tree's character "dominated always by the 'uncanny'"; and decades later so distinguished a critic as Edmund Wilson detects in Svengali's voice, "ventriloquially transferred to the throat of Trilby," that of "our Judeo-Christian God . . . a spirit from an alien world who carries with it uncanny prestige, who may speak in a divine tongue."[126] The uncanny and its inherent hiddenness, secrecy, and strangeness all characterize Svengali's power over Trilby.

It is worth noting that in 1908, aided by the fortune he earned from *Trilby* and concerned by a rising tide of anti-Semitism in Edwardian England, Tree launched his lavish production of *The Merchant of Venice*, consulting with Rabbi Herman Davids to ensure that his use of music and ritual accurately represented the "rich spiritual tradition" of Judaism.[127] It remained an attraction in his annual Shakespeare festivals for years. Thus, if *Merchant* became a cultural "obsession"—and, in Tree's realization, an "unequivocal condemnation of Christian racism"[128]—if *Trilby* catalyzed a "literary mania," and if plays like *Leah, the Forsaken* both accompanied productions of Shakespeare *and* performed Jewishness, then our understanding of the relationship between Jewishness, allo-Semitism, and the performative uncanny must surely be enhanced by a consideration of such contexts as textual rescripting, acting repertory, and cultural celebrity, and their inflection of the transcoding interpretive practices of audiences young and old, affluent and adolescent, urban and provincial. These kinds of texts and performances, coupled with those discussed in the preceding chapter, form a backdrop for the performances of Jewishness—and their relationship to Irishness—in the chapters that follow.

Uncanny Irishness and the Count: A Postscript

The revival of *Monte Cristo* was a failure . . . and it deserved to fail. . . .
Mr. O'Neill is an actor with an Irish name and an Irish accent but
without any Irish sympathy, passion or magnetism.
—*SPIRIT OF THE TIMES*, FEBRUARY 17, 1883

One figure remains to be discussed: the heroic, at times, tragic Irishman on the late nineteenth-century stage who both differs significantly from the Teagues of midcentury immigrant melodrama and haunts Eugene O'Neill's later work, *A Touch of the Poet* (1942) in particular. In many ways, this character shares more in common with Leah and Shylock than with Paddy Miles or Myles-na-Coppaleen—indeed, O'Neill's tortured and psychically split Con Melody in *A Touch of the Poet* reviles country shebeens, peasant brogues, and any trace of the Irishness Boucicault's characters performed[129]—and is perhaps best represented by the protagonists of two plays from the 1880s. One is *Robert Emmet* (1884), often attributed to Dion Boucicault but, as Deirdre McFeely has recently argued, is "first and foremost" the work of Frank Marshall. A text of the play, based on the life, trial, and execution of the martyr who gave his life fighting for Ireland's independence, was given to Boucicault by Henry Irving, who had once considered producing it himself; a financial disaster, it opened and ran for only four nights at Chicago's McVicker's Theatre in November. Audiences, it seems, were expecting the more familiar Boucicauldian comedy and were ill-prepared for the play's somber tone (in fact, the action of three of the play's four acts culminates with a character's death).[130] However unsuccessful in this instance, plays featuring the figure of the heroic Irish nationalist were staged frequently at the end of the century and well into the twentieth, as Ireland's struggle for independence from England provided melodramatists with copious historical materials upon which to base their plays.

The other, for my purposes more resonant, play is *Monte Cristo*, the James O'Neill revision of Charles Fechter's play, first performed by O'Neill in 1883, the same year of Henry Irving's first trip to America. Adapted from the novel, *Monte Cristo* hardly concerns significant moments in Irish history or episodes of life there, but such a fact did not prevent the reviewer from the *Spirit of the Times* from expressing his disappointment that O'Neill's French hero didn't possess "Irish" qualities in sufficient abundance.[131] These defects were quickly remedied, as O'Neill went on to play Edmund Dantès some six thousand times over nearly thirty years, crossing the country and appearing to a cumulative audience of some fifteen million spectators. But the negative assessment of his inaugural performance in the role reveals one significant motif: it seemed impossible for reviewers and spectators alike to forget that O'Neill was Irish, and this insistence goes beyond his dialect. It is also the case that during the week of *Cristo*'s premiere in February 1883, many of the theatrical attractions New Yorkers might have supported involved Irish actors or themes. Irish-American star John Drew (1853–1927) and Ada Rehan (1860–1916) appeared at Daly's Theatre in Daly's *The Squire*; Edward Harrigan and Tony Hart's *McSorley's Inflation* played at the Théâtre Comique, and the comedy *Write in Ireland* appeared at the Cosmopolitan Theatre.[132] How do this context, O'Neill's performance of Irishness in the role of a falsely imprisoned French sailor, and traces of the uncanny inform *Monte Cristo* and audience responses to it?

One answer might trace Dantès's numerous similarities to Marshall and Boucicault's Emmet and to innumerable nationalist heroes in historically based Irish melodrama and romance: all are brave and attractive; all have won the love of estimable and even heroic women; all are betrayed by Judases who presage the infamous betrayer of Liam O'Flaherty's novel *The Informer* (1925) and both Arthur Robison's 1929 and John Ford's 1935 film adaptations; and all ascend to Christ-like dignity through their suffering. Boucicault and Marshall leave no doubt about this comparison, carefully composing the closing tableau of *Robert Emmet* to evoke a messianic comparison. After the condemned Emmet proclaims, "God bless my country!" a volley of shots is fired and he falls to his knees. The stage darkens as a black flag is raised. Then the wall behind the fallen patriot opens and a "vista of blue clouds" appears. The figure of Ireland with a "coronet of shamrocks in her hair" descends and Emmet's head is strategically placed for her to cradle in a picture emulating the *Pietá*.[133] Although Dantès does not perish at the end of O'Neill's *Monte Cristo*, the script of the play contains several allusions to his religious zeal and selflessness. Gazing skyward at the beginning of act 5, for example, he vows to "submit to Thy eternal justice" and repents of a "mean and selfish jealousy" that led to his thought of avenging himself on Fernand by killing his son (66). Instead, he is fully prepared to place himself in danger and, by serving as a martyr, spare the life of Fernand's son Albert, who in actuality is his own son.

The culture of theatrical celebrity provides a context diametrically opposite that of devout self-abnegation, as O'Neill's rise to stardom and his portrayal of Dantès read differently in the context of his scandalous notoriety. By 1883, like Irving and Bernhardt, O'Neill was a star whose admirers routinely crowded train stations to welcome him to their city, as they did in San Francisco, for example, in early 1878. Yet he arrived, much as Bernhardt would two years later, having served as a principal in salacious newspaper reporting about his private life. In this instance, a headline in the September 8, 1877, *New York Times* aptly summarizes the notoriety: "James O'Neil [*sic*] in Court in Chicago to Answer for Deserting His Wife, Nettie O'Neil Adultery with a Deceased Actress also Charged."[134] Informed audiences at the time, therefore, brought to the theater both a knowledge of O'Neill's triumphs playing Shakespearean roles with luminaries like Edwin Booth, Adelaide Neilson, and Charlotte Cushman *and* an awareness of how the once desperately poor son of an Irish father from Kilkenny, a father who abandoned his destitute family in America and returned to Ireland, had also been accused of bigamy by one woman and been the proximate cause of the apparent suicide of an actress with whom he had once been involved.

Edmund Dantès is a kind of amalgam of the tragic stature of a Hamlet and the simmering passion implicit in these newspaper accounts; he is also a far more psychically complex and emotionally riven figure than the Christ-like Emmet. For, in addition to providing a heroic, even swashbuckling opportunity for O'Neill to play a deeply wronged French sailor—in this latter respect, a role not unlike Leah or Irving's ill-used Shylock—*Monte Cristo* also advances several motifs associated with the performative uncanny. One is the sense of concomitant strangeness and unusual familiarity associated with the uncanny, and the possibility of danger or evil residing just beneath the surface of daily activity. In perhaps the best example of this in the play, Albert—Viscount de Morcef, young officer and son of Mercédès—meets Edmund disguised as a priest and befriends him by insisting that a soldier rudely demanding the priest's identification papers demonstrate proper respect for the cloth. Remarkably, Albert finds himself mysteriously drawn to the priest, a feeling he struggles to explain: "Although my reason clearly tells me that we have met to-day for the first time, it seems to me as though we were acquainted before—before united—where I know not." More than this, Albert professes to "love" him, further admitting that when Edmund touched him a "strange emotion thrilled my heart"; he feels emotionally propelled toward Edmund as if moved by a "divine power" (41). Plotting to avenge himself against the three villains who caused his imprisonment and destroyed his plan to marry Mercédès, Edmund tears a card in half and tells Albert that his brother—the Count of Monte Cristo—will later proffer the missing half to him to signal their alliance. But when Edmund is informed that this noble young officer is the son of Mercédès and Fernand, one of the three men who contrived his imprisonment, he makes a startling pledge in an aside to the audience:

> And I grasped his hand and pressed him to my heart! Oh, woe to him! His father must love him, may well be proud of him—it is through his child I will strike Fernand. I will kill his son. (45)

He appears to reiterate this pledge at the end of act 4 even after Mercédès informs him that Albert is really his son; while glaring at Fernand, Edmund insists, "I will kill him!" (65), creating uncertainty about the real object of this threat and the possibility that his plan to kill his own son will be carried out to completion. In the play's final line and after Edmund has dispatched the last of his enemies, however, Mercédès intervenes: "Your prayers have saved your father's life, Albert—you are his son!" (70).

As the final curtain descends, Edmund's revenge has been completed; thus, there is no reason for further violence, especially against Albert, or so audiences must believe. More important, elements of the uncanny, including secrecy, hidden identity, and "gruesome fear" have been resolved. In addition, as in Freud's conception of the uncanny, the hero believed to be dead is actually alive; the son whose strange familiarity with and love for him has survived; and the inversion of life and death has been righted. Of all of the elements Freud attributes to the uncanny, none is more important to *Monte Cristo* than the notion of concealment and hidden identity. Act 4 amplifies the latter notion, as characters speculate about the Count's real identity: Is he a Polish refugee who served in the Egyptian army and became wealthy from a pearl fishery in Ceylon? Or is he really Maltese and made his fortune mining silver in Thessaly? And, of course, audiences want to know if his rage—indicated in stage directions as the action reaches its climax—is so uncontrollable as to lead him to the murder of his innocent son. Who is this count and what passions seethe below the surface of his gentility? If not so self-sacrificing as Robert Emmet, Dantès has at least assured that justice has been done and evil punished; moreover, something potentially dreadful has been averted and something grand achieved.

The performance of Jewishness, in an admittedly small way, supports this process and conclusion. Adamant that the innocent Edmund be freed from the dungeon to which he has been confined for eighteen years, Noirtier, brother of the villainous Villefort who has orchestrated Edmund's imprisonment, gives his brother one month to release him from prison and bring him to the Inn Pont du Gard, where Noirtier will be waiting. Not trusting his brother, Noirtier enters disguised as Solomon Van Gripp, a Jewish diamond merchant and, before retiring to his room and arming himself for trouble, he is asked to appraise a stone Edmund has given the inn's proprietors. Momentarily dropping his accent during the ensuing discussion and thus revealing his true identity, Noirtier reclaims his part by performing a stereotype and haggling over the gem's worth. "More than fifty thousand" is not fifty thousand, he barters, so he offers forty to the proprietors who are anxious to sell it; he must be who he says he is. A comic interlude to the scene's main and climactic business, this performance of Jewishness is *so* stereotypical and predictable, as absurd as some San Francisco reviewers found the stage design's "bobbing chunks of wood" and "supremely ridiculous details."[135]

But no matter—the play became famous, and the son of an Irish peasant became a star on the American stage. With him, more than a self-sacrificing and heroic Irishman, for whom Dantès serves as a surrogate, emerged into the cultural imaginary to displace the hegemony of Irish peasants Boucicault created. Unlike the "bogus" or "pasteboard" peasants and villains Stewart Parker's clown describes in *Heavenly Bodies*, James O'Neill's Count added ambivalent and uncanny complexity to popular conceptions of Irishness not unlike the allo-Semitic qualities of characters like Leah, Shylock, and Svengali. All of these reside in the unconscious of modern American drama as the work of, among other writers, O'Neill's son Eugene so brilliantly demonstrates.

{ 4 }

The Jewish-Irish Modern American Drama

The Irish as a race were greatly improved by the fact that many of the ships of the Spanish Armada foundered on the coast of Ireland, thus producing that group of the Irish people known as the "black Irish". . . . A number of the Spaniards were Maranos [*sic*]—or converted Jews, which resulted in certain admixtures of Jewish and Irish people. Undoubtedly, you are one of the striking examples of this mixture, since you possess all the virtues of Moses, Spinoza, Heine and all the other Jewish prophets. . . . Yes, G.B.S., the truth will out. You too are a Sheeny.

—LAWRENCE LANGNER, LETTER TO
BERNARD SHAW, OCTOBER 7, 1938

After Shaw's heyday [in America] came an international war, and this war had a profound effect on the theatre. . . . Our American theatre—the theatre as a big force—started only after the First World War.

—STELLA ADLER, *STELLA ADLER ON
AMERICA'S MASTER PLAYWRIGHTS*

As is the case with facetious assertions of James Joyce's Jewishness, there is little evidence that Bernard Shaw was a "Sheeny."[1] It *is* certain, however, that Lawrence Langner felt moved to call him one during a 1938 exchange over Shaw's play *Geneva*, a correspondence complicated by the pair's friendship and long collaboration after World War I. As a teenager working at an acting academy in London, Langner (1890–1962) was introduced to Shaw's work and subsequently attended his lecture on Fabian socialism, admiring what he heard.[2] Traveling to New York in 1911 to accept a position as a patent agent in the office of a British-owned firm, his affection for the theater and respect for Shaw continued to grow. Working first with the Washington

Square Players, Langner was a driving force in founding the Theatre Guild in 1918, which, in addition to staging such experimental American plays as Lawson's *Processional* and Elmer Rice's *The Adding Machine*, between 1920 and 1935 produced fourteen of Shaw's plays, starting with *Heartbreak House*.[3] For over a decade between 1920 and 1931, each Guild season featured at least one Shaw play (in 1925 it produced two, *Androcles and the Lion* and *The Man of Destiny*). Thus, however accurate Stella Adler's observation that Shaw dominated the New York stage before World War I—the so-called Bernard Shaw "cult" grew after productions of *Candida, John Bull's Other Island*, and *Mrs. Warren's Profession* in 1904 and 1905[4]—his plays were hardly absent from it after the war. Nor were those of Sean O'Casey and other Irish dramatists at a moment when Eugene O'Neill and Rice—and, slightly later, Clifford Odets, Tennessee Williams, Lillian Hellman, and Arthur Miller—transformed the theater, in Adler's phrasing, into a "big force" in postwar America.

How does modern America drama relate to, in some cases even emerge from, the Irish-Jewishness that animated Langner and Shaw's dialogue? What vestiges of the nineteenth-century stage haunt this drama? Langner's imputation of Shaw's Irish-Jewishness suggests the importance of multidirectional memory both in reading modern American drama and in assessing the work of Irish writers' Jewish-American confederates, Jewish rapparees as it were. Here, "rapparee" is not intended to describe bandits or, more historically delimiting, pike-wielding foot soldiers in the Williamite wars in late seventeenth-century Ireland, but rather to recuperate its use as a largely masculine term of fellowship and affection, as in Shaun's teasing admonition to his boisterous friends in Boucicault's *Arrah-na-Pogue*, "Aisy now, ye rapparees."[5] A Shavian rapparee in this sense, Langner instigated the kerfuffle over a character known as "The Jew" in *Geneva*. After reading a copy of the play in August, Langner was "deeply hurt" by parts of it, particularly by The Jew's adumbration of the "*weaker side* of his case" in refuting the dictator Battler's account of the origins of anti-Semitism: "We Jews have been driven by persecution *into trade and finance* until we have become more skillful at them than our lazy prosecutors" (emphasis in original).[6] Although this exact line does not appear in the final version of *Geneva*—Shaw revised the text several times, rewriting the preface in 1945 and adding an act in 1947—ones similar to it do, such as The Jew's retort, "Why do you exclude the Jew? Because you cannot compete with his intelligence, his persistence, his foresight, his grasp of finance."[7] As if to validate the cogency of the last endorsement in this list, the British foreign secretary Sir Orpheus Midlander, who earlier deemed the act of thinking to be "unEnglish,"[8] accuses the Jew of hastily exiting in act 4 so as to phone his stockbroker and thereby profit from information gleaned from his overhearing of a confidential conference:

> Only the Jews, with the business faculty peculiar to their race, will profit by our despair. Why has our Jewish friend just left us? To telephone, he said. Yes; but to whom is he telephoning? To his stockbroker, gentlemen. (5:753)

Langner is hardly alone in bridling at the intimation of Jews' "peculiar faculty" for business. For David Nathan, this "compliment" amounts not only to "nonsense, and insulting nonsense," but also to "dangerous nonsense" in 1938, leading him to pose two questions with the full knowledge that Shaw abhorred anti-Semitism: "If a characteristic which is usually considered contemptible is attributed to a Jew, but with praise instead of condemnation, is it any the less anti-Semitic? And if not anti-Semitic, is it nevertheless as harmful—or even more harmful—because it lends support to a prejudicial stereotype?"[9]

Geneva contains both expressions of conventional prejudice against Jews and the predicable suppositions about Jewishness that irritated Nathan and Langner. Most of the former are uttered either by Sir Orpheus or a frequently outrageous character known as The Widow. Thoroughly capable of thoughtless remarks and cutting insults—the latter includes the accusation of blood libel—she announces that she is of Aztec descent and demurs that she "should never dream of insulting Quetzalcoatl by sacrificing a Jew to him" (5:704). She also proffers milder aspersions cloaked as compliments, the kind Nathan queries. So, for example, her vanity flattered by The Jew's observation that wherever *his* people dominate the "theatre and the picture gallery" her "type of beauty is supreme," The Widow concedes, "It is true. You have taste, you Jews. You have appetites. You are vital, in your Oriental fashion" (5:709), recalling the relationship between Jews, orientalism, and an innate talent for fashion that informs nineteenth-century drama, tenement fiction like Anzia Yezierska's, and Shaw's depiction of Henrietta Jansenius in *An Unsocial Socialist* some half-century earlier. In his *Revolutionist's Handbook* appended to *Man and Superman* (1905), Jack Tanner in deriding the notion of "progress" argues that "Even the Jews, who, from Moses to Marx and Lassalle, have inspired all the revolutions" have to admit that, more times than not, "Man will return to his idols and cupidities" (3:712). On occasion, a Shaw play not featuring Jewish characters similarly relies upon all-too-predictable depictions; thus, in *You Never Can Tell* (1899) Valentine characterizes his landlord Fergus Crampton as "rich as a Jew and as hard as nails" (6:622), although Crampton's first name and fondness for Irish whiskey imply a different heritage. Nathan's concerns about anti-Semitic stereotyping notwithstanding, even that veiled as praise, more problematic in Langner's view is what *Geneva* and The Jew do *not* say: that Jews have "numbered among the brightest lights of German Culture" (in his letter to Shaw, Langner mentions Albert Einstein, Hertz, Mendel, Mendelssohn, Mahler, Heine, and many more), reducing to an "absurd libel" the notion that they have contributed to German civilization only in the areas of "trade and finance" (Langner, 455).

Parrying this criticism, Shaw began his September 1938, response to Langner with a cantankerous rhetorical question: "Can you wonder at Hitler (and now Mussolini) driving out the Jews?" This provocative barb was followed by Shaw's rationalization that in *Geneva* he had made "ruthless fun" of "British Cabinet

Ministers, of German and Italian dictators and Cockney young women, of the Buchmanite Oxford movement, of Church of England bishops, and of the League of Nations. Everyone laughs. Not a voice is raised in their defence" (Langner, 457). "But," he continued, "I have dared to introduce a Jew without holding him up to the admiring worship of the audience . . . [and] instantly you, Lawrence raise a wail of lamentation." All of this led to Shaw's accusation, "You really are the most thoughtless of Sheenies" (457), a comment that demanded a rejoinder. So, after thanking Shaw for his letter, Langner, as quoted in the epigraph above, responds to his interlocutor in kind: "If I am really one of the most thoughtless of 'Sheenies,' then you are one of the most inconsistent of 'Micks'" (458).

Shaw's colloquy with Langner, like many acerbic remarks in his prefaces and plays, has motivated critical examinations of Shavian views on Jews and Jewishness for nearly a century. Contributors to this inquiry include Stanley Weintraub and Bryan Cheyette, the latter of whom derives a revealing and complex narrative about Jews and Jewishness from over six decades of Shaw's writing. As I have mentioned, this contains early chapters on Shaw's portrayal of the "beautiful and luxurious" Jewess Henrietta Jansenius—and, as Cheyette outlines, to an Arnoldian opposition between Hebraism and Hellenism in the representations of Henrietta's father and her estranged husband[10]—his depiction of Mendoza in *Man and Superman*, and his creation of Dr. Leo Schutzmacher in *Doctor's Dilemma* (1911). It also focuses on his interlocution with French playwright Henry Bernstein in the mid-1920s and on Shaw's views of dictatorial politics during and after the rise of the Nazis as expressed in *Geneva* and its preface, his letters to Langner, and his "Preface on Bosses" to *The Millionairess* (1935). I want to revisit this history, not so much to scold Shaw for callousness or amplify Langner's justifiable concern that, through a character like The Jew, he risks adding "another figure to a collection" including Fagin and Shylock that "breeds intolerance and racial hatred" (456). Instead, expanding upon Langner's identification of Shaw as an Irish sheeny, I want to unpack allo-Semitism and allo-Hibernianism in the work of Elmer Rice, Clifford Odets, and Arthur Miller and explore modern American drama's Irish-Jewish substrate. This begins with a précis of Irishness and Jewishness in Shavian thought, then moves to O'Casey and the ascent of Rice and Odets on the American stage, to a neglected play in Miller's canon, to Stella Adler's reading of Synge's *Riders to the Sea*, and—briefly, as an epilogue—to the residue of nineteenth-century Irishness in O'Neill's later plays.

In a lecture revised for publication as "GBS and the Despots," Stanley Weintraub develops a point fundamental to untangling Shaw's knotty politics: namely, the fact that he "deplored parliamentary democracy as flawed and irreparable."[11] And he found various ways to express his aversion. In "Preface on Bosses," for example, he disparages "modern liberal democracy" as an "unashamed plutocracy" responsible for the "patriotic lying by which the workers of Europe had been provoked to slaughter one another" in World War I (6:178, 186). In his 1945 preface to *Geneva*, Shaw invents such terms as "pseudo-democratic parliamentary mobocracy" to convey his disdain (5:641), arguing that not all "upstart dictators and legitimate monarchs" have been "personal failures" (5:643). Central to this caustic assessment of democracy—and an echo of Sir Orpheus's threat to Battler in act 4 of the play to tread carefully when dealing with England—is Shaw's accusation that England, a supposed bastion of virtuous government, is "capable of anything" when "thoroughly frightened": dropping bombs "weighing ten thousand pounds on dwellings full of women and children" in the name of "heroic patriotism" (5:625), for example; or in the case of the "victorious Allies" after World War II, treating Germany and Japan as ruthlessly "as Catholic Ireland was treated by England in the seventeenth century" (5:631). Only a "veneer of civilization," one worn "dangerously thin," separates democracies from the rebarbative practices of more primitive cultures (5:632); and, for this reason, Shaw not only countenanced dictatorial governance, but was also antipathetic both to nationalist rhetoric and to assertions of ethnic exceptionalism, often deploying Jews and Irishmen interchangeably to illustrate the danger of such collective self-aggrandizement. To be sure, he *did* deplore anti-Semitism and regarded Hitler's belief that the "Germans are a chosen race divinely destined to rule the world" as one of the myriad "delusions" inherent to Nazism (6:639).[12] But, then again, he viewed all such hypernationalistic claims as delusional.

Shaw's use of Jews and the Irish to advance his thesis surfaces in "Irish Nonsense about Ireland" (1916), published in the *New York Times* some two weeks before the Easter Rising. In it, he lambastes a republican manifesto aimed at garnering support for independence from Irish America, deriding the "Irish conviction that the Irish are the salt of the earth and that all other races are comparatively barbarous, degraded, sordid, irreligious." This conceit, he bristles, "shines ridiculously in every paragraph." Ever critical of hubristic nationalisms, Shaw insisted that Ireland must also abandon the notion that a "natural" enmity exists between itself and England—for wars originate in nationalist mythoi and capitalist greed—and embrace instead a "democratic internationalism."[13] In his "Postscript to the Bernstein-Shaw Controversy" a decade later, published in French and translated in *Der Jude*, Shaw denounced philo-Semitism as strenuously as he had objected to Irish nationalists' implicit philo-Hibernianism:

> I must repudiate pro-Judaism as emphatically as I do anti-Semitism. As an Irishman, I know that unhealthy violent sense of national consciousness, called forth by oppression and persecution, too well to encourage the Jews to give themselves up to their dreams. I have often enough been obliged to tell my own countrymen, in the days when they were not free, that they were not a chosen people.

He also vows to "say the same to Jews as often as occasion arises,"[14] as it did when asked in an interview, "Do you believe the Jews to be the chosen race?" Shaw responded with typical peremptoriness, "Certainly not," dismissing the question as dangerously "paranoic."[15] In his 1925 postscript to the Bernstein-Shaw controversy, he also reiterated his contention that the Irish and Jews serve equally as targets of English caricature as he outlined England's "general prejudice" against "all foreigners": "There are continual jokes about the avarice of Jews. . . . The Jew is caricatured with a hooked nose, just as the Irishman with the jaw of a Spanish muleteer."[16] He concluded the postscript with the hope that his views will not be misunderstood as anti-Semitic and an expression of confidence that they are shared by all "enlightened" Jews.

In fact, although seemingly uncritical of Mussolini's rise to power, Shaw sharply condemned anti-Semitism, Hitler's in particular. In his "Preface on Bosses" preceding *The Millionairess*,[17] he also dismantled the concept of ethnic purity in Nazi ideology and anticipated the possibility—one further cultivated in *Geneva*—that Langner was right: Maybe Shaw was a "sheeny." Maybe Hitler was, too. Shaw admonishes "Herr Hitler" for going to the "scandalous length of outlawing, plundering, and exiling Albert Einstein, a much greater man than any politician" (6:189), and challenges the Führer's belief in the fantasy of a "pure bred German race." Shaw reminds his reader, as he might have failed to impress upon the audience of *Geneva*, that the "Mendelssohns and Meyerbeers" were both Germans *and* Jews, and then eviscerates the concept of racial superiority by insinuating that Hitler could claim Jewishness in his own family history and gesturing toward the larger potential of ethnic hybridity:

> I am told that children bred from Irish colleens and Chinese laundrymen are far superior to inbred Irish or Chinese. Herr Hitler is not a typical German. I should not be at all surprised if it were discovered that his very mixed blood . . . got fortified somewhere in the past by that of King David. (6:191)

This notion of a country as always already alloyed—modernity as farrago or jumble—is reiterated by The Judge in *Geneva* who replies to Sir Orpheus's boast that he is an "Englishman from the heart of England" with: "You mean a British islander from Birmingham, the choicest breed of mongrels in the world. You should be proud of your cross-fertilization" (5:708).

Langner's allegation of Shaw's Jewishness is thus, ironically, a Shavian mongrelizing asseveration, one that, to varying degrees, might be applied to Jewish rapparees like Rice, Odets, and even Miller, and to Irish writers like O'Casey who, much as Shaw did, remained a force in the American theater of the 1920s and long afterward. This assertion, though, fails to address David Nathan's disappointment with Shaw's reliance upon stereotypes, however undercut by irony. In identifying the issue, Nathan begs another, perhaps obvious, question: Is it even possible to represent modern tenement life and immigrant subjectivity—topics all of these dramatists explored with such great distinction on the modern American stage—*without* confronting and manipulating the very stereotypes one abhors? So, in his productive exchange with Shaw, Langner supports his hyperbolic claim by referencing his Irish friend's *performance* of Jewishness as evidence that he is a "sheeny." As Langner wryly observes, Shaw not only possesses all the virtues of Moses, Spinoza, and Heine, but also exhibits the Jew's alleged expertise at business: "Nine-tenths of the radical playwrights starve to death; you make a fortune at it." Further, Shaw is a socialist and, "according to Hitler, all Socialists are Jewish." Shaw even *looks* like a Jew, Langner puckishly adds, a medieval Jew in particular who "always had a red beard" (458). Langner was not alone in noticing Shaw's attentiveness to matters of business, his performance of conventional "sheeniness" one might say. Struck by how Joyce, Shaw, and other writers were "preoccupied" with the "merchandising of [their] wares," Rice, one of Shaw's greatest admirers, recalls working with the University Settlement in New York when it sought permission to give three or four performances of *The Shewing-up of Blanco Posnet* (1909): "I have never ceased to marvel at the amount of time and energy expended, by a world famous dramatist, on the licensing of a production to an obscure amateur group."[18] The most esteemed modern writers, Rice concludes, understand royalties and performance rights.

Many of these writers emerge from the Irish-Jewish unconscious of the American theater and of the circum–North Atlantic more generally. In his own way, so does Langner. Born in Swansea, in the opening paragraph of his autobiography he juxtaposes the stark contrast between the "ugliness of the industrial world" of fin de siècle Wales and the "beautiful countryside and a background of Celtic mysticism and imagination" (4). He recalls with great fondness his Irish governess, who "endeavored" to make him and his siblings "speak like little Dubliners" (7). He remembers arriving in New York and living with the family of a retired Irish-American railroad engineer, an experience that instantiated his feelings of being "carefree and happy" as he was now free of the repressions of home (44). And, of course, he and the Theatre Guild would go on to produce some of the greatest work of Shaw and O'Neill, as the uncanniness of Irish-Jewish relationships emerged to shape the modern American drama just as surely as the tour of the Moscow Art Theatre in 1923 exerted a determinative influence on American acting and, later, on the rise of the Group Theatre and its cadre of famous acting coaches: Lee Strasberg, Sanford Meisner, Bobby Lewis, and Stella Adler. This uncanny relationship, I will argue, was frequently expressed in terms encapsulated by the Shaw-Langner interchange: the allo-Semitic and allo-Hibernian ambiguities of Jews and the Irish on stage; the reappearances of stereotypes (flattering and otherwise); the alienations of modernity, immigrant experience, and tenement life; and much more. It is to all of these matters that I now turn.

Tenement Drama, Immigrant Subjectivity, and Affect: O'Casey, Odets, and Rice

> Wasn't he, in a lot of ways, a refugee himself . . . ? He was already half-homeless, and would be homeless altogether, if he didn't succeed in getting American dollars to carry home with him. . . . He was a refugee, for Ireland had cast him forth, England couldn't afford to keep him, so he depended on America now to provide him with a sufficiency to keep him and his family for another year or two.[19]
>
> —SEAN O'CASEY, *ROSE AND CROWN* (1952)

> Closer to his creative heart this year [1926] . . . was a play not by an American but by an Irishman whose folk connections, in his characters and in their talk, resonated in Odets like the Yiddish language of the neighbors. . . . [H]e wrote in his diary: "Wonderful play . . . beautiful humor and revengeful pathos. Best play I've seen yet."
>
> —MARGARET BRENMAN-GIBSON, *CLIFFORD ODETS AMERICAN PLAYWRIGHT: THE YEARS FROM 1906–1940* (1981)

Sean O'Casey was considerably older than Paul Muni and Irving Berlin when they arrived as boys in New York at the turn of the century. But, as was the case with most immigrants then and now, in 1934 O'Casey regarded America as providing an opportunity, perhaps a final one, to support his family. The story of his rise to fame at Dublin's Abbey Theatre and the circumstances leading to his estrangement from it are well known and related with great poignancy in his autobiographical volume *Inishfallen, Fare Thee Well* (1949): the riot caused by *The Plough and the Stars* in 1926, the public debate that ensued, and his decision to emigrate to England.[20] O'Casey's disappointment over William Butler Yeats's negative response to his expressionist World War I play *The Silver Tassie* (1928) and the play's championing by Shaw have similarly been studied exhaustively. As Garry O'Connor puts it, O'Casey forwarded an early draft of *The Silver Tassie* to the "one man alive in England whose literary authority was unquestioned" to seek his "fatherly judgment." In June 1928, Shaw rendered his opinion with unambiguous clarity—"What a hell of a play!"—which in turn prompted his chiding of Yeats and Lady Gregory for treating O'Casey like "a baby."[21] The uneven fate of this "hell of a play," however, as Christopher Murray diagnoses, metastasized into an anger in O'Casey that lingered to influence his next full-length experiment *Within the Gates*, which he began in late 1930 (213). Three years later, he watched the play "hearsed within an atrocious production" in London that closed after only twenty-eight performances, netting him a paltry twenty pounds. If this weren't sufficient punishment, he also endured the savaging of reviewers, most notoriously that of James Agate of the *Sunday Times*, who labeled the play "pretentious rubbish."[22] As O'Casey recounts in *Rose and Crown*, only one desperate possibility remained for this self-described "slum dramatist" and "guttersnipe among the trimly educated and richly clad": travel, cheap suitcase firmly in hand, to America (*Autobiographies* 2:253).

This decision was made less difficult by American responses to *Within the Gates* vastly different from Agate's. George Jean Nathan, whose book *The Critic and the Drama* (1922) O'Casey held in high regard, acquired a type-script of *Within the Gates* in October 1933, and heralded it as "one of the most beautiful plays I have read in a very, very long time," a work of "*overwhelming* beauty." Two months later, Eugene O'Neill praised it as a "splendid piece of work" with a "rare and sensitive poetical beauty."[23] Buoyed by these tributes at a time when "all was dismal"—and when he was "relieved but apprehensive" by Nathan's securing of Richard Madden as an agent and an agreement for a New York production (Murray 231)—O'Casey boarded the *Brittanic* and headed for New York. Like the Irish priests and bishops who eventually became O'Casey's traveling companions on the ocean liner, he might have enjoyed (although, for the most part, he didn't) the luxuries available to the class able to afford cabin tickets: deck chairs, books from the ship's library, drinks from the bar, and so on. By contrast, the less fortunate "steerage mammals" crammed into the bowels of the ship enjoyed precious few amenities, prowling about their "closely caged-in quarters" in an "almost airless" confinement that recalled for O'Casey the nightmarish conditions of passage during the Great Famine (*Autobiographies* 2:394). In a haunting from the past that parallels the traces of melodrama in many of his plays, he fantasized that hordes of "glimmering ghosts" roamed the freezing depths of the North Atlantic, a vision that moved him to visit steerage and reflect upon his kinship with the denizens of the stifling holds of nineteenth-century coffin-ships.

The *Brittanic* docked in New York on September 17, 1934, and O'Casey was met by both Madden and Nathan, with whom the writer developed a "warm, lasting friendship." At this moment, O'Casey's reinvention as an "experimental playwright" (Murray, 233, 227), something he felt necessary but impossible to achieve in London, now seemed within reach in New Island, as Gaelic-speakers once called America. Although this aspiration was not to be fully realized, O'Casey's impact on American drama was considerable, so much so that some scholars and theatrical practitioners like Harold Clurman advanced the notion that Clifford Odets might best be understood as the "Sean O'Casey of America."[24] Such a characterization is consistent with Margaret Brenman-Gibson's contention that Odets, hearing the faint echoes of conversations between his Yiddish-speaking neighbors in O'Casey's dia-logue, held *Juno and the Paycock* close to his "creative heart."[25] And this is tantamount to saying that O'Casey's play might also be considered as a model for both many of Odets's achievements in the 1930s and, to a lesser extent, those of Elmer Rice, both of whom wrote plays steeped in the traditions of tenement literature and progressive political drama: Odets's *Waiting for Lefty* (1935), *Paradise Lost* (1935), *Golden Boy* (1937), and *Awake and Sing!* (1935), and Rice's *Street Scene* (1929), *We, The People* (1933), and even elements of the ear-lier *The Adding Machine* (1923).

The influence on Odets seems especially profound, as Brenman-Gibson's comment underscores, but Rice's theatrical origins are similarly traceable to a Jewish-Irish influence: his viewing of Jacob Adler as Shylock in the Yiddish theater, on the one hand, and, as he recounts in his autobiography, his discov-ery of Bernard Shaw on the other: "Many writers, past and present, influenced my thinking, but it was Bernard Shaw who far exceeded all the rest. I had occasion to describe that influence at a luncheon given by the British Authors' Society on the centenary of Shaw's birth." In particular, *Plays Pleasant and Unpleasant*, Rice reveals, exerted a profound influence on him, as did Shaw's dramatic criticism including *The Quintessence of Ibsenism*.[26] In his 1956 remarks to the Authors and Composers Society in London, Rice relates his refulgent experience as a teenager reading Shaw in the public library, some-thing he cherished as the "most revolutionary" intellectual experience of his life.[27] In addition, as a young playgoer he enjoyed productions of *Caesar and Cleopatra, Man and Superman, Pygmalion*, and others. But even if one were unaware of these details, a reading of Rice's *A Diadem of Snow* (1917), pub-lished under his real name, Elmer L. Reizenstein in the April 1918 issue of *The Liberator*, would almost certainly recall Shaw's own one-act plays treating Russian politics and historical figures: *Great Catherine* (1913) and *Annajanska, The Bolshevik Empress* (1917). After Rice scored a smash success with *On Trial* (1914), which ran for 365 performances and netted the fledgling playwright a handsome sum,[28] publication in *The Liberator* might have seemed an excep-tional and certainly different form of approbation, for the same issue featured John Reed's stories from Petrograd, Max Eastman's comments on socialism, and the promise of an essay by James Weldon Johnson in the next issue. At this moment in his young career, while Elmer Rice was a commercially suc-cessful dramatist, Elmer L. Reizenstein was a committed Shavian socialist and Jewish rapparee.[29]

And in the fall of 1934, O'Casey was something of an "Irish sheeny" himself, an honorary and affectionate description of modern Irish writers—Brendan Behan, for example, who appears in the next chapter—who arrive in New York and find a comfortably familiar new home within the Jewish community. In *Rose and Crown*, O'Casey recounts being conveyed from a rehearsal of *Within the Gates* to a great synagogue at the request of Rabbi Newman, who possessed

a "passionate love" of literature and drama. Invited to speak at a Sabbath service, O'Casey outlined for the congregation the many "curious resemblances"
existing between the Jews and the Irish—similarities between the "rhythm,
emotion, and manner" of Gaelic and Jewish poetry; the mutual "wit and nim-
bleness of mind" of both Jews and the Irish; their analogous diasporic scat-
terings across the globe, migrations necessitated by their parallel histories of
persecutions, and much more—and after his remarks the rabbi imposed upon
him to greet his admiring audience. Shaking hands until his own hand began
to ache, O'Casey was amazed to discover Irish men and woman from almost
every county in the old country (and their Jewish spouses). By the time his
visit to the Temple of Rudolph Sholem had ended, "all Ireland had paraded
before him," an unlikely procession that moved him greatly: "Sean had to
murmur in his heart that the world's best blessings would swarm round the
Shield of David and the Harp of Eireann" (*Autobiographies* 2: 420–21).

This literary-minded intellectual invited to speak at the synagogue is a distant relative of the playwright represented by the New York press when Odets
saw *Juno and the Paycock* at the Mayfair Theatre in the spring of 1926. In a
backhandedly complimentary review in the *New York Sun* entitled "Education
and the Dramatist," O'Casey was proclaimed the exemplar of a movement to
"de-educate" playwrights. After all, the *Sun* observed, he "is a plumber—and
a mighty good plumber too, they say—and he never had any schooling. He
laboriously taught himself to read." Attributing the sentiment to O'Casey that
"Education . . . is a terrible drawback to a playwright," the *Sun* concluded
that *Juno* was the product of an "unspoiled mind." Education and formal
schooling are, of course, hardly synonymous; and, like his working-class
heroes Jack Rocliffe in *The Harvest Festival* (1919) and Ayamonn Breydon in
Red Roses for Me (1942), O'Casey was an avid reader who possessed a capacious knowledge of, among other things, Western literature. Still, for the
Sun reviewer, O'Casey's humble origin would not allow him to indulge in
"Shaw-like jest"; instead, plays like *Juno* exhibited an "absolute seriousness"
made evident through "vivid characters, racy humor, crushing tragedy, and
deep insight into the foibles and warmnesses of the human heart." In spear-
heading this de-education "movement," or so the *Sun* alleged, O'Casey was
"destined perhaps to revolutionize our stage," supplanting the "many polite
and education-ridden playwrights" who then dominated it.[30] One of these
polite dramatists was Anne Nichols, whose *Abie's Irish Rose* was entering its
fifth year on Broadway when *Juno and the Paycock* opened; Nichols's play,
according to *Variety*, earned $8,000 the preceding week, rivaling its substan-
tial box-office take at Boston's Castle Square Theatre, where it had run for
over thirty weeks.

For the young Odets, the *Sun*'s reviewer captured the essence of O'Casey's
drama. And this drama, while scarcely resembling *Abie's Irish Rose*, might be
attributable nonetheless to the uncanny Irish-Jewish relationship Nichols so

successfully portrayed. Brenman-Gibson suggests as much in her biography of Odets, pausing, for instance, to consider a note marked "783 Beck Street" that, in his later years, he placed in a file of play manuscripts, the designation taken from an address in the Bronx where the Odets family moved when he was a child. Like the experiences of so many Jewish-American writers—Henry Roth, Edward Dahlberg, Benjamin Appel—this Bronx neighborhood was constituted of "equal mixtures" of Jewish and Irish families.[31]

There, Odets learned a lexicon of ethnic-based slang—"kike," "sheeny," "mick," and "shanty Irish"—and there, as Brenman-Gibson extrapolates from his later notation, his determination was born to interrogate the "dehumanizing myth of the steadily expanding economy" epitomized by his family's frequent moves to a new address: Was the American dream one in which every house is little more than a temporary "wayside"? Must a new home always deteriorate into a "slagheap" on the way to something better?[32] For Odets, these questions inhered in the project he identified as his goal in writing *Awake and Sing!*: namely, to represent the "struggle for life amidst petty conditions."[33]

In Odets's and O'Casey's earliest, arguably greatest, achievements,[34] "petty conditions" emanate from social inequity and poverty; indeed, throughout O'Casey's "Dublin Trilogy"—*The Shadow of a Gunman* (1923), *Juno and the Paycock* (1924), and *The Plough and the Stars* (1926)—the hardships of tenement life rival the destructive power of historical violence in threatening the survival of the family. Nevertheless, the Irish Civil War ultimately claims Johnny Boyle in *Juno*, just as the struggle for independence from England in 1916 takes Jack Clitheroe in *Plough*. Johnny's "shatthered" arm and the bullet in his hip find a graphic parallel in Moe Axelrod's missing leg in *Awake and Sing!* and serve as constant reminders of the costs of war, civil or global. Moreover, capitalism's dependence upon the profitability of war forms a motif in Odets's play, as in the act 2 conversation between Moe, Morty, and the pacifistic Jacob motivated by Moe's receipt of several wooden legs from the government, a largesse to which Morty objects:

MORTY: Four wooden legs?
MOE: Three
MORTY: What's the big idea?
MOE: Why not? Uncle Sam gives them out free.
MORTY: Say, maybe if Uncle Sam gave out less legs we could balance the budget.
JACOB: Or not have a war so they wouldn't have to give out legs.
MORTY: Shame on you, Pop. Everybody knows war is necessary.[35]

Moe's response—"Don't make me laugh" because the "first time you pick up a dead one in the trench" you realize that "war ain't so damn necessary" (62)—parallels a moment in *The Plough and the Stars* in which Captain Brennan informs the Clitheroes' neighbor Bessie Burgess of Jack's death. Brennan hypothesizes that although Jack has been killed, "Mrs. Clitheroe's grief will be a joy when she realizes that she has had a hero for a husband." Bessie's incredulity—"If you only seen her, you'd know to th' differ" (*CP* 1:244)—collapses the mythology of nationalist sacrifice just as surely as Moe refutes the thesis that war is a necessary cost of democracy.

As it does in Shavian critiques of World War I and of democracy's "unashamed" plutocracy, the relationship between the soldier's broken body and the ledger sheets of industrial capitalism reverberates throughout the Irish-Jewish unconscious and tenement dramas like *Awake and Sing!*, as O'Casey, Odets, and Rice all interrogate corporate investment in war. At times, as Norman Rabkin observes about Rice's *We, The People*, arguments against capitalist-motivated war in 1930s political drama may deliquesce into didacticism, but that scarcely invalidates their basic premises.[36] In this documentary-style play tinctured with elements of agitprop, Rice inveighs against what Philip Roth's Nathan Zuckerman in *American Pastoral* (1997) so aptly refers to as the "dark austerities" of the Depression: the poverty of working people, urban and rural, for example, and the obscene affluence of the ruling class.[37] Rice's play foregrounds these austerities, for while a worker for Mr. Drew painfully explains to his girlfriend in scene 3 that they cannot yet afford to marry, in scene 4 Drew's wife calls from London, where she is off "buying Titians again."[38] As in Odets's *Waiting for Lefty*, the anti-Semitism of such institutions as public universities and the judiciary in *We, The People* is barely concealed; and there is no hiding the quilted, intersecting interests of big business, nationalist ideology, and the military. In scene 12, Applegate, a manufacturer responsible for the firings of workers and, later, the shooting of strikers at his plant, complains that America has "been led astray by a lot of this talk about internationalism" (159). Riding high upon his rhetorical hobby horse, he fumes, "We'd be a damned sight better off . . . if we had an army and navy that was [*sic*] ready and willing to protect the interests of the American investor abroad" (160). In scene 2 of *Waiting for Lefty*, Mr. Fayette, identified only as an "industrialist," defends the same position while justifying the manufacturing of a poison gas with the potential to kill millions: "If big business went sentimental over human life there wouldn't be big business of any sort!" (15).

The broken bodies and debilitating trauma of returning soldiers constitute the most effective refutations of this ideology on the modern stage. The action of *We, The People* is framed by these spectacles as the shell-shocked, alcoholic Larry Collins staggers through scene 5 and the "bedraggled" veteran Ramsay, dressed in a "filthy" and "ragged olive-drab service overcoat," appears before a war memorial in scene 18 to address a crowd about his shattered life as a returning soldier: his bouts of influenza originally contracted during the war, his chronic unemployment, three arrests for vagrancy, and the "bums' rush" from congressmen to whom he appealed for help (236–37). The dilemmas of Rice's servicemen resemble those of O'Casey's war veterans Harry Heegan and Teddy Foran in *The Silver Tassie*. In the final scene, they attend a party held at the Avondale Football Club where Harry was once cheered as a veritable athletic god. Now Harry, paralyzed below the waist, wheels himself in a chair around the dance floor and Teddy, totally blind, enters the party with assistance. Anticipating the physical limitations of Hamm and Clov in Samuel Beckett's *Endgame* (1957), the pair comments on their respective disabilities:

> HARRY: I can see, but I cannot dance.
> TEDDY: I can dance, but I cannot see. (*CP* 2:94)

And, although their injuries are not directly tied to industrial capitalism, the second act of *The Silver Tassie*—much like the spectacle of Mr. Zero crawling upon a giant calculator in Rice's *The Adding Machine*—conveys this sense through its mise en scène and an enormous gun fed with shells by scurrying soldiers. The stage directions describe the weapon as simply a "*big howitzer gun, squat, heavy underpart*" located at the back center of the stage (*CP* 2:35), which at the act's conclusion "*swings around and points to the horizon*" before it is fired, reloaded, and fired again (*CP* 2:56). But in the 2010 production of Galway's Druid Theatre, a production that moved to Lincoln Center in the summer of 2011, the massive weapon inched downstage toward the audience at the end of the act, firing with a deafening roar. O'Casey's soldiers, like Rice's Mr. Zero, are merely so many insect-like pawns in the greater schemes of big business.

The constellation of war, a dehumanizing technology that furthers corporate interests, and the devastated lives of former soldiers inflects agitprop and tenement drama alike, compelling the audience to consider the consequences of nationalism. However, perhaps the most pervasive effect of urban poverty—and a far more damaging cause of suffering in tenement drama—is the riven subjectivity of impoverished residents and their children, many of them immigrants, as explored by novelists and playwrights alike: the intensity of feeling, particularly negative feeling; the projection of desire, much of it frustrated, onto distant locales almost always figured as sites of escape; a consequently heavy psychical investment in mass culture, especially film; and a consciousness fractured either by nostalgia for the past or by a preoccupation with the country of one's origin. Such nostalgia, as I have argued throughout, is the *least* debilitating feature of this subjectivity, but it still scars older characters in tenement drama of the 1920s and 1930s—and, we might recall, still permeates James Tyrone's thoughts in *Long Day's Journey into Night*. A fatuous nostalgia manifests itself in the closing moments of *Juno and the Paycock*, for example, when, drunkenly arriving at the now vacated Boyle home, Joxer Daly evokes several pasts now lapsed into total irrelevance to the tragic present: his allusion to reading "Willy Reilly and his Colleen Bawn," for instance, and his misquoted singing of lines from the 1915 tune, "Pack Up Your Troubles in Your Old Kit-Bag and Smile, Smile, Smile." For many languishing in the squalor of tenement life, memories of a simpler past, however distorted, exaggerated, or inaccurate, offer a refuge from a more complicated modernity, much as trips to the popular theater did or fantasies prompted by popular song lyrics.

In American tenement fiction and immigrant songs from Tin Pan Alley, this internal fracturing produces sadness, nostalgia, and regret. Modern tenement drama, however, much like nineteenth-century immigrant melodrama on the American stage, exhibits little time for such backward glances. And when they occur, they often resonate with xenophobic prejudice, with the ring of maudlin falsity that Joxer's allusions create in the last scene of *Juno and the Paycock*; or, as in Rice's *Street Scene*, with the ineffable sense of their complete irrelevance to modern life. When counseling Rose Maurrant about her relationship with Sam Kaplan, a college student who lives in her building, Lippo Fiorentino, in his broken English, lapses into predictability: "No, ees no good—Jew. 'E's only t'ink about money, money—alla time money." Although Rose objects that Sam "isn't like that a bit," she doesn't point out what must have been obvious to the audience: namely, the contradictory quality of Lippo's argument. For just moments earlier, he had expressed what appears to be nostalgic longing for Italy—"Een Eetaly ees bewtiful, but ees no money"—and concludes that it's "better to 'ave money" than beauty.[39] The irony of Fiorentino's positions illuminates both the pervasiveness of anti-Semitism and its illogic. That is, when bigots in *Street Scene* like the Jones family verbally and physically abuse Sam and other "foreigners," one might attribute it to both their ignorance and malevolence, but when the affable and even generous Fiorentino lapses into the same illogic, Rice's audience gains a new purchase of the inchoate nature of anti-Semitism. At the same time, Sam, a victim of bullying and vicious anti-Semitic slurs, will not countenance philo-Semitism, as he reminds his sister, Shirley: "It's always the same thing. . . . You never can get over your race prejudice. I've told you a hundred times that the Jews are no better than anybody else" (113). Shirley's philo-Semitism underlies her opposition to her brother's relationship with Rose, as she is wary of mixed marriage: "it's much better," she tells Rose later, "to marry with your own kind" (127). *Street Scene* thus portrays the allo-Semitic qualities of tenement life, the philo-Semitic bias of one character and the anti-Semitic ugliness of several others, linking the latter through Fiorentino's florid memories of Italy to the obsolescence of nostalgia.

But anti-Semitism in *Street Scene* is seldom so benignly manifested as this; on the contrary, the Joneses' anti-Semitism serves as a synecdochal figure of a more pervasive hatred of the "foreign" that reverberates throughout Rice's plays of the 1920s and 1930s. Indeed, in one telling line Mrs. Jones hints at Jewishness and Irishness as the origin of chaotic life in the tenement: "It's a fine house to be livin' in, ain't it, between the Maurrants upstairs an' that bunch

FIGURE 4.1 *Sam Kaplan (William Collier Jr.) and Rose Maurrant (Sylvia Sidney) in* Street Scene. *Film directed by King Vidor, 1931.*

o' crazy Jews down here" (93). But her hostility pales in comparison to that of Rice's bourgeois automatons in *The Adding Machine*, who advocate lynching with much the same venom as Lawson's Ku Klux Klan does in *Processional*. At an ill-fated party that ends in Zero's arrest for murder in *The Adding Machine*, the celebrants make their malice clear in a chorus of threats: "Damn foreigners! Damn dagoes! Damn Catholics! Damn sheenies! Damn niggers! Jail 'em! Shoot 'em! Hang 'em! Lynch 'em! Burn 'em!" (19). The rural Collins family in *We, The People* harbors similar resentments as expressed by its matriarch: "Foreigners over-running the land, until there seems to be hardly an American left. What's become of the America your forefathers and mine fought and died for?" (53–54). In the play's closing speech, delivered at a rally in support of the wrongly convicted Allen Davis, his former professor C. Carter Sloane reminds the crowd that America is comprised of immigrants and that his family came to the country on the *Mayflower*, making him just as much a "foreigner" as anyone else. Standing in front of a large American flag, he further insists that the promise of America is to "'promote the general welfare and secure the blessings of liberty'" for all its citizens (253).

At the same time that *Street Scene* contains scenes of ethnic hatred, it also works subtly to invert stereotypes or transpose conventions long associated on the stage with Jewishness and Irishness. So, in one of the Jones family's less vicious examples of anti-Semitism—the bullying Vincent Jones calls Sam a "little kike bastard" before knocking him to the pavement, while his mother tells Mrs. Maurrant, "I'd think twice before I'd let any child o' mine bring a Jew into the family" (103, 119)—Mr. Jones repeats to his neighbors a truism he finds amusing: "Like I heard a feller sayin': the Eye-talians built New York, the Irish run it, an' the Jews own it [*Laughter*]" (86). Almost every aspect of Rice's play undermines the acuity of this punch line. On the contrary, Abraham Kaplan inveighs against private property and capitalism at every turn; Shirley and Sam Kaplan are more or less entrapped by their poverty; and, as Rose has objected, Sam seldom thinks about money and instead ameliorates her daily struggles through his introduction of poetry and beauty into her life. Like the Irish immigrant Kenneth in Miller's *A Memory of Two Mondays*, Sam quotes from Walt Whitman and infuses life with a literary and specifically poetic quality that is in desperately short supply. And Rose (Erin O'Brien-Moore in the original production, who would later go on to play Rosie Redmond in John Ford's film version of *The Plough and the Stars*) similarly represents the innocence of their relationship, although she is hardly a hapless melodramatic heroine; indeed, her self-determination is underscored in her final exit, suitcase in hand. In short and in another instance of Irish-Jewish surrogation, Sam possesses a touch of the Irish poet; Rose, a touch of the independent New Woman found in Yezierska's fiction poised to undertake an independent life away from her family and the tenement.

However admirable these two characters are, material deprivation produces an excess of feeling in many tenement dwellers' lives, leading to the predominance of such negative affects as shame and disgust. Shame in tenement fiction and drama is typically generated by one of two dilemmas: the pregnancy of unmarried young women or the distrainment of a family's property and its relocation to the sidewalk.[40] Both occur in *Juno and the Paycock*. In the last scene, Captain Boyle and Joxer enter the now vacated Boyle home from which almost everything has been removed. The specter of a similar humiliation haunts Yezierska's *Bread Givers* from its opening paragraphs, as Sara fears being "thrown into the street to shame and to laughter from the whole world" (1), which Mrs. Hildebrand and her two children suffer in *Street Scene*. The same fate looms for Leo and Clara Gordon in the final scene of Odets's *Paradise Lost*. Even though they have owned their home for seventeen years, the sheriff has seized their property. Local union organizer—and accomplished drinker—Phil Foley wants the Gordons' furnishings removed from the sidewalk as they might spoil the festive atmosphere of the union-sponsored block party he has planned, but Leo is adamant that they remain. In his closing monologue, he explains why:

> Those people at the block party whisper and point. They're afraid. Let them look in our house. We're not ashamed. Let them look in. Clara, my darling,

listen to me. Everywhere now men are rising from their sleep. . . . Their whispers are growing to shouts! They become an ocean of understanding! *No man fights alone.* (230; emphasis in original)

Collective action and an activist ideology may reverse the performative etiology of shame, which requires the shamed party's exposure of weakness, presumed moral laxity, or fault to others. This conception underlies the unusual description of shame rendered in *Waiting for Lefty* when Agate, rising to rejoin Fatt's strikebreaking arguments and stir his fellow taxi drivers to action, reports that his union button self-combusted on his coat: it "just blushed itself to death! Ashamed!" (30).

Pregnancy, however, is almost always another matter, one that seems to trump poverty or organized labor's inaction when it comes to the affective surplus of feelings of shame, although collective action *may* exercise a curative effect in this instance as well. Like Sadie Cohen in *Processional*, who vows that she is not ashamed to bring a child into the world, the unwed and defiantly pregnant Mary Klobutsko, Allen Davis's lover in *We, The People*, addresses the crowd assembled in the final scene, pledging that she and her unborn child will join the "thousands, millions, the poor and the oppressed everywhere, until we strike off our chains, until we free ourselves of our oppressors, until we win for ourselves the right to live" (250). She reminds her audience that her father came to America from Poland to find "food and freedom for his family" (249), but these are at present nearly impossible projects for too many Americans. Far from being a melodramatic heroine devastated by the shame of pregnancy, Mary is passionately committed to the project of freedom for all, immigrants included, and acts as an alchemist of affect transmuting the base metal of shame into the precious ore of class pride.

These exceptions aside, pregnancy is more often a source of familial shame, as it is in both *Juno and the Paycock* and *Awake and Sing!* In the former, Mary Boyle has had a brief affair with Charles Bentham, who eventually abandons her. In act 3 of O'Casey's play—ironically, just as workers from the Hibernian Furniture Company have arrived to repossess the Boyles' property—Mary returns home and is immediately subjected to her brother's censure: "It's a wondher you're not ashamed to show your face here, afther what has happened" (*CP* 1:79). Her former boyfriend Jerry Devine enters, still hoping he can persuade Mary to marry him, until he learns that she has "fallen as low as that" (*CP* 1:81); after he leaves, Johnny, incredulous that his sister told Jerry the truth, resumes his tirade: "Are you burnin' to tell every one of the shame you've brought on us?" (*CP* 1:82). O'Casey's juxtaposition of these twin origins of shame in tenement subjectivity—the distrainment of property and a pregnancy out of marriage, the affective results of which are instantiated when performed for neighbors—illuminates the analogous impact of these events in working-class Dublin, in the Jewish-American tenements of the Lower

East Side, and in the Berger apartment in the Bronx where, as Bessie observes, "Times is getting worse" and "every day furniture's on the sidewalk" (95).

The multiple ramifications of Hennie's pregnancy in *Awake and Sing!* rival those of Mary Boyle's, while the divergent responses of their mothers mark a major difference. That is, while Juno is determined to rise above feelings of shame—in part, by moving Mary to her sister's away from male disapprobation—Bessie contrives a different solution, one condemned by her father, Jacob: Hennie's marriage to an unsuspecting gull, Sam Feinschreiber. In fact, both of Bessie's children—Hennie and her son Ralph—are sources of acute feelings of shame for her. Ralph begins an argument with his mother in front of his Uncle Morty, and Bessie comments, "You got no shame" (64); he is fond of a girl who happens to be an orphan, and Bessie remarks, "I could die from shame" (65). But the major source of this negative feeling, again, is Hennie's pregnancy. After Sam learns he isn't the baby's father, he echoes Bessie's sentiment—"I could die like this from shame" (79)—which motivates Bessie again to take action to defend against shame by declaring that such news of the baby's paternity is "impossible" and "bughouse," too crazy and unfounded to be taken seriously (80–81). It is within this framework of negative feeling that Hennie accedes to Moe's invitation to run away with him: "Come away. A certain place where it's moonlight and roses. We'll lay down, count stars. Hear the big ocean making noise. You lay under the trees" (98). As the final curtain falls Moe and Hennie, abandoning her baby and family, make their escape to a distant place where a life without shame might just be possible. Unseen, distant locales like Moe's beach play a crucial role in tenement subjectivity. For Andrew Sofer, appropriating a term from modern physics, these invisible sites constitute a "dark matter" in drama and, as such, comprise a "*structural* component of any theatrical performance." Encompassing "*whatever is materially absent onstage but un-ignorable,*" dark matter is not "a finger pointing at the moon, but the tidal force of gravity that pulls at us unseen." The "modus operandi of postclassical Western theatre," dark matter motivates Sofer's "spectral reading" of the "gravitational forces at work in the world of the performance or play" that never materially appear: Moe's exotic tropics or Lefty in Odets's play.[41] My contention is that, more so than most dramatic genres, tenement drama creates its own variety of dark matter where the fulfillment of desire is constructed as remote and difficult to attain. Often constituted of the exotically primitive as represented by such sites as the South Sea Islands in O'Neill's *Mourning Becomes Electra*, dark matter exists outside the tenement building, warehouse, office, or factory, always beckoning one toward it. In tenement drama it is often vague and multifarious, in large part because the desire it represents is more abstract than, say, the hatred of foreigners, especially greenhorns, which typically takes the form of a focused disgust. This is precisely why "sheenies" are dirty, "dagos" are greasy, and "micks" are inconsistent and stupid, drunk or sober; bigots like Fred Whipple in *We, The People* despise them all and don't want a "lot o' crummy foreigners in this country, stinkin' up the place and takin' jobs away from Americans" (124). Such negative feelings as disgust are highly specific, as Sianne Ngai observes. Disgust is "never ambivalent" about the stinky or dirty objects to which it is averse; even when "boiled down to its kernel of repulsion, repulsion itself tends to be a fairly definite response." Working differently, desire "seems capable of being vague, amorphous, and even idiosyncratic, in ways that disgust cannot."[42] It's connected to counting stars, or lying on beaches, or listening to the waves lapping the shore—to the primitive and unrepressed—and is impervious to shame.

Desire is therefore often represented by a kind of exoticized and generalized dark matter that resembles Moe Axelrod's sensual paradise. At times, this site beckons from just across the street or airshaft, as is the case in *The Adding Machine* when Judy O'Grady exposes herself to nightly gawkers like Mr. Zero (here, an Irish-American floozy serves as a surrogate for exotic Jewesses). In the closing moments of *Rocket to the Moon* (1938), Odets uses the red neon lights of the nearby Hotel Algiers to signal the life of desire Ben Stark has foregone: "STARK *turns out the last light, then exits, closing the door behind him. The room is dark, except for red neon lights of the Hotel Algiers and a spill of light from the hall*" (418). Such visual effects, precisely because they are seen, might be disqualified as dark matter, but the hotel nonetheless serves as a synecdochal figure of desire throughout the play. In act 2, Mr. Prince glances out at the hotel when asking the seductive Cleo if she likes Stark; and earlier, at the end of act 1, as her romance with Stark is just evolving, she lights his pipe after he has looked out at the Hotel Algiers while trying to sort out his feelings for her.

This sense of the fulfillment of desire requiring escape—to somewhere, anywhere—finds corollaries in "Eveline" from Joyce's *Dubliners* and, in less mature ways, in "An Encounter," where "real adventures" do not happen "to people who remain at home: they must be sought abroad" (12). It is partially for this reason that the tenement subjectivity contains a strong impulse for the escape popular and mass culture provides. And, just as Henry Roth's Albert Schearl made regular trips to the theater, tenement dwellers also flocked to the movies and other mass entertainment genres. As part of his argument in *Juno and the Paycock* that "religions [*sic*] is passin' away—they've had their day like everything else"—Captain Boyle tells Joxer, as I mentioned in my introduction, that Dublin people "know more about Charlie Chaplin an' Tommy Mix than they do about SS. Peter an' Paul" (1:44). So do Rice's and Odets's characters. Mrs. Zero begins *The Adding Machine* with a monologue delineating her favorite recent films and her knowledge of fan magazine reporting on the lives of stars; Sid and Florrie in *Waiting for Lefty* allude to lines from movies and playact as if they were appearing in one. In *Street Scene*, Mrs. Hildebrand is criticized by a heartless social worker for extravagantly spending seventy-five cents to take her two children to the movies. Moreover, with a by now unsurprising regularity in Rice's and Odets's plays, characters enjoy Irish-Jewish or Irish texts and performers, but this Irish Jewishness is not confined merely to the distal and unseen world of dark matter. In *Awake and Sing!* the family discusses the Irish Sweepstakes as a fantastical means of rising above their economic stagnation, and Morty gently pricks Jacob with, "A real, real Boob McNutt you're getting to be" (72), alluding to the popular character created by cartoonist Rube Goldberg. While Sam is distraught about the possibility that he was hoodwinked into marrying Hennie, Bessie and Myron discuss the movie they have just seen starring Wallace Beery and Polly Moran, the latter an Irish-American comedienne from Chicago. A similar motif informs *Waiting for Lefty* when Sid, in an attempt to cheer up an increasingly despondent Florrie, imitates the soft-shoe routine of entertainer Pat Rooney and whistles "Rosie O'Grady."

At times, such references hearken back to the nineteenth-century stage as do, in a highly ironic fashion, O'Casey and Odets in later plays. So, in Rice's expressionist experiment *The Subway* (1924), written in the wake of his triumph with *The Adding Machine*, Sophie Smith's mechanistic world of work and the urban jungle in which she lives are momentarily displaced in scene 5 by a trip to the movies. Much as Sophie Treadwell would do in *Machinal* (1928)—and Arthur Miller creates in *A Memory of Two Mondays*, to which I shall turn momentarily—Rice evokes Sophie's nightmarish modern world through an at times striking mise en scène: enormous and confining file cabinets, grotesque animal masks, wallpaper with vertical stripes resembling prison bars, carefully calculated lighting and sound, and so on.[43] Lonesome and plagued by guilt, she goes with her artist-admirer Eugene to the cinema to see *Heart of Erin*.[44] There, the orchestra plays "Killarney," and the audience enjoys a comic Irishwoman in the film smoking a pipe—which Rosemary Muldoon (Debra Messing) is doing when she first appears in John Patrick Shanley's *Outside Mullingar*—while the virtuous Kathleen is pursued by Lord Orville, much as Sophie is by her artist-admirer, Eugene.[45] Dialogue from the film melds into Sophie's thoughts; and, as the lines between film and reality blur, she enacts a more complicated version of the melodramatic heroine who cannot decide if she should resist such advances or enjoy them; the couple exits the theater as the orchestral accompaniment swells to a blare.

More important than the plots of *The Subway* and *Heart of Erin*, this scene implies the enduring presence of Irish melodrama in 1920s America, redacted and relocated to the cinema, and its permanent residence in the Irish-Jewish unconscious. If this were not the case, then Odets's prediction about the decline of O'Casey's career could not have been so inaccurate. Writing in January 1940, Odets reports seeing a revival of *Juno and the Paycock* that he enjoyed but which prompted his guarded forecast of its author's continuing success: "The play is really talented, but O'Casey is old news by now. But he'd better get down to writing a good play soon or he will really be old news." Conceding that O'Casey, in a "small way," had influenced him and hypothesizing that they must be "similar men" who live "physically, not with the noodle,"[46] Odets returns several times to O'Casey in *The Time Is Ripe: The 1940 Journal of Clifford Odets* (1988). In late March, he expands his earlier observation of a "certain problem" in both O'Casey and O'Neill's writing: namely, while O'Casey wrote a "vivid" drama about Irish proletarian life, he was "not content to keep repeating these genre pictures and wanted to move out into the wider world where he would have the opportunity of showing other types and the lives they lead."[47] Risks attended this aspiration, as Odets knew. Reeling from the commercial failure of *Paradise Lost*, he attempted to "move away from characters that might be considered 'too Jewish'" by, among other things, heading westward to Hollywood, where despotic studio executives imposed tight strictures on ethnic representations.[48] The predicament confronting O'Casey, Odets theorized, is that in moving to a wider world of genres and representations, a writer's "whole talent may fall off the moving van"; at the same time, he worried that if he continued to write only about Jewish life, he would leave himself vulnerable to the charge of merely replicating the characters, genres, and fictive worlds he had already created and thus being narrowly categorized as a Jewish or "too Jewish" writer.

What Odets did not consider, however, is that audiences and anxious producers might not allow successful writers to hop on the moving van to the larger world *in the first place*. The former group typically wants to see the kinds of plays they had always enjoyed, and the latter often makes certain they have that opportunity so as to better secure their investments. This was O'Casey's fate in America, as the stage history of his plays indicates. While *Within the Gates* enjoyed a modest run of 101 performances ending in January 1935, the Abbey Theatre's tour the same year with a revival of *The Plough and the Stars* earned a greater royalty. So did *Purple Dust*—eventually. Completed in 1940, as Christopher Murray observes, the play was monstrously ill-timed, for who, in the throes of the Battle of Britain and the advent of a world war, was going "to laugh at the prospect" of the destruction of the British Empire no matter how clever the farce?[49] Still, George Jean Nathan worked tirelessly to help broker a staging of the play, complaining that New York producers' snubbing of his friend's later work was "one of the strangest things in our theatre, supposedly the most enterprising in the world."[50] Nathan would have to wait until the last days of December 1956 before *Purple Dust* finally opened off Broadway at the Cherry Lane Theatre, running for 430 performances with Alvin Epstein, fresh from his turn as Lucky in the Alan Schneider-directed *Waiting for Godot*, appearing as the handsome stonemason O'Killigain. And, in the fall of 1957, a fifteen-year-old Barbra Streisand joined the company to work as an assistant stage manager and understudy for the part of Avril, the twenty-one-year-old Irish beauty who wraps men effortlessly around her lit-tle finger.

Purple Dust, as many commentators have observed, recalls Boucicault and replicates the attractions of nineteenth-century Irish melodrama: the clever Irishman O'Killigain outwitting avaricious British fops, an evoca-tion of Ireland's natural beauty, rollicking knockabout comedy, and so on. Garry O'Connor goes so far as to say that the play reawakened O'Casey's "long-neglected Boucicault instincts in playwriting," and argues further that several scenes in his autobiographical writing at the time feature "Boucicault set-pieces."[51] Significant differences obtain, too, between O'Casey's farceu-drama and the Boucicauldian tradition, none more striking than the maneu-verings of Avril and the older Souhan, who, hardly describable as virtuous and helpless colleens, have seduced two British nincompoops only to desert them in the end for more attractive Irishmen (taking their ill-gotten wealth with them). O'Casey's laughable Brits, Basil Stoke and Cyril Poges, not only resemble the prissy Englishmen of immigrant melodrama—Clifford in James Pilgrim's *Paddy Miles* and Arthur Wellesby Vere de Vere Smith in Augustin Daly's *Horizon*, for instance—but also recall the unattractive process servers, British soldiers, debauched gentry, and other pursuers of Irish women seen frequently on the nineteenth-century circum–North Atlantic stage. Equally important, in one scene Poges's actions both mirror those of which the Jew is accused in Shaw's *Geneva* and advance the critique of war profiteering in Rice and Odets. Finally able at the beginning of act 3 to telephone his London assistant from the Tudor home he is having restored in rural Ireland, Poges learns of his failed attempts to acquire stock in a company at the precise moment a bombing might commence, as no shares are available. This news prompts his lamentation, one made more ironic in the context I have tried to delineate here: "One wouldn't imagine there'd be so many trying to cash in on splintered bodies" (*CP* 3:84). Rice, Odets, and O'Casey knew all too well that there were.

Nathan's high regard for *Purple Dust* was not universally shared, although both supporters and detractors of the play recognized its Boucicauldian pad-dywackery. As Murray describes, in Ireland the play "gave offence," leading Denis Johnston to sneer, "In [O'Casey's] early work there was real passion. . . . Now there is spleen, there is tendentiousness, there is charade humour, which are no substitutes for what he left behind him in Ireland."[52] By contrast, Richard Watts Jr. applauded "all the old zest, vitality, rich humor, and comic sense of character" in the play,[53] suggesting that the old "moving van," to use Odets's metaphor, might need to remain in the garage from time to time: to survive, that is, playwrights must occasionally return to successful dramatic formulae. This is hardly news. When making his prediction about O'Casey's need to move past his earlier successes, therefore, Odets did not recognize the extent to which the "old zest" of residual dramatic forms would continue to influence the modern American stage—and the twenty-first-century American theater as well, as reviews of John Patrick Shanley's *Outside Mullingar* make abundantly clear. Finally, much like Odets, who was criticized at times for creating characters that were "too Jewish," O'Casey seemed equally damned by some whether he ventured into expressionist theater as exemplified by *Within the Gates*, or created a "too Irish" rural Ireland—like the one in *Purple Dust*—that New York audiences had enjoyed for over a century, but that many denigrated as an accession to stereotype just as damaging as the one Langner identified in Shaw's *Geneva* about Jews' inherent acumen for business. Yet, regardless or in spite of these controversies, an uncanny Irish-Jewishness and Jewish-Irishness, one intimately related to the immigrant experience, continued to influence the modern American theater. And so it was with Arthur Miller's distinguished career as well.

Poetry, Things, and the Allo-Hibernian: Arthur Miller and Stella Adler

I hoped to define for myself the value of hope, why it must arise, as well as the heroism of those who know, at least, how to endure its absence. Nothing in this book was written with greater love, and for myself I love nothing printed here better than this play.

—ARTHUR MILLER, INTRODUCTION TO *ARTHUR MILLER'S COLLECTED PLAYS* (1957)

You have for the first time in modern literature the highest type of poetic realism. Ireland [the Irish] has always been famous for its poetic language. . . . And the reason for that is there are vast areas in Ireland that are untouched by modernism. You can get a colloquial thing that Odets gets but the industrial thing levels out the people's individual expression.

—STELLA ADLER, "SCRIPT ANALYSIS OF SYNGE'S *RIDERS TO THE SEA*" (1959)

Rather remarkably, given a decade of such singular achievements between 1947 and 1957 as the premieres of *All My Sons, Death of a Salesman,* and *The Crucible*—and his adaptation of Henrik Ibsen's *An Enemy of the People*—Arthur Miller professed his strongest affection, his love in fact, for the often-ignored one-act play *A Memory of Two Mondays*.[54] And, while it is true that writers commonly harbor special feeling for works that reviewers disparage or audiences fail to support—Rice battled to keep *We, The People* running beyond forty-nine performances in 1933, for example, and *Paradise Lost*, although "poorly received," remained Odets's "favorite" early play[55]—Miller's sentiment seems even more unlikely when one considers that *A Memory of Two Mondays* was not only dismissed or neglected altogether by critics but also written in barely two weeks and then only as a *pièce d'occasion*. As Miller explains, Martin Ritt asked him for a short play that he and other actors might perform on a Sunday evening in 1955. Miller responded quickly to the request, also offering Ritt a one-act version of *A View from the Bridge* as a "curtain raiser," something "to round out a full evening" at the theater. It is also true that Miller, who underscores the partly autobiographical nature of all of his plays, regarded *Memory* as a "kind of elegy" for his years in the auto parts warehouse in the early 1930s where he earned enough money after graduating from high school to enroll at the University of Michigan in September 1934, the exact month O'Casey arrived in New York to negotiate an American production of *Within the Gates*.[56]

A *Memory of Two Mondays* is, not surprisingly, more than an elegy; among other things, it is also a play about labor, commodities and value, immigration, assimilation, and, perhaps, given his own descriptions of the play's genesis, an expression of Miller's own psychology as well. He referred to it as a testament to his "need" during the height of the Cold War to "touch again a reality I could understand, unlike the booming, inane America of the present."[57] Like *A View from the Bridge*, he confided, *Memory* lived "in the back of [his] head for many years" and then relocated to an even more central place.[58] In his biography of Miller, Martin Gottfried teases out the deeply personal implications of these comments, noting that although the play is the writer's "most immature and least consequential adult work," it nevertheless resided "closest to his heart, surely because it is so unabashed an ode to his youth." And this ode, Gottfried adds, is both "fanciful" and "Irish," as "most of the characters are from Ireland" and "in the English-speaking theater Irish playwrights enjoy an unparalleled reputation for poetic language."[59]

Well, yes and no—or, rather, no and yes. Stella Adler's script analysis of John Millington Synge's *Riders to the Sea* supports the latter half of Gottfried's contention about Irish writers' association with poetic language, recalling Synge's dictum that "in a good play every speech should be as fully flavoured as a nut or apple."[60] Throughout her actors' workshops on *Riders to the Sea* in 1959 and 1960, Adler lavished praise upon Synge's poetry, which for her enhances the play's magnitude and provides, for our purposes, a resonant context within which to read Miller's "Irish play":

> The turn of phrase [in Synge] for the first time in modern literature has found an epic sense. The common people have found in Synge the poetry of the people. Poetic realism. Only when people are untouched by modern life can they retain this kind of simplicity. (March 25, 1959, 8)

In Adler's reading, the poetry of *Riders to the Sea* is its most overdetermined quality, deriving from such a myriad of factors as its premodern simplicity, its characters' unalienated labor in an economy in which everyday objects have *not* been reduced to their exchange value or status symbols, and the possibility that the "most cosmic idea" may be communicated by the "most humble creature." Poetry and the "tragic" do not—cannot, in Adler's view—originate in plot structure. "Get rid of the plot," she urges; topple all obstacles between "man and death," which in Synge results in poetry that is "pure," "colloquial," and "epic" (March 23, 1959, 2). For his part, Miller similarly admired the language of such Irish writers as O'Casey, commending him and Odets for adding a "lyrical voice" to the modern theater in their capacities as "Marxist prophets" of the 1930s.[61] He also lobbied the Dramatists Guild unsuccessfully in 1950 to mount a counterpicket to the politically motivated protest of the American Legion over the proposed production of O'Casey's *Cock-a-Doodle-Dandy* in America.[62]

It is not the case, however, as Gottfried contends, that most of the characters in *A Memory of Two Mondays* hail from Ireland, although it isn't difficult to understand how he arrived at this misreading.[63] In the play's early moments, Kenneth—who, in fact, *is* from Ireland, having immigrated to America some five and a half months before the action of the play begins—sings the opening lines of Thomas Moore's ballad "The Minstrel Boy," written in memory of the 1798 rising of the United Irishmen. His coworker Patricia asks, "Was that an Irish song?" to which he "shyly" responds, "All Irish here and none of yiz knows an Irish song" (*Collected Plays* 341). When he repeats the lyrics near the end of the play on the second Monday of the play's title, Patricia repeats her question and Kenneth reiterates his incredulity more emphatically: "All Irish here, and none of yiz knows an Irish song!" (371). His coworkers' ignorance of well-known Irish songs like this one, famously recorded by John McCormack and exceptionally popular after World War I, is easily explained: to wit, most of the workers in Miller's Depression-era warehouse are *not* from Ireland, but are Irish- Americans like Raymond Ryan, Tommy Kelly, Willie Hogan, and others. And several characters aren't Irish or Irish-American: the "barrel-bellied" Gus who speaks with a "gruff Slavic accent" (336), for instance, and the Ivy League–educated boss Mr. Eagle, whose visits produce anxiety in many of the workers. And, if it is true, as Miller insisted, that he is "in" all of his plays, then in *Memory* he is quite clearly Bert, an eighteen-year-old boy confronting the twin challenges of reading *War and Peace* and trying to save enough money to enroll in college, as Miller himself did by working at the Chadick-Delameter auto parts warehouse from 1932 to August 1934. The only Jew in a workplace dominated by Irish-Americans, a fact of which he was very much aware, Miller, for perhaps the first time in his life, was exposed to anti-Semitism,which is replaced in the play by a highly ambivalent allo-Hibernianism I hope to explicate here.[64]

Gottfried's assertion of the play's Irishness is nonetheless useful in stressing Miller's efforts to create a kind of romantic, if imperfect and complicated,

Ireland within the grime, dust, and mice-infested confines of a Manhattan warehouse modeled after the one in which he once worked. The stage directions of *Memory* underscore this paradoxical duality. On the one hand, the set must appear "*dirty and unmanageably chaotic*," an unkempt beehive of activity, dominated by "*factory-type windows which reach from floor to ceiling and are encrusted with the hard dirt of years.*" These windows "*seem to surround the entire stage*" (332). On the other, the warehouse shipping room is also "romantic": a "*little world, a home to which, unbelievably perhaps, these people like to come every Monday morning, despite what they say*" (333). The latter half of this description, the notion of a workplace as a home that can mitigate the frustrations of working for inadequate wages or in challenging conditions, is conventional enough; indeed, it is the premise of television situation comedies from *Taxi* to *Cheers*. In Adler's reading of *Riders to the Sea*, labor on the Aran Islands resembles this communitarian ethos, which surfaces frequently in *Memory*.[65] Tommy Kelly has worked in the warehouse for sixteen years; Gus, for twenty-two. Ray Ryan, the manager, sympathizes with his friend Larry's complaints about his salary. The workers care for each other in ways that exceed the routinized interactions of the workplace, as when they attempt to shield the drunken and stupefied Tommy from Mr. Eagle, covering for him by improvising busywork in response to nonexistent invoices. Patricia and Larry enjoy a close, if emotionally uneven, relationship; Jim offers companionship to Gus after his wife's death and is with him when he dies; and they variously encourage Bert's dream of attending college, although he seems disappointed by the tepid farewell he receives in the play's closing moments.

A "home," perhaps, but in what ways is the auto parts warehouse "romantic"? Or, as Miller variously characterized *Memory*, in what ways does it mark a "departure from realism," convey "a story but not a plot," or amount to a "lyrical, even nostalgic" response to McCarthyism?[66] Most importantly, how does it realize what Miller identifies as drama's highest aesthetic priority: "I prize the poetic above else in the theater, and because I do I insist that the poem truly be there"?[67] The answers to these questions, to a considerable extent, reside in by now familiar dimensions of Irish- and Jewish-American interactions and in the surrogation inherent to performance. That is to say, not unlike the adolescent Mike Gold, the teenaged Miller and Bert in *Memory* entered a world of work that, anti-Semitic hiring practices notwithstanding, was in effect an Irish-Jewish construction. At times, this world could prove romantic and at others seem prosaic, even repulsive. As an example of the former instance, recall Gold's refulgent memory in *Jews without Money* of working at the Callahan Transfer Express, quoted so many pages ago and expanded slightly here:

> The expressmen were leather-faced young Irish, the coach drivers were leather-faced young Jews.

> Between jobs these citizens of the two leading persecuted and erratic small nations of the world loafed on a bench. They fought, philosophized and drank buckets of beer together in the sunlight. (269)

In *A Diving Rock on the Hudson*, Ira Stigman's experience at the Polo Grounds selling peanuts and soda at New York Giants baseball games was far less euphoric. On game days, the "vituperative, harried, and tyrannical" Jew Benny Lass handpicked vendors from a mob of kids looking for work; after they were selected, the fortunate few then awaited their assignments as meted out by Walsh and Phil, the Irish-Jewish team that ran the outfit while, simultaneously, the latter chain-smoked and hawked up "yellow-green phlegm" that he spat on the floor (98, 106). Not a lot of sunny philosophizing or romance here.

Crucial to both descriptions, however, is the kind of surrogation of the Irish and Jews prevalent on the nineteenth-century stage. Gold's Irish expressmen and Jewish coach-drivers were equally leather-faced, and in their respites from work drank beer together while solving the problems of the world; conversely, Roth's Polo Grounds' Irishmen and Jews were equally grotesque. Taken together, these two examples reflect the ambivalence that defines both allo-Semitism and allo-Hibernianism, the latter of which describes Miller's Kenneth in *A Memory of Two Mondays*. Surrogation in the play, in at least one respect, is far more romantic. In its final moments Bert's determination to pursue a college education—and his affiliation with literature and the arts more generally—is registered by way of allusion to Moore's "The Minstrel Boy." As Bert leaves the warehouse for the final time, Kenneth "*turns and looks about, [and] sees Bert is gone,*" then sings softly, "The minstrel boy to the war has gone!" At the drop of the curtain, he continues: "in the ranks of death you will find him. / His father's sword he has girded on, / And his wild harp slung behind him" (376). Bert exits the stage carrying the book that will nurture his imagination, itself an avatar of the "wild harp" of Moore's young warrior-bard. In his exodus, the fledgling writer achieves something Kenneth promises to do and only Gus accomplishes through death: escape from the grime of the capitalist machine where people are inventoried like so many automobile carburetors and ignition systems. And he makes his escape as a Jewish rapparee not unlike George Jean Nathan, fighting for a literary or aesthetic ideal that transcends the prison-houses of profit, commercial success, and ethnic tension or hostility.

Besides this process of surrogation in which a Jewish student is metamorphosed into an Irish nationalist—a youthful hero prepared to sacrifice himself for Mother Ireland strikes at the very heart of romance—how does a sense of poetry and possibility inform this enclosed world? Miller brooded over this very issue: "The fact that [*Memory*] was seen as something utterly sad and hopeless as a comment on life quite astonishes me still" ("Introduction" 49). The question is complicated by the play's resemblance both to the nineteenth-century immigrant melodrama, a genre compared earlier to Sir Robert Howard's comedy *The Committee*, and the plight of many Irish unable to earn a living during the Depression. The plots of plays in this genre, you may recall, are simple and direct. In Howard's play, Teague, so destitute he is wearing only a blanket, arrives in the city looking for work. His Irish immigrant successor on the melodramatic stage is equally poor, having failed at other jobs and, given this checkered history, it is difficult to determine what occupation he might pursue successfully. Like Teague, however, the protagonists in plays by James Pilgrim and John Brougham are vivacious, resolute, and blessed with a gift for comic invention. On the nineteenth-century stage, the Irishman's ingenious solution of a Yankee employer's financial or amatory dilemma—and his own entrepreneurial initiative—eventually leads to his assimilation into his new country and often to both a position of financial security and a wife, a romantic comic conclusion also enjoyed by George Henry Jessop's Jewish drummer, Sam'l of Posen.

Kenneth shares many of his predecessors' characteristics and virtues. He arrives in America poor and looking for work; while he has more than a blanket to wear, he is reduced to buying for a quarter a pair of such ill-fitting shoes that he is forced to carve a hole in one to give his little toe "a breath of air." Having been fired from "two or three" jobs in Ireland, thus mirroring the checkered employment histories of his theatrical forebears, he has found employment at the warehouse; and, although he occasionally annoys his irascible coworker Gus, like his predecessors Kenneth is an attractive and vibrant addition to the workplace. He possesses an impressive internal archive of lyrics to sing and recites poetry from memory, although his talents diminish as his days in the warehouse drag on. Unlike his antecedents, however, and in a bittersweet counter to the birth of a new, inclusive social order manufactured by the Irishman in most immigrant melodrama, Kenneth stands alone at the end of the play. When Miller terms the play a "pathetic comedy" lacking a "plot" (49), this is in part what he means, as Kenneth—like Samuel Beckett's Clov in *Endgame* or Winnie in *Happy Days*—remains rooted in the quotidian grind he vows to escape. "Well, you've got to keep movin'" (375), he advises Bert, but it isn't clear that he ever will.

Like Beckett's characters and unlike most immigrants in popular melodrama, Kenneth slowly declines over the short course of the play, and given the cause of his deterioration—drinking—Miller might be accused of reliance upon an all-too-familiar stereotype by turning his character into a modern-day stage Irishman. In an exchange with Tommy Kelly, with whom he had earlier enjoyed a friendly repartee sparked by Tommy's adoption of an exaggerated brogue, Kenneth is forced to confront a terrible possibility:

> TOM. You better get yourself a little will power, Kenny. I think you're gettin' a fine taste for the hard stuff.

KENNETH: Ah, no, I'll never be a drunk, Tommy.

TOM: You're a drunk now.

KENNETH: Oh, don't say that, please!

TOM: I'm tellin' you, I can see it comin' on you. (361–62)

In addition to his gifts of reciting poetry and singing—his coworker Patricia compliments his "terrific" voice—Kenneth thus also succumbs to this cardinal shortcoming of the stage Irishman. Further, like the most invidious of stereotypes, Kenneth reveals an incipient pugnacity, lunging with "one fist ready" at a coworker for calling him "donkey" and threatening more reprisals in the future: "You'll see me later, all right—with one eye closed!" (369). Throughout the nineteenth century and well into the twentieth, this hard-drinking, blathering caricature overwhelmed any sense of the romantic Irishman. If Bert can be figured as an Irish minstrel boy and romantic hero, then this alternative figure of Irishness recalls the much-traveled stereotype used to rationalize anti-Irish prejudice. Like the allo-Semitic figure of the Jew, Kenneth is ambivalence incarnate, simultaneously talented yet also deeply flawed, a figure of both what Bert wants to become and needs to avoid.

In addition, Kenneth resembles not only antecedent stereotypes, but also Depression-era immigrants to America more generally. As Diarmaid Ferriter explains, the "twin pillars" of Irish economic policy in the 1930s and 1940s—"agricultural and industrial self-sufficiency"—failed to improve the economy, a failure that impelled young people in particular to leave the country (Kenneth is twenty-six in Miller's play). By 1944, some two-thirds of Irish men seeking work permits in Britain were under thirty, and during the same period the sharpest rise of emigration demographics was for women under the age of twenty-two.[68] Kenneth, however much he complains about the meager and predictable lunch his landlady packs for him, recounts to Bert the "many and many a time" he went hungry in Ireland (357), and he was clearly not alone in this deprivation, as new immigrants Marco and Rodolpho in *A View from the Bridge* recount to their new American acquaintances. The lack of employment possibilities has other consequences as well, as Rodolpho explains to Catherine in act 1: "I have no money to get married, I have a nice face, but no money" (394). Physical hunger is therefore often paralleled by emotional need—recall that the "Great Hunger" in Patrick Kavanagh's 1942 poem alludes to emotional starvation, not the Famine—with the result that rates of marriage are adversely affected and the ages of those who are able to marry rise.[69] Fired from two or three jobs at home, not unlike Pilgrim's Paddy Miles, who failed at several occupations in Ireland, Kenneth struggled to find gainful employment there, a condition that produces a casualization of labor defined by irregularity, impermanence, and an inconsistent income that falls below a level necessary for subsistence and for marriage. In *A View from the Bridge*, Marco recalls that in Italy he and his brother did "whatever" work there was: fixing bridges, working in the fields at harvest time, even waiting for the train to earn a "few lire" by pushing a taxi of passengers up a hill to the local hotel (392). For Kenneth, however imperfect it may be, a job at the warehouse ends a personal history of casualized labor, although it seems not quite so final as working for the civil service, which he feels inevitably "seals the fate and locks the door" for a worker's lifetime (364).[70] Still, for Kenneth, who fears he is lapsing into inebriety, the prospect of such permanence as the civil service provides has its psychical advantages: "I'll get back to regular there, I think" (375).

Irish historians emphasize that, given these harsh material circumstances, the romantic myth of an agrarian Ireland as represented by the much-heralded Irish peasant was put under exceptional pressure during the Depression and the years of the war. By contrast, and despite such sobering realities as inadequate salaries, cluttered and unhealthy working conditions (Kenneth complains about chronic sneezing caused by an unrelenting "rainin'" of dust from the ceiling), and the routinization of working life, *A Memory of Two Mondays* contains important romantic and poetic elements, particularly if both "romance" and "poetry" are understood to connote, among other things, resistance to the vicissitudes of modernity. In this reading, again one influenced by Stella Adler's workshops on *Riders to the Sea*, the warm summer of work on the first Monday, when the warehouse constitutes a space removed from the outside world by the opacity of the blackened windows, retains several romantic strains. Most obviously, Kenneth's recitation of lines from Norman Macleod's "Courage, Brother" and Walt Whitman's "When Lilacs Last in the Dooryard Bloomed," and his singing of Thomas Moore's ballad, evoke this poetic counterreality. His Irishness itself signals a romantic world remote from the workaday drudgeries of the modern city. So if Jews could be negatively associated with the vicissitudes of modernity, an association made manifest in a myriad of ways, then the Irish could just as easily be viewed, as Adler regards Synge's Aran Islanders, as figures of a premodern simplicity that precedes the alienations of industrial capitalism.

Repeatedly in her script analysis, Adler underscores the poetic dimensions of Synge's play and, by extension, of Irishness understood in a decidedly pre-modern sense. For her, Maurya in *Riders to the Sea* evinces the "purity of poverty," and it is precisely the characters' inability to access "what we call 'modern life'" that "keeps the material pure." Similarly, as in the epigraph above, poetic language has survived in Ireland because "vast areas" of the country are "untouched by modernism" (March 23, 1959, 2, 8). Poetry, finally, is connected to both the common man and to oppressed people; and like surrogation, it returns us to the Irish-Jewish unconscious. In a March 1960 workshop on Synge, Adler remembers going to an Irish fair complete with cattle and "weather beaten" men with red scarves, one of whom looked at her and asked, "Who is this fair appearision [*sic*] among us?" This "character of speech," this "natural endowment," meant for Adler that the Irish, like speakers of Yiddish, cannot be pulled down by words: "You can't belittle them in language" (March 24, 1960, n.p.), because Irish and Yiddish poetry is too strong.

The evocative materiality of stage objects in *Riders to the Sea* complements its linguistic and poetic qualities. In both Adler's reading of Synge and mine of *A Memory of Two Mondays*, stage properties on occasion convey a rich counterdiscourse to modernity and the reign of the commodity. For Adler, in *Riders to the Sea* "everything is symbolic. Everything is important," including the rope, cake, spinning wheel, new coat, halter, and so on as indicated in Synge's stage directions. The gendered domestic economy of Aran Islands peasants is registered in the play's initial set description, as the action begins with Cathleen, Maurya's elder daughter, kneading dough for a cake and then moving to work on the spinning wheel. Such simple and utilitarian objects communicate the timelessness of epic:

> There is a cottage kitchen, with nets, oil-skins, spinning wheel, some new boards. What kind of objects are they? They're eternal but they are poor things that have gone on forever. There is nothing modern. The things have the same poetic thing . . . that the sea has because things connected to the sea have in them an unchangeable quality. (March 25, 1959, 6)

In an odd and slightly nonidiomatic articulation, one reminiscent of Lola Ridge's typology in "The Ghetto" that likened Hester Street Jewish women to "ancient mothers" who had seen the "dawn break over" Egypt,[71] Adler argues that in *Riders to the Sea* "everything has in it already a going back to foreverness" (March 25, 1959, 6). In an equally telling formulation, she adds, in Synge you "can get a colloquial thing that Odets gets but the industrial thing levels out the people's individual expression" (March 25, 1959, 8). Adler's use of "things," of course, long precedes the advent of "thing theory" in the academy, although this cultural theory will prove useful in discussing Miller. For Adler, in other words, objects resonate differently on Synge's Aran Islands than in Odets's tenement apartments and offices.

Yet, while in her reading of *Riders to the Sea* poetic "things" may at first blush *seem* to contrast sharply with the litter of mechanical parts for sale in *A Memory of Two Mondays*, this may not necessarily be the case. More generally, Miller's dusty and mice-infested warehouse appears to be located near the epicenter of an even more objectionable means of production. Overwhelmed by giant black windows rendered opaque by the accumulation of grime, the workers on the warehouse floor are confined within the prison-like warehouse and its mammoth inventory, not unlike O'Casey's soldiers feeding shells to an enormous gun or Rice's Mr. Zero crawling insect-like across a giant adding machine. Yet visible and invisible things in *Memory* are also potentially complicated things, requiring a more careful parsing of their signifying and poetic potentials. Indeed, on the first Monday while encased by darkened windows, the warehouse floor becomes its own kind of island, floating remotely in space with no contact with the world outside; as a result, the objects associated with this island may on occasion take on the poetic qualities of Synge's spinning wheel and fishing nets. A reading of these objects, among other interpretive strategies, might foreground Andrew Sofer's argument in *The Stage Life of Props* (2003) that just as roles are "haunted" by stage histories—Henry Irving's Shylock is preceded by other actors' performances, and his Shylock was contextualized in a repertory including Mathias in *The Bells* and Boucicault's Louis XI—so, too, are stage properties. Borrowing notions from Prague School semioticians and students of performance, Sofer maintains that stage objects "accrue intertextual significance" as they travel across performances, in some cases even acquiring an "independent signifying force" akin to that of the actor.[72] Such notions are compatible with Bill Brown's elaboration of "thing theory" in at least two respects: first, when an object marks a relationship or *encounter* with a subject, its thingness exceeds its materiality; and, second, "We begin to confront the thingness of objects . . . when their flow within circuits of production and distribution, consumption and exhibition, has been arrested, however momentarily."[73] This psychically resonant interruption of the exchange of objects or ever so slight halt in the routinized deadness of inexorable production may confer upon a commodity a new status as thing.

Such is the case in *Memory* when objects momentarily evoke a world outside of the domination of commodities and exchange value. Following Sofer's thesis, this revaluation partially originates in theater history and the connotations stage properties accrue as signifiers; and few objects on the modern stage carry with them more significance than the car. The action of *Memory* occurs literally within the figurative space of the automobile, parts of which surround the action; and on stage the car is especially laden with meaning. A brief chronicle of the automobile on the North Atlantic stage might begin with Henry Straker and Jack Tanner's momentarily broken down "touring car" in act 2 of Shaw's *Man and Superman* (1905). Shaw's second act begins with Tanner addressing a pair of legs attired in dungaree overalls sprawled out from under a car. The legs belong to Straker, the Cockney-accented chauffeur who understands both how to repair machines and how to extract maximum value from them by driving fast. A product of the Polytechnic, not Harrow, Eton, or Oxford, and the possessor of mechanical skills that the social elite conspicuously lack, Straker, as Tanner remarks, marks the "advent of the New Man" (*CPP* 3:566); as such, this competent and thoroughly practical man capable of shattering a brittle class system exemplifies an ascendant masculinity that seems as mobile and fast as the cars he repairs.

For this reason, the automobile transports easily and often tragically to Depression-era America and later in plays like Miller's *Death of a Salesman*

(1949). In the opening scene, Linda Loman's fears of Willy's incipient decline are grounded in his recent difficulties with driving, which motivate her question: "You didn't smash the car, did you?" (*Collected Plays* 131). The sad fact is that Willy no longer drives his 1928 red Chevrolet with the windshield that opens; he no longer glides down roads cut through the beautiful forests of New England as the "warm air bathe[s] over [him]" (132). For Willy, driving can no longer mean leisurely touring; it can no longer be associated with the joyous experience of autumn scenery, sunshine, and motility. Instead, the car now symbolizes his incompetence, professional failure, and delusion. And, of course, it ultimately causes his death.

This direct relationship between cars, manhood, and death informs *Golden Boy* (1937), one of Odets's most vivid portraits of the Great Depression. As Adler observes in her extended commentary on the play, the image of the car in *Golden Boy* speaks directly to the immigrant experience, just as stage props demand the concerted attention of the actor. "Before using a prop," she advises, "you have to know what the life of the prop is." If the script calls for a gun, the actor needs to know how to use it, how to take it apart and reassemble it; if the role involves swordplay, the actor needs to master every aspect of the "whole tradition [that] surrounds the wearing of a sword."[74] Cars, I would submit, require a similar committed understanding for the actor, even if a role does not require the changing of a flat tire or replacement of a spark plug. For Adler, like all immigrant young men, Odets's Joe Bonaparte "wanted to be an American" but couldn't thrive as one easily because all immigrant men were, first and foremost, "a wop, a sheeny, a mick, or a spic."[75] As a consequence, for Joe, as for so many, the car becomes the ultimate symbol of success. But not just any car, as Adler explains:

> Now, any *pisher* can buy a car. A man of [Joe's] size wants to buy a car? When you sit in a nice car, you can look down on the world. Joe is in a long tradition of strong men who want to be important, and that's his symbol of success.[76] (*Master Playwrights* 134)

Odets's dialogue confirms Adler's thesis and thickens it. Joe wants to buy the same Duesenberg Gary Cooper drives, a car too expensive to purchase new but perhaps, as he tells Lorna early in the play, he could find a secondhand one. At the same time, he is keenly aware that as an aspiring violinist he could never afford such a car; only by boxing and winning sizable purses could he acquire one. For this reason, fast cars for Joe are "poison in my blood" (266); he *has* to have one even if it kills him. And it eventually does.

Fast cars and "speed" itself accrue a rich significance in *Golden Boy*, and Adler's aside that from an expensive car one can "look down on the world," taken from Odets's dialogue, is apposite in the context of the Irish-Jewish (or mick-sheeny, as she might phrase it) unconscious. In this metaphor, speed on the highways of America parallels the airy verticality of corporate skyscrapers that former tenement dwellers inhabit as they ascend to the summits of power in American business. In Rice's *Counsellor-at-Law* (1931), for example, George Simon occupies a suite of law offices "*high up in a skyscraper*" that affords a view of "*several tall buildings in the middle distance, and the Hudson River and New Jersey shore in the background.*"[77] So as to reiterate the connotation of this verticality, its distance from the pushcarts and poverty of his youth—and from the stifling immigrant basement in Gold's *Money*—Simon's interior office in scene 2 allows for "*a panoramic view of lower Manhattan.*"[78] In John Howard Lawson's *Success Story*, the action occurs in the "*richly furnished*" offices of the Raymond Merritt Company, located on the fortieth floor of a building in which "*big windows . . . look out on an uninterrupted expanse of blue sky.*"[79] And the verticality of corporate success inherent to this figure of speech informs Joe's paean to the virtues of speed in *Golden Boy*: "When you sit in a car and speed you're looking down at the world. Speed, speed, everything is speed—nobody gets me!" (266).

Speed, then, implies both elevation, ascent up the social ladder, and escape. It also connotes affluence, autonomy, and a complete separation from the rest of society. Joe repeats this sentiment in the scene before his fatal accident, as he exhorts Lorna to steal away with him after his final victory in the boxing ring:

> We'll drive through the night. When you mow down the night with head-lights, nobody gets you! You're on top of the world then—nobody laughs! That's it—speed! We're off the earth—unconnected! We don't have to think! That's what speed is for, an easy way to live! (316)

For Christopher Herr, *pace* the theories of Jean Baudrillard, such speeches reflect a larger mythology that if one drives fast enough and far enough into the great deserts of the American West, crippling obsessions and oppressive structures can be relegated to the rearview mirror—they can be escaped. The formula is simple: "to be famous is to be rich is to be fast is to be free, or so Joe's fantasy would have it."[80] Such rootlessness and the possibility of severing connections and leaving no trace behind—a notion crucial to tenement subjectivity—also informs Baudrillard's social theory and Adler's notion that in American drama "nothing is fixed": not religion, not family, not property (*Master Playwrights* 18).

A history of cars in modern drama, therefore, precedes the appearance of parts in *Memory*. And in this history, the car conveys more than the operations of supply and demand, or the need to get from one place to another; and, while car parts may not connote the "foreverness" Adler detects in Syngean properties—while every prop may not be "symbolic" or constitute a "thing"—several in Miller's play gesture toward such a poetic sensibility. This alternative economy surfaces in the opening scene when Raymond Ryan asks Bert what he can "get" out of a book like *War and Peace*, and Bert answers, "Well, it's—it's literature" (334). Its value may not be quantifiable or immediate. This is precisely the noninstrumental response Larry gives Gus, who is amazed that Larry would be foolish and impractical enough to buy an Auburn:

GUS: You crazy? Buy Auburn?

LARRY, *with depth—a profound conclusion*: I like the valves, Gus.

GUS: Yeah, but when you gonna go sell it who gonna buy an Auburn?

LARRY: Didn't you ever get to where you don't care about that? I *always* liked those valves, and I decided, that's all.

GUS: Yeah, but when you gonna go sell it—

LARRY: I don't care. (342)

For Larry, Auburns have the most "beautifully-laid out valves in the country" and are worth more than their exchange value. Later, after his wife's death, Gus seems finally to appreciate Larry's point, returning in a new suit and hauling a pair of new Ford fenders still in wrapping paper, which he and Jim carefully lean against the wall. Jim explains that Gus spent "all Saturday buyin' new clothes to go to the cemetery; then all the way the hell over to Long Island City to get these damned fenders for that old wreck of a Ford he's got" (363). He never successfully affixed them to the car, but instead carries them with him, almost as if they possessed a talismanic significance no one but he can fathom. Like Maurya's spinning wheel and Bartley's fishing nets, Larry's valves and Gus's fenders exist outside the parameters of commercial exchange; like literature, they cannot be reduced or quantified; and, like Brown's "things," they momentarily—and dramatically—arrest circuits of production and consumption.

But there is, sadly, a profound sense in *Memory* that these disruptive moments will occur less frequently after Bert, the Jewish-Irish bard, leaves. More than the instrumentalized materiality of car parts or nonthings suggest this possibility; the play's unseen outside world, most often a site of freedom and escape, reasserts the indomitability of capitalism and the commodity form. This invisible "dark matter," again appropriating Sofer's concept, propels the action in a trajectory just the opposite of the gravitational pull of Pacific islands and other exotic sites of fulfilled desire back into the workaday realities from which workers cannot be extricated and from which no speed can facilitate a permanent rupture. By the end of the play, Kenneth appears to languish, his poetic Irishness overwhelmed by drink, work, or merely discouragement. Gus is dead. The frisson between Patricia and Larry, a tension in part symbolized by a drive in the country in his beautiful Auburn that never occurs, seems dissipated by the revelation that Larry intends to sell the car he can no longer "afford." When things revert to commodities, poetry and romance die.

This is especially true of love, as is reflected in the play's dominant scenic effect—the washing of the grimy windows and the introduction of bright sunlight into the once dark island of the warehouse (see figure 4.2). Initiated

FIGURE 4.2 *Kenneth and Bert Washing Windows in* A Memory of Two Mondays, *Steve Fedoruk, Director, September 9–October 17, 2010, Eclipse Theatre Company, Chicago*
Scott Cooper, photographer.

by Kenneth and completed by Bert, washing the windows is transformative, but in a surprising, unintended way:

> *A rag in hand, Bert mounts the table; they [Bert and Kenneth] make one slow swipe of the window before them and instantly all the windows around the stage burst into the yellow light of summer that floods into the room.* (357)

The warmth of this sun lasts less than a minute: "*Gradually, as they speak all light hardens to that of winter*" (357). Now, for the first time, the community of workers is able to see outside—to watch cats "walk dainty in the snow" yet also to experience an "ice-cold city" in the grip of the Depression (359). The clearest emblem of this malaise, of the distinct absence of romance and poetry, exists just outside the newly cleaned windows: a brothel, with women provocatively displayed as so many commodities. Kenneth is especially upset by the spectacle and pleads with his coworker Agnes not to look at it: "Oh, that's a terrible thing to be lookin' at. Oh, Agnes you best not be comin' back here any more now" (366). Kenneth repeats his admonition to Patricia and, when Tommy demurs—"It's only a lot of naked women"—Kenneth seems amazed that Patricia is amused by the thought of a "cathouse" operating in plain view for all to see.

A Memory of Two Mondays, Miller's protestations notwithstanding that the play is not "utterly sad" (49), suggests that, once a clear view of the city is enabled, modernity remains inimical to poetry and individual happiness. It is difficult *not* to see this mise en scène as influenced by the closing tableau of Ibsen's *Ghosts* as the sun's piercing of the play's predominant grayness finally reveals Oswald's condition to devastating effect. As warm summer brightness turns to hardened and cold light in *Memory*, affectively resonant things, including sex, are reduced to mere objects to exchange, as the now visible prostitutes confirm. More important for my purposes, the Irish-Jewish unconscious, the surrogation of Irish and Jewish characters, and the allo-Hibernian all inform Miller's play, which, admittedly, is a relatively minor achievement in comparison to Miller's landmark works *Death of a Salesman* and *The Crucible*. But contextualizing *Memory* with Synge, especially as Adler regards him, creates an Irish Miller we seldom see in the rest of his distinguished canon of plays.

Further, along with *A View from the Bridge*, Miller's Irish play repositions him in a roster including O'Casey, Rice, and Odets—and such nineteenth-century Irish and Irish-American playwrights as Brougham, Jessop, and Augustin Daly—who depict the immigrant experience so central to the development of American drama. This experience, psychically fragmenting and "pathetic" in the way Miller suggests, is also, like other representations of tenement subjectivity in the circum–North Atlantic, prone to the emotional excess that destroys Eddie Carbone in *A View from the Bridge*. In *View*, Miller's narrator Alfieri offers what is by now an unsurprising analysis of Eddie's self-destructive impulses: "Every man's got somebody that he loves, eh," he explains. "But sometimes . . . there's too much" (409). Like other Jewish and Irish immigrants, including Kenneth, Eddie embodies this excess of feeling. This affective surplus, posited some pages ago as inherent to the immigrant/tenement subjectivity more generally, combined with the challenge of securing meaningful work and the fantasy of a possible romantic escape from workaday reality, helps define this significant genre of modern American drama. So, too, does Bert's insight into the ambivalent working world he so briefly inhabits. As Kenneth polishes the now clear windows, singing softly and contentedly before seeing the ugliness outside, Bert notes, "There's something so terrible here! There always was, and I don't know what" (358). Something, in other words, is concealed beneath the surface of *A Memory of Two Mondays*, it seems, something dreadful momentarily held in abeyance by the grandeur of Irish poetry and song.

Coda: On the Late Eugene O'Neill

> Oh the praties they grow small
> Over here, over here,
> Oh, the praties they grow small
> Over here.
> Oh the praties they grow small
> And we dig them in the fall
> And we eat them skins and all
> Over here, over here.

—FROM A TRADITIONAL IRISH SONG IN EUGENE O'NEILL,
A MOON FOR THE MISBEGOTTEN (1943)

The opening stage directions of *Long Day's Journey into Night* have always seemed to me a kind of interpretive trap, a feint for which too credulous readers (more so than viewers unable to make out the fine print of O'Neill's descriptions) might fall at their peril. For from the specificity of the titles shelved in the set's twin bookcases, readers might be tempted to construct an opposition that cannot be sustained as a template for unpacking the play's complexities and those of the characters they are about to meet. That is, one bookcase on the right seems irreducibly modern save for the picture of Shakespeare above it; in fact, Shakespeare is present in both libraries, as three sets of his works are housed in the rival bookcase as well. The more modern catalog of titles features novels by Balzac, Zola, and Stendhal, and philosophical volumes by Schopenhauer, Nietzsche, Marx, and others like the anarchist Petr Kropotkin. Its large "glassed-in" counterpart, by contrast, seems laden with more antique fiction by Hugo, Dumas, and the popular mid-nineteenth-century Irish writer Charles Lever (1806–72), digests of the world's best literature, and "miscellaneous volumes of old plays, poetry, and several histories of Ireland" (11). This personal library, in effect, is a small repository of mostly nineteenth-century titles, a gesture to the past that is still very much present.

After meeting the characters, it becomes obvious that the first library houses books belonging to O'Neill's fictive persona Edmund Tyrone; the latter, prominently featuring well-thumbed and even musty texts, to his father, James. If there were any doubts about the owners of these respective collections, they are quickly demolished by the elder Tyrone's disparagement of his son's "Socialist gabble" (23) and "damned Socialist anarchist sentiments"

(25), and by Edmund's quoting from *Thus Spake Zarathustra* in act 2. But like most binaries, this one begins to collapse in light of O'Neill's later plays, for like O'Casey and Joyce he could never quite abandon an Ireland that, in several respects, more resembles his father's peasant roots in the nineteenth century than the modernist thought represented by many of his books. Or, more accurately, his late plays, especially *A Moon for the Misbegotten* and *A Touch of the Poet*, evoke a familiar world of Irish melodrama and combine it with a kind of politics shared by O'Casey, Rice, and Odets, all the while retaining the psychical complexity of his earlier plays.

The lyrics of the well-known Famine anthem Phil Hogan drunkenly stumbles through and repeats several times in *A Moon for the Misbegotten*, first produced with unfortunate results by the Theatre Guild in 1947, suggest the play's atavism even though it set in early September 1923.[81] Hogan's rendition of "Oh the praties they grow small / Over here, over here," the only verse he knows, is but one of several variants, including the more profane version Brendan Behan's father invented, which ends, "[But] they were better than fugh-all over here."[82] Samuel Lover (1797–1868) is generally credited with putting a less vulgar combination of these lines to music from an extant song, and the well-known refrain evolved into an oblique commentary on the dire circumstances of the Great Famine.[83] But even if American theatergoers were unaware of the song's history, they would have had no difficulty coming to a conclusion similar to that John Henry Raleigh reached about *A Moon for the Misbegotten*: "O'Neill's last play [was] one of the most Irish, if not the most Irish, of all his plays. Only *A Touch of the Poet* is comparable."[84] As Raleigh outlines, in *A Moon for the Misbegotten* O'Neill offers a "miniature dramatization" of the lives of one large segment of the Irish diaspora in America—the Irish peasant family—and its struggles to survive in its new home.[85]

Set at a historical remove from the tragedy of starvation and disease that ravaged mid-nineteenth-century Ireland, *A Moon for the Misbegotten* nevertheless retains several conventions Dion Boucicault successfully employed in such plays as *The Colleen Bawn*: a home imperiled by the peasant's inability to pay rent, a landlord threatening eviction, comic relief provided by hard-drinking and verbally dexterous stage Irishmen, the loyalty of these Irishmen to their friends, and much more. Here, the distinction between Irish melodrama of the Boucicauldian variety and nineteenth-century immigrant drama, the latter of which figures prominently in the genealogy of Miller's *A Memory of Two Mondays*, accrues interpretive significance. In the latter, the fate of the immigrant arriving in the city eager to find work and thereby progress into a *new* life drives the plot; in the former, retention of an *old* life symbolized by the family home and the centrality of the melodramatic heroine—innocent, pursued, and endangered—predominates. There are, needless to say, enormous differences between Eily O'Connor in *The Colleen Bawn* and Josie Hogan in *A Moon for the Misbegotten*, between Hardress

Cregan and Jim Tyrone, and between the intrepid Myles-na-Coppaleen and Phil Hogan, however similar their thirsts and nimble wits.

Raleigh is hardly alone in recognizing O'Neill's atavistic "turn" in his later plays, one registered in his setting *A Touch of the Poet* a century earlier complete with pre-Famine immigrant Con Melody's inebriate pretensions to nobility and his revulsion at anything resembling the peasantry: his daughter Sara's exaggerated brogue, which she deploys in a calculated fashion as a response to his especially bad behavior, for example, and his wife Nora's once beautiful black hair, now "*streaked with gray*" and straggling "*in untidy wisps.*"[86] In truth, however, it is not Nora's fading beauty that sickens him, but rather her association with the peasantry. When she comes near him early in the play, a "*sudden revulsion of feeling convulses his face. He bursts out with disgust, pushing her away from him*": "For God's sake, why don't you wash your hair? It turns my stomach with its stink of onions and stew!" (42). His equally sudden apology for this cruelty, however, cannot disguise his disgust with a certain class of Irish immigrant. So, when Nora misconstrues his embittered wish that America will one day "drive the English from the face of the earth [for] their shameless perfidy" as a polemic advocating the freedom of Ireland, Melody contemptuously asks, "Ireland? What benefit would freedom be to her unless she could be freed from the Irish?" (40). Hardly a Robert Emmet who loves his country and his peasant neighbors equally, Melody and his anti-Hibernianism provide a counter to Jim Tyrone's philo-Hibernianism (and that of his father, for that matter). Moreover, given his predilection for mirrors that metaphorize his internal division as, alternatively, admired Byronic hero and despised shebeen keeper, Melody and his narcissism diametrically oppose the generosity and self-sacrificing heroism of a Robert Emmet or Edmund Dantès.

Jim in *A Moon for the Misbegotten* is as fully capable of displays of instantaneous revulsion and disgust as Con Melody, but the specific objects of these feelings are different from those that instantiate Melody's truly excessive feelings. In his fantasy construction of Josie Hogan as a virginal colleen and peasant ideal, for instance, Jim will not countenance any "rough stuff" from her that implies sexual promiscuity, questionable "Broadway" experience, or any semblance of self-deprecation. When she insists upon drinking bourbon with him, "*a strange bitter disgust*" fills his eyes and his voice hardens with "*repulsion*": "I've slept with drunken tramps on too many nights!" he exclaims, as he knocks a tumbler of liquor from her hand (78). A complicated composite picture—part earth mother with large and nurturing breasts, part peasant colleen—Josie also resembles Christine Ell, a voluptuous woman whom O'Neill used as a model for several characters.[87] But the thrust of this comparison of Melody's and Tyrone's surplus and decidedly negative affect is both to recall this element of the immigrant subjectivity and to suggest an allo-Hibernianism comparable to allo-Semitism: the Irish, in this case, as figures of striking ambivalence.

The composite picture of Harder, the Hogans' antagonist in *A Moon for the Misbegotten*, similarly attains new complexity when placed in the context of the Jewish-Irish unconscious. Harder is an extension of the character alluded to as Harker in *Long Day's Journey*, the blue-blooded adversary of a tenant named Shaughnessy, a precursor of Phil Hogan, the "wily Shanty mick" who is always complaining and never pays his rent until threatened with eviction (22). At the same time, James Tyrone Sr. cannot conceal his considerable pleasure at hearing from Edmund that Shaughnessy has won a "glorious victory" over the Standard Oil millionaire, a "king of America," in a dispute over the Irishman's pigs breaking through a fence and wallowing in Harker's pond (23). Before considering the "serious trouble" Shaughnessy might cause him and lapsing into irascibility, Tyrone *"Admiringly"* exclaims, "The damned old scoundrel! By God, you can't beat him!" (25).

A Moon for the Misbegotten references this episode, adding political dimension to the wealthy antagonist of the Irish peasant tenant farmer. For Harder is not merely a representative of the corporate class depicted by Rice and Odets, complete with their affluence and privilege; he also represents the defeat that so many popular audiences in the nineteenth century longed to celebrate: the trouncing of the English by the Irish. Harder appears at the ramshackle Hogan home late in act 1, a somber and less entertaining version of O'Casey's Stoke and Poges. Attired in a *"beautifully tailored English tweed coat"* and *"immaculately polished English riding boots"* complete with riding crop in hand, Harder is *"naturally lethargic, a bit stupid."* His Ivy League education, affluence, and pampered life as a "country gentleman" have rendered him no match for the aggressive wit and tag team roistering of the Hogans. Indeed, as the stage directions specify, *"It would be hard to find anyone more ill-equipped for combat with them"* (36), unless one ventured back to the nineteenth century and characters like the Honorable Smith in Augustin Daly's *Horizon*, who feels he can "manage" interactions with Native Americans because he has read Fenimore Cooper. And to make certain audiences don't miss the English-Irish connotations of this confrontation, Hogan alludes pointedly to that "English bastard" Simpson in Harder's employ and promises Harder he will think "He's the King of England at an Irish wake" before he's through with him (41). In this scene, then, O'Neill offers a highly charged satisfaction for his audience similar to that in *Purple Dust*: a performance of Irishness that can not only defeat the English, but also secure the victory of the poor over the idle and self-indulgent rich who can afford to pay $10,000 for property worth far less simply to get their way. As Harder retreats ingloriously from the field of discursive battle, Hogan cannot suppress his glee: "O Jaysus, this is a great day for the poor and oppressed. I'll do no more work! I'll go down to the Inn and spend money and get drunk as Moses" (42). After all, doesn't everyone know that Moses was a hard-drinking Irish tenant farmer?

So, as it turns out, were Eugene O'Neill and Edmund Tyrone. Even after all their reading of Marx and Nietzsche, their study of Freudian and Jungian psychoanalysis as manifested in such plays as *Strange Interlude* (1928) and *Mourning Becomes Electra* (1931), and their commitment to modernist thought as represented by Strindberg and Nietzsche, Zola and Stendhal, neither author nor character could quite leave his father's Ireland and melodrama behind—or the romantic heroism of *Monte Cristo* and *Robert Emmet*, for that matter, both of which undergo massive revision in *A Touch of the Poet*. Nineteenth-century Irish theater and the socialism O'Neill discussed with Mike Gold drinking in the Hell Hole in New York so many years previously never left him. In the later years of his career, when he wrote his most significant work, he remained as drunk as Moses with both.

The New Wandering Rocks

[In the "Wandering Rocks" episode] Bloom has withdrawn to the centre in every sense: at the city's physical centre, and at the central point of the novel, he is brought to full awareness of the nub of his psychic and bodily concerns. In the city's sanctum, the undercover porn-shop, *Sweets of Sin* is produced from behind the curtain, like the ark of the tabernacle.

—CLIVE HART

I've always admired these two sentences written by the distinguished Joyce scholar Clive Hart, which both reassert the centrality of the tenth episode of *Ulysses* to the novel and posit hiddenness, secrecy, and a paradoxical sanctity/profanity as central to the "nub" of Leopold Bloom's psyche.[1] The moment to which Hart refers is well known to readers of the novel: at Molly's request, Bloom has returned to a seedy Dublin bookshop to inquire about the availability of titles like *Sweets of Sin*, a sexually explicit novel she has enjoyed. The shop's wares, including such titillating possibilities as *The Awful Disclosures of Maria Monk* (1836), are both "undercover" and shelved "behind the curtain": secret *and* hidden, these texts are doubly concealed from the bright lights of orthodoxy and repression. Yet, in Hart's trope this subversive site also constitutes a profane ark of the tabernacle, its salacious diversions analogues of the ark's sacred relics. The "centre" of Dublin and of *Ulysses* is thus spiritual and sexual, psychical and bodily, Christian and explicitly Jewish—and it is represented in Joyce's chapter as both inert (a rocky "nub") and constantly in motion ("wandering"). It is also, it must be said, a little strange, for more than pornography is available for purchase at this site; in fact, in addition to finding naughty stories of young nuns compromised sexually by priests in confessionals, customers can thumb the pages of Aristotle's *Masterpieces* to gaze at "crooked botched print" and plates of "infants cuddled in a ball in bloodred wombs" (*U* 10.585–86). Or acquire Leopold von Sacher-Masoch's *Tales of the Ghetto*—Joyce and the Blooms have read Masoch's (in)famous *Venus in Furs* (1870)—which connects the Jewish community with the sexual and trans-gressive, even though these short narratives, however enticing and attractive many of their central female characters, are hardly scandalous and have been accurately described as philo-Semitic.[2] Such titles meet with the approbation of a grotesque bookseller, with his "ruined mouth," reeking breath, and abys-mal grammar: "Them are good ones" (*U* 10.595), he tells Bloom in a subliterate promotion of his perversely sacred library.

Paradoxically, the "nub" of Bloom's "psychic and bodily concerns" is also inher-ently performative (wandering) and evocative of the tropes of Irish Jewishness exemplified by the writers and texts considered here, all of which relocate us from the American stage to the more contemporary circum–North Atlantic world. So, for example, although Bloom is not so much a Jew skulking in the shadows like the villain in Augustin Daly's *Leah* or one perpetuating a sophisticated deception like the impostor-protagonist of John Banville's *Shroud* (2002), Joyce seems to insist on Bloom's subjective plurality: Jew and Christian, Leopold Paul and Paula, native Irishman and foreigner at one and the same time. Banville's Axel Vander in *Shroud* embodies a similar plurality of selves and is a distinguished theoreti-cian of this very interior construction. Stealing his name from a friend who had died mysteriously some half-century earlier—Had he been killed fighting in the resistance against the Nazis? Had he committed suicide over a "love affair gone wrong"?[3]—Vander has pursued an academic career resolutely denying the exis-tence of any "sticky imago" that resided within and defined him:

> I spent the best part of what I suppose I must call my career trying to drum into those who would listen . . . the simple lesson that there is no self: no ego, no precious individual spark breathed into each one of us by a bearded patriarch in the sky, who does not exist either. (18)

Instead, selfhood is realized through "gaudy and increasingly chaotic perfor-mances of who and what" Vander is, a quotidian theatrics "carried on with-out interval" (35).[4] Through "poses" and "brilliant pretenses," he impressed his late wife Magda, whom he wooed in New York's Lower East Side (40), though such performances reduced him, he thought, to something that was "not so much a person as a contingency, misplaced and adrift in time" (44). Yet, like the titles in Joyce's bookshop and unlike the more extreme subjec-tive contingency of a character like Nathan Zuckerman in Philip Roth's *The Counterlife* (1986), who claims, "I am a theater and nothing more than a the-ater,"[5] crouching in the nub of Vander's "contingency" is something central and secret: "The past, my own past . . . is still there, a secret chamber inside me, like one of those sealed rooms, behind a false wall, where a whole family might live in hiding for years" (151).

In Vander's case, a Jew (and perhaps his entire family) cowers inside his myriad displays of selfhood. But, at the beginning of Banville's novel, his closely guarded secret may be exposed, as a young Irishwoman, Cass Cleave, has discovered his past and arranged a meeting with him in Turin. Vander is anxious about this prospect and contemplates its more ominous consequences, although he need not have been, as he takes the "child-woman" to bed almost as soon as his "old friend libido stirred anew" (63). As this assignation suggests, Cass had actually initiated the meeting not to ruin him, but rather to inaugurate a process of caring for him, marshaling "all of her energy and attention" toward him (191). As spring turned into summer in the three-odd months of their tryst, she became "his colleen, his Cathleen Ni Houlihan, his wild Irish girl" (199)—and he grew to love her although he knew from their first meeting that something was terribly wrong. For, like him, she had a Jew speaking in a multitude of voices inside of her head; researching mental disorders, he discovered that the cause of Cass's illness was Mandelbaum's syndrome: "Mr. Mandelbaum occupies a redoubt three-quarters of the way toward the bad end of the scale between manic depression and full-blown dementia" (202). In fact, Mandelbaum had taken up residence in Cass long before this, as her father recounts in *Eclipse* (2000), producing a symptomology often confused with epilepsy; in *Eclipse*, she returned from a frightening seizure "with the bloody froth still on her mouth" and a look on her face dominated by an "unearthly smile."[6] Things get worse in *Shroud*, as Cass's already troubled psyche deteriorates into a "battleground where uncontainable forces waged constant war" leading her, pregnant and desperate, to suicide (203). Prior to this, Vander had hoped to banish the "interloper" Mandelbaum; he foolishly believed that a good "Herr Doktor Jungfreud" could cure Cass, allowing her to "deliquesce" in his arms in a union of "desire and adoration" (209). Throwing herself off a cliff near the novel's conclusion, Cass could not be saved, and Vander reflected darkly upon the implications of the nightmare: "in her belly there had already sprung the new beginnings of my people, my lost people. It was as simple as that. . . . Oh, fond old man! How could I have thought this world would allow for such redemption?" (240).

My project in this chapter is twofold: first, to sketch the contours of psychical architectures like Axel's and Cass's, structures that, while at times resembling Vander's pastiches of postmodern subjectivity, hearken back to an older model of uncanny Irish-Jewish and Jewish-Irish relationships: the putative Irish identity of Abie Levy and Jewish identity of Rosemary Murphy in *Abie's Irish Rose*, for example.[7] This secret Jewishness or Irishness informs subjectivity and selfhood in oddly familiar, even strange ways. In an expression of agency that seemingly contradicts his more philosophically nuanced view of the human subject, Axel believes himself capable of cobbling together a persona from scraps of mass culture, as he boasts when relating that he "*chose* to present" himself in postwar New York "as a character out of the pictures, a fat cigarette lolling in my lips and a tumbler of bourbon at my elbow" (37; my emphasis). This "intellectual as tough guy" makes a cameo appearance in this chapter in the brawling escapades of Norman Mailer and Brendan Behan. But the self as simulation is less important to my concerns here than the topics introduced so many pages ago: the Freudian uncanny, allo-Semitism and allo-Hibernianism, performance, and excess. Put another way, how has the hostility between the Irish and Jews—as well as their unusual affinity for each other—that shaped immigrant melodrama of the nineteenth century, tenement fiction, and modern American drama continued to inform texts produced later in the twentieth and twenty-first centuries? Second, as this meditation progresses, subjectivity and affect recede into the background as the diasporic parallels of the Jews and Irish outlined by Professor MacHugh in *Ulysses*, particularly their histories as a dominated people similarly seeking freedom and independence, take center stage. How might a multidirectional reading contribute to a greater understanding of both? How is collective memory inflected by the construction of analogies between the Famine and the Holocaust—or between the "Troubles" in late twentieth-century Northern Ireland and the Holocaust? In this way, the uncanny in all of its furtiveness and eeriness, its ambivalence and intensity, surrenders the limelight to more historical and collective considerations; yet, at times, these very histories also function as psychical remainders, indelible and determinative of feeling, nubs amid contingencies.

Like Bloom at the bookshop in "Wandering Rocks," then, the narrative that follows considers various writers and texts—at times in small, floating narrative sections—from the late twentieth century and the beginning of our own, attempting to illuminate the determinative presence of the Irish-Jewish unconscious, the uncanny, and the dreadful grandeur of more recent writing. And, finally, this odyssey ends more or less where it began: with the experiences of later immigrants to America and their resemblance to new arrivals at Ellis Island decades earlier. In most cases, the tenements are gone, but the diasporic subject—with all of her internal fractures, affective intensities, and popular cultural investments—remains.

Brendan Behan, Borscht Belt Comedian

New York humour is largely an Irish-Jewish creation.[8]

—ULICK O'CONNOR, *BRENDAN BEHAN*

It was inevitable that Brendan should fall in love with New York, for it was nearer to his dream of the Never-Never Land than he would ever find elsewhere. . . . It was inevitable, too, that the Americans should fall in love with Brendan.[9]

—RAE JEFFS, *BRENDAN BEHAN, MAN AND SHOWMAN*

One of the "gentlemen" of the press writing for *Time* magazine reported the chaotic events of the evening this way:

> Washington's scruffy Ambassador Theatre, normally a pad for psychedelic frolics, was the scene of an unscheduled scatological solo last week in support of the peace demonstrations . . . .
>
> Slurping liquor from a coffee mug, [he] faced an audience of 600, most of them students. . . . "I don't want to grandstand unduly," he said, grandly but barely standing.
>
> It was one of the few coherent sentences. Mumbling and spewing obscenities as he staggered about the stage . . . [he] described his search for a usable privy on the premises.[10]

The obscenity-spewing guzzler in this passage is *not* Brendan Behan, but Norman Mailer on the eve of the march on the Pentagon on October 21, 1967 in protest of America's role in the Vietnam War. Among the estimated 50,000–100,000 protestors were peace activists, academics, public figures like Dr. Benjamin Spock, poets Robert Lowell and Allen Ginsberg, and hundreds of young men who threw their draft cards in a bag that was then dumped on the doorstep of the US government. What began as a peaceful demonstration eventually devolved into confrontations with US marshals armed with tear gas, rifles, and fixed bayonets. Nearly seven hundred people were arrested, Mailer among them. The night before, however, it appeared that he might not be welcomed by this predominantly younger crowd of aspiring demonstrators. As the reporter for *Time* observed, Mailer stumbled about the stage, drunk and barely coherent, when he experienced a kind of epiphany. His earlier deployment of an Irish brogue elicited laughter and, referring to himself in the third person, "He was beginning to recognize for the first time that bellowing without a mike demanded a more forthright style—'I shall now *engage* in confession.' More Irish accent. (He blessed Brendan Behan for what he had learned from him)."[11] More laughter followed, and occasional booing. And when Mailer, not necessarily renowned for his keen sense of comedic timing, procrastinated in delivering the verbal goods the audience wanted, several screamed, "The confession. The confession!" Thanks to Behan's tutelage, he had managed to gain their attention—and win their approbation.

The next morning greeted Mailer with more than a hangover, however, as cultural critic and former editor of the *Partisan Review* Dwight Macdonald, on the podium with him the night before, asked if he had read newspaper accounts of the evening. He had, he admitted, and sandwiched in the accounts was a "short but cutting reference to Macdonald" that Mailer found diverting. Mildly amused himself but also chafed at the slight, Macdonald believed Mailer had been transformed into a veritable "hero" at his expense, and he didn't like it: "Yes, it's all very funny . . . for *you*, my God it is, you stand up there and carry on like some absolute *hybrid* between William Burroughs and Brendan *Behan*, and don't even let Lowell and me *speak*."[12] This moment in *The Armies of the Night*, like Mailer's epiphany about comic performance the night before, suggests the extent of Brendan Behan's penetration of the cultural imaginary of postwar America. For more than three years after his death in 1964, Mailer turned to Behan's comic technique, and his audience clamored for more Irish "confession"; further, intellectuals like Macdonald immediately recognized Behan's haunting of Mailer's performance, however hybridized it might have been by the added suggestion of figures from the Beat movement like Burroughs. This connection between Behan and the Beats was made well before Macdonald alluded to it, particularly by Mailer, and Behan knew and admired figures like Ginsberg, whom he first met in New York in 1959 (see figure 5.1).

But Behan shared more—and much less—with postwar American culture than the Bohemian predilections and iconoclastic politics of the Beat movement; hence, he is as misplaced in this context as he is in the slippery notion of the Irish literary tradition in which he is inevitably situated, albeit often in rather different places. As John Brannigan outlines, Behan has been variously described as the heir to Joycean linguistic invention, as a cross between Dion Boucicault and Sean O'Casey, and as the practitioner of an irreverent strain of Irish writing represented by Oliver St. John Gogarty,

FIGURE 5.1 *Peter Orlovsky and Allen Ginsberg with Brendan Behan and Beatrice Behan, poets, playwright, and painter, New York, September 28, 1960*
Photograph by Richard Avedon. @The Richard Avedon Foundation.

Shaw, and Oscar Wilde.[13] While all of these comparisons are illuminating, none seems quite adequate. Casting Behan as a Beat writer is fraught with its own set of difficulties, especially if one agrees with aspersions like Norman Podhoretz's of those "Know-Nothing Bohemians" Ginsberg, Burroughs, and especially Jack Kerouac. For Podhoretz, these "new" Bohemians evinced a kind of "know-nothing populist sentiment" in which "whores" and "junkies" were viewed as more interesting than most educated and professional people (as the former are in Behan's *The Hostage*). In this indictment the Beats are little more than epigones of the literary bohemians of the 1920s and 1930s (T. S. Eliot, Ezra Pound, Ernest Hemingway); and perhaps most seriously, the Beat "predilection for bop language" and jazz signals a contempt for "rational discourse" and language itself. "To be articulate," in Podhoretz's snide ventriloquizing, "is to admit that you have no feelings (for how can real feelings be expressed in syntactical language?)." And then there is the "darker side" of this essentially solipsistic enterprise that privileges sensation and excess, "violence and criminality, main-line drug addiction and madness."[14]

Such characterizations of or analogies to Behan are, alternatively, incisive—what Anthony Cronin terms Behan's "voracious appetite" for "public notice," for example, defines his own solipsism[15]—and wildly distortive, perhaps none more so than the charges of anti-intellectualism and inarticulateness. On the contrary, Behan was acutely aware of literary and theatrical traditions and greatly respected such figures as Oscar Wilde—to whose grave in Paris he and Cronin "made a pilgrimage" where they "asked his protection on our knees by the graveside" (Cronin, 43)—O'Casey, and Samuel Beckett. And, far from being inarticulate, although he was often reduced to such by alcohol abuse in the last years of his life, he became a television celebrity in North America because of his skills in the art of conversation and his vivid use of language, appearing on two of the early 1960s' most popular and controversial shows, *The Jack Paar Show* and David Susskind's *Open End*. His candor on such shows was often provocative as, for example, his pronouncement on Canadian television that Lord Beaverbrook was an "idiot" and that Englishmen, who typically lived "dull" and "rather mean" existences at home, flourished in colonial environments like Africa through their unprincipled use of "arms and armaments." In the same remarks, he compared English colonial exploitation to German domination of Poland and Czechoslovakia during the war, a comparison of ruthlessness and brutal force to which I shall return later.[16]

However imperfect, analogical theses often inform the best cultural criticism, for without it such basic concepts as discrete periods of artistic achievement or discernible aesthetic "movements"—romanticism, aestheticism, absurdism—would be literally inconceivable. And so the seemingly fanciful analogy between Brendan Behan and Borscht Belt comedians might also prove of explanatory value, though the notion suffers from some obvious liabilities.

Behan was *not* a professional "stand-up" comedian, although he possessed the wit and performative skills to succeed as one, as he proved countless times in Dublin pubs and onstage at the Blue Angel in New York to an apprecia- tive audience that included Shelley Berman, who in fact *was* a Borscht Belt comedian.[17] Behan therefore was not a headliner at popular resort nightclubs in the Catskill Mountains located some one hundred miles north-northwest of New York City known as the "Borscht Belt" because of its clientele of Jews of Eastern European heritage. At the height of its popularity in the 1950s and 1960s, the "Borscht Belt" included nearly a thousand lodging houses, smaller hotels, and swanky hotel-resorts complete with restaurants, golf courses, and nightclubs where such entertainers as Jerry Lewis, Milton Berle, Henny Youngman, Alan King, Totie Fields, Joey Bishop, Buddy Hackett, and scores of others honed their skills. This summer holiday destination became popu- lar earlier in the century, offering working- and middle-class Jews an escape from the stifling heat of the city. Impecunious vacationers rented *cookaleins* (or *kuchaleyns*), rooms with a kitchen for the renters' use, while more afflu- ent visitors enjoyed sprawling hotels with planned social activities like those depicted in the film *Dirty Dancing* (1987).[18] As Stefan Kanfer notes, two tech- nological advances in the mid-1950s—television and affordable air condition- ers—"conspired to change the Catskills forever." That is, "guests who [spent] good money to watch comedians and singers in the resorts cold now see them for free in their own bedrooms."[19] And that bedroom was longer sweltering and unbearable in the "dog days" of summer. By the 1980s, the Borscht Belt would be reduced to one-tenth of its former glory.

When Behan returned to New York in the spring of 1960, however, like many Borscht Belt comedians, he quite quickly became an even more lumi- nous star, in part, because television was emerging as a mass cultural force. *The Ed Sullivan Show* (1948–71), a variety program that ran for an hour on Sunday night, became *the* venue for singers, comedians, and especially emer- gent music groups like The Beatles, whom Sullivan introduced to screaming teenyboppers in 1964. Media historians also discuss Sullivan's promotion of Broadway musicals, the songs and choreography from which were performed to eager audiences across the country. But he similarly booked comedians rising to prominence, like the husband–wife team of Jerry Stiller and Anne Meara, who appeared some thirty-seven times between 1962 and 1969. Stiller remembers a partially improvised skit they performed of a young Jewish man matched by a computer on a first date with an Irish-American Catholic girl; predictably enough, the skit humorously magnified the inevitable miscom- munication between the pair caused by their different backgrounds. Stiller and Meara's agents initially warned them that Sullivan would never allow the skit on his show, as the country was predominantly Protestant and wouldn't find Catholic and Jewish banter amusing, even though *Abie's Irish Rose* had been such an enormous hit a few decades earlier. The agents were wrong, and a year later Stiller and Meara took their act to London, where they met Behan's brother Dominic, who proclaimed their comedy "terrific."[20]

But why? Why was it terrific? What did Dominic Behan find so entertaining in Stiller and Meara's comedy? In part, I think, familiarly hyperbolic performances of Irishness and Jewishness that paralleled features of his brother's comic arsenal. I want to inventory and assess these devices, extrapolating from my epigraph from Ulick O'Connor that New York humor is and was largely an Irish-Jewish creation, in the process making three additional and complementary claims. One is that Behan's affection for New York originates not only in his frequent visits to Irish bars on Third Avenue to meet his many Irish-American buddies, as Michael O'Sullivan observes.[21] In fact, many Irish-Americans deplored Behan's public antics and were moved to write letters charging him with bringing "disgrace and shame" on them and recommending that he "just fuck off back to Dublin."[22] Rather, his affection for America in general and New York in particular is equally attributable to his interactions with his large cadre of Jewish-American friends and his uncanny familiarity with and enjoyment of aspects of Jewish culture. Here, I intend for "uncanny" to resonate in at least one of the ways Freud defines: namely, the point at which a paradoxical strange familiarity exists; the emergence of a comfortable and homely feeling (*heimlich*) in a surprising or foreign (*unheimlich*) setting, even to the point where something secret or concealed comes into the revealing glare of daylight. (Freud's observations about the fearful and eerie elements of the uncanny are clearly less relevant here.) My second assertion pertains to what O'Sullivan terms Behan's "bad boy image" in America, Britain, and Canada fostered by his appearances on television. Recent theorizing of celebrity make it possible, I think, to examine this image with a more fine-grained particularity, one result of which will return us to the kinship between Behan and Mailer, who shared, as many biographers have observed, a kind of notoriety that in some ways defined their relationship. Indeed, along with Podhoretz, Allen Ginsberg, Grove Press publisher Barney Rosset, bandleader Peter Duchin, and other celebrities, Behan was invited to the November 19, 1960, party where, in the early morning hours, Mailer stabbed his wife Adele.[23] He was arrested at the hospital where she was recovering, as he had been the week before on a disorderly conduct charge.[24] How is the kind of celebrity Mailer and Behan shared, what O'Connor terms their "odd notoriety," relevant to New York's Jewish-Irish humor?

Such questions underlie my third and perhaps largest claim that Behan, the inveterate entertainer, was more than an avatar of the nineteenth-century stage Irishman enacting an offensive "paddywhackery" that many Irish-Americans despised.[25] Rather, like Mailer that tumultuous night in Washington—and like the younger Henry Roth or his fictional counterpart Ira Stigman—he performed an eccentric Irish Jewishness or, if you prefer, a Jewish Irishness, a claim premised in part by the notion that both terms share performative qualities outlined in the opening chapter. In particular, as I mentioned earlier, both "Irish" and "Jew" can be uniquely used as a verb or verbal: to "Irish up" means to enliven something, thus implying an "action," "practice," or "performance,"[26] whereas "Jew" can be wielded disparagingly as in the infinitive phrase "to Jew down," or to haggle unscrupulously in commercial negotiation with the aim of increasing one's own profit. This stereotype has informed performances of Jewishness for centuries, as Behan knew and exploited in his radio play *The Big House* (1957). Moreover, in a sentiment attributed to his mother, Behan regarded Irishness as inherently performative, as the following exchange from owners of the "big house" implies:

> ANANIAS: You forget, Boadicea, that I am Irish. Like my ancestors before
> me, I was born here.
> MRS. BALDCOCK: If an ass is born in a stable, does that make it a horse?[27]

Here, Mrs. Baldcock, the haughty English owner of the big house, references Behan's notion that ethnic identity is not rooted in national origin, as his brother Dominic recalls when quoting the same familiar quip to Gainor Crist on the topic of Anglo-Irishmen:

> Anyway, there's no such animal as the Anglo/Irishman. . . . A bloke is either
> Irish or not Irish. It hasn't got much to do with where you were born; as my
> mother says, "because yeh were born in a stable doesn't make yeh a horse."[28]

If this is so, if performance corroborates or even defines ethnic identity, not the circumstances of one's birth, then Brendan Behan might be regarded as an honorary Borscht Belt comedian.

***

> [He'd] been a brain guy once in this city of New York, Jew York, Jew
> Cork Ireland.[29]
>
> —BENJAMIN APPEL, *THE DARK STAIN* (1943)

Brendan Behan's New York (1964), however often it has been disparaged,[30] clarifies that his New York was very much like the place punningly renamed in Benjamin Appel's crime novel, *The Dark Stain*—namely, an Irish-Jewish city. In the opening pages, Behan recalls eating lunch with Frank S. Hogan, the district attorney, and later dining with Bernie Hoffer, a "strong Zionist" who sent his family for a time to Israel. He alludes to the Protestant schoolteacher from Country Antrim who founded the annual St. Patrick's Day Parade, which in part began as a "piece of defiance against the Ku Klux Klan and other kinds of nutty people of that sort who didn't like the Irish very much at the time" (18). He goes with a Jewish friend to the Blue Angel, and, as they enter the club, Behan asks the Irish doorman if "many of our own" were inside, to which his friend responded, "I hate that expression, 'our own,' Brendan . . . Everyone is your own" (19). He considers the different ways Irish and Jews celebrate St. Patrick's Day and Yom Kippur, and buys an expensive coat at Brooks Brothers to attend a bar mitzvah. His account of the experience underscores his uncanny familiarity with "Jew York": "At the service I was beside Frank Loesser . . . and there was Ethel Merman, the singer, Paddy Chayefsky, the author of Marty and The Tenth Man, and numerous other notabilities, so I felt quite at home" (24).[31] Like Roth's Ira Stigman, who could "loll at ease" in Irish culture, or the older and irascible Edward Dahlberg surrounded by Irish friends, Behan felt unusually comfortable with Jewish friends and cultural practices. At the banquet hall after the bar mitzvah, he discovered that kosher cuisine was "cooked rather in the same way that the Catholic Irish used to cook it at home when I was a kid." And dancing the hora for the first time seemed to him "much the same thing" as dancing the sixteen-handed reel (25). He later recalls that modern Broadway emerges from a nineteenth-century theatrical repertory in which "fully fifty percent" were Irish plays, "good old melodrama," echoes from which still linger in the air (42).[32] For Behan, "Jew Cork," aka New York, was just that: an Irish-Jewish city and an enjoyable mélange of Irish and Jewish cultures, friends, events, and theatrical ghosts.[33]

Behan's affinity for Jewish culture—and the similar affinity Jewish entertainers like Groucho Marx and intellectuals like Mailer felt for him—has origins that predate the 1960s. In *Borstal Boy*, for example, Behan encounters three young Polish Jews and views them with sympathy and affection. Looking frozen from the cold, the shivering boys became refugees simply "because they are Jewish," leading him to quip, "Out of the frying pan into the refrigerator." Insulted by a Y. P. (young prisoner), one of the Poles "gave the English fellow a good look" with the result that the Y. P. "looked away first." Such grit (chutzpah?) went a long way with the young Behan, motivating him to direct an oddly phrased, but sincere, prayer in their direction: "Ah well, God is good and His Mother is very decent, and it won't be long before the three of yous are burning your bellies beneath the sun of David."[34] In *Dead as Doornails*, Anthony Cronin recalls visits to Ralph Cusack's house in County Wicklow overlooking the banks of the Avoca River where Cusack, married to a Jewish woman, inveighed against anti-Semitism, a veritable "capital charge" in his household (24). Behan required no such homily, however, as his equanimity would not allow him to embrace this prejudice; and like Douglas Hyde in the 1890s and O'Casey in the 1930s, he grew to regard Jews and Irishmen as enjoying an especially close kinship.[35]

Anti-Semitism, and the stereotyping that supports it, is subtly introduced and quickly collapsed in *The Big House* when Chuckles Genockey, a "man from the slums of Dublin that never had as much land as would fill a window-box" (*Behan's Island* 99), is hired as an agent to preside over the sale of the big house (Tonesollock House) Mrs. Baldcock can no longer abide. Always eager to make a little extra money, Chuckles and his Cockney partner Angel strip lead material from the roof of the house and sell it through a fence, an Irish Jew from Dublin known as "Eyes of Green." When Angel responds that he has never heard of an Irish Jew, Chuckles replies, "Well you don't notice, I suppose. Most Dublin Jews have an accent like mine, only a bit worse" (104), implying that the Jewish go-between sounds *more* Irish than he does (perhaps an Irishman lurks secretly in him?). And when the negotiation over the value of the "bluey," the pile of scrap Chuckles has pilfered, begins, the inevitable disagreement over its value has to be settled, Chuckles setting its value at 100 quid and the fence dismissing the sum as too high:

> EYES OF GREEN: I say eighty [pounds], what's the difference?
> CHUCKLES: A score of pounds.
> EYES OF GREEN: Split it. I'll give you ninety.
> CHUCKLES: Done, and I hope the odd ten nicker chokes you.
> EYES OF GREEN: That's real decent of you. (*Counts money.*) Here you are. And many thanks for your Christian sentiments.
> CHUCKLES: *Shalom alechim*, Eyes of Green.
> EYES OF GREEN: *Slawn latt*, Chuckles. (105)

Two elements of this dialogue limn the argument I'm attempting to make. One is that, when they weren't derogated as cheating naive gamblers or swindling the unsuspecting by selling them worthless goods at inflated prices, characters in many nineteenth- and twentieth-century texts fostered the stereotype of Jews' penchant for haggling over prices and unfairly seizing the advantage in such negotiations.[36] Behan's scene rejoins these representations. The second pertains to the notion of surrogation so central to performance: that is, an actor on stage, a comedian performing a skit, or an inebriated Mailer promising an Irish "confession" takes the place of someone else in a crucial substitution. At the end of this exchange, Chuckles expresses a traditional courtesy in Hebrew ("peace be upon you"); Eyes of Green, in Irish ("health to you"). The Irish thief is a surrogate of the Jewish fence and vice versa.

So, in that tense moment on the stage of the Ambassador Theatre, why did Mailer silently bless Behan? What had he learned from him? Several things, not the least of which is Mailer's assumption of a part that Behan had honed to perfection, what, returning to Sharon Marcus, might be termed a variety of "impudent celebrity." Theorizing celebrity through the careers of Oscar Wilde and Sarah Bernhardt, Marcus's thesis is equally helpful in providing a context for Behan's conquest of America in the early 1960s. For Marcus, "celebrity" and "fame" do not describe the same cultural status or phenomenon. While fame implies a kind of "permanent renown," something "genuine," "masculine," and "dignified," celebrity—one might say *mere* celebrity—connotes the "factitious, superficial, and transient, associated with feminine artifice and the shameless public display of actions that should be kept private."[37] Because Marcus's distinction is rooted in the careers of Bernhardt and Wilde—the former, an object of salacious newspaper reporting about a myriad of lovers and a son born out of wedlock; the latter, involved in a sensationalized trial in part sparked by the allegation of being a sodomite—it is not difficult to understand her privileging of gender in these definitions. Mailer's and Behan's performances worked differently. Both tended to meld "shameless public display" (shame, again, as in nineteenth-century melodrama and tenement literature associated with the feminine) with a hypermasculinized pugnacity, humor with an edgy politics that effaced the line between propriety and audacity. Mailer's allusion to bathroom activities, for example, in his inebriate ranting the night before the Pentagon march and his frequent recourse to the retort "Fuck you" when hecklers accused him of being a "publicity hound" come immediately to mind. Like Wilde and America's Beat writers, impudent celebrities, as Marcus defines them, flaunt their "indifference to popular opinion and middle-class conventions."[38] Moreover, as Anthony Cronin observes, "Brendan was neither a woman nor a hysteric, but he constantly used the hysteric's weapon of a public scene from which only one party could be the gainer" (110). Mailer's "confession," then, might regarded be as complexly gendered, an amalgam of tough-guy bravado and a propensity for the kind of public spectacle associated with hysteria.

By performing the irreverent alcoholic to brawling perfection, Mailer and Behan also offered audiences the possibility that something naughty and wildly inappropriate might occur. They might just get arrested, then add texture to their iconoclastic personas by dissecting the very public imbroglio to reporters the next day. Violence might erupt, as in the cases of Mailer's attack of his wife or Behan's assault of detectives in Toronto after creating a scene in his hotel over the management's refusal to send a bottle of whiskey to his room. Indeed, such terms as "rumpus," "pandemonium," and "mêlée" inform Rae Jeffs's and other accounts of Behan's public behavior as his alcoholism worsened. In its own uncritical way, *The Catskill Mountain News*' retrospective of Behan's 1961 visit to the Catskills might have put it best under the headline "Famous Irish Playwright Found Haven Here Following Escapades": "Brendan Behan, controversial young Irish playwright and a famous personality because of a number of famous escapades in this country, and Mrs. Behan were four-day guests of Mr. and Mrs. Joseph Brill over the weekend."[39] This notice's pleonastic quality captures the point beautifully: Behan was *famous*, his "escapades" were *famous*, and with both him and Mailer the possibility of another *famous* adventure was only a drink or punch or arrest away. And American audiences in the 1960s just couldn't wait to see what might happen.

But perhaps the most significant lessons Mailer learned from Behan originate in well-established comic strategies, some of which were perfected in the nightclubs of the Borscht Belt. One of these involves a comedian playing his own ethnicity in hyperbolic and often self-deprecatory ways, exceeding comically the expectations of an audience by engagement with their knowledge of stereotypes, and another is performing another quite different ethnicity, as Mailer did when adapting a broad Irish brogue. Adept at both, Behan was clearly expert in exploiting the latter strategy, as Anthony Cronin recalls in *Dead as Doornails* as an original form of "*cabaret intime.*" This spontaneous form was composed of several conventions: the impersonation of a character or multiple characters different from the comedian himself; vocal changes designed to match the impersonations and, when required, an exaggerated dialect; grotesque humor; and a comic trajectory ranging from witty observation to satirical evisceration. These "miniature dramas" resembled playlets or skits; in one of these, "The Childhood of D. H. Lawrence," Behan played "scurrilous father," "anxious mother," and "patronizing" little boy "in various postures and with accents varying from broad Yorkshire to badly cultivated middle-class English." At times, minor properties, costumes, and exaggerated gestures would enhance the performance, as when Behan employed a towel as a veil in "Maud Gonne at the Microphone." Cronin adds that, where possible, these set playlets were "embellished" by songs and the melding of patriotic or left-wing political sentiment with "scurrilous comic pieces" (17–18). Mailer's improvised "confession" replicates this *cabaret intime*, with all of its ridiculous surrogation and exaggerated dialect, punctuated by profanity and impudent indifference to middle-class values.

Behan and Borsht Belt entertainers had other tricks up their sleeves, too, the most provocative of which was the laceration of historical pieties, including the worst tragedies in modern times for both the Irish and Jews. So, in *Borstal Boy*, Behan recalls his father's irreverent redaction of the song Phil Hogan sings in O'Neill's *A Moon for the Misbegotten*:

> Oh, the praties they were small over here,
> Oh, the praties they were small over here,
> Oh, the praties they were small, but we ate them skin and all
> They were better than fugh-all over here. (72)

The elder Behan's wife used to scold him that it was a "disgrace and a shame" to be "making game" of his countrymen who suffered during Black Forty-Seven, but the younger Behan couldn't help but be amused: "But honest to Jesus, you'd have to laugh at my old fellow" who would insert such desacralizing lines as "fugh-all" into texts associated with an event like the Famine (72). Equally undaunted in wresting humor from historical nightmares, Jewish comics of the Cold War years like Alan King worked allusions to Adolf Hitler and Nazis into their stand-up routines or, in Mel Brooks's case, into the song "Springtime for Hitler" from his musical *The Producers* (1968). King, for example, couldn't resist the temptation to needle fellow comedian Don Rickles by linking him to Nazi Germany in outrageous ways. In an uproarious "roast" at New York's famous Friars' Club in 1968, King mockingly praised Rickles for displaying such a precocious writing ability at a very young age that he was retained as a ghost writer to "punch up" *Mein Kampf*.[40] At another roast of Johnny Carson, King referred to Rickles as the "Heinrich Himmler" of comedy.

Yet another strategy, one conventional to the *cabaret intime*, featured self-deprecations of "Irishness" or "Jewishness" and the exaggeration of each's foibles. So, in one memorable line from *The Big House*, the Baldcocks' butler, Dionysus O'Looney, exclaims, "Sure God help the Irish, if it was raining soup, they'd be out with forks" (98); and the same source of laughter emerges from innumerable exchanges between such comic creations as Mrs. Brennan and Mr. Crippen in Behan's columns in the *Irish Press* in the early 1950s. Similarly, many Borscht Belt stars like self-proclaimed "Ultimate Jew" and former rabbi Jackie Mason achieved tremendous success lampooning the vicissitudes of Jewish marriages and laughing at Jews' mechanical inability, obsessions, and emotional insecurities: their incredulity at the results of weighing themselves; their recourse to "nose jobs" to change their appearance; their need for psychiatric or psychoanalytic help, especially about sex; and much, much more.[41]

Performing Irishness or Jewishness involved all of these strategies and comedic possibilities for "confession."[42] Behan knew them all, enacting them in performances that Americans loved and remembered—and one of his many admirers was Norman Mailer, who, for one night anyway, stood as a surrogate Irish comedian.

***

An animated correspondence spanning some five issues of the *New Statesman* in the winter of 1962 motivated Behan to perform his Irish Jewishness (no hyphens here, which he could abide) in a more polemical way. Reviewing Cecil Woodham-Smith's *The Great Hunger* in an essay entitled "Genocide," A. J. P. Taylor ignited a colloquy to which Leonard Woolf contributed twice, accusing Taylor of "whitewashing" Hitler and the Nazis by alluding to Ireland in 1846 as a "Belsen." Supporting Taylor's positing of this analogy and writing somewhat belatedly to the *New Statesman* in December, Behan challenged several of Woolf's contentions, one of which concerned the relationship between working-class Irishmen and Brits. And there was no question that Behan fully endorsed the multidirectional memorial operation of juxtaposing what he regarded as genocidal intentions of the British government in nineteenth-century Ireland to those of Hitler's government during the Holocaust of World War II:

> [The Famine] was, I will admit, a more primitive attempt at a final solution than Himmler's. At the same time, Lord Russel's [*sic*] score wasn't bad. He reduced the population [of Ireland] from eight million to four and a half in five years.[43]

In the same letter, Behan recalls meeting two Jewish boys "pinched" in New York for sending weapons to Israel in packets of clothing. He points out

that the Irish sergeant who arrested the boys called them "good kids," add-
ing that he wished "we had a few more like them in County Mayo in 1920."[44]
Analogy here drifts into a homology, one that adapts Professor MacHugh's
construction in *Ulysses* to a post–World War II politics: English imperialism
is to Nazi brutality as Irish victims of the Famine are to Jewish victims of the
Holocaust. A half-century later in *The Famine Plot: England's Role in Ireland's
Greatest Tragedy* (2012), Tim Pat Coogan, who eulogized Behan in the *Evening
Press* in 1964, revisits the controversy of Taylor's allusion to Ireland as a
Belsen, accusing Irish historians of a craven silence about anti-Irish prejudice
in London at the time of the Famine.[45] If New York humor is an Irish-Jewish
creation, victims of genocide in these examples are similarly Irish and Jewish
targeted simply because, like the Polish boys Behan meets at the borstal, they
are "who they are."

Great comedians like Behan often base their antics, their comic bits, on
such matters of historical substance, even of collective trauma. And, when
not honoring their self-imposed obligation to speak truth to power, comedians like Behan, Mel Brooks, Lenny Bruce, Jackie Mason, and Alan King
impudently challenge middle-class hypocrisies, as they perform identities that rub against the grain of orthodoxy and reveal truths many of us
don't really want to recognize. This includes the terms "Irish" and "Jewish,"
which are always available for self-deprecation, caricature, exaggeration,
and exchange. But the star power of impudent celebrities is irresistible and
people listen. Thus it is that an uncanny Borscht Belt comedian like Brendan
Behan emerged in Cold War America with his "fugh-all" abrasiveness and
brilliance.

Pinter's Irish Romance and the Hidden

> Ireland wasn't golden always, but it was golden sometimes and in
> 1950 it was, all in all, a golden age for me.[46]
>
> —HAROLD PINTER, "MAC" (1966)

The title of this section of my argument deliberately, and I hope productively,
conveys ambiguity. How are we to understand the phrase "Pinter's Irish
romance"? What precisely is "hidden," secret, or waiting to erupt? Answers to
the former question include, first, how Aidan Higgins's 1966 novel *Langrishe,
Go Down*, as adapted by Pinter for the BBC in 1978, functions as a peculiarly
Irish romance; second, how this teleplay, screened at a festival at Lincoln
Center in 2001 and later released as a feature film, constitutes what director
David Jones termed a "love poem to Harold's own time in Ireland";[47] and
last, how Ireland, in turn, has returned this affection, almost to the point of
claiming him as one of its own. Like my assertions of Behan as a Borscht Belt

comedian and of his uncommon feeling of ease in Jewish culture, one of the claims I want to make about Pinter involves a similar and uncanny mirroring: namely, that he is an Irish, or rather, Irish-Jewish writer even though he has no discernible lineage leading to an Irish ancestry. The fact that Pinter was born to lower-middle-class Jewish parents in London's East End should prove no impediment to my suggestion that he is, if not de facto then de jure, an Irish writer. Remember old witticism about horses and stables.

This gesture of asserting Pinter's Irishness or Immaculate Reconception is hardly unique. Anthony Roche, for example, has admirably outlined Pinter's long-standing affection for Ireland, and Ireland's requital of this affection, beginning with the three Dublin theater festivals devoted to his work in 1991, 1994, and 2005, the last of which also featured a star-studded celebration of his seventy-fifth birthday.[48] Roche develops his argument from two additional sources: Pinter's accounts of touring Ireland as a young actor in the early 1950s in a repertory company headed by the actor-manager Anew McMaster; and the well-documented influence on his writing of such Irish writers as William Butler Yeats, James Joyce, and—especially—Samuel Beckett, whom Pinter's widow Antonia Frasier acknowledges he "revered."[49] Roche archly notes that McMaster, much like the actor-manager Micheál MacLiammóir—famous for his portrayal of Iago in Orson Welles's 1952 film version of *Othello* and cofounder of Dublin's Gate Theatre—promoted himself as being born in Ireland, when in fact both he and MacLiammóir were actually English, born, respectively, in Birkenhead and London.[50] To my knowledge, Pinter never claimed an Irish birth, nor was his most important performance the "daily masquerade" of pretending to be Irish; thus, following Clive Hart's articulation of the bookshop in "Wandering Rocks" and the nub or center of Bloom's psychical concerns, I am merely making this assertion in his stead, one paralleling the concealed amalgam of Irishness and Jewishness in Behan, Joyce, Henry Roth, Elmer Rice, and others.

But why make this claim at all? What difference does it make to our readings of Pinter, modernism, or modernity? Some answers seem obvious. As Roche points out, the genealogy of several of Pinter's most enduring characters may be traced to his acting experiences in Ireland. Max and Mac in *The Homecoming* (1965) resemble the figure Pinter evokes in his memorial essay for McMaster entitled simply "Mac"; and, albeit more mysteriously, Goldberg and McCann in *The Birthday Party* (1958) emerge from the same imaginary gene pool. In particular, one passage in "Mac" illustrative of McMaster's ambivalence about Ireland evokes Max's similarly outrageous and paradoxical descriptions of his dead wife, Jessie. In "Mac," the older actor asks Pinter to look out at an Irish town from his hotel window: "Look out the window at this town. What a stinking diseased abandoned Godforsaken bog. . . . But you see one thing the Irish peasantry really appreciate[s] is style, grace and wit" ("Mac" 77). This striking instance of allo-Hibernianism—stink and disease on the one hand, an appreciation of grace and wit on the other—defines Max's bluster and Pinter's memories of midcentury Ireland.

And, on occasion in Pinter's oeuvre, as in the arrivals of Goldberg and McCann in *The Birthday Party* and the odd eruptions of Irish-Jewishness in his last play, *Celebration* (2000), a more direct and excessive Irish-Jewish dyad informs his writing and, at the same time in the latter case, is mapped onto modernity in surprising ways. *Celebration*, set in a contemporary and expensive London restaurant, features an intrusive waiter who regales diners with rambling and obscure monologues about his grandfather's long acquaintance with modernism's greatest artists: Yeats, Eliot, Pound, Picasso, Kafka, and—somewhat incongruously—the Three Stooges, recalling faintly Behan's friendships with Groucho and Harpo Marx. The waiter absurdly claims that his grandfather was James Joyce's "godmother,"[51] and then makes an even more bizarre statement concerning his grandfather's experience of Hollywood before and during the Big Studio era:

> Of course there was a very well established Irish Mafia in Hollywood in those days. And there was a very close connection between some of the famous Irish film stars and some of the famous Irish gangsters in Chicago. Al Capone and Victor Mature, for example. They were both Irish. Then there was John Dillinger, the celebrated gangster, and Gary Cooper, the celebrated film star. They were Jewish.[52]

These figures, quite clearly, were *not* Irish—or Jewish. What are we to make of this imagined Irish-Jewish mob of film icons and notorious gangsters? Is this notoriety related to that of Behan and Mailer—or to a Sarah Bernhardt–like sensational and "impudent" celebrity? Is domination of the cultural imaginary in general and the film industry in particular an inherently Irish-Jewish project, much as Tin Pan Alley–era popular music, modern American drama, and New York comedy of the Cold War era can be usefully regarded as largely Irish-Jewish creations?

Penelope Prentice poses several biographical possibilities as answers to such questions. For her, this monologue "may recall" Pinter's adolescence growing up in a Jewish neighborhood in London's East End, and may even possess "resonance" with the atrocities of World War II, a matter obliquely intimated in his earlier play *Ashes to Ashes* (1996) when a character recounts being led to trains and having her baby taken from her. Prentice also recalls Pinter's "youthful fascination with gangster films,"[53] making this allusion in *Celebration* a kind of homage to a film genre he greatly admired. It is also the case that while Victor Mature was of Italian heritage and Gary Cooper was the son of English immigrants, arguably the three greatest stars of gangster films during the studio era were Irish- and Jewish-American: James Cagney, George Raft, and Edward G. Robinson. Further, the fictive biographies of Hollywood icons, decontextualized radically in Pinter's texts, mix promiscuously with adversions to World Wars I and II: Matt's singing of a refrain from a well-known World War I marching song ("Wash me in the water / Where you washed your dirty daughter") and the waiter's references to the Austro-Hungarian Empire, the archduke, Benito Mussolini, and Winston Churchill.[54] Behind or underneath the dramatic action in a posh restaurant at the beginning of a new millennium, then—and existing somewhere in Matt's memory, as in Rebecca's in *Ashes to Ashes*—these collective traumas of the twentieth century reside, however remote they might be and *even if*, as Rebecca makes exceedingly clear, "Nothing has ever happened to me. Nothing has ever happened to any of my friends. I have never suffered. Nor have my friends."[55] A relative of Cass Cleave's Mr. Mandelbaum lurks somewhere beneath the discursive battleground of Pinter's text.

Another answer, perhaps, returns us to the premise that both "Irish" and "Jewish" are largely performances—from the stage Irishman to the stage Jew or exotic Jewess, from Behan at a bar mitzvah to Mailer at "confession." Moreover, imagined or hidden ethnicity functions widely as a motif in contemporary fiction and drama, and our challenge is to contemplate this motif's connection to modernity. Insofar as Pinter is concerned, we should not be surprised that Patrick Lonergan's *Theatre and Globalization: Irish Drama in the Celtic Tiger Era* (2009) begins not with the plays of Brian Friel, Marina Carr, or Frank McGuinness, but with the Gate Theatre's 2005 festival of Pinter's work and Jeremy Irons's reading of a passage from "Mac" in which Pinter characterizes every member of a 1950s' provincial Irish audience as being "drunk" at a performance of *Othello* in which he and McMaster starred ("Mac" 79). At one time Pinter's denigration of Irish playgoers might have cut too close to the bone of stereotype and thus incited conflict. But not now. Today, Lonergan speculates, the "contemporary Irish audience seems to identify much more with Pinter than [with] the Irish people he describes."[56] This identification may be construed as a result of globalization or a symptom of the increased homogeneity of a population bombarded by a World Wide Web of electronic simulacra.[57] Or, it may be that Pinter's Irish sensibilities have grown increasingly legible given the formidable roster of writers and literary characters whose Jewishness masks a hidden Irishness or vice versa: Irish figures who harbor a hidden and uncanny Jewishness that lurks in texts and performances alike.

Pinter seems to intimate this uncanny relationship in the interactions of Goldberg and McCann; further, *The Birthday Party* more generally operates through what are by now familiar motifs of psychical complexity, plurality of selfhood, and hiddenness. One clear direction in productions of the play over the past twenty-five years or so has been to underscore these elements while simultaneously reducing the play's gestures toward naturalism. So, in her 1989 production at the Classic Stage Company in New York, Carey Perloff paired *The Birthday Party* with Pinter's later *Mountain Language* (1988), using the juxtaposition as a way of reading the earlier text through the lens of the later. This pairing—and the casting strategy of reversing the roles of the same actors for both plays—allowed spectators a revised purchase of characters in *The Birthday Party*; so, for example, the same actor (Peter Riegert) played both Goldberg and the brutalized prisoner in *Mountain Language*. In this way, Perloff argues, it was possible not only to perceive bleakly comic moments in the later play, but also to blur the lines between oppressor and oppressed, victim and victimizer in the earlier play. The company's "first work" on *The Birthday Party* was the construction of "masks" to conceal "the emotional truths hidden below the surface," which meant, among other things, a blunting of such tenets of method acting as psychological training and the designing of a sparse, slightly raised setting with "absolutely minimalist furnishings."[58]

The 2013 production of *The Birthday Party* at Chicago's Steppenwolf Theatre operated similarly by emphasizing the play's uncanny psychical reality over a more realistic representation. To be sure, such recurrent descriptions of the play as a comedy of "menace," as one dominated by senses of claustrophobia and imminent danger, apply well to the Steppenwolf production. But like Perloff, Steppenwolf director Austin Pendleton and designer Walt Spangler elected to avoid insofar as it is possible most naturalistic detail; in fact, Spangler admits to researching "what a boarding-house room would literally look like" and then discarding almost everything he had learned. Instead of creating a place where one might even for a second feel "cozy" in a very "English-looking room," Spangler opted for something more like an elevated "boxing ring," one realized as such when Goldberg and McCann arrive (see figure 5.2). Surrounded by an audience on three sides enveloped in blackness, action occurred on a slightly canted and raised "alley configuration" that seemed to be floating uneasily in space.[59] Sitting on three sides of the action, the audience is unable to fully witness Goldberg and McCann's interrogation of Stanley, thus creating the sense of unease that we both know and yet do not fully know what is transpiring.

All of these staging devices helped deepen the anxiety generated by Goldberg and McCann's arrival. Like the composite pictures of dreams, Goldberg is either Nat or Simey or Benny, depending upon the moment and the story he is relating, several of which take on a decidedly Jewish inflection such as outings with his uncle on Shabbos and fond memories of his mother's gefilte fish. Similarly, McCann harbors nostalgic affection for Roscrea and Tullamore, and he asks Stanley, whom he refers to as a Judas who has "betrayed our land," "What about Drogheda?" to which Goldberg immediately adds, "You betray our breed."[60] There is, of course, no way to corroborate such accusations, but what *does* seem clear are Goldberg and McCann's uncanny relationship and the Irish Jewishness they represent: our "land" or Ireland becomes our Irish-Jewish "breed." The uncanniness continues in

FIGURE 5.2 *Goldberg (Francis Guinan) and McCann (Marc Grapey) from* The Birthday Party, *Steppenwolf Theatre, Chicago, Austin Pendleton, Director, January 24–April 28, 2013*

both Stanley and McCann's whistling of the tune "The Mountains of Morne," the lyrics of which trace the nostalgia of an immigrant in London who longs to return home. This eeriness devolves into weirdness when Lulu describes Goldberg as "the dead image of the first man I ever loved" (61), and when Goldberg asks McCann to blow air in his mouth, as if it were a revitalizing cocktail. Given a purposefully dehistoricized set with action on an elevated stage enveloped in darkness, scenes and lines like these only reinforce the psychical and affective resonance of Pinter's play; as a result, the violent eruptions of the Irish-Jewish unconscious find a space more rife with possibility and nuance than a narrowly circumscribed, photographically realistic setting could provide.

***

Aidan Higgins's *Langrishe, Go Down*, by contrast, is both as Irish as a novel gets and deeply rooted in the history of international modernity. Set in 1937–38 and in flashbacks to 1932, its dramatic action concerns the dissolution of a once affluent Kildare family, now represented by three middle-aged sisters living in the decrepit family home in which they were raised. As John Banville quips, Higgins tells "an old story in the annals of the landed Irish: the dog days are sweet but eventually all goes to the dogs."[61] As the novel begins, the surviving members of the Langrishe family include Helen and her younger sisters Lily and Imogen, the latter of whom at age thirty-nine was involved five years earlier in a torrid affair with a visiting German graduate student, Otto Beck, who occupied a cottage on the declining family estate, studied Irish folklore, and survived mostly by poaching and fishing. The action of the novel and film begins and ends in 1937–38, bookended by newspaper head- lines announcing, first, violence during the Spanish Civil War and, later, the "downfall" of Austria culminating in Hitler's triumphant arrival in Vienna. A long section in the middle from 1932 traces the beginning, passionate mid- dle, and what Banville describes as an "inevitable" end to the affair between Otto and Imogen.[62] This inevitability is linked, in part, to the presence of death that haunts the book: a fourth Langrishe sister, Emily, has committed suicide before the novel begins, and several scenes take place at the cemetery in which she and her parents are buried; at forty-three, Helen is dying and will eventually succumb to both hepatitis and a stroke; and the cessation of Imogen and Otto's intimacies is represented by the stillborn child Imogen will eventually deliver.

In *Langrishe, Go Down*, Higgins infuses a Chekhovian plot of aristocratic decline and enervation with the sexual frisson of D. H. Lawrence's *Lady Chatterley's Lover*. Yet more so than the closing pages of Higgins's novel, Pinter's screenplay recasts Imogen as an avatar of Samuel Beckett's Krapp, with a bundle of unmailed letters to which she constantly returns replacing Krapp's spools of tape. As the narrative begins, Imogen's affair with Otto has been over for years. In the intervening time, she has purposefully avoided con- tact with the outside world, a point Higgins reinforces in a kind of Beckettian deconstructive sentence in which she happens across her mother's obituary while rummaging through a desk drawer: "She sat there, empty of feeling. Kindly and considerate. No, a hard cold woman really who kept her feelings to herself."[63] Like Krapp, who once frequented a pub and enjoyed a minimally active social life, Imogen has become a recluse; and, like Krapp, she drinks excessively and returns to scenes of lost love, as Pinter's closing shots confirm. Higgins presents this matter very differently, as in the novel's last chapter Imogen returns to the abandoned lodge in which her intimate congress with Otto Beck was conducted, a site now redolent with the "smell of poverty, dis- use . . . and dirty beds" (252). By contrast, the last shots in Pinter's screen- play capture Imogen reading: a long shot of her at her desk is followed by another of her in profile, another high-angle shot of her, and then a close-up of her lips "moving silently" as she mouths each word of Otto's letter. Finally, much as Krapp retrieves another spool of tape to play on his recorder, in a last long shot Imogen replaces one letter in an envelope and reaches for another.[64] Like Krapp, who professes not to want to relive his youth yet does, Imogen is fated to revisit the one period in her adult life where love seemed possible. Her miming of old letters performs what is left of a gestural repertory in an emotionally arid life led in isolation, a veritable trope in so much Irish writing from Synge to Jennifer Johnston's *The Railway Station Man* (1992), Edna O'Brien's *The House of Splendid Isolation* (1994), and Martin McDonagh's *The Beauty Queen of Leenane* (1996).

In a novel and screenplay reminiscent of the Big House tradition of creaky estates and declining hegemonies, *Langrishe, Go Down* seems—indeed *is*— irreducibly Irish. As Vera Kreilkamp explains, another convention of this subgenre is the juxtaposition of a Catholic antagonist with the Protestant ascendancy, a convention Higgins extends in complex and global directions through the introduction of Otto Beck. Reading Beck's role allegorically, Kreilkamp sees him not only as subversive of the enclosed Langrishe world, but also as indicative of the death of a broader European culture; in fact, he transports a post–World War I German intellectual milieu of Heideggerian philosophy, contemporary German fiction, and a rising Naziism into the declining ambit of the Anglo-Irish.[65] It is within this context—one including the terrors of *Kristallnacht*—that the Irish-Jewish relationship emerges. Otto reminds Imogen that under British imperial rule the "native" Irish, "having lost their country, their lands and homes," were forced to forfeit their own names, "their contact with the past, their blood identity" (Higgins 168). They renamed themselves after a color, trade, science, or town, hence the proliferation of such surnames as Carpenter, Butler, Green, and so on. Similarly, Beck mentions in a later scene that, as Naziism rages in Germany, Jews have "taken the names of trees and mountains. They want to hide themselves, the Rosenblums and Lowenthals" (197). Much like Behan's linking of the Holocaust with the Great Famine, then, Pinter and Higgins construct a familiar homology in which Jews and the Irish are equivalent victims of a ruthless British-Nazi domination.

This particular variety of hidden Irishness and hidden Jewishness, however, like my assertion of Pinter as an Irish writer, is not precisely the issue I want to explore here. For this kind of "passing," like most forms of masquerade, embodies a conscious strategy employed either to succeed socially or economically in a racist or otherwise unjust society, or—quite simply—to survive in one. More relevant to this discussion, as in the case of Banville's Axel Vander, are those occasions when the trope of cloaked ethnicity emerges in psychically complex or thematically nuanced contexts like the one in Pinter's *Celebration*. Consider, again, Declan Kiberd's twin hypotheses about James Joyce's creation of Leopold Bloom, one of which concerns psychical complexity and the other, sociohistorical malaise and unease. On the one hand, Kiberd remarks, "In making the central character of *Ulysses* an ordinary Jewish citizen, [Joyce] may have foreseen that the Jews could easily become victims of the general disenchantment with the complications of modernity"; on the other, he speculates that "*Ulysses*, in recreating the effects of such chance meetings [as Stephen Dedalus's and Bloom's], connects the reader with his or her inner strangeness, helping us to make friends with our buried selves, epitomised perhaps by the Wandering Jew."[66] The implications of Kiberd's hypotheses are immense, as they suggest that the figure of the Jew in *Ulysses* serves either as an exemplar of modernity's multiple alienations or as a means for the subject to access her more authentic self. The swirl of affects is almost dizzying: in one of Kiberd's theses, Jewishness stands in for an alienating modernity that carries us away from ourselves; in the other, Jewishness facilitates our entry into subjective truth and buried authenticity. And, not infrequently, so does Irishness, however hidden.

This paradox constitutes a theme in both modern theoretical discourse and modernist representation. It does in the twenty-first century as well. For example, hidden Irishness and Jewishness forms a motif in Howard Jacobson's 2010 novel *The Finkler Question*. The novel's protagonist, a womanizing divorcé appropriately named Julian Treslove, is misrecognized at a Jane Austen costume party not as Colin Firth impersonating Mr. Darcy but rather as, alternatively, Dustin Hoffman, Billy Crystal, and Adam Sandler. It is clear from the beginning of the scene that the drunken American woman responsible for these misrecognitions will treat him to the "jolliest night of sex" he had ever enjoyed (71),[67] but in the sobering light of dawn Treslove wonders how someone who bore only the slightest resemblance to these and other Jewish actors or entertainers—Jeff Goldblum, Jerry Seinfeld—could be mistaken for a Jewish celebrity. The resemblance, he concludes, must have been "of another order. It must have been a matter of spirit and essence. *Essentially* he was like them. *Spiritually* he was like them" (72). Jacobson develops this motif later when Treslove is randomly attacked on the street by a female assailant who says to him only, "You Jew." Treslove can parse the accusation in only two ways: either the woman was venting her "irrepressible rage" at Jews through this attack, or she was providing him with a piece of vital information, something like "*I have a sneaking little feeling (don't ask me why) that you might not have known it, you're a Jew*" (108–9). Given this possibility of hidden Jewishness, it is hardly surprising that later in the novel Treslove falls in love with the curator of a Holocaust Museum, Hephzibah Weizenbaum, whose close friends call her Juno after the matriarch in Sean O'Casey's *Juno and the Paycock*. Astonished at this revelation, Treslove believes this nickname possesses magical significance, which if he knew how to decode properly might indicate that his hour for commitment to a single woman had finally arrived.

It is thus possible that all his life he has been waiting for this uncannily concealed Jewish-Irishness to complete his performance of selfhood.

This motif of the hidden Irish / hidden Jew in *The Finkler Question* is quite different from the consciously self-concealing Irish and Jews alluded to in *Langrishe, Go Down*—that is, groups of colonized and oppressed subjects who share a spiritual kindred and a heritage of hiding so as to survive. Characters like Treslove and Hephzibah, by contrast, more closely resemble the Leopold Bloom Kiberd theorizes in *Ulysses and Us*; that is, as figures of a hidden strangeness and uncanny affinity. This precise affinity, I think, is not usefully theorized through what are by now familiar critical lenses like diaspora studies or even critical race studies, however illuminating these might be in other contexts (like the analogical positioning of the Holocaust and the Great Famine, for example). So, when Eric Goldstein, speaking of the Jewish immigrant experience in fin de siècle America, describes Jews as a "mirror of American modernity," he underscores their frequent association with the effects of urban life: he lists, among other possibilities, nervousness, intellectualism, even underdeveloped physical strength.[68] (Something Joyce's Bloom considers in *Ulysses* and comedians like Woody Allen, Jackie Mason, and others regularly exploited on nightclub stages and television sets.) Such associations might literally be construed as "racist," given the discourse at the time that typically construed Jews and Irish as distinct races, or as merely the result of the demographic reality that a preponderance of both kinds of immigrants resided in the city—New York, Boston, Philadelphia—not in rural villages and towns, and often in the same neighborhoods competing for the same scarce resources. It should thus come as no surprise that both can be marked as "hidden" in ways that resemble each other. But the kind of hiddenness to which I have been gesturing becomes more legible in the domains of psychoanalysis and affect theory than in demographics or diaspora study.

All of which returns us to Pinter's obnoxious waiter in *Celebration* and his fallacious genealogies of Gary Cooper, Victor Mature, Al Capone, and John Dillinger. Are these non-Jews and non-Irish performing another hidden ethnicity? Are they performing ambivalence or desire in some strange way? Or are the waiter's several monologues examples of disorder and disruption that, after Joseph Litvak's meditations, define Jewishness as a style "transgressing norms of gender and nationality at once, since whatever goes further than the strict requirements of getting the job done, whatever introduces an element of luxury into the performance of the task at hand" might be so marked?[69] For Pinter's waiter, as in so many examples offered here, Irishness is similarly luxuriant and excessive in operation, much as Goldberg and McCann's interrogations are in *The Birthday Party*. As it was at the beginning of Pinter's career in the late 1950s, so it was with *Celebration* at the end: if one's birthday party is to be so thoroughly disrupted by an Irish-Jewish explosion, then an expensive dinner celebrating a wedding anniversary can be too. And however bizarre this iteration or performance of the Irish-Jewish unconscious, we can't help but be engaged by it and baffled at the same time.

MacLaverty's Holocaust: Affect, Memory, and the "Troubles"

Everyday life is not simply the material relationships. . . . It is about
how you can move across those relationships, where you can and
cannot invest, where you can stop/rest and where you can move and
make new connection, what matters and in what ways.[70]

—LAWRENCE GROSSBERG (2010)

Situated as it is in a moment of cultural trauma, Bernard MacLaverty's oeu-vre, which began with the publication of *Secrets and Other Stories* in 1977 and his poignant novel *Lamb* (1980), might be illuminated by two emergent intel-lectual projects, both of which endeavor to address the lived experience of the "Troubles" in Northern Ireland. These projects or interpretive "turns" include, first, the proliferation of studies of collective memory since the events of September 11, 2001, a scholarly complement to what theologian and former political prisoner Miroslav Volf regards as a larger "memory boom" in the fast-paced, "entertainment-saturated culture in which we live."[71] The second returns us to affect theory, which, although a quite different critical enterprise, might be articulated with studies of collective memory in read-ing MacLaverty's most significant representations of the "Troubles," his nov-els *Cal* (1983) and *Grace Notes* (1997).[72] This articulation might help us better understand both MacLaverty's depiction of personal, emotional truths, if not specific historical ones, and his strategy of adding resonance to these truths by juxtaposing them to those of other historical moments and traumas, a strategy Michael Rothberg has related to the operation of "multidirectional memory": memory that is "subject to ongoing negotiation, cross referencing, and borrowing"; memory that is "productive, not privative."[73] MacLaverty's evocation of the Holocaust in *Grace Notes* serves as an exemplar of the very productive memorial operations Rothberg describes and, as such, represents a different use for the uncanny Irish Jewishness that this book has outlined.

Among his many virtues as a writer, MacLaverty is extraordinarily adept at relating a character's intense feeling.[74] The opening section of *Cal*, for exam-ple, emphasizes the inner life of an alienated young working-class Catholic living in a Protestant neighborhood, its narration relying literally and repeat-edly upon the verb "felt": Cal "*felt* the muscles of his stomach relax" after lighting a cigarette and thereby quelling the nausea occasioned by his visit to the abattoir where his father works (8; my emphasis); as "he turned down into his street he *felt* the eyes on him" (9, my emphasis); he *felt* the red, white, and blue kerbstones were aimed at him and his father (9); and as the sense of

Protestant hegemony grew ominously around him, Cal and his father "felt" increasingly "excluded and isolated" (9). Given this experience, fear, a "feeling he had had ever since childhood," predominates his life; moreover, "there were times when he experienced fear more than others" (53), and he does so throughout the novel. Later when contemplating his complicity in Robert Morton's murder, he fears he "would lose his dignity" if he were apprehended by the police and tortured (88); and in one scene after taking residence at the Morton farm, he is worried that Marcella will catch him peeping into her window, a temptation he seems powerless to resist.

Fear and anxiety, however, do not comprise the entirety of Cal's repertoire of feelings; so, in one awkward encounter with Marcella at the library as his love for her becomes all-consuming, Cal "*felt* himself begin to blush and fought it helplessly." To "be out of his own control" in Marcella's company irritates and embarrasses him (79), and all that remains for him to do is to stare helplessly at the floor hoping to avert her gaze. This momentary loss of control serves as a prelude to the more devastating shame of impotence as Cal's relationship with Marcella evolves. Even his recovery of sexual competence is marred by premature excitation, his subjective instrumentation requiring more fine tuning to become fully functional. These moments of unease later in the novel are juxtaposed to moments of Cal's nascent sense of self-satisfaction—emotive places, Grossberg might call them, where Cal can stop for a moment and rest—and a newfound sense of confidence. Soon after moving into the Mortons' cottage and enjoying the "cleansing" effect of work, Cal "felt a surge of his own power to direct his life into whatever path he wanted." Yet, almost immediately, just as he "felt safe from the world," he began to be "attacked from within his own head" (117). Like fear, the anxiety that disturbs his dreams also undermines his confidence, anticipating the dispiriting subjective truth of the novel's final paragraph: he was "grateful that at last someone was going to beat him to within an inch of his life" (170). Better a present comprised of brutal certainty than one marked by constant fear; better to be visible than to live in hiding in an abandoned cottage, however transformed by Marcella's attentions. It is difficult not to see Cal, given the terms of this argument, as a surrogate of the Jews in hiding we have seen; thus, it should not be surprising that MacLaverty would later choose to develop this analogy in *Grace Notes*, albeit in a very different way.

Like *Cal*, *Grace Notes*, at least for one critic, represents the "Irish colonialist problematic" as a "specific historical instance of a deeper human problematic, one focused on the relations between the unique and the general in human affairs."[75] I'd like to revise the problematic to which Gerry Smyth alludes while retaining one of his emphases: namely, the relation of specific *human* truths to general ones, and, more particularly, the relation between one specific history—the "Troubles" in Northern Ireland—and another, Nazi atrocities against Jews during World War II, a relationship forming a powerful, in some ways disturbing leitmotif in MacLaverty's novel. The relationality of these two historical traumas emerges violently during the performance of the protagonist's, Catherine McKenna's, musical triumph in the book's final pages, and it is a connection that MacLaverty cultivates throughout the novel, in part to help Catherine transform her feelings about Orangemen and the local history of sectarian violence she carries in her memory. Both this history and her response to it, not surprisingly, are connected to her father, whose death requires Catherine's return home for his funeral, hence the dimensions of a deeper "human problematic" Smyth identifies.

Related to this problematic and to the thickening of its textures are both the multidirectional memory linking the Troubles in Northern Ireland to the Holocaust of World War II and the notion that a musical composition can be reified into something more substantial, into a *thing* resembling a headstone or memorial dedicated to an individual or event that has passed into our collective memory. Following Volf and Rothberg, I want to pursue the "multidirectional" matter of reading the Troubles by way of the Holocaust and the concept of "remembering rightly," underscoring the relationship between memory and affect. "Remembering rightly," Volf postulates, means not only remembering the traumatic event but, in an echo of Augustine, "also forgetting—forgetting how suffering and evil *felt*."[76] This assertion is in itself controversial, and MacLaverty implicitly responds to it by not presenting Catherine's "emotionless recollection" (Volf's phrase), but rather her transposition of emotion from one "key" or register to another. That is to say, in the end Catherine's ability as a composer not only to incorporate the Troubles into her music, but also to recircuit the emotion produced by sectarian violence and simple bullying both redacts collective memory and matters greatly to her own psychical well-being.

Grace Notes marks MacLaverty's most significant contribution to a growing catalog of texts addressing the conjoined issues of trauma, collective and personal memory, and—ultimately—healing and the even more complex project of reparation. Reflection on the Holocaust is crucial to this conversation. As Theodor Adorno, speaking of the Holocaust, notes, "One wants to get free of the past . . . since one cannot live in its shadow, and since there is no end to terror if guilt and violence are only repaid, again and again, with guilt and violence." At the same time, he asks, how does one enact a "serious working through of the past, the breaking of its spell through an act of clear consciousness?"[77] How does one achieve more than a shallow "coming to terms," a concept Adorno denigrates as implying less than a serious engagement with histories personal and collective? A perhaps surprising answer suggested by Paul Ricouer and implicitly endorsed by Primo Levi in *Survival in Auschwitz* (1947/1958) involves a complex formula of memory and its putative opposite, forgetting. In *Memory, History, Forgetting* (2004), Ricouer argues that forgetting and forgiveness form an important tandem: "for forgetting, the problematic of memory and faithfulness to the past; for forgiveness, guilt and reconciliation with the past."[78] Contrary to the idea that forgetting is a form of dysfunctionality, Ricouer posits it as a necessary adjunct to, not an "enemy of," memory; and weighs the possibility that one must find an appropriate balance between the two, suggesting that "appropriate memory" may entail the "renunciation of total reflection."[79] For his part, enduring the privations of the concentration camp or "Lager," as he calls it, Levi describes memories of the "world outside" pervading his "sleeping and waking hours." He and his fellow inmates had "forgotten nothing," as every memory rose "in front of us painfully clear."[80] Happy recollections of their former homes, Levi notes, are as painful to internees "as the thrusts of a sword." Perhaps for this reason, he grew determined to erase from his mind the abusive conditions of the camp: "Many things were then said and done among us," Levi recalls, "but of these it is better that there remain no memory."[81]

In assessing the intervention in critical memory MacLaverty makes in *Grace Notes*, then, and in particular the effectiveness of the Troubles/ Holocaust analogy in this process, one must ask how the latter facilitates "remembering rightly" or a serious working through of historical atrocity. These projects, as I have tried to suggest, inevitably put pressure on such issues as memorializing, narrative, and what Ricouer terms the "mnestic trace": the imprinted historical image that persists precisely because it has "struck us, touched us, affected us, and the affective mark remains in our mind."[82] Such traces often remain isolated, shorn of context, and are therefore inimical to Miroslav Volf's notion of "remembering rightly." In *The End of Memory*, Volf recalls his 1984 arrest in then-Communist Yugoslavia on the charge of being a spy working for the United States, his subsequent interrogation, and torture by a security officer known only as Captain G. Describing himself as broken into pieces, Volf was eventually driven to contemplate the thorny question of how to remember his confinement and abuse. "To remember a wrongdoing," he advises, is to "struggle against it"; and to "remember rightly" must mean "also what is right for those who have wronged that individual and for the larger community."[83] The former project relocates one's tormentor, the one who has grievously wronged the victim, into the larger and more sympathetics contexts of expanded biography—the perpetrator of the wrong has a life outside the prison—and of Christian salvifics.

MacLaverty takes a very different tack as conveyed by three relevant motifs in *Grace Notes*: first, its several references to the 1941 Nazi massacre of 33,000 men, women, and children at Babi Yar, a ravine outside the city of Kiev, the vast majority of whom were guilty of nothing but being Jews;[84] second, a deliberative repetition in *Grace Notes* of interrupted linearity or teleology gestured to, in part, by the novel's title; and third, as I have suggested, the notion, contemplated by the novel's protagonist, Catherine Anne McKenna, of a musical composition forming a kind of memorial to a specific historical moment or episode. This last matter raises an obvious question: namely, what kind of memorial or collective remembering *does* Catherine's *Vernicle*, the title of her composition, form? One answer resides in the kinds of music Catherine prefers and writes herself, all of which are noted for their non-linearity; thus, her memorial to the "Troubles" might be viewed as similarly resistant to larger narratives, just the opposite of Volf's strategies of remembering rightly through a purposeful insertion of traumatic events into the larger master narratives of biography and the New Testament.

Grace Notes foregrounds numerous instances of Catherine's privileging of a denarrativizing and minimalizing aesthetic. Visiting the cemetery in which her father will be interred—a visit that actually occurs *after* the broadcast of her symphony on BBC Radio—Catherine spies the headstone of Paddy Fleck, a young IRA soldier she once knew. Seeing this, she immediately thinks of Leoš Janáček's "Adagio" commemorating the shooting of a boy by Austrian troops in 1905. "She wondered about writing something for Paddy Fleck—what would it be like? . . . Was the nationalism Janáček represented different from the kind espoused by the Provisional IRA?" (85). Does it differ from the politics of Yevgeny Evtushenko's poem "Babi Yar" or Dimitri Shostakovich's Thirteenth Symphony, based on the poem, both of which Catherine's mentor Melnichuck had recalled during her earlier study with him:

> You know Babi Yar? [he asked].
> No, not . . .
> Maybe you are too young. Babi Yar is a place of death. In 1941 the Nazis made all the Jews of Kiev come together and they took them to Babi Yar—thirty-five thousand—men, women, children—and they shot them and put them down in a ravine to be buried. Evtushenko wrote a poem and Shostakovich put it in a symphony. (126)

Catherine's *Vernicle* is intimately related to this memorializing project—the representation of history and historical atrocity in music—a relation underscored as she listens to the four Orangemen drummers she retained for her concert. As they pound their mammoth Lambeg drums near the end of the novel, she immediately makes the connection between their brutal gestures and Nazi atrocities:

> Their aggression, their swagger put her in mind of Fascism. She was not trying to copy the vulgarity of Shostakovich Seven—the March of the Nazis on Leningrad—but that was the effect. A brutalising of the body, the spirit, humanity. Thundering and thundering and thundering and thundering. When the drums stopped . . . the only thing that remained was a feeling of depression and darkness. Utter despair. (272–73)

In this moment of performance, at least for Catherine, Nazi violence and Protestant domination merge, but to what end? How does this production of "utter despair," however fleeting, achieve meaningful cultural—or psychical—work?

It may be the case that this climactic moment was prepared for by the larger, two-part structure of *Vernicle*. Still, the description of the drumming emphasizes its disruptive, violent quality: the strings' ascent to an F sharp apex allows no larger "vista," as the "short bursts" of drums "like machine-gun fire" destroy the view (271). The merciful silence or respite that follows is shattered by a second volley of drum "fire," a sustained "burst" creating a "throbbing" of echoes in the nonpalliative second moment of silence that follows. Eventually, all the instruments in the orchestra yield, giving way to the superior force of the drums; they have triumphed and effectively silenced all.

And here is where theories of memorialization, traumatic memory, and "remembering rightly" collide in a vertiginous spiral of possibility. One *could* say that, in terms of the novel's privileging of nonlinearity, fragmentation, and, most obviously, of grace notes—"notes which were neither one thing nor the other. A note between the notes" (133)—the thunderous drumming in *Vernicle* is consistent with the aesthetic Catherine admires. This mnestic and aural image, one Catherine recalls early in the novel as something far more "thrilling" than an example of "bloody bigotry," as her father had once characterized Orangemen drumming, has survived in her memory as inflected by another mode of representation: one marked by interruption and spasmodic rhythm, not narrative coherence. Indeed, she "loved" Melnichuck's "spareness and austerity" and purposive "fragments" (62); equally pertinent, from the teaching of Huang Xaio Gang, she adhered to the conviction that "Music was not linear as some people would have us believe" (41). Neither is history nor historical memory, she seems to say. As Catherine advises the four Lambeg drummers during rehearsal, "You're accompanying a tune which doesn't exist any more" (259). Eventually, though, in performance "everything is cut short by the entrance of the Lambegs" (271), just as Catherine's reflection on the writing process before the concert underscores the one thing she hates the most: interruption. A telephone ringing, a baby crying—interrupted writing and interrupted sex. That's the interrupted reality of *Vernicle*.

Yet another interpretive possibility concerns the capacity of "grace notes" themselves—a potentiality akin to the miracle of transubstantiation in the Catholic mass, as the novel's narrator observes—to be two things at once, or, more properly, "the ability unique to music to say two or more things at once" (275). Or is MacLaverty making a subtler point about collective memory of and memorials to the Troubles being healed by way of reference to Evtushenko, Shostakovich, and Babi Yar? Does "remembering rightly" depend upon an exhaustive memory and a narrative capable of encompassing the wide array of historical facts it might accumulate? Or, heeding Ricoeur's admonition concerning the delicate balance between memory and forgetting, are testimony and narrative simply too susceptible to ideology, which could manipulate memory in not only inaccurate, but destructive ways? MacLaverty and Catherine MacKenna imply that a serious "working through" of a traumatic past, does *not* require an Aristotelian narrative with a beginning, middle, and end, all the events of which are linked by probability and necessity. It requires no salvific apotheosis, but rather both a multidirectional recontextualization of traumatic events and maybe a little forgetting. A mnestic trace or image exploding into a collective consciousness might also engender memory: not a cursory or shallow remembering, but one that revises the initial intensities of feeling caused by the trauma into something more productive. For, as oppressive as the drumming is, its performance ultimately leads not to Catherine's collapse but to her rise to receive the audience's enthusiastic applause.

In this way, MacLaverty seems to answer a resounding no to one of the questions that animates Michael Rothberg's *Multidirectional Memory*: "When memories of slavery and colonialism bump up against memories of the Holocaust in contemporary multicultural societies, must a competition of victims ensue?"[85] Rejecting the notion that identities are "pure" and "authentic," Rothberg insists that memory's "multi-directionality encourages us to think of the public sphere as a malleable discursive space in which groups do not simply articulate established positions but actually come into being through their dialogical interactions with others."[86] Memory is labor, a form of work, and victimization is not a "zero-sum" game. And *all* contextualizations of contemporary traumas with the Shoah are not equally valid or efficacious, as the outrage caused by Caryl Churchill's *Seven Jewish Children: A Play for Gaza* suggests. In *Grace Notes*, though, one thing is certain: grace notes saying more than one thing at the same time, in this case creating an Irish Catholic-Jewish surrogation, help heal Catherine McKenna at the considerable risk of casting Orangemen as Nazis. And MacLaverty's juxtaposition of the Troubles and the Holocaust, his transposing the negative affect associated with traumatic experience in Northern Ireland into a new register of feeling and memory, may constitute a crucial step in the reparative process that, whatever the risk, is well worth taking.

Epilogue: Nubs, Contingencies, and More Recent Immigrants

> In fact, the idea is so old-hat in Ireland, that it was almost courageous
> to tackle it again. Everybody has tried an emigrant play. But then
> again, I don't think it was altogether an emigrant play.[87]
>
> —BRIAN FRIEL (1968)

Brian Friel's comments about his first major success across the circum–North Atlantic theater, *Philadelphia, Here I Come!* (1964), are evocative for several reasons. The very idea of basing a fictive text on immigration, an affliction

Mary E. Daly attributes to the "slow failure" of Irish economic policy to address chronic unemployment and the lack of opportunity, particularly for young people, is indeed "old-hat." The first sentence of her book on population decline in postindependence Ireland puts the matter in terms as stark as they are clear: "In 2004 the population of the Republic of Ireland was in excess of four million for the first time since 1871."[88] This sentence smacks the reader in the head, and its concussive effect continues long after the punch is delivered. How is such a thing possible? And, just a bit later, she supplies sobering detail to her assertion of Ireland's unique status as the only European country in the modern era to endure such a sustained loss of its own people:

> Between 1851 and 1961, every census recorded a fall in the population in the area that constitutes the Republic of Ireland (with the exception of the years 1946–51, when the population rose by 5,000). By 1961 the population was 10 percent below the 1911 figure, and probably lower than in 1800.[89]

By 1964, when *Philadelphia, Here I Come!* opened at Dublin's Gaiety Theatre, this issue had grown into a veritable national obsession; among other governmental efforts to ameliorate the problem in the young republic, a Commission on Emigration and Population Problems was convened in 1948 and remained in place until 1954.[90] And Friel is right, too, in remarking that, if not *everybody* has written an immigrant play, a myriad of playwrights *have* found immigrants, immigration, assimilation, nativist prejudice, ethnic stereotyping, and related matters rife with dramatic potential. These include John Brougham, James Pilgrim, Augustin Daly, George Henry Jessop, Eugene O'Neill, Elmer Rice, Clifford Odets, Arthur Miller, Tennessee Williams, Tom Murphy, and many more. Immigrant plays and fiction continue in contemporary America, treating Chinese immigrants "Fresh off the Boat" (David Henry Hwang's *FOB* 1979), Latino/a workers and families in the plays of Luis Valdez and Cherríe Moraga, and other new or recent arrivals to the country.

Philadelphia, Here I Come!, as Friel implies, is also much more than an immigrant play; the relationship between Gareth ("Gar") O'Donnell and his father S. B. O'Donnell, "old Screwballs," as his son calls him, for example, recalls the preeminence of this relationship in Irish literature great and small. Yet, while inaccurately characterized as an immigrant play, Friel's play nonetheless captures quintessential elements of modern immigrant literature, relying upon and revising what are by now familiar motifs, conventions, and problematics. One of these, and its most apparent contribution to such a corpus of texts, is the fractured nature of immigrant and diasporic subjectivity, something Friel concretizes through his creation of two characters to represent the younger O'Donnell's wounded psyche: Public Gar and his double, Private Gar, a persona hidden from sight that only Public Gar can see and hear. But Private Gar is hardly a typical doppelgänger, whom both Freud and Otto Rank link to the uncanny, to concealed and eerie apparitions located at the nexus of the oddly familiar and the frighteningly unfamiliar. Unlike his antecedents, Private Gar provides no direct opposition to Public Gar's attainment of his objectives and no estranging evidence of the *unheimlich*, but rather lives inside his head to comment and chide, incite and offer sardonic, even entertaining, commentary. Friel allows his audience access to this internal dialogue, much of which reveals Public Gar's fantasies and still open psychical wounds. One of the former, discussed so many page ago, concerns America as a site not only of material plenitude, but also of emotional and sexual fulfillment. It is hardly surprising that both possibilities are characterized as excessive and therefore potentially corrupting, as Private Gar humorously insinuates early in the play when, in the guise of a judge declaiming from the bench, he interrogates Public Gar about moving to a "profane, irreligious, pagan country of gross materialism":

> PUBLIC: I am fully sensitive to this, Sir.
> PRIVATE: Where the devil himself holds sway, and lust—abhorrent lust—is everywhere indulged in shamelessly? (*Public winks extravagantly and nudges an imaginary man beside him.*)
> PUBLIC: Who are you tellin'? (*Poker-stiff again.*) Shamelessly, Sir, shamelessly.[91]

In this exchange, Private Gar mockingly gives voice to long-standing paradisiacal fantasies about an America paved with streets of gold and awash with the libidinal gratifications money brings. The equation is so simple and inviolable that everyone from James Pilgrim's Paddy Miles to John Dos Passos's sailors in *Manhattan Transfer* repeats it: "gross materialism" leads to sexual excess. Lots of money and lots of sex—America, a site of excess inherent to so many texts discussed throughout these chapters, promises both to Friel's poor and emotionally starved twenty-five-year-old protagonist.

We quickly learn why both attractions exert such an uncommon force on Public Gar. Ten months before the play's opening scene, the nascent romance between Gar and Kate Doogan appeared to be leading toward their engagement, or at least Gar hoped it would. He nurtured the dream of their marriage and starting a large family with fourteen children. But after Kate, the daughter of a senator, inquired about his professional ambitions and prospects for earning a suitable income, the dream could no longer be sustained. "We could never live on that" (40), she explained flatly, when learning of his salary of three pounds, fifteen shillings a month. Desperate to change her mind, to prove that he actually could support the large family he envisions, he reveals an additional "source of income" few people know about: his purchase of eggs directly from small farmers and sale at a profit to a local hotel. This entrepreneurial initiative, much like the casualized and sundry labors of nineteenth-century Irish immigrants and Arthur Miller's Rodolpho and Marco in *A View from the Bridge*, has netted him as much as one pound per month, but its impermanence hardly constitutes a career. And how could the occasional pound added to his meager wages as a clerk in his father's store amount to a salary capable of sustaining a large family? Unimpressed, Kate soon marries someone else and Gar is shattered.

Gar's dream of happiness with Kate and the family they might create together is replaced, as Richard Rankin Russell observes, with fantasies fueled by Hollywood movies and American popular culture more generally: being elected to the Senate and conducting subcommittee inquiries, cavorting with great "big sexy dames," frequenting "night clubs" and enjoying "high living and films" (55), "swaggering" down Fifty-Sixth Street "with this big blonde nuzzling up" to him (81), and more.[92] What Russell refers to as Gar's "media-influenced imagination" might also be metaphorized in the ways with which this chapter began: Public Gar, however routinized his daily life, drifts as a contingent identity biding his time between deadly monotony and a nub of unfulfilled desires. America, shining in the distance like the neon hotel sign in Odets's *Rocket to the Moon*, is the place where desires are fulfilled and a man can earn enough to find his love requited. The play's concluding line, uttered the night before his departure in which Public Gar admits that he doesn't know why he has to leave, acquires added resonance in the context of the immigrant and diasporic subject. For like so many tenement dwellers, Gar is saturated with popular culture; indeed, he frequently sees life as a film and this internal reality, this other nub of identity, clashes jarringly with the mundane drudgeries of a rural general store and the arcane world his father represents. This is why he has to leave.

We never actually know if Gar O'Donnell makes it to the "promised land," as Mona Chang does when her family moves to the Bronx River Parkway at the beginning of Gish Jen's novel *Mona in the Promised Land* (1996), like *Philadelphia, Here I Come!* set in the 1960s. Chinese immigrants in 1968 America, as Jen's narrator proclaims, are the "New Jews, after all, a model minority and Great American Success. They know they belong in the Promised Land."[93] And like Jewish immigrants almost a century earlier, her family despises greenhorns who come after them. Describing her parents, Mona observes, "They think [the word 'immigrant'] means people who try to bring live chickens on buses and don't own real suitcases" (27). Gar's musty suitcase, smelling of cat urine after years of disuse, resembles this ersatz and shabby variety made of cardboard. And like Eilis's luggage in Colm Tóibín's *Brooklyn*, which is "too Irish" and communicates too much, those bags Chinese immigrants carry convey the same unfortunate message described in Hwang's *FOB*: that their owners are "Clumsy, ugly, greasy"; "loud" and "stupid"; "Someone you wouldn't want your sister to marry."[94] In addition, consistent with the convention of tenement literature nearly a century earlier, in *Mona in the Promised Land* Chinese daughters, even if they aspire to convert to Judaism, still bring "shame" on their families, as Mona's mother complains.

And, as Mona speculates, "Orientals"—like Anzia Yezierska's Sonya Vrunsky in *Salome of the Tenements*—are supposed to be "exotically erotic," as several of her Jewish girlfriends are, although she worries she may fall short of this standard (76). But if Chinese are the new Jews, the Irish can't be too far away, as deep in Mona's thoughts the famous line from Eugene O'Neill's *Long Day's Journey into Night* echoes to signal her sense of displacement in a late 1960s Jewish community: "A stranger in a strange land, that's her, she concludes" (33). Mona Chang, in short, is a Chinese immigrant with a desire to be Jewish whose thoughts include the sentiments of an Irish-American who preceded her and is secreted in her psyche. In other words, and not unlike Axel Vander in Banville's *Shroud*, Mona, who outwardly performs Jewishness as guided by rabbinical instruction, is inhabited by a legion of immigrants, their histories, and feelings.

It is therefore scarcely a surprise that the inaugural story of one of Gish Jen's later collections of short fiction is "Who's Irish?" (1999). At the dawn of a new millennium, the American story—and the circum–North Atlantic story as well—however changed, continues to be one of immigration, diaspora, textual circulation, and uncanny affinity. If the Jews and Irish played significant roles in creating nineteenth-century theater, American popular music during the Tin Pan Alley era, modern drama, and nightclub comedy, they still influence the narrative of immigration today. And, in our new millennium, this narrative continues to be grand, and at times, dreadful.

{ NOTES }

Chapter 1

1. Irving Berlin, *The Complete Lyrics of Irving Berlin*, ed. Robert Kimball and Linda Emmet (New York: Applause, 2005), 69. In *Bert Williams, Black-on-Black Minstrelsy, and the African Diaspora* (Durham, NC: Duke University Press, 2006), Louis Chude-Sokei notes that Berlin also wrote "I Want to See a Minstrel Show," as performed successfully by Bert Williams and Eddie Cantor. Chude-Sokei observes, "The image of both the Negro and the Jew sharing a stage in burnt cork is an image of modernist American popular culture that still awaits consideration and analysis" (21). The study of Irish-Jewish popular culture here complements such an endeavor.

2. Anne Nichols, *Abie's Irish Rose* (New York: Samuel French, 1924), 17. All quotations from the play come from this edition and will be followed by page numbers in the text.

3. Paul Muldoon, *Moy Sand and Gravel* (New York: Farrar, Straus and Giroux, 2002), 94. All quotations from this volume will be followed by page numbers in the text.

4. "Surrogation" is one of several concepts I have borrowed from Joseph Roach, *Cities of the Dead: Circum-Atlantic Performance* (New York: Columbia University Press, 1996).

5. For brief discussions of this theme in early twentieth-century American music, see the liner notes to Mick Moloney, *If It Wasn't for the Irish and the Jews* (New York: Compass Records, 2009); and Ted Merwin, "The Performance of Jewish Ethnicity in Anne Nichols' *Abie's Irish Rose*," *Journal of American Ethnic History* 20 (Winter 2001): 10–11. Merwin also describes intermarriage, the device that drives the comic plot of *Abie's Irish Rose*, as a "multivalent symbol" in numerous songs of the decade that preceded the premiere of Nichols's play (11).

6. Keir Keightley, "Tin Pan Allegory," *Modernism/Modernity* 19 (November 2012): 718.

7. Citing a May 26, 1922, review of the play in *Variety*, Merwin argues that the play's "fantasy of an end to ethnic strife seems to have been one of its biggest draws." *Variety* reported that Father Whalen's speech about "various religions" being "paths to the same goal" elicited the "biggest applause of the evening" (18).

8. The appeal of *Abie's Irish Rose* originates not only in familiar routines and the conventions of romantic comedy, but also in amusing domestic battles analogous to those waged by the comic strip Irish couple Maggie and Jiggs, which Levy's neighbor Isaac Cohen greatly enjoys and describes to his disapproving wife in the play's opening scene. Although its humor owed much to class differences between shanty and middle-class Irish immigrants to America, *Bringing Up Father*, better known by the names of its marital combatants as "Maggie and Jiggs," was the product of an Irish-Jewish team, George McManus and Zeke Zekley. By the 1930s, McManus, who created the strip, turned over most of the work on it to Zekley, who contributed substantially to its success well into the 1950s. The strip was distributed by King Syndicate from 1913 to 2000.

9. See Merwin, "Performance of Jewish Ethnicity," 17–22.

10. This quotation appears on the back of the dust jacket of Nichols's novel, first published by Grosset and Dunlap in 1927. Later printings included photographs of the 1928 Paramount film version of *Abie's Irish Rose* directed by Victor Fleming, and a later version was produced in 1946. In 1926, Universal Studios released *The Cohens and the Kellys*, prompting Nichols's unsuccessful lawsuit *Nichols v. Universal Pictures Corp.* Six Cohen and Kelly movies were produced between 1926 and 1933.

11. See Paul Muldoon, "Getting Round: Notes toward an *Ars Poetica*," *Essays in Criticism* 48 (April 1998): 107–28.

12. These connotations of "genealogy" come from Michel Foucault, "Nietzsche, Genealogy, History," in *Language, Counter-Memory, Practice*, ed. Donald F. Bouchard (Ithaca: Cornell University Press, 1977), 146.

13. Merwin, "Performance of Jewish Ethnicity," 10.

14. Helen Vendler, "Anglo-Celtic Attitudes," *New York Review of Books*, November 6, 1997, 58.

15. Roach, *Cities of the Dead*, 4.

16. Roach, *Cities of the Dead*, 26.

17. Here I am referring to Patricia Yaeger, "Circum-Atlantic Superabundance: Milk as World-Making in Alice Randall and Kara Walker," *American Literature* 78 (December 2006): 769–98; and Keith Cartwright, *Sacral Grooves, Limbo Gateways: Travels in Deep Southern Time, Circum-Caribbean Space, Afro-Creole Authority* (Athens: University of Georgia Press, 2013). The designation "cis-Atlantic," as David Armitage explains, might serve as well as "circum–North Atlantic": the cis-Atlantic describes the "history of any particular place—a nation, a state, a region, even a specific institution—in relation to the wide Atlantic world." See Armitage, "Three Concepts of Atlantic History," in *The British Atlantic World, 1500–1800*, 2nd ed., ed. Armitage and Michael J. Braddick (Houndmills, Basingstoke: Palgrave Macmillan, 2009), 24.

18. J. H. Elliott, "Atlantic History: A Circumnavigation," in Armitage and Braddick, *British Atlantic World*, 255–56.

19. Much later Brendan Behan and, later still in *The Famine Plot: England's Role in Ireland's Greatest Tragedy* (2012), Tim Pat Coogan draw genocidal analogies between the Famine and the Holocaust. This topic is discussed in the last chapter.

20. Yaeger, "Circum-Atlantic Superabundance," 770, 774.

21. Sean O'Casey, *Juno and the Paycock*, in *Collected Plays*, 4 vols. (London: Macmillan, 1952), 1:44. All further quotations from O'Casey's plays come from this edition and will be followed in the text by volume and page numbers.

22. See David Marcus, *Oughtobiography: Leaves from the Diary of a Hyphenated Jew* (Dublin: Gill & Macmillan, 2001), 20. Marcus also enjoyed the music of Frank Sinatra, Bing Crosby, the Gershwins, and many more America artists.

23. Diarmaid Ferriter, *The Transformation of Ireland* (Woodstock: Overlook Press, 2005), 360.

24. James Joyce, *Dubliners*, introduced by Terence Brown (London: Penguin, 1992), 158–59. See also Claudia Rosenhan, "'Grace' and the Idea of 'the Irish Jew,'" *James Joyce Quarterly* 47 (Fall 2009): 71–86. Rosenhan points to the "many convergences between Irish and Jewish identities," including their commonly serving as "the subject of an ideological discourse in which identity is fixed by multiple relationships between internal and external forces" (71).

25. All quotations from *Ulysses* come from *Ulysses: The Corrected Text*, ed. Hans Walter Gabler (New York: Vintage, 1986) and will be followed in the text by chapter and line numbers, as in this case: *U* 10.581.

26. Hélène Cixous and Mireille Calle-Gruber, *Hélène Cixous Rootprints: Memory and Life Writing*, trans. Eric Prenowitz (London and New York: Routledge, 1997), 184.

27. Cixous, *Hélène Cixous Rootprints*, 204.

28. Slavoj Žižek, "'I Hear You with My Eyes'; or, The Invisible Master," in *Gaze and Voice as Love Objects*, ed. Renata Saleci and Slavoj Žižek (Durham, NC: Duke University Press, 1996), 108.

29. Mark Quigley, "White Skin, Green Face: House of Pain and the Modern Minstrel Show," in *The Black and Green Atlantic: Cross-Currents of the African and Irish Diasporas*, ed. Peter D. O'Neill and David Lloyd (Houndmills, Basingstoke: Palgrave Macmillan, 2009), 70.

30. Ciaran Carson, *Belfast Confetti* (Winston-Salem: Wake Forest University Press, 1989), 33.

31. Lionel Pilkington, *Theatre & Ireland* (Houndmills, Basingstoke: Palgrave Macmillan, 2010), 3.

32. Aoife Monks, "Comely Maidens and Celtic Tigers: *Riverdance* in Performance," *Goldsmith's Performance Research Pamphlets 1* (London: University of London Press, 2007), 1.

33. See, for example, Noel Ignatiev, *How the Irish Became White* (New York: Routledge, 1995), esp. 34–59. Ignatiev notes that in Ireland the distinction between "race" and "nation" was much clearer in the eighteenth century, in part as a result of the Penal Laws imposed by England. In America and elsewhere "race" was also used as an informal substitute for gender, as in the John Brougham's *Love and Murder: A Farce in One Act* (New York: Samuel French, 1856): "It ain't you, love, that he objects to, but the whole female race" (3).

34. Eric L. Goldstein, *The Price of Whiteness: Jews, Race, and American Identity* (Princeton: Princeton University Press, 2006), 21–22.

35. Friedrich Kolbenheyer, "Jewish Blood," *American Jewess* 2 (July 1896): 507.

36. Quoted in Edna Nahshon, "Israel Zangwill: Child of the Ghetto," in *From the Ghetto to the Melting Pot: Israel Zangwill's Jewish Plays*, ed. Edna Nahshon (Detroit: Wayne State University Press, 2006), 29–30. All further quotations from Zangwill's plays come from this edition and will be followed in the text by page numbers.

37. Marilyn Reizbaum, "Urban Legends," *Éire-Ireland* 45 (Spring–Summer 2010): 247.

38. See, for example, Tony Kushner and Alisa Solomon, who defended Churchill from charges of blood-libel and blatant anti-Semitism in "Tell Her the Truth," *Nation* 288 (April 13, 2009): 11–16.

39. As Keogh describes, Father John Creagh of Limerick leveled *all* of these accusations in his sermons in 1904, alleging that although "nowadays" Jews "dare not kidnap and slay Christian children," they continue to "pass off their miserable goods" at exorbitant prices to unwitting housewives in their practice as peddlers going door to door. See *Jews in Twentieth-Century Ireland: Refugees, Anti-Semitism and the Holocaust* (Cork: Cork University Press, 1998), 28–29.

40. See Émile Zola, "A Plea for the Jews," in *The Dreyfus Affair: "J'Accuse" and Other Writings*, ed. Alain Pagès and trans. Eleanor Levieux (New Haven: Yale University Press,

1996), 3. In this 1896 essay Zola rehearses the allegation that Jews are believed to comprise "a sort of international sect which has no real mother country."

41. See Cormac Ó Gráda, *Jewish Ireland in the Age of Joyce: A Socioeconomic History* (Princeton: Princeton University Press, 2006), 32. Ó Gráda estimates that between 1871 and 1901 the number of Jews living in Dublin rose from 189 to 2,129. In *The Jews of Ireland: From Earliest Times to the Year 1910* (Shannon: Irish University Press, 1972), Louis Hyman presents similar but not identical data on the Jewish population of Ireland, with helpful discussions on communities in Belfast, Cork, and Limerick.

42. James Joyce, *A Portrait of the Artist as a Young Man*, ed. R. B. Kershner (1916; New York: St. Martin's Press, 1993), 95. All further quotations from *Portrait* come from this edition and will be followed in the text by page numbers.

43. Reizbaum, "Urban Legends," 248.

44. See Marilyn Reizbaum, *James Joyce's Judaic Other* (Stanford: Stanford University Press, 1999), 109–12. For further discussion of sexual fantasy in *Ulysses*, see my essay "'Nothing for a Woman in That': James Lovebirch and Masochistic Fantasy in *Ulysses*," in *Joyce and Popular Culture*, ed. R. B. Kershner (Gainesville: University Press of Florida, 1996), 74–88.

45. Janelle Reinelt, "The Politics of Discourse: Performativity Meets Theatricality," *SubStance* 31 (2002): 201–15.

46. Reizbaum, "Urban Legends," 249, 252; Roach, *Cities of the Dead*, 3, 36.

47. James Joyce, *Dubliners*, 78. Joyce is hardly the only Irish writer to deploy the "Oriental" in this way. In *An Unsocial Socialist* (1884; London: Virago, 1980), as I discuss in a later chapter, Bernard Shaw's narrator describes Henrietta Jansenius, a young Jewish wife whose husband has abandoned her, as possessing "delicately sensuous lips," a "very slender figure moving with serpent-like grace," and a conspicuous "Oriental taste" as displayed in her dress. Her husband, who views her as a "beautiful and luxurious creature," finds it impossible to work when "the spell" of her presence is "upon" him (9, 10).

48. Madeleine Bingham, *Henry Irving and the Victorian Theatre* (London: George Allen & Unwin, 1978), 139.

49. Sir Edward Bulwer-Lytton, *The Lady of Lyons* in *Nineteenth-Century British Drama*, ed. Leonard R. N. Ashley (Glenview, IL: Scott, Foresman, 1967), 153.

50. See Alan S. Downer, *The Eminent Tragedian: William Charles Macready* (Cambridge: Harvard University Press, 1966), 75. One of the "stock successes of the Victorian theatre" (174), *The Lady of Lyons* was revived frequently in Dublin during the years of Joyce's theatergoing.

51. Gordon Bowker, *James Joyce: A Biography* (London: Weidenfeld & Nicolson, 2011), 1. All further quotations from this book will be followed by page numbers in the text. Bowker's anecdote involving an 1898 production of *Sweet Briar* is historically accurate, as the play was staged at the Gaiety Theatre during the week of August 8–14. See also David Kurnick, *Empty Houses: Theatrical Failure and the Novel* (Princeton: Princeton University Press, 2012). Besides providing an engaging reading of Joyce's *Exiles*, Kurnick, while discussing W. M. Thackeray's *Vanity Fair*, argues that the theater "becomes an emblem for what stubbornly resists accommodation in the domestic sphere," in part by "luring its inhabitants out into the streets" and "by symbolizing, and occasioning, the persistence of pre- or extramarital attachments" (42). The young Joyce found this subversive aspect of the theater enormously appealing.

52. Declan Kiberd, *Ulysses and Us: The Art of Everyday Life in Joyce's Masterpiece* (New York: W.W. Norton, 2009), 29.

53. Kiberd, *Ulysses and Us*, 6.

54. Quoted in Kerby A. Miller, *Ireland and Irish America: Culture. Class, and Transatlantic Migration* (Dublin: Field Day Press, 2008), 10. All further quotations from Miller's book will be followed by page numbers in the text.

55. Douglas Hyde, "The Necessity for De-anglicizing Ireland," in *Irish Literature: A Reader*, ed. Maureen O'Rourke Murphy and James MacKillop (Syracuse: Syracuse University Press, 1987), 147.

56. Hyde, "Necessity for De-anglicizing Ireland," 137.

57. Gregory Dobbins, *Lazy Idle Schemers: Irish Modernism and the Cultural Politics of Idleness* (Dublin: Field Day Press, 2010), 8.

58. As Steinberg and other scholars have noted, many writers of the Irish Literary Movement advanced an "explicit identification" between Moses and fallen Irish leader Charles Steward Parnell (27).

59. Rosenhan makes the point that during the "last two decades" Joyce studies "have generated several authoritative accounts of the representation and construction of Jewishness in *Ulysses*," in the process emphasizing "the parallels between Joyce's own fractured cultural identity and that of Jews" (71).

60. Kiberd, *Ulysses and Us*, 300–301.

61. Zygmunt Bauman, "Allosemitism: Premodern, Modern, Postmodern," in *Modernity, Culture and "the Jew*," ed. Bryan Cheyette and Laura Marcus (Cambridge: Polity Press, 1998), 146–47.

62. See Sianne Ngai, *Ugly Feelings* (Cambridge: Harvard University Press, 2005), esp. 332–45; and Sara Ahmed, *The Cultural Politics of Emotion* (New York: Routledge, 2004), esp. 92–100.

63. The terms "political unconscious" and "buried reality" come from Fredric Jameson's *The Political Unconscious: Narrative as a Socially Symbolic Act* (Ithaca: Cornell University Press, 1981), 20.

64. This epigraph and the following biographical information come from Jerome Lawrence, *Actor: The Life and Times of Paul Muni* (New York: George Putnam's Sons, 1974), 15–30.

65. John Dos Passos, *Manhattan Transfer* (1925; Boston: Houghton Mifflin, 2000), 335.

66. In her introduction, Edna Nahshon describes Roosevelt's enthusiastic response to the play when produced at Washington's Columbia Theatre on October 5, 1908, Zangwill's lunch at the White House the next day, and Roosevelt's praise of Jewish soldiers, among other topics. See *From the Ghetto*, 241–43.

67. Zangwill renders "Kishinev" as "Kishineff" in the text, and I have quietly changed the spelling for the purpose of consistency. In 1903, in a pogrom of some 2,750 families, 47 people were killed and 424 wounded; houses were burned to the ground, and Jewish shops were pillaged. See Leonard Dinnerstein and David M. Reimers, *Ethnic Americans: A History of Immigration*, 5th ed. (New York: Columbia University Press, 2009), 58. In *Within the Pale: The Story of Anti-Semitic Persecutions in Russia* (London: Hurst and Blackett, 1903), Irish nationalist Michael Davitt recounted the "saturnalia of ruffianism" and "revolting deeds"—including the rape of girls and murder of children—perpetrated

against Jews. In Davitt's slightly different estimate, forty-four Jews were murdered, some five hundred injured, and their property destroyed or looted. See Davitt, 101–88.

68. Kathleen originates in Zangwill's experience in East London where "Poor women, frequently Irish, and known as *Shabbos-goyahs* or *fire-goyahs*, acted as stokers to the Ghetto at twopence a hearth." Such women "did everything required on the Sabbath." See Zangwill, *Children of the Ghetto* (1895; Cambridge: Black Apollo Press, 2004), 107.

69. Cristanne Miller, "Tongues 'Loosened in the Melting Pot': The Poets of *Others* and the Lower East Side," *Modernism/Modernity* 14 (Fall 2007), 458; Kerby Miller, *Ireland and Irish America*, 7, 67. The largest segments of these immigrants were from eastern Europe, followed by Italian Catholics; and between 1700 and the 1920s over 7 million Irish emigrated to North America.

70. Irving Howe, *World of Our Fathers: The Journey of East European Jews to America and the Life They Found and Made* (1976; London: Phoenix Press, 2000), 31. All further quotations from Howe will be followed in the text by page numbers. In describing mid-Victorian London, Nahshon notes the similar reluctance of established Jews to embrace new arrivals, some viewing the immigrants' "penury and foreignness" as not only "distasteful" but also potentially "detrimental" to their own recently won positions in British society ("Israel Zangwill," 8).

71. David Fitzpatrick, "Irish Emigration in the Later Nineteenth Century," *Irish Historical Studies* 22 (September 1980): 129, 134.

72. Howe, *World of Our Fathers*, 69.

73. Stephen Crane, *Maggie, A Girl of the Streets*, in *The Complete Novels of Stephen Crane*, ed. Thomas A. Gullason (Garden City: Doubleday, 1967); Anzia Yezerska, *Salome of the Tenements* (1923; Urbana: University of Illinois Press, 1995), 34; and Yezierska, *Bread Givers* (1925; New York: Persea Books, 1975), 2. All quotations come from these editions and will be followed by page numbers in the text. Crane's *Maggie* was originally published in 1893 and then revised in 1896.

74. Henry Roth, *Call It Sleep* (1934; New York: Picador, 1991), 9. All further quotations from this novel come from this edition and will be followed by page numbers in the text.

75. See, for example, Steven G. Kellman, *Redemption: The Life of Henry Roth* (New York: Norton, 2005), 24–28, who discusses this strained meeting between husband and wife at the beginning of *Call It Sleep*.

76. Lola Ridge, *The Ghetto and Other Poems* (New York: B.W. Huebsch, 1918), 49. All other quotations from Ridge's poems come from this edition and will be followed by page numbers in the text.

77. See Peter Brooks, *The Melodramatic Imagination: Balzac, Henry James, Melodrama, and the Mode of Excess* (New York: Columbia University Press, 1985). Brooks's discussion at times mirrors Maggie's response. Melodrama "not only employs virtue persecuted as a source of its dramaturgy, but also tends to become the dramaturgy of virtue misprized and eventually recognized" (27).

78. Pnina Werbner, "Introduction: The Materiality of Diaspora—between Aesthetic and 'Real' Politics," *Diaspora* 9.1 (2000): 5–6.

79. James Clifford, "Diasporas," *Cultural Anthropology* 9.3 (1994): 304.

80. Eugene O'Neill, *Long Day's Journey into Night* (New Haven: Yale University Press, 1956), 147. All further quotations from this play will be followed by page numbers in the text.

81. Louis Sheaffer, *O'Neill: Son and Playwright* (Boston: Little, Brown, 1968), 8. Lola Ridge seemed to share a nostalgic and nationalist subjectivity with O'Neill's father. *The Ghetto and Other Poems* concludes with the short poem "Tidings" written on the occasion of the Easter 1916 "Rising" by Irish nationalists in Dublin. The last two lines lament, in an effusion of emotion indicated by italics and an exclamation point, *"They are fighting to-night in Sackville Street / And I am not there!"* (107).

82. See Mary E. Daly, *The Slow Failure: Population Decline and Independent Ireland, 1920–1973* (Madison: University of Wisconsin Press, 2006), 142. Daly believes, as I do, that Miller emphasizes "perhaps to excess" the "ties binding Irish Catholic emigrants," especially men, to home (14). In a plenary lecture simply entitled "Diaspora" at the June 2014 meeting of the American Conference for Irish Studies at University College Dublin, Kevin Kenny echoed this belief. He sketched a tripartite model of diaspora: (involuntary) exodus, connectivity, and return, suggesting that the last stage—return—did not apply well to either Irish or Jewish immigrants, whose rates of return were among the lowest recorded for those leaving Europe for America.

83. James T. Farrell, *Studs Lonigan: A Trilogy* (New York: Library of America, 2004), 206, 209. All quotations from *Young Lonigan* (1932), *The Young Manhood of Studs Lonigan* (1934), and *Judgment Day* (1935) come from this edition and will be followed by page numbers in the text.

84. Colm Tóibín, *Brooklyn* (New York: Scribner, 2009), 52, 5.

85. Tóibín, *Brooklyn*, 241.

86. See, for example, Brian Massumi, *Parables for the Virtual: Movement, Affect, Sensation* (Durham, NC: Duke University Press, 2002), 23–45.

87. Seth Moglen, *Mourning Modernity: Literary Modernism and the Injuries of American Capitalism* (Stanford: Stanford University Press, 2007), 5.

88. Immigrants often feared precisely this "tell" of their class, national, or ethnic origins. In *Haunted in the New World: Jewish American Culture from Cahan to the Goldbergs* (Bloomington: Indiana University Press, 2005), Donald Weber describes Abraham Cahan's protagonist in *The Rise of David Levinsky* (1917) issuing a "series of self-lacerating injunctions" that "reveal the dynamic of latent denial in the immigrant ordeal of Americanization: 'Don't be excited'; 'Speak in a calm, low voice as these Americans do'" (18).

89. Lauren Berlant, *Cruel Optimism* (Durham, NC: Duke University Press, 2011), 1.

90. Ahmed, *Cultural Politics of Emotion*, 103.

91. Massumi, *Parables for the Virtual*, 27, 25.

92. Berlant, *Cruel Optimism*, 5.

93. Massumi, *Parables for the Virtual*, 25.

94. For a juxtaposition of Ridge's poetry with Eliot's and a brief discussion of the latter's anti-Semitism, see Daniel Tobin, "Modernism, Leftism, and the Spirit: The Poetry of Lola Ridge," *New Hibernia Review* 8 (Autumn 2004): 73–75. See also Anthony Julius, *T. S. Eliot, Anti-Semitism, and Literary Form*, new ed. (London: Thames & Hudson, 2003). Julius's thesis is exceedingly clear: "Eliot did not reflect the anti-Semitism of his time, he contributed to it" (xiii).

95. Jacob A. Riis, *How the Other Half Lives* (1890; New York: Penguin, 1997), 21. Riis adds: "The Irishman is the true cosmopolitan immigrant. All-pervading, he shares his lodging with perfect impartiality with the Italian, the Greek, and the 'Dutchman'" (23).

96. George Bornstein, *The Colors of Zion: Blacks, Jews, and Irish from 1845 to 1945* (Cambridge: Harvard University Press, 2011), 2.

97. Quoted in Bornstein, *Colors of Zion*, 44. In this case, Cheyette's *Constructions of "The Jew" in English Literature and Society: Racial Representations, 1875–1945* (Cambridge: Cambridge University Press, 1993).

98. Bornstein, *Colors of Zion*, 7, 74, 87.

99. Sigmund Freud, "The Uncanny," in *The Standard Edition of the Complete Psychological Works of Sigmund Freud*, gen. ed. James Strachey, 24 vols. (London: Hogarth Press and the Institute of Psychoanalysis, 1953–74), 17:219. All further quotations from this essay will be followed by page numbers in the text.

100. See Mike Gold, "A Jewish Childhood in the New York Slums," in *Mike Gold: A Literary Anthology*, ed. Michael Folsom (New York: International Publishers, 1972), 292–94. Please note that I have rendered Gold's first name as "Michael" throughout. All further quotations from Gold's "Childhood" come from this volume and will be followed in the text by page numbers.

101. Michael Gold, *Jews without Money*, 2nd ed. (1930; New York: Carroll & Graf, 1996), 168. All further quotations from this novel will be followed by page numbers in the text.

102. James T. Farrell, "Lest We Forget: Jim Larkin, Irish Labor Leader" (1961), in *On Irish Themes*, ed. Dennis Flynn (Philadelphia: University of Pennsylvania Press, 1982), 150.

103. Arthur and Barbara Gelb, *O'Neill: Life with Monte Cristo* (New York: Applause Books, 2000), 502. Material in this paragraph on Gold's relationship with O'Neill comes from the Gelbs' earlier biography, *O'Neill* (New York: Perennial, 1960), 358–61.

104. Edward Dahlberg, *Because I Was Flesh: The Autobiography of Edward Dahlberg* (1959; New York: New Directions, 1967), 77.

105. Edward Dahlberg, *"Bottom Dogs," "From Flushing to Calvary," "Those Who Perish," and Hitherto Unpublished and Uncollected Works* (New York: Thomas Y. Crowell, 1976), 193. All further quotations from *Bottom Dogs* come from this text and will be followed by page numbers in the text.

106. In a letter to Kay Boyle on January 27, 1967, in which he complained vehemently about James Joyce, Dahlberg added, "I don't wish you to think I am roaming the globe with nothing in my pate but this sort of feeling. My real friends are seldom Jewish, but almost entirely Irish, including the lovely darling [Julia Lawlor] I live with who was born in County Cavan, Ireland. And why that is I cannot tell." This letter can be found in the Kay Boyle collection, Ransom Humanities Center, the University of Texas at Austin, Box 1.6.

107. Ira has periods of Jewish self-loathing and a fetishizing of all things Irish and Christian. "Oh, they made meat look so nice in a *goyish* butcher store," he notes, unlike a "kosher butcher store where meat looked dead" (49). He adds later when contemplating Arthurian romance and the Holy Grail: "So everything beautiful was Christian, wasn't it?" (66).

108. Lori Harrison-Kahane, "'Drunk with the Fiery Rhythms of Jazz': Anzia Yezierska, Hybridity, and the Harlem Renaissance," *MFS: Modern Fiction Studies* 51 (Summer 2005): 424, 422.

109. Harold Billings, Introduction to Dahlberg, *Bottom Dogs*, xvi.

110. Edward Dahlberg, "Ariel in Caliban," in *Bottom Dogs*, 131. All further quotations from this essay will be followed by page numbers in the text.

111. Herbert Read and Edward Dahlberg, *Truth Is More Sacred: A Critical Exchange on Modern Literature* (London: Routledge and Kegan Paul, 1961), 18. All further quotations from this book will be followed by page numbers in the text.

112. See the liner notes to Mick Moloney, *If It Wasn't for the Irish*.

113. Edward Jablonski, *Irving Berlin: American Troubadour* (New York: Henry Holt, 1999), 106.

114. See Jablonski, *Irving Berlin*, 105–34.

115. Thomas H. O'Connor, *The Boston Irish: A Political History* (Boston: Northeastern University Press, 1995), 204.

116. Willis Barnstone, *We Jews and Blacks* (Bloomington: Indiana University Press, 2004), 15.

117. Theodor W. Adorno and Max Horkheimer, *Dialectic of Enlightenment*, trans. John Cumming (1944; New York: Continuum, 1993), 185.

118. See Robert K. Landers, *An Honest Writer: The Life and Times of James T. Farrell* (San Francisco: Encounter Books, 2004), 109–36, for details of these events.

119. Quoted in Landers, *An Honest Writer*, 352.

120. James T. Farrell, *It Has Come to Pass* (New York: Theodor Herzl, 1958), 284.

121. Quoted in Bornstein, *Colors of Zion*, 132.

122. I have borrowed the notion of O'Neill's atavistic return to Irishness from John Henry Raleigh, "The Irish Atavism of *A Moon for the Misbegotten*," in *Eugene O'Neill: A World View*, ed. Virginia Floyd (New York: Frederick Ungar, 1979), 229–36.

Chapter 2

1. Augustin Daly, *Under the Gaslight* (1867), in *American Drama: Colonial to Contemporary*, ed. Stephen Watt and Gary A. Richardson (Fort Worth: Harcourt Brace, 1995), 175.

2. John Howard Lawson, *Processional: A Jazz Symphony of American Life in Four Acts* (New York: Thomas Seltzer, 1925), 74. All quotations from this play and from Lawson's preface to it will be followed by page numbers in the text.

3. Quoted in Watt and Richardson, *American Drama*, 157.

4. Quoted in Rebecca L. Walkowitz, *Cosmopolitan Style: Modernism beyond the Nation* (New York: Columbia University Press, 2006), 4.

5. Walkowitz, *Cosmopolitan Style*, 4–8, 9.

6. Christine Sypnowich, "Cosmopolitans, Cosmopolitanism, and Human Flourishing," in *The Political Philosophy of Cosmopolitanism*, ed. Gillian Brock and Harry Brighouse (Cambridge: Cambridge University Press, 2005), 57.

7. See Gerald Horne, *The Final Victim of the Blacklist: John Howard Lawson, Dean of the Hollywood Ten* (Berkeley: University of California Press, 2006). Horne notes that, while visiting Vienna, Lawson had "sought vainly" to meet Freud (30) and that in the 1920s and later in the 1960s he had compared the form of *Processional* to that of the Brechtian epic theater.

8. Ryan Jerving, "An Experiment in Modern Vaudeville: Archiving the Wretched Refuse in John Howard Lawson's *Processional*," *Modern Drama* 51 (Winter 2008): 543–44, 547–48.

9. Julia A. Walker, *Expressionism and Modernism in the American Theatre: Bodies, Voices, Words* (Cambridge: Cambridge University Press, 2005), 188–206.

10. See Walker, *Expressionism and Modernism*, 199–206. Like Lori Harrison-Kahan, who considers Yezierska's use of "black" in *Bread Givers*, Walker traces the connections between black and evil, and black and unalienated labor, in *Processional*. Horne notes that by the later 1960s Lawson conceded that *Processional* contains "caricatures of Negro and Jewish personalities" originating in a "vaudeville or cartoon method" of characterization (34) and for this reason did not want the play included in a published collection of his works.

11. Thomas Postlewait, *The Cambridge Introduction to Theatre Historiography* (Cambridge: Cambridge University Press, 2009), 14.

12. Jonathan L. Chambers, *Messiah of the New Technique: John Howard Lawson, Communism, and the American Theatre, 1923–1937* (Carbondale: Southern Illinois University Press, 2006), 61. See also Lawrence E. Mintz, "Humor and Ethnic Stereotypes in Vaudeville and Burlesque," *MELUS* 21 (Winter 1996): 19–28.

13. John Brougham, *The Lottery of Life: A Story of New York* (1868; New York: Samuel French, 1875), 9.

14. Dion Boucicault, *After Dark: A Drama of London Life in 1868* (New York: De Witt, 1869), 12.

15. Quoted in Postlewait, *Cambridge Introduction*, 15.

16. In *The Tenement Saga: The Lower East Side and Early Jewish-American Writers* (Madison: University of Wisconsin Press, 2004), Sanford Sternlicht describes the often conflicted relationship between immigrant daughters and the family patriarch, 17–21.

17. See Harley Erdman, *Staging the Jew: The Performance of an American Ethnicity, 1860–1920* (New Brunswick: Rutgers University Press, 1997), 40–60. In the next chapter, I will return in more detail to Erdman's history of the "belle juive" on the American stage.

18. Henry J. Byron, *Ivanhoe, An Extravaganza* (London: Thomas Hailes Lacy, 1862), 23. For an introduction to Byron and burlesque, see Jim Davis, introduction to *Plays by H.J. Byron* (Cambridge: Cambridge University Press, 1984), especially 2–14. As Davis notes, the popularity of burlesque in the middle and later decades of the century rivaled that of melodrama and domestic comedy; and Byron, like John Brougham, was adept at burlesquing contemporary dramatic forms like melodrama and romantic opera. In "Representing Ethnic Identity on the Antebellum Stage, 1825–61," in *The Oxford Handbook of American Drama*, ed. Jeffrey H. Richards with Heather S. Nathans (New York: Oxford University Press, 2013), Nathans argues that "fueled by the craze" for Scott's *Ivanhoe* and Rebecca, British and American playwrights "flooded the stage with a new ethnic stereotype: the exotic Jewess" (103).

19. Ann Mikkelsen, "From Sympathy to Empathy: Anzia Yezierska and the Transformation of the American Subject," *American Literature* 82 (June 2010): 362.

20. Mikkelsen, "From Sympathy to Empathy," 361–62.

21. Shaw, *An Unsocial Socialist*, 9, 10–11. Such signifiers as "luxurious," "deeply sensuous," and "serpent-like" combine to meld desire and temptation in the figure of the Jewess, though as Bryan Cheyette perceptively observes, "Henrietta's serpent-like eroticism does not preclude her, in a pleasing Shavian paradox, from representing the height of conventionality." See Cheyette, "Superman and Jew: Semitic Representations in the

Work of Bernard Shaw," *SHAW: The Annual of Bernard Shaw Studies*, vol. 12 (University Park: Pennsylvania State University Press, 1992), 242.

22. John Howard Lawson, *Success Story* (1932; New York: ReGroup Theatre, 2013), 9–10. In its 2013 revival of the play, New York's ReGroup Theatre, committed to recovering lost plays from the Group Theatre's repertoire, portrayed Agnes as a "heartless" flapper, not as the "blonde bombshell" Lawson described. See David Sheward, "Melodramatic 'Success Story' Hasn't Aged Well," *Backstage*, March 7, 2013. www.backstage.com/reviews.

23. As Julius Novick observes in *Beyond the Golden Door: Jewish American Drama and the Jewish American Experience* (New York: Palgrave Macmillan, 2008), "To many of the Jews from Eastern Europe, America was the *goldene medina*, the golden land, but to others it was the *treyfene medina*, the un-kosher land, a place inimical to the practice of the Jewish religion" (10). In other words, David Quixano's enthusiasm for the melting pot in Zangwill's play wasn't shared by all new arrivals to America.

24. Walker, *Expressionism and Modernism*, 200–201.

25. Joyce Flynn, "Sites and Sighs: The Iconology of the Subterranean in Late Nineteenth-Century Irish-American Drama," *MELUS* 18 (Spring 1993): 8. A similar metaphor of verticality informs *Success Story*. The "richly furnished" office in which Sol Ginsberg works is located on the fortieth floor, and the large windows at the rear "look out on an uninterrupted expanse of blue sky" (9). In the final scene, Sol relates a dream-parable to Sarah in which Christ took him to a high mountain and asked, "Do you want the earth, Solomon Ginsberg, or do you want to join me in a cellar, sweating and plotting with a few close friends?" (112).

26. Augustin Daly, *A Flash of Lightning*, in *Plays by Augustin Daly*, ed. Don B. Wilmeth and Rosemary Cullen (Cambridge: Cambridge University Press, 1984), 71.

27. Michael Gold, *Money*, in *One-Act Plays*, ed. Barrett H. Clark and Thomas R. Cook (Boston: D. C. Heath, 1929), 205. All further quotations from this play will be followed by page numbers in the text. My thanks to Brooks Heflin for recommending this play to me.

28. Gold refers to "foreign coolies" in "The Second American Renaissance," an address to the Fourth Congress of American Writers in 1941. This address continued Gold's attack on such writers as Thornton Wilder, whose work "offers a good synthetic pastiche of the tastes of the bourgeois decade." Gold was no more generous with T. S. Eliot's "snobbism" or the "beer-garden aristocracy" of H. L. Mencken, preferring the work of John Steinbeck and Richard Wright. See *Gold: A Literary Anthology*, 243–54. For a discussion of the ways in which the desire for material goods, even wealth, exists problematically in working-class literature, see Pamela Fox, *Class Fictions: Shame and Resistance in the British Working-Class Novel, 1890–1945* (Durham, NC: Duke University Press, 1994), esp. 1–20.

29. See Thomas Postlewait, "From Melodrama to Realism: The Suspect History of American Drama," in *Melodrama: The Cultural Emergence of a Genre*, ed. Michael Hays and Anastasia Nikolopoulou (New York: St. Martin's Press, 1996), 39–60.

30. See Deirdre McFeely, *Dion Boucicault: Irish Identity on Stage* (Cambridge: Cambridge University Press, 2012), 13–14. If a question exists about the term "Irish drama" as it pertains to John Patrick Shanley's *Outside Mullingar*, it is equally ironic to consider that Boucicault's career as the author of Irish plays actually began in America.

31. Scott Boltwood, introduction to Dion Boucicault, *Arrah-na-Pogue; or, The Wicklow Wedding* (London: Methuen, 2010), n.p. Quotations from the play come from this edition and will be followed by page numbers in the text. Revivals of *The Colleen Bawn* and the

productions of plays and operettas derived from it held the New York, London, Dublin, and other stages well into the twentieth century. See, for example, the "Dublin Theatrical Calendar, 1898–1904," in my *Joyce, O'Casey, and the Irish Popular Theatre* (Syracuse: Syracuse University Press, 1991), 201–39. For a calendar of melodramas, including productions of *The Colleeen Bawn*, in such other Irish cities as Cork and Belfast between 1895 and 1904, see Christopher Fitz-Simon, *"Buffoonery and Easy Sentiment": Popular Irish Plays in the Decade Prior to the Opening of the Abbey Theatre* (Dublin: Carysfort Press, 2011), 4–18.

32. See McFeely, *Dion Boucicault*, 70–74. While accepting my thesis about the chameleon nature of the politics of Boucicault's *The Shaughraun*, she quite helpfully revises my reading of the later play *Robert Emmet*, the authorship of which is more complicated than I had allowed. See 139–52.

33. John P. Harrington, *The Irish Play on the New York Stage, 1874–1966* (Lexington: University of Kentucky Press, 1997), 7.

34. Maureen Murphy, "From Scapegrace to Grásta: Popular Attitudes and Stereotypes in Irish American Drama," in *Irish Theater in America: Essays on Irish Theatrical Diaspora*, ed. John P. Harrington (Syracuse: Syracuse University Press, 2009), 24

35. Harrington, *Irish Play*, 13.

36. William Winter, *The Wallet of Time*, vol. 1 (New York: Moffat, Yard, 1913), 134.

37. These descriptions of Brougham's style come from William Winter, *Other Days: Being Chronicles and Memories from the Stage* (New York: Moffat, Yard, 1908), 101.

38. Edward Said, *On Late Style: Music and Literature against the Grain* (New York: Vintage, 2006), 85.

39. Such data should perhaps be accompanied by mild disclaimers. Dinnerstein and Reimers set the number of Irish immigrants entering America at nearly 2.2 million between 1840 and 1870, a figure that approached 4 million by 1900 (*Ethnic Americans*, 24, 26). In *The Famine Plot: England's Role in Ireland's Greatest Tragedy* (London: Palgrave Macmillan, 2012), Tim Pat Coogan, using Irish census data, observes that the population of Ireland decreased from 8,175,124 in 1841 to 6,552,365 in 1851, 985,000 of whom perished (10). But he quickly adds that these figures are hardly certain, given the lack of roads in the west of the country and the living conditions of many peasants. Underreporting is evident here, he argues, perhaps by as much as 100 percent, and the largest number of emigrants left after 1851.

40. Miller, *Ireland and Irish America*, 10.

41. John O'Brien and Al Dubin, "'Twas Only an Irishman's Dream" (1916), liner notes to Mick Moloney, *If It Wasn't for the Irish and the Jews*, n.p. See also Joseph Roach, "Barnumizing Diaspora: The 'Irish Skylark' Does New Orleans," *Theatre Journal* 50 (1998): 39–51, which concerns the appearances of Catherine Hayes in antebellum New Orleans. Roach discusses the lyrics of Thomas Moore's "The Last Rose of Summer," a poem written in 1805 that was later set to music and published in *Irish Melodies* (1807). In the refrain, "Oh! Who would inhabit this bleak world alone," he detects a "dark Celtic sorrow" beneath the "luminous skin" of the "skylark" that suggests the diasporic longing Miller describes (51).

42. Werbner, "Introduction: The Materiality of Diaspora," 5, 7.

43. Miller, *Ireland and Irish America*, 25.

44. Fitzpatrick, "Irish Emigration," 129. In "Discipline, Sentiment, and the Irish-American Public: Mary Ann Sadlier's Popular Fiction," *Éire-Ireland* 40 (Spring/

Summer 2005), Marjorie Howes puts the matter of Irish immigrants' capacity to succeed a bit more delicately: "The massive waves of famine immigrants were generally literate and were not the very poorest people in Ireland. But they were poorer, less Anglicized, and less skilled than previous immigrant generations" (145).

45. Tyler Anbinder, "Moving beyond 'Rags to Riches': New York's Irish Famine Immigrants and Their Surprising Savings Accounts," *Journal of American History* 99 (December 2012): 743.

46. Anbinder, "Moving beyond 'Rags to Riches,'" 744.

47. See chapter 1 for a brief discussion of the comparatively low rates of return immigration of both Irish- and Jewish-Americans. As Diarmaid Ferriter explains, it would take until the 1960s and early 1970s before the number of people entering or returning to Ireland exceeded the number of Irish leaving it (542). Increasing international investment in Ireland played a major role in this demographical reversal.

48. Miller, *Ireland and Irish America*, 18.

49. See David Sheward, "'Loud Speaker' Hits Us over the Head," *Backstage*, March 13, 2013. www.backstage.com/review/ny-theatre/off-off-broadway/loud-speaker-regroup-theatre-john-howard-lawson/.

50. Quoted in Roach, *Cities of the Dead*, 25.

51. Here, Byron is most likely referring to Edmund Falconer's Irish play *Peep O' Day; or, Savourneen Deelish*, which premiered at the Lyceum Theatre in November, 1861.

52. Byron, *Plays by H. J. Byron*, 45, 48.

53. George Farquhar, *The Beaux' Stratagem*, ed. Helen M. Burke, in *The Broadview Anthology of Restoration and Early Eighteenth-Century Drama*, gen. ed. J. Douglas Canfield (Peterborough, Ontario, Canada: Broadview, 2001), 1282.

54. Farquhar, *The Beaux' Stratagem*, 1281.

55. Farquhar, *The Beaux' Stratagem*, 1298.

56. For a brief discussion of the stage history of the play and the sources of Teague, see *Sir Robert Howard's Comedy "The Committee,"* ed. Carryl Nelson Thurber (Urbana: Graduate School of the University of Illinois, 1921), 9–46.

57. See Thurber, *Sir Robert Howard's Comedy*, 39–45.

58. Sir Robert Howard, *The Committee*, ed. Cheryl L. Nixon, in *The Broadview Anthology of Restoration and Early Eighteenth-Century Drama*, gen. ed. J. Douglas Canfield, 477. All further quotations from *The Committee* will be followed by page numbers in the text.

59. Thurber, *Sir Robert Howard's Comedy*, 44.

60. For Boucicault's commentary on his efforts to "abolish" the clownish stage Irishman from the stage, see Robert Hogan, *Dion Boucicault* (New York: Twayne, 1969), 79–96. See also the "Editorial Remarks" prefatory to Pilgrim's *Shandy Maguire; or, the Bould Boy of the Mountain* (Boston: William V. Spencer, 1855). First produced in Philadelphia in 1851, this play, according to an anonymous editor, entertains "without the performer being caricatured in filth and rags, which we regret to say is too often the case. The piece is a true picture of life . . . without the extreme and disgusting scenes of poverty, which are exhibited in some Irish plays" (n.p.).

61. Helen Burke, "Teague and the Ethnicization of Labor in Early Modern British Culture," *Eighteenth Century: Theory and Interpretation* 46.3 (2005): 239.

62. Burke, "Teague," 241.

63. John Brougham, *Temptation, or, The Irish Emigrant: A Comic Drama in Two Acts* (New York: Samuel French, 1856), 7. All further quotations from this play will be followed by page numbers in the text.

64. Bruce A. McConachie, *Melodramatic Formations: American Theatre and Society, 1820–1870* (Iowa City: University of Iowa Press, 1992), 162.

65. McConachie, *Melodramatic Formations*, 163, 167, 177.

66. Quoted in Donald C. King, *The Theatres of Boston: A Stage and Screen History* (Jefferson, NC: McFarland, 2005), 37.

67. George C. D. Odell, *Annals of the New York Stage*, 15 vols. (New York: Columbia University Press, 1927–49), 5. 246. All further references from Odell will be followed by volume and page numbers in the text.

68. Joseph N. Ireland, *Records of the New York Stage from 1750–1860*, 2 vols. (New York: Benjamin Blom, 1866), 2.332. Ireland describes Powers's successful appearances at the Park Theatre in 1833 and later in 1836 and 1839 before his untimely death in 1841. All further references to these records will be followed by volume and page numbers in the text.

69. Thomas H. O'Connor, *Boston Catholics: A History of the Church and Its People* (Boston: Northeastern University Press, 1998), 91.

70. James Pilgrim, *Eveleen Wilson, the Flower of Erin* (Boston: William V. Spencer, 1858), 26. All further quotations from the play will followed by page numbers in the text.

71. See Robin Bernstein, "Toward the Integration of Theatre History and Affect Studies: Shame and the Rude Mechs's *The Method Gun*," *Theatre Journal* 64 (May 2012): 215. The reference in *Eveleen Wilson* to shame as a "living death" anticipates Bernstein's argument that death, performance, and shame are interrelated as the predicate "mortify" suggests. That is, one is "mortified" by shame, which in turn is typically performed to an audience, real or imagined.

72. Howes, "Discipline, Sentiment," 142.

73. Mary Anne Sadlier, *Bessy Conway; or, The Irish Girl in America*, ed. Liz Szabo (1861; Charlottesville: University of Virginia American Studies, 1997), 5. Note here that Sadlier's middle name is spelled variously as "Anne" or "Ann."

74. James Pilgrim, *Paddy Miles, The Limerick Boy*, rev. ed. (London: Thomas Hailes Lacy, 1856), p. 3; *Irish Assurance and Yankee Modesty* (New York: Samuel French, 1864), 4.

75. James Pilgrim, *Ireland and America; or, Scenes in Both* (New York: Samuel French, 1856), 19.

76. Bruce McConachie, "The Cultural Politics of 'Paddy' on the Midcentury American Stage," *Studies in Popular Culture* 10 (1987): 1–2.

77. Augustin Daly, *Horizon*, in *Plays by Augustin Daly*, 113.

78. Joseph Valente, *The Myth of Manliness in Irish National Culture, 1880–1920* (Urbana: University of Illinois Press, 2011), 2.

79. In his introduction to *The Condition of the Working-Class in England* (1845; Moscow: Progress Publishers, 1973), for example, Engels recounts the peaceful agrarian life enjoyed by agricultural laborers before the advent of machines. Workers led a "passably comfortable existence" and "did not need to overwork"; they "did no more than they chose to do, and yet earned what they needed" (41). Midcentury melodrama frequently begins with just the opposite depiction: namely, the financial exigency of tenants and other farmers.

80. C. H. Hazlewood, *Jessy Vere; or, The Return of the Wanderer* (London: Thomas Hailes Lacy, 1856), 3.

81. Jim Davis and Victor Emeljanow, *Reflecting the Audience: London Theatregoing, 1840–1880* (Iowa City: University of Iowa Press, 2001), 59.

82. Nahshon, "Israel Zangwill," 7–8.

83. Quoted in Nahshon, "Israel Zangwill," 26. Boucicault recognized the potential of this emergent audience and added a note to a New York edition of *After Dark: A Drama of London Life in 1868*, which, as I have mentioned, features the Jewish gambler Dicey Morris. Praising Dominick Murray's portrayal of the character, Boucicault notes that a successful "imitation of the salient peculiarities of the low-lived London Jew's speech and mannerisms" clearly "strengthened the attractions and made a perceptible proportion of the audience be of that race" (7).

84. Davis and Emeljanow, *Reflecting the Audience*, 92.

85. Davis and Emeljanow, *Reflecting the Audience*, 69.

86. These scenes and incidents are highlighted in boldface on playbills advertising the play.

87. Quoted in Nahshon, *From the Ghetto*, 242.

88. See Nahshon, *From the Ghetto*, 228–32 on the stage Jew, 221–23 on intermarriage.

89. Jameson, *The Political Unconscious*, 40.

90. C. H. Hazlewood, *The Stolen Jewess, or Two Children of Israel* (London: Samuel French, 1872), 4. Licensed with a slightly different title, all further quotations from this play will be followed by page numbers in the text.

91. Colin Hazlewood, *Never Too Late to Mend* (New York: Samuel French, 1859), 5. All further quotations from this play will be followed by page numbers in the text. On occasion, Hazlewood's plays were attributed to his full name "Colin," rather than his initials, C. H.

92. This convention is less common, but drives the insensitivities of, among other characters, Sara Smolinsky's father in *Bread Givers*. In *Children of the Ghetto* (1899) Zangwill introduces "Reb" Shemuel, who is so attentive to the particulars of Jewish marital law that he hazards the loss of his daughter Hannah's affection. But even before this, Hannah makes her antipathy to her father's world clear in such lines as, "I hate your snuffy scholars and poets" (Nahshon, 171).

93. Here I refer to Harley Erdman, "M.B. Curtis and the Making of the American Stage Jew," *Journal of American Ethnic History* 15 (Fall 1995): 28–45. As Erdman explains, the facts of Curtis's early life are somewhat uncertain, and this uncertainty extends to the actual years of his lifespan as well. In both this article and his book, Erdman designates his lifespan as 1852–1921, whereas *The Cambridge Guide to American Theatre*, ed. Don B. Wilmeth and Tice Miller (Cambridge: Cambridge University Press, 1993) lists it as 1851–1920 (528).

94. Erdman, *Staging the Jew*, 88. Erdman notes that these traits were described in a review in the *New York Dramatic Mirror*, May 21, 1881.

95. Dinnerstein and Reimers, *Ethnic Americans*, 24.

96. See Howe, *World of Our Fathers*, 401–5 for a discussion of the commercial traveler as Jewish comic.

97. George Henry Jessop, *Sam'l of Posen; or, the Commercial Drummer*, in *Davy Crockett and Other Plays*, ed. Isaac Goldberg and Hubert Heffner (Princeton: Princeton

University Press, 1940), 160. This volume is included in *America's Lost Plays*, vol. 4 (Bloomington: Indiana University Press, 1975). All quotations from *Sam'l of Posen* will be followed by page numbers in the text.

98. Erdman, "M. B. Curtis," 32.

99. "The Home Stage," *Boston Daily Globe*, December 19, 1882.

100. See King, *The Theatres of Boston*, 63, 74.

Chapter 3

1. James Shapiro, *Shakespeare and the Jews* (New York: Columbia University Press, 1996), 15. In *Blood Relations: Christian and Jew in "The Merchant of Venice"* (Chicago: University of Chicago Press, 2008), Janet Adelman makes a similar observation about "conversos" that I discuss below in relation to Shylock.

2. Shapiro, *Shakespeare and the Jews*, 20. As Shapiro notes in regard to the etymology of "temporize," the word appears to have entered into use in the later sixteenth century meaning, as the *OED* defines it, "to adopt some course for the time or occasion," thereby linking it to acting or improvisation. Later in Georgian England, as Michael Ragussis discusses in *Theatrical Nation: Jews and Other Outlandish Englishmen in Georgian Britain* (Philadelphia: University of Pennsylvania Press, 2010), "The supertheatricality of the Jew suggests the Jew as actor, as dissembler, he is the outsider trying to pass himself off as an insider, a gentleman" (47).

3. Thomas Postlewait, "Theater Events and Their Political Contexts: A Problem in the Writing of Theater History," in *Critical Theory and Performance*, rev. ed., ed. Janelle G. Reinelt and Joseph R. Roach (Ann Arbor: University of Michigan Press, 2007), 198, 211.

4. George Taylor, "Svengali: Mesmerist and Aesthete," in *British Theatre in the 1890s: Essays on Drama and the Stage*, ed. Richard Foulkes (Cambridge: Cambridge University Press, 1992), 93.

5. Bauman, "Allosemitism," 143.

6. Bauman, "Allosemitism," 147.

7. Stewart Parker, *Heavenly Bodies*, in *Stewart Parker Plays: 2* (London: Methuen, 2000), 154–55. For a fuller discussion of the play, see Marilynn Richtarik, *Stewart Parker: A Life* (Oxford: Oxford University Press, 2012), 288–95.

8. For a discussion of this dialectic, see Lawrence Grossberg, *Dancing in Spite of Myself: Essays on Popular Culture* (Durham, NC: Duke University Press, 1997), especially 1–26. While Grossberg is primarily interested in contemporary music—and the fans devoted to it—his observations are helpful in considering fan culture and the rise of star-actors on the nineteenth-century stage.

9. Quoted in Robert Gottlieb, *Sarah: The Life of Sarah Bernhardt* (New Haven: Yale University Press, 2010), 118–19.

10. Quoted in Erdman, *Staging the Jew*, 88.

11. Erdman lists several similar plays featuring Jewish protagonists in the 1880s including *Moses Levy* (1882), and *Morris Cohen, The Commercial Drummer* (1882), 90–92.

12. Relying upon data from the *Annual Reports* of the Immigration and Naturalization Service, Dinnerstein and Reimers note that the 207,654 Irish immigrants to America in the 1830s jumped to 780,719 in the 1840s, and 914,119 in the 1850s. Although significant,

the number subsided to 435,697 in the 1860s, spiking again in the 1880s to over 650,000 (*Ethnic Americans*, 24).

13. Dinnerstein and Reimers, *Ethnic Americans*, 24. The number of immigrants from Italy also rose during this period, particularly during the first decade of the twentieth century. For discussion of this population's effect on New York, see Mary Elizabeth Brown, "A Separate Feast: The Italian Influence on Catholic New York," in *Catholics in New York: Society, Culture, and Politics, 1808–1946*, ed. Terry Golway (New York: Fordham University Press / Museum of the City of New York, 2008), 27–39.

14. Augustin Daly, *A Memoir of Miss Bateman* (New York: Wynkoop, Hallenbeck, and Thomas Printers, 1863), 1. All further quotations from this memoir will be followed by page numbers in the text.

15. As Donald C. King describes in *The Theatres of Boston*, the "second' Boston Theatre, which opened in September, 1854, had a capacity of some 3,140 spectators and was adorned in 1856 by a large, expensive chandelier displayed conspicuously in the center of the auditorium (45–50).

16. According to the "Hand-List of Plays" in Allardyce Nicoll's *A History of English Drama, 1660–1900*, vol. 5 (Cambridge: Cambridge University Press, 1946), 253, Mrs. H. L. Bateman's play was licensed for an 1865 performance in London's Adelphi Theatre as *Geraldine; or, The Master Passion*.

17. See, for example, Gottlieb, *Sarah*; Cornelia Otis Skinner, *Madame Sarah* (Boston: Houghton Mifflin, 1966); and Gerda Taranow, *Sarah Bernhardt: The Art within the Legend* (Princeton: Princeton University Press, 1972). Taranow's study is especially valuable in understanding the actress's technique, much of which is applicable to Leah.

18. Lawrence Hutton, "Infant Phenomena," *American Magazine* 21 (1886): 444.

19. Hutton, "Infant Phenomena," 445.

20. McConachie, *Melodramatic Formations*, 212. See also the calendar of plays appended to my *Joyce, O'Casey, and the Irish Popular Theater* (Syracuse: Syracuse University Press, 1991), compiled from Dublin newspapers at the end of the century.

21. Michael Foster and Barbara Foster, *A Dangerous Woman: The Life, Loves, and Scandals of Adah Isaacs Mencken, 1835–1868, America's Original Superstar* (Guilford, CT: Lyons Press, 2011), 84.

22. Quoted in Foster and Foster, *A Dangerous Woman*, 85.

23. Sharon Marcus, "Salomé!! Sarah Bernhardt, Oscar Wilde, and the Drama of Celebrity," *PMLA* 126 (October 2011): 1010.

24. Erdman, *Staging the Jew*, 40, 42.

25. See Cornelia Otis Skinner, *Madam Sarah* (Boston: Houghton Mifflin, 1966), 155ff.

26. Bernard Shaw, "Duse and Bernhard" (1895), in *Our Theatre in the Nineties*, 3 vols. (London: Constable and Company, 1932), 1:149. All further quotations from Shaw's drama criticism will come from these volumes and be followed by volume and page numbers in the text.

27. Patricia Marks, *Sarah Bernhardt's First American Theatrical Tour* (Jefferson, NC: McFarland, 2003), 29, 12.

28. Skinner, *Madam Sarah*, 163–64.

29. Augustin Daly, *Leah, the Forsaken* (New York: Samuel French and Son, 1863), 3. All further quotations from the play will be followed by page numbers in the text.

30. Lori B. Harrison, "Bloodsucking Bloom: Vampirism as a Representation of Jewishness in *Ulysses*," *James Joyce Quarterly* 36.4 (1999): 782.

31. Harrison, "Bloodsucking Bloom," 783.

32. Religious buildings and Christian symbols "in ruins," particularly Catholic ones, appear regularly in Irish melodrama and, later, in plays like J. M. Synge's *The Well of the Saints* (1905), which takes place on a set with a "ruined" church doorway at left. The action of Boucicault's *Arrah-na-Pogue* opens in front of the ruins of St. Kevin's Abbey.

33. Boucicault's *The Vampire* opened at the Princess's Theatre, London, in 1852.

34. Dion Boucicault, *The Phantom* (London: Dick's Standard Plays, 1856), 5. All further quotations from this play will be followed in the text by page numbers.

35. "Amusements," *New York Times*, January 20, 1863.

36. "Amusements," *New York Times*, October 31, 1878.

37. Quoted in Marks, *Sarah Bernhardt's Tour*, 192. In a speech to New York's Lotos Club in his first tour of America, Irving cited Clara Morris and Lawrence Barrett as American actors who would be warmly welcomed by London audiences. See Joseph Hatton, *Henry Irving's Impressions of America, Narrated in a Series of Sketches, Chronicles, and Conversations* (Boston: James R. Osgood, 1884), 91. All further quotations from Hatton will be followed by page numbers in the text.

38. "Union-Square Theatre," *New York Times*, March 2, 1887. The review of Clara Morris as Leah appeared in the *Times* on November 23, 1875.

39. Gottlieb reports that while in Paris an anonymous letter advised her not to show her "horrible Jewish nose" in public (*Sarah*, 77); and during a tour of North America, she was the object of "violent attack" in the "intensely Catholic and deeply anti-Semitic community" of Montreal (13).

40. "Music and Drama," *Chicago Daily Tribune*, March 1, 1892. The reviewer for the *New York Herald* similarly praised Bernhardt's appearance as Leah in Boston the preceding January, noting her "reserve of strength" and "unquestioned genius." See "Sarah's Leah Seen in Boston," *New York Herald*, January 9, 1892.

41. Mladen Dolar, *A Voice and Nothing More* (Cambridge, MA: MIT Press, 2006), 14.

42. Mrs. Patrick Campbell, *My Life and Some Letters* (London: Hutchinson, 1922), 137.

43. For Bernhardt's early vocal instruction, see Taranow, *Sarah Bernhardt*, esp. 7–14.

44. "Amusements," *Chicago Daily Tribune*, September 13, 1883.

45. "At the Play," *The Theatre: A Monthly Review and Magazine* 1 (December 1, 1878): 387.

46. Marvin Carlson, *The Haunted Stage: The Theatre as Memory-Machine* (Ann Arbor: University of Michigan Press, 2001), 3.

47. Carlson, *The Haunted Stage*, 10.

48. Carlson, *The Haunted Stage*, 62.

49. Gottlieb, *Sarah*, 80–81.

50. Shaw, *Our Theatres in the Nineties*, 3:150. Comparing Bernhardt unfavorably to Eleonora Duse, Shaw observed: "The dress, the title of the play, the order of the words may vary; but the woman is always the same."

51. Henry Wadsworth Longfellow, "Evangeline: A Tale of Acadie," in *The Complete Poetical Works of Henry Wadsworth Longfellow* (Boston: Houghton Mifflin, 1848), 79. All further quotations from the poem will be followed by page numbers in the text.

52. This analogy between the Famine and the Holocaust is discussed in the final chapter.

53. Adelman, *Blood Relations*, 11.

54. Arnold Wesker, preface to *The Merchant* (London: Methuen, 1983), L.

55. See, for example, Madeleine Bingham, *Henry Irving and the Victorian Theatre* (London: George Allen & Unwin, 1978), 93.

56. See Janet Clare and Stephen O'Neill, "Interpreting Shakespeare in Ireland," in *Shakespeare and the Irish Writer*, ed. Janet Clare and Stephen O'Neill (Dublin: UCD Press, 2010), 4 ff.

57. See J. C. Trewin, *Benson and the Bensonians* (London: Barry & Rockliff, 1960), 73–93. The phrase "more tightly organized programme" is from Trewin.

58. William Archer, "Shakespeare and the Public," in *About the Theatre* (London: T. Fisher Unwin, 1886), 239.

59. For a discussion of Archer's criticism of Irving, see Jim Davis, "'He Danced, He Did Not Merely Walk—He Sang by No Means Merely Spoke'—Irving, Theatricality and the Modernist Theatre," in *Henry Irving: A Re-evaluation of the Pre-eminent Victorian Actor-Manager*, ed. Richard Foulkes (London: Ashgate, 2008), 27–36.

60. Hatton, *Henry Irving's Impressions*, 54.

61. Linda Rozmovits, *Shakespeare and the Politics of Culture in Late Victorian England* (Baltimore: Johns Hopkins University Press, 1998), 2–3.

62. See Hesketh Pearson, *Beerbohm Tree: His Life and Laughter* (New York: Harper Brothers, 1956), 116–28.

63. Deirdre McFeely, "Shakespeare on the Dublin Stage, 1660–1904," paper presented at the conference "Performing Shakespeare in Ireland, 1660–1922," National University of Ireland–Galway, September 5, 2010.

64. Keogh, *Jews in Twentieth-Century Ireland*, 9. Keogh sets the 1911 figure at nearly 4,000 Jews. In *Jewish Ireland in the Age of Joyce: A Socioeconomic History*, Cormac Ó Gráda, using the decennial census of the population (North and South), cites the number of Jews living in Ireland in 1911 as 5,148, up from 285 in 1871.

65. Bryan Cheyette, "Jewish Stereotyping and English Literature, 1875–1920: Towards a Political Analysis," in *Traditions of Intolerance: Historical Perspectives on Fascism and Race Discourse in Britain*, ed. Tony Kushner and Kenneth Lunn (Manchester: University of Manchester Press, 1989), 14–15.

66. Fred F. Schrader, "Henry Irving in Three Great Roles," *Washington Post*, January 3, 1904, A6. Schrader was referring to Irving's portrayal of Shylock in his American tour in the winter of 1903–4; he appeared later that May in Dublin in all three of the roles Schrader lauds: Louis XI, Shylock, and Conan Doyle's Corporal Brewster.

67. Bram Stoker, *Personal Reminiscences of Henry Irving* (London: William Heinemann, 1907), 92.

68. Charles H. Shattuck, *Shakespeare on the American Stage: From Booth and Barrett to Sothern and Marlowe* (Washington, DC: Folger Shakespeare Library, 1987), 160. In "Blaming the Bard," *Our Theatres in the Nineties*, 2:198, Shaw similarly complains that Irving's Shylock wasn't Shakespeare's character "at all."

69. Ellen Terry, *The Story of My Life* (London: Hutchinson, 1908), 186.

70. Quoted in Hatton, *Henry Irving's Impressions*, 53, 225–27.

71. "Stock evil buffoon" comes from Rozmovits, *Shakespeare*, 62. Macklin's portrayal of Shylock has been written about voluminously, with most commentators stressing its monstrous dimensions as in Mrs. Inchbald's much-quoted observation: "No fiend-like

malice, no outrageous cruelty, no diabolical joy in human misery, seemed too excessive for the nature of mankind." Some years ago Denis Donoghue in "Macklin's Shylock and Macbeth," *Studies: An Irish Quarterly Review* 43 (1954), argued that by even considering Shylock seriously Macklin, who was best known for his comic roles, "was setting himself directly against the contemporary theatrical treatment of Jews" (424).

72. Shapiro, *Shakespeare and the Jews*, 220.

73. See Shapiro, *Shakespeare and the Jews*, 213–24; and Emily Hodgson Anderson, "Celebrity Shylock," *PMLA* 126.4 (2011): 940–45.

74. Anderson takes this quotation from Edward Abbot Parry, *Charles Macklin* (London: Kegan Paul, 1891), qtd. on 941.

75. See Ragussis, *Theatrical Nation*, esp. 45–61.

76. Mrs. Patrick Campbell, *My Life and Some Letters*, 133–34. Looking back on Irving's influence on her self-described "simple" 1895 portrayal of Juliet opposite Forbes Robertson, she applauds aspects of this modern acting style, comparing it favorably to its musty opposite: "In those days, as in these, a declamatory style, exaggerated gesture, rhodomontade in any form, were . . . ridiculous."

77. Quoted in Stephen Watt, "Historical Drama and the 'Legitimate' Theatre: Tom Taylor and W. G. Wills in the 1870s," in *When They Weren't Doing Shakespeare: Essays on Nineteenth-Century British and American Theatre*, new edition, ed. Judith L. Fisher and Stephen Watt (Athens: University of Georgia Press, 2011), 199.

78. Terry, *Story of My Life*, 338.

79. Eric Jones-Evans, "With Irving and *The Bells*," in *Henry Irving and "The Bells"*, ed. David Mayer (Manchester: Manchester University Press, 1980), 22. Jones-Evans remembers the exact lines as uttered somewhat differently.

80. In *Performing Shakespeare in the Age of Empire* (Cambridge: Cambridge University Press, 2002), Richard Foulkes underscores the success of Irving's *Merchant* outside of New York. It was "hailed for its Zola-esque modernity" in Chicago and was so well received in Washington that President Chester Arthur invited Irving to the White House. See Foulkes, 128.

81. "Irving in 'The Merchant of Venice' at Abbey's," *New York Times*, November 28, 1893.

82. All quotations from *The Merchant of Venice* come from the Folger Shakespeare Library edition, ed. Barbara A. Mowat and Paul Werstine (New York: Washington Square Press, 1992). See Shattuck, *Shakespeare on the American Stage*, 162–64.

83. Herbert Beerbohm Tree, *Thoughts and Afterthoughts* (New York: Funk & Wagnalls, 1913), 197.

84. Hatton, *Henry Irving's Impressions*, 227, 230. For an account of Irving's thoughts about Shylock, see Hatton, 224–36.

85. Stephen Cockett, "Serenade in a Gondola: Music and Interpolated Action in Irving's Production of *The Merchant of Venice*," in Foulkes, *Henry Irving: A Re-Evaluation*, 135.

86. Quoted in Cockett, "Serenade in a Gondola," 142.

87. Quoted in Shattuck, *Shakespeare on the American Stage*, 162.

88. Quoted in Cockett, "Serenade in a Gondola," 146.

89. Shattuck, *Shakespeare on the American Stage*, 163.

90. This is not merely my opinion. Carlson quotes Booth biographer William Winter, who regards Irving as inextricably associated with Matthias (*The Haunted Stage*, 65).

91. Lisa Fitzpatrick, "Staging *The Merchant of Venice* in Cork," *Modern Drama* 50 (Summer 2007): 170. Fitzpatrick borrows the concept of an "apologist tradition" from Avraham Oz and quotes from an 1879 review of the play in the *Spectator*.

92. Quoted in Davis, "He Danced," 29–30.

93. Quoted in Fitzpatrick, "Staging *The Merchant of Venice*," 170.

94. Dion Boucicault, *Louis XI*, in *Forbidden Fruit and Other Plays*, ed. Allardyce Nicoll and F. Theodore Cloak (Bloomington: Indiana University Press, 1963), 58.

95. Shattuck, *Shakespeare on the American Stage*, 164.

96. Adelman, *Blood Relations*, 114.

97. Peter Thomson, "The Secret Self of Henry Irving," in *Shakespeare and the Victorian Stage*, ed. Richard Foulkes (Cambridge: Cambridge University Press, 1986), 103.

98. Harry Berger Jr., *Fury in the Words: Love and Embarrassment in Shakespeare's Venice* (New York: Fordham University Press, 2013), 31.

99. Alan Hughes, "Henry Irving's Tragedy of Shylock," *Educational Theatre Journal* 24.3 (1972): 253.

100. Wesker, *The Merchant*, 4.

101. Martin Harvey, *The Autobiography of Sir John Martin-Harvey* (London: Sampson, Low, Marston, 1933), 348–49.

102. Trewin, *Benson and the Bensonians*, 80–81.

103. See Lawrence Grossberg, "Is There a Fan in this House? The Affective Sensibility of Fandom," in *The Adoring Audience: Fan Culture and Popular Media*, ed. Lisa A. Lewis (New York: Routledge, 1992), 50–65.

104. Stoker, *Personal Reminiscences*, 27.

105. Stoker, *Personal Reminiscences*, 193.

106. This letter is included in Wesker's preface to *The Merchant*.

107. Wesker, preface to *The Merchant,* lii.

108. Ernst Bloch, *The Principle of Hope*, vol. 1, trans. Neville Plaice, Stephen Plaice, and Paul Knight (Cambridge: MIT Press, 1995), 117.

109. Hughes, "Henry Irving's Tragedy," 262.

110. "Irving as Shylock," *Chicago Daily Tribune*, October 3, 1893.

111. Quoted in Emily Jenkins, "*Trilby*: Fads, Photographers, and 'Over-Perfect Feet,'" *Book History* 1 (1998): 235.

112. See Alexander Woollcott, "An All-Star 'Trilby," *New York Times*, April 4, 1915.

113. Hokey-Pokey, "Crazes Die Young: 'Trilby's' Reign Is O'er," *Irish Playgoer*, April 5, 1900, 17.

114. For a description of this phenomenon, see Tracy C. Davis's introduction to Paul Potter's *Trilby* in *The Broadview Anthology of Nineteenth-Century British Performance* (Peterborough, Ontario: Broadview Press, 2012), 577–87. All quotations from *Trilby* come from this edition and will be followed by page numbers in the text.

115. See Jenkins, 221–34.

116. "Mr. Beerbohm Tree in 'Trilby,'" *Times*, September 9, 1895, 10.

117. George Du Maurier, *Trilby* (1894; rpt. Oxford: Oxford University Press, 1998), 133. All quotations from the novel come from this edition and will be followed by page numbers in the text.

118. Quoted in Daniel Pick, *Svengali's Web: The Alien Encounter in Modern Culture* (New Haven: Yale University Press, 2000), 12.

119. "New Theatrical Bills—Paul Potter's 'Trilby' Greeted with Loud Hurrahs," *New York Times*, April 16, 1895.

120. See, for example, Heidi J. Holder, "Nation and Neighborhood, Jews and Englishmen: Location and Theatrical Ideology in Victorian London," in *The Performing Century: Nineteenth-Century Theatre's History*, ed. Tracy C. Davis and Peter Holland (Houndmills, Basingstoke: Palgrave Macmillan, 2007), esp. 110–12.

121. Maurice Willson Disher, *The Last Romantic: The Authorised Biography of Sir John Martin-Harvey* (London: Hutchinson, 1944), 121.

122. In "'Hypnosis Redivivus': Ernest Hart, "British Medical Journal,' and the Hypnotism Controversy," *Victorian Periodicals Review* 34 (Summer 2001): 104–27, Mary Elizabeth Leighton outlines several contexts for *Trilby*. One is Julia Frankau's 1887 novel *Dr. Phillips: A Maida Vale Idyll*, in which a Jewish doctor, involved in an extramarital affair, murders his wife by interfering with her surgery. "Attentive readers," Leighton argues, may have detected a resemblance between the fictional doctor and Ernest Hart, a successful Jewish physician and editor of the *British Medical Journal* whose wife died "under mysterious circumstances" in 1861 (108). Hart promoted controversial medical issues, one of which was the "foreign practice" of hypnotism, and Potter relied upon several sources on the subject in writing his play (115).

123. Here, Bauman is quoting E. M. Cioran ("Allosemitism," 146, 148). Another aspect of allo-Semitism in the novel occurs when Little Billee considers marrying his neighbor, Alice. He refers to her father as "no Jephthah" but a man who "loves his daughter as much as Shylock loved his" (182), casting him not as an example of a monster, but of a father who dearly loves his daughter.

124. Daniel Pick, *Svengali's Web*: 4.

125. Joseph Litvak, "Jew Envy," *Women's Studies Quarterly* 34 (Fall–Winter 2006): 83–84.

126. The review from the *Scotsman* is quoted in Davis's introduction to the play (584). The quotation from Edmund Wilson's *A Piece of My Mind: Recollections at Sixty* (1957) is from Taylor, "Svengali," 97.

127. John Ripley, "Sociology and Soundscape: Herbert Beerbohm Tree's 1908 *Merchant of Venice*," *Shakespeare Quarterly* 56 (Winter 2005): 397.

128. Ripley, "Sociology and Soundscape," 387.

129. See Eugene O'Neill, *A Touch of the Poet* (1946; New Haven: Yale University Press, 1957). Melody despises his daughter's "damned peasant brogue," which she exaggerates at times to "tease" him (41); he admonishes Paddy O'Dowd for entering his inn as if it were a "dirty shebeen" (53); and when his wife suggests that his revenge against England might lead to the freeing of Ireland, he sneers contemptuously, "Ireland? What benefit would freedom be to her unless she could be freed from the Irish?" (40).

130. McFeely, *Dion Boucicault*, 4.

131. Quoted in Gelb and Gelb, *O'Neill*, 49. It was also O'Neill's misfortune, as many scholars describe, to have had the benefit of just three rehearsals before the play opened. I will use the spelling Edmund Dantès as in *James O'Neill's Version of "Monte Cristo"* in *America's Lost Plays*, vol. 16, ed. J. B. Russak (Bloomington: Indiana University Press, 1940). Quotations from the play come from this edition and will be followed by page numbers in the text.

132. See Myron Matlaw, "James O'Neill's Launching of *Monte Cristo*," in Fisher and Watt, *When They Weren't Doing Shakespeare*, 94–95.

133. See *Robert Emmet* in *Selected Plays: Dion Boucicault*, introduced by Andrew Parkin (Gerrards Cross: Colin Smythe; Washington, DC: Catholic University of America Press, 1987), 397.

134. For a summary of these tumultuous moments and allegations, see Gelb and Gelb, *O'Neill*, 69–78.

135. Quoted in Gelb and Gelb, *O'Neill*, 50.

Chapter 4

1. In both the epigraph and here, I have quietly corrected Langner's "sheenie" to its more common spelling, "sheeny." Langner's correspondence with Shaw about *Geneva* constitutes "Appendix II" to his *The Magic Curtain: The Story of a Life in Two Fields: Theatre and Invention by the Founder of the Theatre Guild* (New York: E. P. Dutton, 1951), 454–58.

2. Like so many artists and socialists, Langner was also appalled by the "repellent poverty" of London slums, which "awakened" his "social instincts." See Langner, *The Magic Curtain*, 26.

3. See "Appendix VIII" to Langner, *The Magic Curtain*, 473–80. Over a decade later, the Guild produced *You Never Can Tell* in 1948.

4. For a discussion of the "Bernard Shaw cult" of early twentieth-century New York, see Harrington, *Irish Play*, 34–54.

5. Dion Boucicault, *Arrah-na-Pogue*, 29. In late nineteenth-century melodrama and fin de siècle historical melodramas a rapparee occasionally plays a role similar to those of the stage Irishman in Boucicault's Irish plays. In J. W. Whitbread's *Sarsfield: The Siege of Limerick* (1905), for example, a rapparee named Gallopin' Terry Hogan thwarts his Dutch adversaries at every turn, rescuing women and nationalist heroes in peril while adding comic vitality to the play. Boucicault also wrote a play set during the Williamite wars, *The Rapparee, or, The Treaty of Limerick* (1870).

6. Langner, *The Magic Curtain*, 454–55. The epigraph and all other quotations from Langner and this exchange come from this volume and will be followed by page numbers in the text.

7. Bernard Shaw, *Geneva*, in *Complete Plays with Prefaces*, 6 vols. (New York: Dodd, Mead and Company, 1963), 5:731. All quotations from Shaw's plays and their prefaces come from this edition and will be followed in the text by volume and page numbers. For a discussion of Shaw's revisions of *Geneva*, see David Nathan, "Failure of an Elderly Gentleman: Shaw and the Jews," *SHAW: Shaw and Politics* 11 (1991): 233–37.

8. While this line suggests Sir Orpheus's foppish nature, St. John Ervine, who disparages *Geneva* as "saddening stuff to read," regarded him as the "most impressive person in the play," largely because he "almost casually" deflates Battler's dictatorial hubris by warning him (and others) that the British Empire is "capable of anything" when frightened. See *Bernard Shaw: His Life, Work and Friends* (New York: William Morrow, 1956), 564, 567.

9. Nathan, "Failure of an Elderly Gentleman," 234, 222.

10. See Bryan Cheyette, "Superman and Jew: Semitic Representations in the Work of Bernard Shaw," *Shaw* 15 (1995): 211–29.

11. Stanley Weintraub, "GBS and the Despots," *TLS: Times Literary Supplement*, August 22, 2011, online.

12. Numerous articles of the 1930s and 1940s allude to Shaw's criticism of both Hitler's government and its doctrine of ant-Semitism: "Hitlerites Acting Like 'Madmen' in Persecuting Jews, Says Shaw," *New York American*, June 11, 1933, for example; and "Shaw Compares Hitler Acts to Witchburning," *New York Journal-American*, March 26, 1938.

13. Bernard Shaw, "Irish Nonsense about Ireland," in *The Matter with Ireland*, ed. David H. Greene and Dan H. Laurence (London: Rupert Hart-Davis, 1962), 100–101, 106. Some historians argue that at the turn of the century and later, such promotion of internationalism was often viewed as an inherently Jewish position. See, for example, David Biale, "Masochism and Philosemitism: The Strange Case of Leopold von Sacher-Masoch," *Journal of Contemporary History*, April 1982, 305–23. Biale notes in regard to Sacher-Masoch's Galicia, "[His] identification with the ethnic mix of Galicia led to an internationalist philosophy in opposition to exclusivist nationalism. Such an anti-nationalist position naturally favoured the Jews, the quintessential example of a people without a nation-state" (307).

14. Bernard Shaw, "On the Jews," a reprinted account of a 1925–26 exchange, ed. Desmond Harding, *SHAW: Shaw and the City*, 32 (2012): 25.

15. Shaw Collection, Box 2.14 (no date), Ransom Humanities Center, University of Texas at Austin.

16. Shaw, "On the Jews," 24.

17. Shaw frequently, and at times oddly, excoriated Hitler personally for his anti-Semitism. So, for example, in a 1939 interview he declared Hitler "terribly handicapped by his anti-Semitism, which is a crazy fad and not a political system." Quoted in Hesketh Pearson, *Bernard Shaw: His Life and Personality* (London: Collins, 1950), 411.

18. Elmer Rice, *The Living Theatre* (New York: Harper & Brothers, 1959), 4.

19. Sean O'Casey, *Rose and Crown*, in *Autobiographies 2: Inishfallen, Fare Thee Well, Rose and Crown, Sunset and Evening Star* (London: Pan Books, 1980), 400–401. All quotations from O'Casey's later autobiographies will be followed in the text by volume and page numbers.

20. This narrative of a "sudden" rise to prominence is overstated, as well before the productions of his "Dublin Trilogy"—*The Shadow of a Gunman, Juno and the Paycock*, and *The Plough and the Stars*—O'Casey submitted plays to the Abbey Theatre with little success, most notably *The Harvest Festival* (1919). See my *Joyce, O'Casey, and the Irish Popular Theater*, 32; and Christopher Murray, *Seán O'Casey: Writer at Work—a Biography* (Montreal: McGill-Queen's University Press, 2004), 125–27. The manuscript of *The Harvest Festival* is the only one of these to survive.

21. Garry O'Conner, *Sean O'Casey: A Life* (New York: Atheneum, 1988), 259–60.

22. For a summary of these reviews, see Murray, *Seán O'Casey*, 226–27. Agate's remarks about *Within the Gates* earned him O'Casey's enmity—O'Casey described him as "heavy, clumsy-looking," and lacking innate grace, a "refined son of a refined Caliban" (2:265)— and he directed letters to several London newspapers in defense of his play. *Within the Gates* also received a positive review from the *Times*, and in a December 27, 1933, letter to George Jean Nathan, O'Casey alludes to an offer from a young producer backed by Jewish

friends to give it a less "commercial" production. See David Krause, ed., *The Letters of Sean O'Casey 1910–1941* (New York: Macmillan, 1975), 480, 485.

23. Robert G. Lowery and Patricia Angelin, eds., *My Very Dear Sean: George Jean Nathan to Sean O'Casey, Letters and Articles* (Rutherford: Fairleigh Dickinson University Press, 1985), 32; Krause, *Letters of Sean O'Casey*, 482.

24. See, for example, Gerald Weales, *Odets the Playwright* (New York: Methuen, 1985), 77–82.

25. Of course, other American playwrights felt similarly. In her lecture at a conference delivered some two weeks before the 1959 Broadway opening of *A Raisin in the Sun*, Lorraine Hansberry—who had first seen *Juno and the Paycock* years earlier while an undergraduate at the University of Wisconsin—began with a quotation from O'Casey's autobiographical volume *Sunset and Evening Star* and returned to him and Tennessee Williams throughout. See her "The Negro Writer and his Roots: Toward a New Romanticism" published in *The Black Scholar* 12 (March–April 1981): 2–12.

26. Elmer Rice, *Minority Report: An Autobiography* (New York: Simon and Schuster, 1963), 85.

27. A five-page typescript of Rice's "Extemporaneous Remarks Made at a Luncheon at the Hotel Savoy, London, Given by the British Society of Authors and Composers on the 100th Anniversary of Bernard Shaw's Birth," July 26, 1956, is cataloged in the Harry Ransom Center, Box 93.1. His fuller description of discovering Shaw's plays reads thusly: "The effect was cataclysmic. Doors and windows opened, bells rang, lights went on and horizons widened. It was the most revolutionary event to happen in my life in an intellectual sense" (2).

28. In *Minority Report*, Rice specifies $100,000 as his profit from *On Trial*, 87.

29. Rice's admiration for Irish writing extends beyond his fondness for Shaw. In *The Living Theatre*, after denigrating Dublin as a kind of "provincial backwater," he lauds the exceptional caliber of modern Irish drama: "Yet in poetic beauty, imaginativeness, insight and theatrical effectiveness, it would be hard to match in any country of the contemporary world the plays of J.M. Synge, Lady Gregory, W.B. Yeats, Lord Dunsany, Lennox Robinson, and Sean O'Casey" (76). He purposefully omits Shaw, Wilde, and St. John Ervine from this roster, he notes, because they are "usually identified" with the English theatre.

30. "Education and the Dramatist," *New York Sun*, April 8, 1926, 26.

31. Discussion of Roth's similar experience growing up in an Irish neighborhood, as lived by his surrogate Ira Stigman, and that of Edward Dahlberg with Irish kids appears in chapter 1.

32. Brenman-Gibson, *Clifford Odets American Playwright: The Years from 1906–1940* (New York: Atheneum, 1981), 38. Here, she is also quoting from a note in Odets's file. It is perhaps ironic that, in this later notation, the older Odets echoes the thesis developed by George Jean Nathan and H. L. Mencken in their thoughtful preface to the otherwise whimsical *The American Credo: A Contribution toward the Interpretation of the National Mind* (1920; rpt., London: Dodo Press, 2008). For them, the "dominant passion" of the American is "to lift himself [*sic*] by at least a step or two in the society that he is a part of—a passion to improve his position, to break down some shadowy barrier of caste. . . . The American is a pusher. His eyes are ever fixed on some round of the ladder that is just beyond his reach" (xii).

33. Quoted in Brenman-Gibson, *Clifford Odets*, 251.

34. Here I am excluding O'Casey's pre-Abbey efforts like *The Harvest Festival* and Odets's O'Neill-inspired one-act plays *Dawn* and *At the Water Line*, begun in 1925 (Brenman-Gibson, *Clifford Odets*, 91).

35. Clifford Odets, *Awake and Sing!* in *"Waiting for Lefty" and Other Plays* (New York: Grove Press, 1994), 62. All quotations from Odets's plays come from this volume and will be followed by page numbers in the text.

36. Norman Rabkin, *Drama and Commitment: Politics in the American Theatre of the Thirties* (Bloomington: Indiana University Press, 1964), 249–51.

37. Philip Roth, *American Pastoral* (1997; New York: Vintage, 1998), 7.

38. Elmer Rice, *We, The People* (New York: Coward-McCann, 1933), 47. All quotations from the play come from this edition and will be followed by page numbers in the text.

39. Elmer Rice, *Three Plays: "The Adding Machine," "Street Scene," "Dream Girl"* (New York: Hill and Wang, 1965), 116–17. All quotations from *The Adding Machine* and *Street Scene* come from this volume and will be followed by page numbers in the text.

40. In *Not for Children* (1934) from *Other Plays and Not for Children* (London: Victor Gollancz, 1935), Rice alludes almost mockingly to the convention of dramatizing the problems of pregnant women through Ambrose Atwater, a former professor fired for having an elicit relationship with a female student, who quips, "If the heroines of plays ever learn the technique of contraception, half our dramatists will have to go back to the prairies" (436).

41. Andrew Sofer, "Spectral Readings," *Theatre Journal* 64 (October 2012): 332, 333.

42. Ngai, *Ugly Feelings*, 335.

43. For a summary of the play and these effects, see Anthony F. R. Palmieri, *Elmer Rice: A Playwright's Vision of America* (Rutherford: Fairleigh Dickinson University Press, 1980), 77–86.

44. This fictional film should not be confused with Victor Herbert's comic opera *Hearts of Erin*, renamed *Ellen*, after its 1917 opening on Broadway and based on Samuel Lover's novel *Rory O'Moore*.

45. The rural Irish setting suggested by both the orchestra's playing of "Killarney" and the presence of a pipe-smoking Irishwoman, along with the snippets of plot revealing a lord's attempted seduction of a heroine, recall "The Lass of Aughrim," the singing of which affects Gretta Conroy near the conclusion of Joyce's "The Dead." In this way, perhaps, Rice places an Irish ballad with all of its romantic quality in the center of his protagonist's efforts to escape a machine-dominated modernity.

46. Clifford Odets, *The Time Is Ripe: The 1940 Journal of Clifford Odets* (New York: Grove Press, 1988), 16.

47. Odets, *The Time Is Ripe*, 87.

48. For a discussion of Odets's efforts to avoid this "certain problem," see Mary Elizabeth Phillips, "Clifford Odets: Writing around Jewishness," Ph.D. dissertation, National University of Ireland–Galway, 2012. Her third chapter, "Odets in Hollywood," is especially incisive on this topic.

49. Murray, *Seán O'Casey*, 265.

50. Lowery and Angelin, *My Very Dear Sean*, 172, 173.

51. O'Connor, *Sean O'Casey:* 333.

52. Murray, *Seán O'Casey*, 266. Johnston's rebuke is quoted on the same page.

53. Quoted in Murray, *Seán O'Casey*, 382.

54. Miller explains his affection for *A Memory of Two Mondays* in his introduction to *Arthur Miller's Collected Plays* (New York: Viking Press, 1957), 49, adding that the play was "dismissed so thoroughly that in one of the reviews, and one of the most important, it was not even mentioned as having been played" (48). All quotations from his introduction to *A Memory of Two Mondays* and *A View from the Bridge* will be followed by page numbers in the text.

55. For a brief discussion of Rice's efforts, see Palmieri, *Elmer Rice*, 125–26, and Clifford Odets, preface, in *Waiting for Lefty and Other Plays*, vii.

56. Arthur Miller, *Timebends: A Life* (New York: Grove Press, 1987), 353.

57. Miller, *Timebends*, 353. See also the opening pages of Christopher Bigsby, *Arthur Miller, 1962–2005* (Ann Arbor: University of Michigan Press, 2011). Bigsby begins his first chapter with this quotation from Miller: "The plays are my autobiography. I can't write plays that don't sum up where I am. I'm in all of them. I don't know how else to go about writing" (1).

58. Arthur Miller, "On Social Plays," in *The Theater Essays of Arthur Miller*, ed. Robert A. Martin (New York: Viking Press, 1978), 65.

59. Martin Gottfried, *Arthur Miller: His Life and Work* (Cambridge, MA: Da Capo Books, 2003), 252, 249.

60. Stella Adler, Script Analysis of J. M. Synge's *Riders to the Sea*, March 23, 1959–March 26, 1959. Box 15.4, Ransom Humanities Center, University of Texas at Austin. Further quotations from this archive will be followed by date and page numbers in the text. Synge made this comment in his preface to *The Playboy of the Western World*, in *Collected Works*, gen. ed. Robin Skelton, 4 vols. (London: Oxford University Press, 1961–68); vol. 4, ed. Ann Saddlemyer, 4:54.

61. Gottfried, *Arthur Miller*, 249. Miller's praise of O'Casey and Odets as Marxist prophets with lyrical voices was excerpted in "Ibsen and the Drama of Today" in the program of Dublin's Gate Theatre 2013 production of Miller's *Enemy of the People* (9). In this program, director Wayne Jordan recognizes the relevance of Miller's adaptation to "our own broken little country" at a historical moment when the "many must take the consequences for the risks taken by the few" (3).

62. Christopher Bigsby, *Arthur Miller, 1915–1962* (Cambridge: Harvard University Press, 2009), 402.

63. In *Arthur Miller, 1915–1962*, Bigsby makes the same point about the young Miller's work at an auto warehouse: "The warehouse personnel were almost exclusively Irish and suspicious of Miller" (68). Little of this suspicion surfaces in the play, and most distinctions between the Irish and Irish-Americans seem effaced save for the latter's ignorance of Irish songs.

64. Bert's reading of *War and Peace* is hardly accidental, as Miller's own enthusiasm for literature was sparked by such Russian novels as Dostoyevsky's *Crime and Punishment* and *The Idiot*. Like Gottfried, Bigsby also refers to the predominantly Irish world at the warehouse Miller entered (Bigsby, *Arthur Miller, 1915–1962*, 65–71), emphasizing that Miller may have been somewhat oblivious to anti-Semitism until his graduation from high school and search for a job (68). Miller came to view the warehouse workers' anti-Semitism as "not as important as their contempt for themselves" (70). More important for my purposes, Miller's philo-Hibernian pull overwhelms other considerations.

65. See Nelson Ó Ceallaigh Ritschel, *Shaw, Synge, Connolly, and Socialist Provocation* (Gainesville: University Presses of Florida, 2011), 17–27. Ritschel argues that, in his trips to the Aran Islands, particularly Inishmaan, "Synge found workers not destroyed, or alienated, by their work." Due to their remoteness, the islands had no industry, land agents, or even "bosses"; consequently, laborers did not feel "valueless" or exploited by a "modern capitalist system" (18).

66. The first two quotations about *A Memory of Two Mondays* come from Miller's introduction to the *Collected Plays*, 5, 50, and last one is taken from his 1965 essay "What Makes Plays Endure?" published in the *New York Times* and reprinted in *The Theater Essays of Arthur Miller*, 260.

67. Miller, *Theater Essays*, 119.

68. Ferriter, *The Transformation of Ireland*, 381, 383. This exodus of young Irish continued during the postwar years. As Mary E. Daly reports in *The Slow Failure: Population Decline and Independent Ireland, 1920–1973* (Madison: University of Wisconsin Press, 2006), *The Report of the Royal Commission on Population* (1949) predicted that Britain would require some 140,000 young adult immigrants each year for a decade to re-constitute a viable labor force (151).

69. Ferriter notes that in 1933, the time of the first Monday of Miller's play, a group of Cork farmers informed the Irish Ministry of Agriculture that only twelve marriages had occurred in the previous year (*The Transformation of Ireland*, 375).

70. Working for the civil service is thus as highly ambivalent as allo-Semitism and allo-Hibernianism. For Kenneth, it represents a final move, the end of mobility and the closing of a door of employment possibility. At the same time, as R.F. Foster explains in *Modern Ireland, 1600–1972* (London: Penguin, 1988), in 1932 Irish president Eamon de Valera attempted to cut the salaries of civil servants because he felt they were earning more than the country could afford. A committee at the time likened the "'impoverished country with such an elaborate governmental machine" to a "Tin Lizzie fitted with a Rolls-Royce eight-cylinder engine.'" See Foster, 342–45.

71. See chapter 1.

72. Andrew Sofer, *The Stage Life of Props* (Ann Arbor: University of Michigan Press, 2003), 2, 9. Sofer takes the latter point from the theoretical work of Jiří Veltruský.

73. Bill Brown, "Thing Theory," *Critical Inquiry* 28 (Autumn 2001): 4.

74. Stella Adler, *The Art of Acting*, ed. Howard Kissel (New York: Applause Books, 2000), 78.

75. Stella Adler, *Stella Adler on America's Master Playwrights*, ed. Barry Paris (New York: Vintage Books, 2012), 125. All further quotations will be followed by page numbers in the text.

76. Adler's point might be extended to include weaker men as well, for whom cars—especially expensive makes and models—function similarly as symbols of success. In Rice's *The Adding Machine*, for example, when Zero fantasizes about confronting his boss and asking for a raise, he also plans on buying a "place in Jersey" and "maybe a little Buick. No tin Lizzie for me" (12).

77. Elmer Rice, *Counsellor-at-Law*, in *Awake and Singing: Seven Classic Plays from the American Jewish Repertoire*, ed. Ellen Schiff (New York: Mentor Books, 1995), 93.

78. Rice, *Counsellor-at-Law*, 109.

79. Lawson, *Success Story*, 9.

80. Christopher J. Herr, *Clifford Odets and the American Political Theatre* (Westport, CT: Praeger, 2003), 87. Jean Baudrillard discusses speed in *America*, trans. Chris Turner (New York: Verso, 1988): for example, "Speed is the triumph of effect over cause, the triumph of instantaneity over time as depth, the triumph of surface and pure objectality over the profundity of desire." Speed has only one rule: "leave no trace behind" (6).

81. Eugene O'Neill, *A Moon for the Misbegotten* (New York: Vintage Books, 1974), 47. All quotations from this play will be followed by page numbers in the text.

82. Brendan Behan, *Borstal Boy* (New York: Alfred A. Knopf, 1959), 72. All further quotations from this volume will be followed by page numbers in the text. This comic invention is discussed in more detail in the next chapter.

83. See William H. A. Williams, *'Twas Only an Irishman's Dream* (Champaign: University of Illinois Press, 1996), 29–30.

84. Raleigh, "Irish Atavism," 229.

85. Raleigh, "Irish Atavism," 230.

86. Eugene O'Neill, *A Touch of the Poet* (New Haven: Yale University Press, 1957), 20. All further quotations from this play will be followed by page numbers in the text.

87. For a discussion of Christine Ell and Josie Hogan, see Sheaffer, *O'Neill*, 330–31, 435, and 442–43.

Chapter 5

1. Clive Hart, "Wandering Rocks," in *James Joyce's Ulysses*, ed. Clive Hart and David Hayman (Berkeley: University of California Press, 1974), 187.

2. See David Biale, "Masochism and Philosemitisim: The Stange Case of Leopold von Sacher-Masoch," *Journal of Contemporary History* 17 (1982): 305–23. Biale discusses Sacher-Masoch's Jewish stories as a "vehicle for his erotic fantasies" (313) and observes that the subgenre *ghettogeschichten* typically includes tales of powerful Jewish wives or "beautiful 'semitic' girls," foregrounding their "romantic problems." In addition, Jewish and non-Jewish readers alike were presented with "a sentimentalized and romanticized community that might satisfy their need for a *recherché du temps perdu*" (306). Selections in Sacher-Masoch's *Jewish Tales*, trans. Harriet Lieber Cohen (1878; Chicago: A.C. McClurg, 1894) confirm these observations, as several depict simple times in villages and towns. While many of the stories do not concern the amatory dilemmas of beautiful young women, several do. In "How Sloba Married Her Sister," two beautiful sisters whose good looks and taste help sell gowns and bonnets in the family dry goods store—a familiar convention—attract numerous suitors. Sloba, the younger sister, falls for a young bookseller who seeks her hand in marriage, but her father will not agree to the match until his elder—and haughty—daughter Bella is also betrothed. The story follows Sloba and her fiancé acting as matchmakers for Bella, contriving successfully to produce a double marriage at the story's conclusion.

3. John Banville, *Shroud* (2002; New York: Vintage Books, 2004), 27. All further quotations from this novel will be followed by page numbers in the text.

4. For an articulation of the performativity of Jewishness and Paul de Man's "hermeneutics of suspicion," see Elmer Kennedy-Andrews, "Representations of the Jew in the Modern Irish Novel since Joyce," *Irish University Review* 43 (Autumn–Winter 2013): 322–25.

5. Philip Roth, *The Counterlife* (1986; New York: Vintage, 1996), 321. Like Vander, Nathan Zuckerman insists that there is no self, hence all is "impersonation." Moderating his claim slightly in the novel's later pages, he also observes that if there is "an irreducible self, it is rather small" (320).

6. John Banville, *Eclipse* (2000; New York: Vintage Books, 2002), 141.

7. For a discussion of subjectivity in Banville and Baudrillardian simulation, see Hedda Friberg, " '[P]assing through Ourselves and Finding Ourselves in the Beyond': The Rites of Passage of Cass Cleave in John Banville's *Eclipse* and *Shroud*," *Irish University Review* 36 (Spring–Summer 2006): 151–64.

8. Ulick O'Connor, *Brendan Behan* (1970; London: Abacus, 1993), 282–83.

9. Rae Jeffs, *Brendan Behan: Man and Showman* (Cleveland: World Publishing, 1968), 142–43.

10. Norman Mailer, *The Armies of the Night: History as a Novel, The Novel as History* (New York: Plume, 1968), 3.

11. Mailer, *Armies of the Night*, 37.

12. Mailer, *Armies of the Night*, 64.

13. See John Brannigan, *Brendan Behan: Cultural Nationalism and the Revisionist Writer* (Dublin: Four Courts Press, 2002), 24–28.

14. Norman Podhoretz, "The Know-Nothing Bohemians," in *The Norman Podhoretz Reader*, ed. Thomas L. Jeffers (New York: Free Press, 2004), 31–33.

15. Anthony Cronin, *Dead as Doornails* (1976; Dublin: Lilliput Press, 1999), 66. All further quotations from this book will be followed by page numbers in the text.

16. Thanks to the Internet, these remarks and exchanges are widely available online.

17. See Brendan Behan, with drawings by Paul Hogarth, *Brendan Behan's New York* (Boston: Little, Brown, 1964), 20. Quotations from this book will be followed by page numbers in the text.

18. For a representation of a 1930s-era vacation in the Catskills, see Will Eisner's "Cookalein" in his graphic novel *The Contract with God Trilogy* (1978; New York: W.W. Norton, 2006), 125–80. At the opposite end of the economic spectrum, Grossinger's Hotel and Country Club, one of the area's best-known resorts, was spread over eight hundred acres with six hundred rooms and a 1,700-seat dining room. See Stefan Kanfer, *A Summer World: The Attempt to Build a Jewish Eden in the Catskills, from the Days of the Ghetto to the Rise and Decline of the Borscht Belt* (New York: Farrar, Straus and Giroux, 1989), 7–8.

19. Kanfer, *A Summer World*, 227.

20. See Jerry Stiller, *Married to Laughter: A Love Story Featuring Anne Meara* (New York: Touchstone, 2000), 199–200, 205.

21. Michael O'Sullivan, *Brendan Behan: A Life* (Dublin: Blackwater Press, 1999), 264.

22. These quotations are from Janet Behan's play *Brendan at the Chelsea* (2011 script), *Irish University Review* 44 (Spring–Summer 2014): 20. The play, first produced in 2008, treats Behan's residency at the Chelsea Hotel in New York during the spring of 1963. In this scene, he reads these letters with his Jewish musician-friend George, whom he sardonically asks, "Well isn't it great to have the support of your own people?" (20).

23. See Mary V. Dearborn, *Mailer: A Biography* (Boston: Houghton Mifflin, 1999), 161–64.

24. "Norman Mailer Arrested in Stabbing of Wife at Party," *New York Times*, November 22, 1960.

25. This antipathy, as both Ulick O'Connor and Michael O'Sullivan chronicle, manifested itself in Behan's banning from the 1961 St. Patrick's Day Parade in New York. See O'Connor, *Brendan Behan*, 296–98, and O'Sullivan, *Brendan Behan*, 275–77.

26. Pilkington, *Theatre & Ireland*, 3.

27. Brendan Behan, *The Big House*, in *Brendan Behan's Island: An Irish Sketch-book* (London: Hutchinson, 1962), 94. All further quotations from this radio play will be followed by page numbers in the text.

28. Dominic Behan, *My Brother Brendan* (New York: Simon and Schuster, 1965), 100.

29. Benjamin Appel, *The Dark Stain* (New York: Dial Press, 1943), 32.

30. As is widely known, Behan narrated *Brendan Behan's New York* and *Brendan Behan's Island: A Sketch-book* into a tape recorder, as he was no longer able to write in any sustained way during the latter years of his life. Frank O'Connor in early 1964 said that he wished he "had it in [his] power to suppress *Brendan Behan's New York*. . . . It will not be New York and it will not be Brendan." See E. H. Mikhail, ed., *Interviews and Recollections*, 2 vols. (Totowa, NJ: Barnes and Noble, 1982), 2:260. In 1965, Benedict Kiely referred to *Brendan Behan's New York* as a "sad book" (*Interviews and Recollections* 2:306).

31. It should be noted that Ethel Merman was not Jewish; thus, both Jewishness and celebrity may be equally responsible for Behan's sense of ease and familiarity.

32. This praise of "good old melodrama" is hardly surprising given the careers of his uncle P. J. Bourke and his cousin Jimmy, also known as Séamus de Búrca. Jimmy took great pride in popular theater and in Behan, as he expressed to me several times in letters or over lunch. See his book *The Queen's Royal Theatre, Dublin, 1829–1969* (Dublin: de Búrca, 1983).

33. Writing from Hollywood on May 19, 1961, to his half-brother Rory Furlong, Behan praises New York as a "real city," while Los Angeles has "no navel" because it has no Broadway. Still, he enjoyed California sunshine and swimming pools: "I just leave my suite and go down in the lift wearing my togs with the Jews and smart Irish." See *The Letters of Brendan Behan*, ed. E. H. Mikhail (Houndsmills, Basingstoke: Macmillan, 1992), 196.

34. Brendan Behan, *Borstal Boy*, 120. This is merely one of Behan's many expressions of good will to his Jewish associates.

35. See chapter 1.

36. As discussed in chapter 2, in Boucicault's play, *After Dark: A Drama of London Life in 1868* and John Brougham's *The Lottery of Life: A Story of New York*, Jews play unscrupulous gamblers; in George Henry Jessop's *Sam'l of Posen; or, The Commercial Drummer*, the protagonist enters the play selling inexpensive goods at a profit.

37. Marcus, "Salomé!!" 1010.

38. Marcus, "Salomé!!" 1011.

39. "Ten Years Ago," *Catskill Mountain News*, August 5, 1971: 1.

40. This roast of Don Rickles is commercially available under several titles such as *Friars Club Roast of Don Rickles 1968*.

41. In a 1967 monologue on television, King reviews the fourteen "nose jobs" his family members have received, his sister having two though her nose is still not "permanent"; in his bit "Jews and Gentiles," Mason magnifies differences between the two, which includes Jews' mechanical ineptitude and their anxieties over weighing themselves.

42. In *A Summer World*, Stefan Kanfer introduces another comic tactic, something he terms "physical Yiddish" or Yiddish body language. This strategy, exemplified by what became the stock "bewildered look" of Ed Wynn or the "bared teeth" exaggerated smile of Milton Berle, became a vehicle for expressing Jewish humor without words. One might ask if a similar "physical Irish" exists as a complement to this device. See Kanfer, 224–26.

43. *Letters of Brendan Behan*, 217.

44. *Letters of Brendan Behan*, 220.

45. Tim Pat Coogan, *The Famine Plot: England's Role in Ireland's Greatest Tragedy* (New York: Palgrave Macmillan, 2012), 3.

46. Harold Pinter, "Mac," in *Poems and Prose, 1949–1977* (London: Eyre Methuen, 1978), 82.

47. Quoted in Michael Billington, *Harold Pinter* (London: Faber and Faber 2007), 268.

48. Anthony Roche, "Pinter and Ireland," in *The Cambridge Companion to Harold Pinter*, 2nd ed., ed. Peter Raby (Cambridge: Cambridge University Press, 2009), 195–215.

49. I discuss the influence of Joyce's *Ulysses* on Pinter's early writing in "Things, Voices, Events: Harold Pinter's *Mountain Language* as Testamental Text," *Modern Drama* 52.1 (2009): 38–56. See also Antonia Fraser, *Must You Go? My Life with Harold Pinter* (New York: Doubleday, 2010), 57. Here she describes the way her husband revered Beckett and includes a photograph of Pinter at Joyce's gravesite in Zurich.

50. Roche, "Pinter and Ireland," 196.

51. Harold Pinter, *Celebration and The Room* (New York: Grove Press, 2000), 31.

52. Pinter, *Celebration*, 47.

53. Penelope Prentice, *The Pinter Ethic: The Erotic Aesthetic* (New York: Garland, 2000), 403.

54. Pinter, *Celebration*, 16, 61.

55. Harold Pinter, *Ashes to Ashes* (New York: Grove Press, 1996), 41.

56. Patrick Lonergan, *Theatre and Globalization: Irish Drama in the Celtic Tiger Era* (Houndmills, Basingstoke: Palgrave Macmillan, 2009), 2.

57. See, for example, Fredric Jameson, *The Seeds of Time* (New York: Columbia University Press, 1994).

58. Carey Perloff, "Pinter in Rehearsal: From *The Birthday Party* to *Mountain Language*," in *Pinter at Sixty*, ed. Katherine H. Burkman and John L. Kundert-Gibbs (Bloomington: Indiana University Press, 1993), 3–6.

59. See "Revelation," an edited conversation between designer Walt Spangler and artistic director Martha Lavey, in the Steppenwolf program for *The Birthday Party* (2013), 21–22.

60. Harold Pinter, *The Birthday Party and The Room* (New York: Grove Press, 1959), 52. All further quotations from *The Birthday Party* will be followed by page numbers in the text. It isn't entirely clear why Drogheda, located near Dublin, entered the conversation; however, that fact that it is the site of the so-called Massacre of the Innocents, an atrocity perpetrated by Cromwellian forces in 1649, adds historical resonance to its inclusion.

61. John Banville, "The Missing Link," in *Aidan Higgins: The Fragility of Form*, ed. Neil Murphy (Champaign and London: Dalkey Archive Press, 2010), 45.

62. Banville, "The Missing Link," 49.

63. Aidan Higgins, *Langrishe, Go Down* (1966; Normal, IL: Dalkey Archive Press, 2004), 47.

64. Harold Pinter, *Langrishe, Go Down* in *Collected Screenplays One* (London: Faber and Faber, 2000), 660.

65. Vera Kreilkamp, "Reinventing a Form: The Big House in Aidan Higgins' *Langrishe, Go Down*," *Canadian Journal of Irish Studies* 11 (December 1985): 34.

66. Kiberd, *Ulysses and Us*, 6, 29.

67. Howard Jacobson, *The Finkler Question* (New York: Bloomsbury, 2010), 71. All quotation from this novel will be followed by page numbers in the text.

68. Goldstein, *The Price of Whiteness*, 36–37.

69. Litvak, "Jew Envy," 96.

70. Lawrence Grossberg, interviewed by Gregory J. Seigworth and Melissa Gregg, "Affect's Future: Rediscovering the Virtual in the Actual," in *The Affect Theory Reader*, ed. Melissa Gregg and Gregor J. Seigworth (Durham, NC: Duke University Press, 2010), 313.

71. Miroslav Volf, *The End of Memory: Remembering Rightly in a Violent World* (Grand Rapids, MI: William B. Eerdmans, 2006), 39–40.

72. Quotations from MacLaverty's fiction come from *Cal* (London: George Braziller, 1983), and *Grace Notes* (New York: W.W. Norton, 1997). All quotations come from these editions and will be followed by page numbers in the text.

73. Michael Rothberg, *Multidirectional Memory: Remembering the Holocaust in the Age of Decolonization* (Stanford: Stanford University Press, 2009), 3.

74. Patricia T. Clough, "The Affective Turn: Political Economy, Biomedia, and Bodies," in Gregg and Seigworth, *The Affect Theory Reader*, 209. Here, Clough is discussing the work of Brian Massumi who, like Grossberg, is a major contributor to this theoretical conversation.

75. Gerry Smyth, " 'The Same Sound but with a Different Meaning': Music, Repetition, and Identity in Bernard MacLaverty's *Grace Notes*," *Éire-Ireland* 37 (2002): 15.

76. Volf, *The End of Memory*, 23.

77. Theodor W. Adorno, "What Does Coming to Terms with the Past Mean?" in *Bitburg in Moral and Political Perspective*, ed. Geoffrey H. Hartman (Bloomington: Indiana University Press, 1986), 115.

78. Paul Ricoeur, *Memory, History, Forgetting*, trans. Kathleen Blamey and David Pellauer (Chicago: University of Chicago Press, 2004), 412.

79. Ricoeur, *Memory, History, Forgetting*, 413.

80. Primo Levi, *Survival in Auschwitz* (1958; New York: Classic House, 2008), 46.

81. Levi, *Survival in Auschwitz*, 4.

82. Ricoeur, *Memory, History, Forgetting*, 427.

83. Volf, *The End of Memory*, 11.

84. See James E. Young, "Memory and Monument," in Hartman, *Bitburg*, 105, 112. Young cites an inscription on the monument in Denver's Babi Yar Park that 100,000 "citizens of Kiev and prisoners of war" died there. He observes that 33,000 people died at the Babi Yar ravine (MacLaverty's Melnichuck sets this number at 35,000) and notes that 100,000 people were murdered in and around Kiev by Nazi troops between 1941 and 1943. He also makes the important point that such descriptors as "prisoners of war" and "citizens" obscure the fact that "almost all were killed for having been Jews" (105).

85. Rothberg, *Multidirectional Memory*, 2.

86. Rothberg, *Multidirectional Memory*, 5.

87. Lewis Funke, "Interview with Brian Friel," in *Brian Friel in Conversation*, ed. Paul Delaney (Ann Arbor: University of Michigan Press, 2000), 61.

88. Daly, *The Slow Failure*, 3.

89. Daly, *The Slow Failure*, 4.

90. See Ferriter, *The Transformation of Ireland*, 472–81 for a discussion of immigration, unemployment, and other related social maladies.

91. Brian Friel, *Philadelphia, Here I Come!*, in *Brian Friel: Plays 1* (London: Faber and Faber, 1996), 32. All further quotations from this play will be followed by page numbers in the text.

92. See Richard Rankin Russell, *Modernity, Community, and Place in Brian Friel's Drama* (Syracuse: Syracuse University Press, 2014), 30–63.

93. Gish Jen, *Mona in the Promised Land* (1996; New York: Vintage, 1997), 3. All further quotations come from this edition and will be followed by page numbers in the text.

94. David Henry Hwang, *"FOB" and Other Plays* (New York: New American Library, 1990), 6.

{ BIBLIOGRAPHY }

Adelman, Janet. *Blood Relations: Christian and Jew in "The Merchant of Venice."* Chicago: University of Chicago Press, 2008.

Adler, Stella. *The Art of Acting.* Edited and compiled by Howard Kissel. New York: Applause Books, 2000.

Adler, Stella. Script Analysis of Synge's *Riders to the Sea.* March 23, 1959–March 26, 1960. Harry Ransom Center, University of Texas at Austin. Box 15.4.

Adler, Stella. *Stella Adler on America's Master Playwrights.* Edited by Barry Paris. New York: Vintage Books, 2012.

Adorno, Theodor W. "What Does Coming to Terms with the Past Mean?" In *Bitburg in Moral and Political Perspective*, edited by Geoffrey H. Hartman, 114–29. Bloomington: Indiana University Press, 1986.

Adorno, Theodor W., and Max Horkheimer. *Dialectic of Enlightenment.* 1944. Translated by John Cumming. New York: Continuum, 1993.

Ahmed, Sara. *The Cultural Politics of Emotion.* New York: Routledge, 2004.

"Amusements." *Chicago Daily Tribune*, September 13, 1883.

"Amusements." *New York Times*, January 20, 1863.

"Amusements: Broadway Theatre." *New York Times*, October 31, 1878.

"Amusements: Wallack's Theatre." *New York Times*, June 11, 1867.

Anbinder, Tyler. "Moving beyond 'Rags to Riches': New York's Irish Famine Immigrants and Their Surprising Savings Accounts." *Journal of American History* 99 (December 2012): 741–70.

Anderson, Emily Hodgson. "Celebrity Shylock." *PMLA* 126.4 (2011): 935–49.

Angoff, Charles S., ed. *The World of George Jean Nathan: Essays, Reviews, and Commentary.* New York: Applause Books, 1998.

Appel, Benjamin. *The Dark Stain.* New York: Dial Press, 1943.

Appel, Benjamin. *Hell's Kitchen.* New York: Pantheon, 1977.

Archer, William. *About the Theatre.* London: T. Fisher Unwin, 1886.

Armitage, David. "Three Concepts of Atlantic History." In *The British Atlantic World, 1500–1800*, 2nd ed., edited by David Armitage and Michael J. Braddick, 13–29. Houndmills, Basingstoke: Palgrave Macmillan, 2009.

"At the Play." *The Theatre: A Monthly Review and Magazine* 1 (December 1, 1878): 372–87.

Banville, John. "The Missing Link." In *Aidan Higgins: The Fragility of Form*, edited by Neil Murphy, 42–53. Champaign and London: Dalkey Archive Press, 2010.

Banville, John. *Eclipse.* 2000. New York: Vintage Books, 2002.

Banville, John. *Shroud.* 2002. New York: Vintage Books, 2004.

Barnstone, Willis. *We Jews and Blacks.* Bloomington: Indiana University Press, 2004.

Baudrillard, Jean. *America.* Translated by Chris Turner. New York: Verso, 1988.

Bauman, Zygmunt. "Allosemitism: Premodern, Modern, Postmodern." In *Modernity, Culture and "the Jew,"* edited by Bryan Cheyette and Laura Marcus, 143–58. Cambridge: Polity Press, 1998.

Behan, Brendan. *Borstal Boy.* New York: Alfred A. Knopf, 1959.

Behan, Brendan. *Brendan Behan's Island: An Irish Sketch-book.* London: Hutchinson, 1962.

Behan, Brendan. *Brendan Behan's New York.* Boston: Little, Brown, 1964.

Behan, Dominic. *My Brother Brendan.* New York: Simon and Schuster, 1965.

Behan, Janet. *Brendan at the Chelsea,* 2011 script. *Irish University Review* 44 (Spring–Summer 2014): 6–58.

Berger, Harry, Jr. *Fury in the Words: Love and Embarrassment in Shakespeare's Venice.* New York: Fordham University Press, 2013.

Berlant, Lauren. *Cruel Optimism.* Durham, NC: Duke University Press, 2011.

Berlin, Irving. *The Complete Lyrics of Irving Berlin.* Edited by Robert Kimball and Linda Emmet. New York: Applause, 2005.

Bernstein, Robin. "Toward the Integration of Theatre History and Affect Studies: Shame and the Rude Mechs's *The Method Gun." Theatre Journal* 64 (May 2012): 213–30.

Bigsby, Christopher. *Arthur Miller, 1915–1962.* Cambridge, MA: Harvard University Press, 2009.

Bigsby, Christopher. *Arthur Miller, 1962–2005.* Ann Arbor: University of Michigan Press, 2011.

Billings, Harold. Introduction to *"Bottom Dogs," "From Flushing to Calvary," "Those Who Perish," and Hitherto Unpublished and Uncollected Works by Edward Dahlberg,* xiii–xx. New York: Thomas Y. Crowell, 1976.

Billington, Michael. *Harold Pinter.* London: Faber and Faber, 2007.

Bingham, Madeleine. *Henry Irving and the Victorian Theatre.* London: George Allen & Unwin, 1978.

Bloch, Ernst. *The Principle of Hope.* Vol. 1. Translated by Neville Plaice, Stephen Plaice, and Paul Knight. 1959. Cambridge, MA: MIT Press, 1995.

Boltwood, Scott. Introduction to Dion Boucicault, *Arrah-na-Pogue.* London: Methuen, 2010, n.p.

Bornstein, George. *The Colors of Zion: Blacks, Jews, and Irish from 1845 to 1945.* Cambridge, MA: Harvard University Press, 2011.

Boucicault, Dion. *After Dark: A Drama of London Life in 1868.* New York: DeWitt, 1869.

Boucicault, Dion. *Arrah-na-Pogue; or, The Wicklow Wedding.* 1867. London: Methuen, 2010.

Boucicault, Dion. *Louis XI.* In *Forbidden Fruit and Other Plays,* edited by Allardyce Nicoll and F. Theodore Cloak, 51–106. Bloomington: Indiana University Press, 1963.

Boucicault, Dion. *The Phantom.* London: Dicks' Standard Plays, 1856.

Boucicault, Dion. *Robert Emmet.* In *Selected Plays Dion Boucicault,* introduced by Andrew Parkin, 331–97. Gerrards Cross: Colin Smythe; Washington, DC: Catholic University Press of America, 1987.

Bowker, Gordon. *James Joyce: A Biography.* London: Weidenfeld & Nicolson, 2011.

Boyle, Kay. Correspondence with Samuel Beckett and Edward Dahlberg. Harry Ransom Center, University of Texas at Austin. Box 1.6.

Brannigan, John. *Brendan Behan: Cultural Nationalism and the Revisionist Writer.* Dublin: Four Courts Press, 2002.

Brenman-Gibson, Margaret. *Clifford Odets American Playwright: The Years from 1906 to 1940*. New York: Atheneum, 1981.

Brock, Gillian, and Harry Brighouse, eds. *The Political Philosophy of Cosmopolitanism*. Cambridge: Cambridge University Press, 2005.

Brooks, Peter. *The Melodramatic Imagination: Balzac, Henry James, Melodrama, and the Mode of Excess*. New York: Columbia University Press, 1985.

Brougham, John. *The Lottery of Life: A Story of New York*. 1868. New York: Samuel French, 1875.

Brougham, John. *Love and Murder: A Farce in One Act*. New York: Samuel French, 1856.

Brougham, John. *Temptation, or, the Irish Emigrant: A Comic Drama in Two Acts*. New York: Samuel French, 1856.

Brown, Bill. "Thing Theory." *Critical Inquiry* 28 (Autumn 2001): 1–22.

Brown, Mary Elizabeth. "A Separate Feast: The Italian Influence on Catholic New York." In *Catholics in New York: Society, Culture, and Politics 1808–1946*, edited by Terry Golway, 27–39. New York: Fordham University Press / Museum of the City of New York, 2008.

Bulwer-Lytton, Sir Edward. *The Lady of Lyons*. In *Nineteenth-Century British Drama*, edited by Leonard R. N. Ashley, 138–92. Glenview, IL: Scott, Foresman, 1967.

Burke, Helen. "Teague and the Ethnicization of Labor in Early Modern British Culture." *Eighteenth Century: Theory and Interpretation* 46.3 (2005): 237–44.

Byron, Henry J. *Ivanhoe, An Extravaganza*. London: Thomas Hailes Lacy, 1862.

Campbell, Mrs. Patrick. *My Life and Some Letters*. London: Hutchinson, 1922.

Canfield, J. Douglas, gen. ed. *The Broadview Anthology of Restoration and Early Eighteenth-Century Drama*. Peterborough, Ontario: Broadview Press, 2001.

Carlson, Marvin. *The Haunted Stage: The Theatre as Memory-Machine*. Ann Arbor: University of Michigan Press, 2001.

Carson, Ciaran. *Belfast Confetti*. Winston-Salem: Wake Forest University Press, 1989.

Cartwright, Keith. *Sacral Grooves, Limbo Gateways: Travels in Deep Southern Time, Circum-Caribbean Space, Afro-Creole Authority*. Athens: University of Georgia Press, 2013.

Chambers, Jonathan L. *Messiah of the New Technique: John Howard Lawson, Communism, and American Theatre, 1923–1937*. Carbondale: Southern Illinois University Press, 2006.

Cheyette, Bryan. *The Constructions of "The Jew" in English Literature and Society: Racial Representations, 1875–1945*. Cambridge: Cambridge University Press, 1993.

Cheyette, Bryan. "Jewish Stereotyping and English Literature, 1875–1920: Towards a Political Analysis." In *Traditions of Intolerance: Historical Perspectives on Fascism and Race Discourse in Britain*, edited by Tony Kushner and Kenneth Lunn, 12–32. Manchester: Manchester University Press, 1989.

Cheyette, Bryan. "Superman and Jew: Semitic Representations in the Work of Bernard Shaw." In *SHAW: The Annual of Bernard Shaw Studies* 12: 241–60. University Park: Pennsylvania State University Press, 1992.

Chude-Sokei, Louis. *Bert Williams, Black-on-Black Minstrelsy, and the African Diaspora*. Durham, NC: Duke University Press, 2006.

Cixous, Hélène, and Mireille Calle-Gruber. *Hélène Cixous Rootprints: Memory and Life Writing*. Translated by Eric Prenowitz. New York: Routledge, 1997.

Clare, Janet, and Stephen O'Neill, eds. *Shakespeare and the Irish Writer*. Dublin: UCD Press, 2010.

Clifford, James. "Diasporas." *Cultural Anthropology* 9 (1994): 302–38.

Clough, Patricia T. "The Affective Turn: Political Economy, Biomedia, and Bodies." In *The Affect Theory Reader*, edited by Melissa Gregg and Gregory J. Seigworth, 206–25. Durham, NC: Duke University Press, 2010.

Cockett, Stephen. "Serenade in a Gondola: Music and Interpolated Action in Irving's Production of *The Merchant of Venice*." In *Henry Irving: A Re-evaluation of the Pre-eminent Victorian Actor-Manager*, edited by Richard Foulkes, 135–48. London: Ashgate, 2008.

Coogan, Tim Pat. *The Famine Plot: England's Role in Ireland's Greatest Tragedy*. New York: Palgrave Macmillan, 2012.

Crane, Stephen. *Maggie, A Girl of the Streets*. In *The Complete Novels of Stephen Crane*, edited by Thomas A. Gullason, 99–154. Garden City, NY: Doubleday, 1967.

Cronin, Anthony. *Dead as Doornails*. 1976. Dublin: Lilliput Press, 1999.

Dahlberg, Edward. *Because I Was Flesh: The Autobiography of Edward Dahlberg*. 1959. New York: New Directions, 1967.

Dahlberg, Edward. *"Bottom Dogs," "From Flushing to Calvary," "Those Who Perish," and Hitherto Unpublished and Uncollected Works*. New York: Thomas Y. Crowell, 1976.

Daly, Augustin. *A Flash of Lightning*. In *Plays by Augustin Daly*, edited by Don B. Wilmeth and Rosemary Cullen, 48–102. Cambridge: Cambridge University Press, 1984.

Daly, Augustin. *Horizon*. In *Plays by Augustin Daly*, edited by Don B. Wilmeth and Rosemary Cullen, 103–62. Cambridge: Cambridge University Press, 1984.

Daly, Augustin. *Leah, the Forsaken*. New York: Samuel French & Son, 1863.

Daly, Augustin. *A Memoir of Miss Bateman; Being a Brief Chronicle of the Early Successes and Later Triumphs of the Great Tragic Artiste*. New York: Wynkoop, Hallenbeck, and Thomas, 1863.

Daly, Augustin. *Under the Gaslight*. In *American Drama: Colonial to Contemporary*, edited by Stephen Watt and Gary A. Richardson, 157–91. Fort Worth: Harcourt, Brace, 1995.

Daly, Mary E. *The Slow Failure: Population Decline and Independent Ireland, 1920–1973*. Madison: University of Wisconsin Press, 2006.

Davis, Jim. "'He Danced, He Did Not Merely Walk—He Sang, by No Means Merely Spoke': Irving, Theatricality and the Modernist Theatre." In *Henry Irving: A Re-Evaluation of the Pre-Eminent Victorian Actor-Manager*, edited by Richard Foulkes, 27–35. London: Ashgate, 2008.

Davis, Jim. Introduction to *Plays by H.J. Byron*, edited by Jim Davis, 1–32. Cambridge: Cambridge University Press, 1984.

Davis, Jim, and Victor Emeljanow. *Reflecting the Audience: London Theatregoing, 1840–1880*. Iowa City: University of Iowa Press, 2001.

Davis, Tracy C. Introduction to Paul Potter's *Trilby*. In *The Broadview Anthology of Nineteenth-Century British Performance*, edited by Tracy C. Davis, 577–87. Peterborough, Ontario: Broadview Press, 2012.

Davitt, Michael. *Within the Pale: The Story of Anti-Semitic Persecutions in Russia*. London: Hurst and Blackett, 1903.

Dearborn, Mary V. *Mailer: A Biography*. Boston: Houghton Mifflin, 1999.

Delaney, Enda. "The Vanishing Irish? The Exodus from Ireland in the 1950s." In *The Lost Decade: Ireland in the 1950s*, edited by Dermot Keogh, Finbarr O'Shea, and Carmel Quinlan, 80–86. Douglas Village, Cork: Mercier Press, 2004.

Dinnerstein, Leonard, and David M. Reimers. *Ethnic Americans: A History of Immigration.* 5th ed. New York: Columbia University Press, 2009.

Disher, Maurice Willson. *The Last Romantic: The Authorised Biography of Sir John Martin-Harvey.* London: Hutchinson, 1944.

Dobbins, Gregory. *Lazy Idle Schemers: Irish Modernism and the Cultural Politics of Idleness.* Dublin: Field Day Press, 2010.

Dolar, Mladen. *A Voice and Nothing More.* Cambridge, MA: MIT Press, 2006.

Donoghue, Denis. "Macklin's Shylock and Macbeth." *Studies: An Irish Quarterly Review* 43 (Winter 1954): 421–30.

Dos Passos, John. *Manhattan Transfer.* 1925. Boston: Houghton Mifflin, 2000.

Downer, Alan S. *The Eminent Tragedian: William Charles Macready.* Cambridge: Harvard University Press, 1966.

Du Maurier, George. *Trilby.* 1894. Rpt. Oxford: Oxford University Press, 1998.

Dziemianowicz, Joe. "*Outside Mullingar.*" *New York Daily News*, January 23, 2014.

"Education and the Dramatist." *New York Sun*, April 8, 1926, 26.

Eisner, Will. *The Contract with God Trilogy.* 1978. New York: W.W. Norton, 2006.

Elliott, J. H. "Atlantic History: A Circumnavigation." In *The British Atlantic World, 1500–1800*, 2nd ed., edited by David Armitage and Michael J. Braddick, 253–70. Houndmills, Basingstoke: Palgrave Macmillan, 2009.

Engels, Friedrich. *The Condition of the Working-Class in England.* 1845. Moscow: Progress Publishers, 1973.

Erdman, Harley. "M.B. Curtis and the Making of the American Stage Jew." *Journal of American Ethnic History* 15 (Fall 1995): 28–45.

Erdman, Harley. *Staging the Jew: The Performance of an American Ethnicity, 1860–1920.* New Brunswick: Rutgers University Press, 1997.

Ervine, St. John. *Bernard Shaw: His Life, Work and Friends.* New York: William Morrow, 1956.

Farquhar, George. *The Beaux' Stratagem.* Edited by Helen M. Burke. In *The Broadview Anthology of Restoration and Early Eighteenth-Century Drama*, J. Douglas, Canfield, general editor, 1278–1331. Peterborough, Ontario: Broadview Press, 2001.

Farrell, James T. *It Has Come to Pass.* New York: Theodor Herzl, 1958.

Farrell, James T. "Lest We Forget: Jim Larkin, Irish Labor Leader." 1961. In *On Irish Themes*, edited by Dennis Flynn, 143–51. Philadelphia: University of Pennsylvania Press, 1982.

Farrell, James T. *Studs Lonigan: A Trilogy.* 1932–35. New York: Library of America, 2004.

Fechter, Charles. *James O'Neill's Verison of "Monte Cristo".* In *America's Lost Plays*, vol. 16, edited by J. B. Russak, 1–70. Bloomington: Indiana University Press, 1940.

Ferriter, Diarmaid. *The Transformation of Ireland.* New York: Overlook Press, 2005.

Fisher, Judith L., and Stephen Watt, eds. *When They Weren't Doing Shakespeare: Essays on Nineteenth-Century British and American Theatre.* 1989. Athens: University of Georgia Press, 2011.

Fitzpatrick, David. "Irish Emigration in the Later Nineteenth Century." *Irish Historical Studies* 22 (September 1980): 126–43.

Fitzpatrick, Lisa. "Staging *The Merchant of Venice* in Cork: The Concretization of a Shakespeare Play for a New Society." *Modern Drama* 50 (Summer 2007): 168–83.

Flynn, Joyce. "Sites and Sighs: The Iconology of the Subterranean in Late Nineteenth-Century Irish-American Drama." *MELUS* 18 (Spring 1993): 5–19.

Foster, Michael, and Barbara Foster. *A Dangerous Woman: The Life, Loves, and Scandals of Adah Isaacs Mencken, 1835–1868, America's Original Superstar*. Guilford, CT: Lyons Press, 2011.

Foster, R. F. *Modern Ireland, 1600–1972*. London: Penguin, 1988.

Foucault, Michel. "Nietzsche, Genealogy, History." In *Language, Counter-Memory, Practice*, edited by Donald F. Bouchard, 139–64. Ithaca: Cornell University Press, 1977.

Foulkes, Richard. *Performing Shakespeare in the Age of Empire*. Cambridge: Cambridge University Press, 2002.

Foulkes, Richard, ed. *Henry Irving: A Re-evaluation of the Pre-eminent Victorian Actor-Manager*. London: Ashgate, 2008.

Fox, Pamela. *Class Fictions: Shame and Resistance in the British Working-Class Novel, 1890–1945*. Durham, NC: Duke University Press, 1994.

Fraser, Antonia. *Must You Go? My Life with Harold Pinter*. New York: Doubleday, 2010.

Freud, Sigmund. "The Uncanny" (1919). In *The Standard Edition of the Complete Psychological Works of Sigmund Freud*, translated by James Strachey. 24 vols., 17:217–56. London: Hogarth Press and the Institute of Psychoanalysis, 1953–1974.

Friberg, Hedda. " '[P]assing through Ourselves and Finding Ourselves in the Beyond': The Rites of Passage of Cass Cleave in John Banville's *Eclipse* and *Shroud*." *Irish University Review* 36 (Spring–Summer 2006): 151–64.

Friel, Brian. *Brian Friel: Plays 1*. London: Faber, 1996.

Funke, Lewis. "Interview with Brian Friel." In *Brian Friel in Conversation*, edited by Paul Delaney, 51–71. Ann Arbor: University of Michigan Press, 2000.

Gate Theatre, Dublin. Program to Arthur Miller's adaptation of *An Enemy of the People*. Opening Night, May 28, 1913.

Gelb, Arthur, and Barbara Gelb. *O'Neill*. New York: Perennial, 1960.

Gelb, Arthur, and Barbara Gelb. *O'Neill: Life with Monte Cristo*. New York: Applause Books, 2000.

Gold, Michael. "A Jewish Childhood in the New York Slums." In *Mike Gold: A Literary Anthology*, edited by Michael Folsom, 292–319. New York: International Publishers, 1972.

Gold, Michael. *Jews Without Money*. 2nd ed. 1930. New York: Carroll & Graf, 1996.

Gold, Michael. *Money*. In *One-Act Plays*, edited by Barrett H. Clark and Thomas R. Cook, 205–29. Boston: D. C. Heath, 1929.

Gold, Michael. "The Second American Renaissance." In *Mike Gold: A Literary Anthology*, edited by Michael Folsom, 243–54. New York: International Publishers, 1972.

Goldstein, Eric L. *The Price of Whiteness: Jews, Race, and American Identity*. Princeton: Princeton University Press, 2006.

Gottfried, Martin. *Arthur Miller: His Life and Work*. Cambridge, MA: Da Capo, 2003.

Gottlieb, Robert. *Sarah: The Life of Sarah Bernhardt*. New Haven: Yale University Press, 2010.

Green, Jesse. "*Outside Mullingar* Is a Shamrock Shake." *Vulture*, January 23, 2014. www.vulture.com/2014/01/theater-review-outside-mullingar.html.

Gregg, Melissa, and Gregory J. Seigworth, eds. *The Affect Theory Reader*. Durham, NC: Duke University Press, 2010.

Grossberg, Lawrence. *Dancing in Spite of Myself: Essays on Popular Culture*. Durham, NC: Duke University Press, 1997.

Grossberg, Lawrence. "Is There a Fan in the House? The Affective Sensibility of Fandom." In *The Adoring Audience: Fan Culture and Popular Media*, edited by Lisa A. Lewis, 50–65. New York: Routledge, 1992.

Grossberg, Lawrence. "Affect's Future: Rediscovering the Virtual in the Actual." Interview by Gregory J. Seigworth and Melissa Gregg. In *The Affect Theory Reader*, edited by Melissa Gregg and Gregory J. Seigworth, 309–38. Durham, NC: Duke University Press, 2010.

Hansberry, Lorraine. "The Negro Writer and His Roots: Toward a New Romanticism." 1959. *The Black Scholar* 12 (March–April 1981): 2–12.

Harrington, John P. *The Irish Play on the New York Stage, 1874–1966*. Lexington: University of Kentucky Press, 1997.

Harrington, John P., ed. *Irish Theatre in America: Essays on Irish Theatrical Diaspora*. Syracuse: Syracuse University Press, 2009.

Harrison, Lori B. "Bloodsucking Bloom: Vampirism as a Representation of Jewishness in *Ulysses*." *James Joyce Quarterly* 36 (Summer 1999): 781–97.

Harrison-Kahan, Lori. "'Drunk with the Fiery Rhythms of Jazz': Anzia Yezierska, Hybridity, and the Harlem Renaissance." *MFS: Modern Fiction Studies* 51 (Summer 2005): 416–36.

Harrison-Kahan, Lori. *The White Negress: Literature, Minstrelsy, and the Black-Jewish Imaginary*. New Brunswick: Rutgers University Press, 2011.

Hart, Clive. "Wandering Rocks." In *James Joyce's Ulysses: Critical Essays*, edited by Clive Hart and David Hayman, 181–216. Berkeley: University of California Press, 1974.

Harvey, Martin. *The Autobiography of Sir John Martin-Harvey*. London: Sampson, Low, Marston, 1933.

Hatton, Joseph. *Henry Irving's Impressions of America, Narrated in a Series of Sketches, Chronicles, and Conversations*. Boston: James R. Osgood, 1884.

Hazlewood, C. H. *Jessy Vere; or, the Return of the Wanderer*. London: Thomas Hailes Lacy, 1856.

Hazlewood, C. H. *Never Too Late to Mend*. New York: Samuel French, 1859.

Hazlewood, C. H. *The Stolen Jewess; or, Two Children of Israel*. New York: Samuel French, 1872.

Herr, Christopher J. *Clifford Odets and the American Political Theatre*. Westport, CT: Praeger, 2003.

Higgins, Aidan. *Langrishe, Go Down*. 1966. Normal, IL: Dalkey Archive Press, 2004.

Hogan, Robert. *Dion Boucicault*. New York: Twayne, 1969.

"The Home Stage." *Boston Daily Globe*, December 19, 1882.

Hokey-Pokey. "Crazes Die Young: *Trilby's* Reign Is O'er." *Irish Playgoer*, April 5, 1900, 7.

Holder, Heidi J. "Nation and Neighborhood, Jews and Englishmen: Location and Theatrical Ideology in Victorian London." In *The Performing Century: Nineteenth-Century Theatre's History*, edited by Tracy C. Davis and Peter Holland, 105–20. Houndmills, Basingstoke: Palgrave Macmillan, 2007.

Horne, Gerald. *The Final Victim of the Blacklist: John Howard Lawson, Dean of the Hollywood Ten*. Berkeley: University of California Press, 2006.

Howard, Sir Robert. *The Committee*, edited by Cheryl L. Nixon. In *The Broadview Anthology of Restoration and Early Eighteenth-Century Drama*, J. Douglas, Canfield, general editor, 472–525. Peterborough, Ontario: Broadview Press, 2001.

Howe, Irving. *World of Our Fathers: The Journey of East European Jews to America and the Life They Found and Made.* 1976. London: Phoenix Press, 2000.

Howes, Marjorie. "Discipline, Sentiment, and the Irish-American Public: Mary Ann Sadlier's Popular Fiction." *Éire-Ireland* 40 (Spring–Summer 2005): 140–69.

Hughes, Alan. "Henry Irving's Tragedy of Shylock." *Educational Theatre Journal* 24.3 (1972): 248–64.

Hutton, Lawrence. "Infant Phenomena." *American Magazine* 21 (1886): 439–48.

Hwang, David Henry. *"FOB" and Other Plays.* New York: New American Library, 1990.

Hyde, Douglas. "The Necessity for De-anglicizing Ireland." In *Irish Literature: A Reader,* edited by Maureen O'Rourke Murphy and James MacKillop, 137–47. Syracuse: Syracuse University Press, 1987.

Hyman, Louis. *The Jews of Ireland: From Earliest Times to the Year 1910.* Shannon: Irish University Press, 1972.

Ignatiev, Noel. *How the Irish Became White.* New York: Routledge, 1995.

Ireland, Joseph N. *Records of the New York Stage from 1750–1860.* 2 vols. New York: Benjamin Blom, 1866.

"Irving as Shylock." *Chicago Daily Tribune,* October 3, 1893.

"Irving in 'The Merchant of Venice' at Abbey's." *New York Times,* November 28, 1893.

Irving, Laurence. *Henry Irving: The Actor and His World.* New York: Macmillan, 1952.

Isherwood, Charles. "Weary, Brooding, and Made for Each Other." *New York Times,* January 23, 2014.

Jablonski, Edward. *Irving Berlin: American Troubadour.* New York: Henry Holt, 1999.

Jacobson, Howard. *The Finkler Question.* New York: Bloomsbury, 2010.

Jameson, Fredric. *The Political Unconscious: Narrative as a Socially Symbolic Act.* Ithaca: Cornell University Press, 1981.

Jeffs, Rae. *Brendan Behan: Man and Showman.* London: Hutchinson, 1966.

Jen, Gish. *Mona in the Promised Land.* New York: Vintage, 1997.

Jenkins, Emily. "Trilby: Fads, Photographers, and 'Over-Perfect Feet.'" *Book History* 1 (1998): 221–67.

Jerving, Ryan. "An Experiment in Modern Vaudeville: Archiving the Wretched Refuse in John Howard Lawson's *Processional.*" *Modern Drama* 51 (Winter 2008): 528–54.

Jessop, George Henry. *Sam'l of Posen; Or, the Commercial Drummer.* 1881. In *"Davy Crockett" and Other Plays,* edited by Isaac Goldberg and Hubert Heffner, 149–85. Princeton: Princeton University Press, 1940. *America's Lost Plays,* volume 4. Bloomington: Indiana University Press, 1975.

Jones-Evans, Eric. "With Irving and *The Bells.*" In *Henry Irving and "The Bells,"* edited by David Mayer, 17–29. Manchester: Manchester University Press, 1980.

Joyce, James. *Dubliners.* Introduction by Terence Brown. London: Penguin, 1992.

Joyce, James. *A Portrait of the Artist as a Young Man.* Edited by R. B. Kershner. New York: St. Martin's, 1993.

Joyce, James. *Ulysses: The Corrected Text.* Edited by Hans Walter Gabler. New York: Vintage, 1986.

Julius, Anthony. *T. S. Eliot, Anti-Semitism, and Literary Form.* New ed. London: Thames & Hudson, 2003.

Kanfer, Stefan. *A Summer World: The Attempt to Build a Jewish Eden in the Catskills, from the Days of the Ghetto to the Rise and Decline of the Borscht Belt.* New York: Farrar, Straus and Giroux, 1989.

Keightley, Keir. "Tin Pan Allegory." *Modernism/Modernity* 19 (November 2012): 717–36.

Kellman, Steven G. *Redemption: The Life of Henry Roth.* New York: Norton, 2005.

Kennedy-Andrews, Elmer. "Representations of the Jew in the Modern Irish Novel since Joyce." *Irish University Review* 43 (Autumn–Winter 2013): 307–26.

Keogh, Dermot. *Jews in Twentieth-Century Ireland: Refugees, Anti-Semitism and the Holocaust.* Cork: Cork University Press, 1998.

Kiberd, Declan. *Ulysses and Us: The Art of Everyday Life in Joyce's Masterpiece.* New York: W.W. Norton, 2009.

King, Donald C. *The Theatres of Boston: A Stage and Screen History.* Jefferson, NC: McFarland, 2005.

Kolbenheyer, Friedrich. "Jewish Blood." *American Jewess* 2 (July 1896): 507ff.

Krause, David, ed. *The Letters of Sean O'Casey 1910–1941.* New York: Macmillan, 1975.

Kreilkamp, Vera. "Reinventing a Form: The Big House in Aidan Higgins' *Langrishe, Go Down.*" *Canadian Journal of Irish Studies* 11 (December 1985): 27–38.

Kurnick, David. *Empty Houses: Theatrical Failure and the Novel.* Princeton: Princeton University Press, 2012.

Kushner, Tony, and Alisa Solomon. "Tell Her the Truth." *Nation*, April 13, 2009, 11–16.

Landers, Robert K. *An Honest Writer: The Life and Times of James T. Farrell.* San Francisco: Encounter Books, 2004.

Langner, Lawrence. *The Magic Curtain: The Story of a Life in Two Fields, Theatre and Invention by the Founder of the Theatre Guild.* New York: E. P. Dutton, 1951.

Lawrence, D. H. Introduction to Edward Dahlberg's *Bottom Dogs*. 1929. In *"Bottom Dogs," "From Flushing to Calvary," and "Those Who Perish," and Hitherto Unpublished and Uncollected Works by Edward Dahlberg*, 147–52. New York: Thomas Y. Crowell, 1976.

Lawrence, Jerome. *Actor: The Life and Times of Paul Muni.* New York: G. P. Putnam, 1974.

Lawson, John Howard. *Loud Speaker.* 1927. New York: ReGroup Theatre Company, 2013.

Lawson, John Howard. *Processional: A Jazz Symphony of American Life in Four Acts.* New York: Thomas Seltzer, 1925.

Lawson, John Howard. *Success Story.* 1932. New York: ReGroup Theatre Company, 2013.

Leighton, Mary Elizabeth. "'Hypnosis Redivivus': Ernest Hart, 'British Medical Journal,' and the Hypnotism Controversy." *Victorian Periodicals Review* 34 (Summer 2001): 104–27.

Levi, Primo. *Survival in Auschwitz.* 1958. New York: Classic House Books, 2008.

Levin, Harry. *James Joyce: A Critical Introduction.* Norfolk, CT: New Directions, 1941.

Linett, Maren. "Introduction: Modernism's Jews/Jewish Modernisms." *MFS: Modern Fiction Studies* 51 (Summer 2005): 249–57.

Litvak, Joseph. "Jew Envy." *Women's Study Quarterly* 34 (Fall–Winter 2006): 82–106.

Lonergan, Patrick. *Theatre and Globalization: Irish Drama in the Celtic Tiger Era.* Houndmills, Basingstoke: Palgrave Macmillan, 2009.

Longfellow, Henry Wadsworth. *The Complete Poetical Works of Henry Wadsworth Longfellow.* Boston: Houghton Mifflin, 1848.

Lowery, Robert G., and Patricia Angelin, eds. *My Very Dear Sean: George Jean Nathan to Sean O'Casey, Letters and Articles.* Rutherford, NJ: Fairleigh Dickinson University Press, 1985.

MacLaverty, Bernard. *Cal.* London: George Braziller, 1983.

MacLaverty, Bernard. *Grace Notes.* New York: W. W. Norton, 1997.

Mailer, Norman. *The Armies of the Night: History as a Novel The Novel as History*. New York: Plume, 1968.

Marcus, David. *Oughtobiography: Leaves from the Diary of a Hyphenated Jew*. Dublin: Gill & Macmillan, 2001.

Marcus, Sharon. "Salomé!! Sarah Bernhardt, Oscar Wilde, and the Drama of Celebrity." *PMLA* 126 (October 2011): 999–1021.

Marks, Patricia. *Sarah Bernhardt's First American Theatrical Tour*. Jefferson, NC: McFarland, 2003.

Martin, Robert A., ed. *The Theater Essays of Arthur Miller*. New York: Viking, 1978.

Massumi, Brian. *Parables for the Virtual: Movement, Affect, Sensation*. Durham, NC: Duke University Press, 2002.

Matlaw, Myron. "James O'Neill's Launching of *Monte Cristo*." In *When They Weren't Doing Shakespeare*, edited by Judith L. Fisher and Stephen Watt, 88–104. 2nd ed. Athens: University of Georgia Press, 2011.

McConachie, Bruce A. "The Cultural Politics of 'Paddy' on the Midcentury American Stage." *Studies in Popular Culture* 10 (1987): 1–13.

McConachie, Bruce A. *Melodramatic Formations: American Theatre and Society, 1820–1870*. Iowa City: University of Iowa Press, 1992.

McFeely, Deirdre. *Dion Boucicault: Irish Identity on Stage*. Cambridge: Cambridge University Press, 2012.

McFeely, Deirdre. "Shakespeare on the Dublin Stage, 1660–1904." Paper presented at Conference "Performing Shakespeare in Ireland, 1660–1922." National University of Ireland–Galway, September 5, 2010.

Merwin, Ted. "The Performance of Ethnicity in Anne Nichols' *Abie's Irish Rose*." *Journal of American Ethnic History* 20 (Winter 2001): 3–37.

Mikhail, E. H., ed. *Brendan Behan: Interviews and Recollections*. 2 vols. Totowa, NJ: Barnes and Noble, 1982.

Mikhail, E. H., ed. *The Letters of Brendan Behan*. London: Macmillan, 1992.

Mikkelsen, Ann. "From Sympathy to Empathy: Anzia Yezierska and the Transformation of the American Subject." *American Literature* 82 (June 2010): 361–88.

Miller, Arthur. *Arthur Miller's Collected Plays*. New York: Viking Press, 1957.

Miller, Arthur. *Timebends: A Life*. New York: Grove Press, 1987.

Miller, Cristanne. "Tongues 'Loosened in the Melting Pot': The Poets of *Others* and the Lower East Side." *Modernism/Modernity* 14 (Fall 2007): 455–76.

Miller, Kerby. *Ireland and Irish America: Culture, Class and Transatlantic Migration*. Notre Dame: Field Day Press, 2008.

Mintz, Lawrence E. "Humor and Ethnic Stereotypes in Vaudeville and Burlesque." *MELUS* 21 (Winter 1996): 19–28.

Moglen, Seth. *Mourning Modernity: Literary Modernism and the Injuries of American Capitalism*. Stanford: Stanford University Press, 2007.

Moloney, Mick. *If It Wasn't for the Irish and the Jews: Irish-American Songs from Vaudeville and Early Tin Pan Alley*. Nashville: Compass Records, 2009.

Monks, Aoife. "Comely Maidens and Celtic Tigers: *Riverdance* in Performance." *Goldsmith's Performance Research Pamphlets* 1. London: University of London Press, 2007.

"Mr. Beerbohm Tree in 'Trilby.'" *Times* (London), September 9, 1895, 10.

Muldoon, Paul. "Getting Round: Notes toward an *Ars Poetica*." *Essays in Criticism* 48 (April 1998): 107–28.

Muldoon, Paul. *Moy Sand and Gravel.* New York: Farrar, Straus and Giroux, 2002.

Murphy, Maureen. "From Scapegrace to Grásta: Popular Attitudes and Stereotypes in Irish American Drama." In *Irish Theater in America: Essays on Irish Theatrical Diaspora,* edited by John P. Harrington, 19–37. Syracuse: Syracuse University Press, 2009

Murray, Christopher. *Seán O'Casey: Writer at Work—a Biography.* Montreal: McGill-Queen's University Press, 2004.

"Music and Drama." *Chicago Daily Tribune,* March 1, 1892, 4.

Nahshon, Edna. "Introduction. Israel Zangwill: Child of the Ghetto." In *From the Ghetto to the Melting Pot: Israel Zangwill's Jewish Plays,* edited by Edna Nahshon, 5–57. Detroit: Wayne State University Press, 2006.

Nathan, David. "Failure of an Elderly Gentleman: Shaw and the Jews." *SHAW: Shaw and Politics* 11 (1991): 219–38.

Nathan, George Jean. *The Critic and the Drama.* New York: Alfred A. Knopf, 1922.

Nathan, George Jean, and H. L. Mencken. *The American Credo: A Contribution toward the Interpretation of the National Mind.* 1920. Rpt., London: Dodo Press, 2008.

Nathans, Heather S. "Representing Ethnic Identity on the Antebellum Stage, 1825–61." In *The Oxford Handbook of American Drama,* edited by Jeffrey H. Richards with Heather S. Nathans, 97–113. New York: Oxford University Press, 2013.

"New Theatrical Bills—Paul Potter's 'Trilby' Greeted with Loud Hurrahs." *New York Times,* April 16, 1895.

Ngai, Sianne. *Ugly Feelings.* Cambridge, MA: Harvard University Press, 2005.

Nichols, Anne. *Abie's Irish Rose* [play script]. New York: Samuel French, 1924.

Nichols, Anne. *Abie's Irish Rose* [novel]. New York: Grosset & Dunlap, 1927.

Nicoll, Allardyce. *A History of English Drama, 1660–1900.* 5 vols. Cambridge: Cambridge University Press, 1946.

"Norman Mailer Arrested in Stabbing of Wife at Party." *New York Times,* November 22, 1960.

Novick, Julius. *Beyond the Golden Door: Jewish American Drama and the Jewish American Experience.* New York: Palgrave Macmillan, 2008.

O'Casey, Sean. *Autobiographies 1: I Knock at the Door, Pictures in the Hallway, Drums under the Window.* 1939, 1942, 1945. London: Pan Books, 1980.

O'Casey, Sean. *Autobiographies 2: Inishfallen, Fare Thee Well, Rose and Crown, Sunset and Evening Star.* 1949, 1952, 1954. London: Pan Books, 1980.

O'Casey, Sean. *Collected Plays.* 4 vols. London: Macmillan, 1950.

O'Connor, Garry. *Sean O'Casey: A Life.* New York: Atheneum, 1988.

O'Connor, Thomas H. *Boston Catholics: A History of the Church and Its People.* Boston: Northeastern University Press, 1998.

O'Connor, Thomas H. *The Boston Irish: A Political History.* Boston: Northeastern University Press, 1995.

O'Connor, Ulick. *Brendan Behan.* 1970. London: Abacus, 1993.

Odell, George C. D. *Annals of the New York Stage.* 15 vols. New York: Columbia University Press, 1927–49.

Odets, Clifford. *The Time Is Ripe: The 1940 Journal of Clifford Odets.* New York: Grove Press, 1988.

Odets, Clifford. *"Waiting for Lefty" and Other Plays.* New York: Grove Press, 1994.

Ó Gráda, Cormac. *Jewish Ireland in the Age of Joyce: A Socioeconomic History.* Princeton: Princeton University Press, 2006.

O'Neill, Eugene. *Long Day's Journey into Night*. New Haven: Yale University Press, 1956.

O'Neill, Eugene. *A Moon for the Misbegotten*. New York: Vintage, 1974.

O'Neill, Eugene. *A Touch of the Poet*. New Haven: Yale University Press, 1957.

O'Sullivan, Michael. *Brendan Behan: A Life*. Dublin: Blackwater Press, 1999.

Palmieri, Anthony F. R. *Elmer Rice: A Playwright's Vision of America*. Rutherford: Fairleigh Dickinson University Press, 1980.

Parker, Stewart. *Heavenly Bodies*. In *Stewart Parker Plays: 2*, 83–168. London: Methuen, 2000.

Pearson, Hesketh. *Beerbohm Tree: His Life and Laughter*. New York: Harper Brothers, 1956.

Pearson, Hesketh. *Bernard Shaw:His Life and Personality*. London: Collins, 1950.

Perloff, Carey. "Pinter in Rehearsal: From *The Birthday Party* to *Mountain Language*." In *Pinter at Sixty*, edited by Katherine H. Burkman and John L. Kundert-Gibbs, 3–17. Bloomington: Indiana University Press, 1993.

Phillips, Mary Elizabeth. "Clifford Odets: Writing around Jewishness." Ph.D. dissertation, National University of Ireland–Galway, 2012.

Pick, Daniel. *Svengali's Web: The Alien Enchanter in Modern Culture*. New Haven: Yale University Press, 2000.

Pilgrim, James. *Eveleen Wilson, The Flower of Erin*. Boston: William V. Spencer, 1858.

Pilgrim, James. *Ireland and America; or, Scenes in Both*. New York: Samuel French, 1856.

Pilgrim, James. *Irish Assurance and Yankee Modesty*. New York: Samuel French, 1864.

Pilgrim, James. *Paddy Miles, The Limerick Boy*. Rev. ed. London: Thomas Hailes Lacy, 1856.

Pilgrim, James. *Shandy Maguire; or, the Bould Boy of the Mountain*. Boston: William V. Spencer, 1855.

Pilkington, Lionel. *Theatre & Ireland*. Houndmills, Basingstoke: Palgrave Macmillan, 2010.

Pinter, Harold. *Ashes to Ashes*. New York: Grove Press, 1996.

Pinter, Harold. *The Birthday Party and The Room*. New York: Grove Press, 1959.

Pinter, Harold. *Celebration and The Room*. New York: Grove Press, 2000.

Pinter, Harold. *Langrishe, Go Down*. In *Collected Screenplays One*, 557–660. London: Faber & Faber, 2000.

Pinter, Harold. *Poems and Prose, 1949–1977*. London: Eyre Methuen, 1978.

Podhoretz, Norman. "The Know-Nothing Bohemians." 1958. In *The Norman Podhoretz Reader*, edited by Thomas L. Jeffers, 29–40. New York: Free Press, 2004.

Postlewait, Thomas. *The Cambridge Introduction to Theatre Historiography*. Cambridge: Cambridge University Press, 2009.

Postlewait, Thomas. "From Melodrama to Realism: The Suspect History of American Drama." In *Melodrama: The Cultural Emergence of a Genre*, edited by Michael Hays and Anastasia Nikolopoulou, 39–60. New York: St. Martin's Press, 1996.

Postlewait, Thomas. "Theater Events and Their Political Contexts: A Problem in the Writing of Theater History." In *Critical Theory and Performance*, rev. ed., edited by Janelle G. Reinelt and Joseph R. Roach, 198–222. Ann Arbor: University of Michigan Press, 2007.

Potter, Paul. *Trilby*. In *The Broadview Anthology of Nineteenth-Century British Performance*, edited by Tracy C. Davis, 577–642. Toronto: Broadview Press, 2012.

Prentice, Penelope. *The Pinter Ethic: The Erotic Aesthetic*. New York: Garland, 2000.

Quigley, Mark. "White Skin, Green Face: House of Pain and the Modern Minstrel Show." In *The Black and Green Atlantic: Cross Currents of the African and Irish Diasporas*, edited by Peter D. O'Neill and David Lloyd, 64–80. London: Palgrave Macmillan, 2009.

Rabkin, Norman. *Drama and Commitment: Politics in the American Theatre of the Thirties.* Bloomington: Indiana University Press, 1964.

Ragussis, Michael. *Theatrical Nation: Jews and Other Outlandish Englishmen in Georgian Britain.* Philadelphia: University of Pennsylvania Press, 2010.

Raleigh, John Henry. "The Irish Atavism of *A Moon for the Misbegotten.*" In *Eugene O'Neill: A World View*, edited by Virginia Floyd, 229–36. New York: Frederick Ungar, 1979.

Read, Herbert, and Edward Dahlberg. *Truth Is More Sacred: A Critical Exchange on Modern Literature.* London: Routledge and Kegan Paul, 1961.

Reinelt, Janelle. "The Politics of Discourse: Performativity Meets Theatricality." *Sub-Stance* 31 (2002): 201–15.

Reizbaum, Marilyn. *James Joyce's Judaic Other.* Stanford: Stanford University Press, 1999.

Reizbaum, Marilyn. "Urban Legends." *Éire-Ireland* 45 (Spring–Summer 2010): 242–65.

Rice, Elmer. *Counsellor-at-Law.* In *Awake and Singing: Seven Classic Plays from the American Jewish Repertoire*, edited by Ellen Schiff, 85–213. New York: Mentor Books, 1995.

Rice, Elmer. "Extemporaneous Remarks Made at a Luncheon at the Hotel Savoy, London, Given by the British Society of Authors and Composers on the 100th Anniversary of Bernard Shaw's Birth." July 26, 1956. Harry Ransom Center, University of Texas at Austin. Box 93.1.

Rice, Elmer. *The Living Theatre.* New York: Harper & Brothers, 1959.

Rice, Elmer. *Minority Report: An Autobiography.* New York: Simon and Schuster, 1963.

Rice, Elmer. *Other Plays and Not for Children.* London: Victor Gollancz, Ltd., 1935.

Rice, Elmer. *Three Plays: "The Adding Machine," "Street Scene," "Dream Girl."* New York: Hill & Wang, 1965.

Rice, Elmer. *We, The People.* New York: Coward-McCann, 1933.

Richtarik, Marilynn. *Stewart Parker: A Life.* Oxford: Oxford University Press, 2012.

Ricoeur, Paul. *Memory, History, Forgetting.* Translated by Kathleen Blamey and David Pellauer. Chicago: University of Chicago Press, 2004.

Ridge, Lola. *"The Ghetto" and Other Poems.* New York: B.W. Huebsch, 1918.

Riis, Jacob A. *How the Other Half Lives.* 1890. New York: Penguin, 1997.

Ripley, John. "Sociology and Soundscape: Herbert Beerbohm Tree's 1908 *Merchant of Venice.*" *Shakespeare Quarterly*, 56 (Winter 2005): 385–410.

Ritschel, Nelson Ó'Ceallaigh. *Shaw, Synge, Connolly, and Socialist Provocation.* Gainesville: University Presses of Florida, 2011.

Roach, Joseph. "Barnumizing Diaspora: The 'Irish Skylark' Does New Orleans." *Theatre Journal* 50 (1998): 39–51.

Roach, Joseph. *Cities of the Dead: Circum-Atlantic Performance.* New York: Columbia University Press, 1996.

Roach, Joseph. "Performance: The Blunders of Orpheus." *PMLA* 125 (October 2010): 1078–86.

Roche, Anthony. *Brian Friel: Theatre and Politics.* Houndmills, Basingstoke: Palgrave Macmillan, 2011.

Roche, Anthony. "Pinter and Ireland." In *The Cambridge Companion to Harold Pinter*, 2nd ed., edited by Peter Raby, 195–215. Cambridge: Cambridge University Press, 2009.

Rosenhan, Claudia. "'Grace' and the Idea of 'the Irish Jew.'" *James Joyce Quarterly* 47 (Fall 2009): 71–86.

Roth, Henry. *An American Type*. Edited by Willing Davidson. New York: W. W. Norton, 2010.

Roth, Henry. *Call It Sleep*. 1934. New York: Picador, 1991.

Roth, Henry. *A Diving Rock on the Hudson*. New York: Picador, 1995.

Roth, Henry. *From Bondage*. New York: Picador USA, 1997.

Roth, Henry. *Requiem for Harlem*. New York: Picador USA, 1998.

Roth, Henry. *A Star Shines over Mt. Morris Park*. New York: Picador, 1994.

Roth, Philip. *American Pastoral*. New York: Vintage, 1997.

Roth, Philip. *The Counterlife*. 1986; New York: Vintage, 1996.

Rothberg, Michael. *Multidirectional Memory: Remembering the Holocaust in the Age of Decolonization*. Stanford: Stanford University Press, 2009.

Rozmovits, Linda. *Shakespeare and the Politics of Culture in Late Victorian England*. Baltimore: Johns Hopkins University Press, 1998.

Russell, Richard Rankin. *Modernity, Community, and Place in Brian Friel's Drama*. Syracuse: Syracuse University Press, 2014.

Sadlier, Mary Anne Madden. *Bessy Conway; or, The Irish Girl in America*. Edited by Liz Szabo. 1861. Charlottesville: University of Virginia American Studies, 1997.

Said, Edward. *On Late Style: Music and Literature against the Grain*. New York: Vintage, 2006.

"Sarah's Leah Seen in Boston." *New York Herald*, January 9, 1892.

Schrader, Fred F. "Henry Irving in Three Great Roles." *Washington Post*, January 3, 1904, A6.

Shakespeare, William. *The Merchant of Venice*. Edited by Barbara A. Mowat and Paul Werstine. Folger Shakespeare Library Edition. New York: Washington Square Press, 1992.

Shanley, John Patrick: *Outside Mullingar*. New York: Theatre Communications Group, 2014.

Shapiro, James. *Shakespeare and the Jews*. New York: Columbia University Press, 1996.

Shattuck, Charles H. *Shakespeare on the American Stage: From Booth and Barrett to Sothern and Marlowe*. Washington, DC: Folger Shakespeare Library, 1987.

Shaw, Bernard. *Complete Plays with Prefaces*. 6 vols. New York: Dodd, Mead, 1963.

Shaw, Bernard. Interview about Jews, no date. Harry Ransom Center, University of Texas at Austin. Box 2.14.

Shaw, Bernard. "On the Jews." 1925. In *Shaw and the City*, edited by Desmond Harding, 16–30. Vol. 32 of *SHAW: The Annual of Bernard Shaw Studies*. University Park: Pennsylvania State University Press, 2012.

Shaw, Bernard. *The Matter with Ireland*. Edited by David H. Greene and Dan H. Laurence. London: Rupert Hart-Davis, 1962.

Shaw, Bernard. *Our Theatres in the Nineties*. 3 vols. London: Constable, 1932.

Shaw, Bernard. *An Unsocial Socialist*. 1884. London: Virago, 1980.

Sheaffer, Louis. *O'Neill: Son and Playwright*. Boston: Little, Brown, 1968.

Sheward, David. "'Loud Speaker' Hits Us over the Head." *Backstage*, March 13, 2013. www.backstage.com/reviews.

Sheward, David. "Melodramatic 'Success Story' Hasn't Aged Well." *Backstage*, March 7, 2013. www.backstage.com/reviews.

Skinner, Cornelia Otis. *Madame Sarah*. Boston: Houghton Mifflin, 1966.

Smyth, Gerry. "'The Same Sound but with a Different Meaning': Music, Repetition, and Identity in Bernard MacLaverty's *Grace Notes*." *Éire-Ireland* 37 (Fall–Winter 2002): 5–24.

Sofer, Andrew. "Spectral Readings." *Theatre Journal* 64 (October 2012): 323–36.

Sofer, Andrew. *The Stage Life of Props*. Ann Arbor: University of Michigan Press, 2003.

Spangler, Walt, and Martha Lavey. "Revelation." 20–22. Program for *The Birthday Party*. Chicago: Steppenwolf Theatre Company, 2013.

Stasio, Marilyn. "Broadway Review: *Outside Mullingar*." *Variety*, January 23, 2014. www.variety.com/2014/legit/reviews/broadway-review-outside-mullingar-1201066197/

Steinberg, Erwin R. "James Joyce and the Critics Notwithstanding, Leopold Bloom Is Not Jewish." *Journal of Modern Literature* 9 (1981): 27–49.

Sternlicht, Sanford. *The Tenement Saga: The Lower East Side and Early Jewish-American Writers*. Madison: University of Wisconsin Press, 2004.

Stiller, Jerry. *Married to Laughter: A Love Story Featuring Anne Meara*. New York: Touchstone, 2000.

Stoker, Bram. *Personal Reminiscences of Henry Irving*. London: William Heinemann, 1907.

Synge, J. M. *Collected Works*. General editor Robin Skelton. 4 vols. London: Oxford University Press, 1961–68.

Sypnowich, Christine. "Cosmopolitans, Cosmopolitanism, and Human Flourishing." In *The Political Philosophy of Cosmopolitanism*, edited by Gillian Brock and Harry Brighouse, 55–74. Cambridge: Cambridge University Press, 2005

Taranow, Gerda. *Sarah Bernhardt: The Art within the Legend*. Princeton: Princeton University Press, 1972.

Taylor, George. "Svengali: Mesmerist and Aesthete." In *British Theatre in the 1890s: Essays on Drama and the Stage*, edited by Richard Foulkes, 93–110. Cambridge: Cambridge University Press, 1992.

"Ten Years Ago." *Catskill Mountain News*, August 5, 1971, 1.

Terry, Ellen. *The Story of My Life*. London: Hutchinson, 1908.

Thomson, Peter. "'Weirdness That Lifts and Colours All': The Secret Self of Henry Irving." In *Shakespeare and the Victorian Stage*, edited by Richard Foulkes, 96–105. Cambridge: Cambridge University Press, 1986.

Thurber, Carryl Nelson, ed. *Sir Robert Howard's Comedy "The Committee."* Urbana: Graduate School of the University of Illinois, 1921.

Tobin, Daniel. "Modernism, Leftism, and the Spirit: The Poetry of Lola Ridge." *New Hibernia Review* 8 (Autumn 2004): 65–85.

Tóibín, Colm. *Brooklyn*. New York: Scribner, 2009.

Tree, Herbert Beerbohm. *Thoughts and Afterthoughts*. New York: Funk & Wagnalls, 1913.

Trewin, J. C. *Benson and the Bensonians*. London: Barry & Rockliff, 1960.

"'Trilby' on the [Boston] Stage." *New York Times*, March 12, 1895.

"Union-Square Theatre." *New York Times*, March 2, 1887, 5.

Valente, Joseph. *The Myth of Manliness in Irish National Culture, 1880–1920*. Urbana: University of Illinois Press, 2011.

Vendler, Helen. "Anglo-Celtic Attitudes." *New York Review of Books*, November 6, 1997, 57–60.

Volf, Miroslav. *The End of Memory: Remembering Rightly in a Violent World*. Grand Rapids, MI: William B. Eerdmans, 2006.

Von Sacher-Masoch, Leopold. *Jewish Tales.* Translated by Harriet Lieber Cohen. Chicago: A. C. McClurg, 1894.

Walker, Julia A. *Expressionism and Modernism in the American Theatre: Bodies, Voices, Words.* Cambridge: Cambridge University Press, 2005.

Walkowitz, Rebecca L. *Cosmopolitan Style: Modernism beyond the Nation.* New York: Columbia University Press, 2006.

Watt, Stephen. "Historical Drama and the 'Legitimate' Theatre: Tom Taylor and W.G. Wills in the 1870s." In *When They Weren't Doing Shakespeare*, edited by Judith L. Fisher and Stephen Watt, 187–211. Athens: University of Georgia Press, 2011.

Watt, Stephen. *Joyce, O'Casey, and the Irish Popular Theater.* Syracuse: Syracuse University Press, 1991.

Watt, Stephen. "'Nothing for a Woman in That': James Lovebirch and Masochistic Fantasy in *Ulysses.*" In *Joyce and Popular Culture*, edited by R. B. Kershner, 74–88. Gainesville: University Press of Florida, 1996.

Watt, Stephen. "Things, Voices, Events: Harold Pinter's *Mountain Language* as Testamental Text." *Modern Drama* 52.1 (2009): 38–56.

Weales, Gerald. *Odets the Playwright.* New York: Methuen, 1985.

Weber, Donald. *Haunted in the New World: Jewish American Culture from Cahan to The Goldbergs.* Bloomington: Indiana University Press, 2005.

Weintraub, Stanley. "GBS and the Despots." *TLS: Times Literary Supplement*, August 22, 2011. Online.

Werbner, Pnina. "Introduction: The Materiality of Diaspora—between Aesthetic and 'Real' Politics." *Diaspora* 9.1 (2000): 5–20.

Wesker, Arnold. *The Birth of Shylock and the Death of Zero Mostel.* London: Quartet Books, 1997.

Wesker, Arnold. *The Merchant.* London: Methuen Student Edition, 1983.

Williams, William H. A. *'Twas Only an Irishman's Dream.* Champaign: University of Illinois Press, 1996.

Wilmeth, Don B., and Tice Miller, eds. *The Cambridge Guide to American Theatre.* Cambridge: Cambridge University Press, 1993.

Winter, William. *Other Days: Being Chronicles and Memories from the Stage.* New York: Moffat, Yard, 1908.

Winter, William. *The Wallet of Time.* Vol. 1. New York: Moffat, Yard, 1913.

Woollcott, Alexander. "An All-Star 'Trilby.'" *New York Times*, April 4, 1915.

Yaeger, Patricia. "Circum-Atlantic Superabundance: Milk as World-Making in Alice Randall and Kara Walker." *American Literature* 78 (December 2006): 769–98.

Yezierska, Anzia. *Bread Givers.* 1925. New York: Persea, 1975.

Yezierska, Anzia. *Salome of the Tenements.* 1923. Urbana: University of Illinois Press, 1995.

Young, James E. "Memory and Monument." In *Bitburg in Moral and Political Perspective*, edited by Geoffrey H. Hartman, 103–13. Bloomington: Indiana University Press, 1986.

Zangwill, Israel. *Children of the Ghetto: A Study of a Peculiar People.* 1895. Cambridge: Black Apollo Press, 2004.

Zangwill, Israel. *From the Ghetto to the Melting Pot: Israel Zangwill's Jewish Plays.* Edited by Edna Nahshon. Detroit: Wayne State University Press, 2006.

Žižek, Slavoj. "'I Hear You with My Eyes'; or, The Invisible Master." In *Gaze and Voice as Love Objects*, edited by Renata Saleci and Slavoj Žižek, 90–126. Durham, NC: Duke University Press, 1996.

Zola, Émile. *The Dreyfuss Affair: "J'Accuse" and Other Writings*. Edited by Alain Pagès. New Haven: Yale University Press, 1996.

{ INDEX }